Deception in the Digital Age

Deception in the Digital Age

Exploiting and Defending Human Targets Through Computer-Mediated Communications

Cameron H. Malin
Terry Gudaitis
Thomas J. Holt
Max Kilger

ACADEMIC PRESS

An imprint of Elsevier

Academic Press is an imprint of Elsevier
125 London Wall, London EC2Y 5AS, United Kingdom
525 B Street, Suite 1800, San Diego, CA 92101-4495, United States
50 Hampshire Street, 5th Floor, Cambridge, MA 02139, United States
The Boulevard, Langford Lane, Kidlington, Oxford OX5 1GB, United Kingdom

Notices
Knowledge and best practice in this field are constantly changing. As new research and experience
broaden our understanding, changes in research methods, professional practices, or medical
treatment may become necessary.

Practitioners and researchers must always rely on their own experience and knowledge in
evaluating and using any information, methods, compounds, or experiments described herein.
In using such information or methods they should be mindful of their own safety and the safety
of others, including parties for whom they have a professional responsibility.

To the fullest extent of the law, neither the Publisher nor the authors, contributors, or editors,
assume any liability for any injury and/or damage to persons or property as a matter of products
liability, negligence or otherwise, or from any use or operation of any methods, products,
instructions, or ideas contained in the material herein.

Library of Congress Cataloging-in-Publication Data
A catalog record for this book is available from the Library of Congress

British Library Cataloguing-in-Publication Data
A catalogue record for this book is available from the British Library

ISBN: 978-0-12-411630-6

For information on all Academic Press publications
visit our website at https://www.elsevier.com/books-and-journals

Working together
to grow libraries in
developing countries

www.elsevier.com • www.bookaid.org

Publisher: Sara Tenney
Acquisition Editor: Elizabeth Brown
Editorial Project Manager: Anna Valutkevich
Production Project Manager: Priya Kumaraguruparan
Cover Designer: Matthew Limbert

Typeset by TNQ Books and Journals

With deepest appreciation and gratitude, we give thanks and dedicate this book to our loving spouses:

Adrienne Malin
Stasi Poulos
Karen Holt
Christine Kilger

They supported us, served as inspiration and motivation through late nights, supplied lots of caffeine, and encouraged us to finish this book successfully.

Contents

About the Authors

Cameron H. Malin is a Certified Ethical Hacker (C|EH) and Certified Network Defense Architect (C|NDA), as designated by the International Council of Electronic Commerce Consultants (EC-Council); a GIAC Certified Intrusion Analyst (GCIA), GIAC Certified Forensic Analysis (GCFA), GIAC Certified Incident Handler (GCIH), GIAC Certified Reverse Engineering Malware professional (GREM), GIAC Penetration Tester (GPEN), and GIAC Certified Unix Security Administrator (GCUX), as designated by the SANS Institute; and a Certified Information Systems Security Professional (CISSP), as designated by the International Information Systems Security Certification Consortium ((ISC)2).

From 1998 through 2002, Mr. Malin was an Assistant State Attorney (ASA) and Special Assistant United States Attorney in Miami, Florida, where he specialized in computer crime prosecutions. During his tenure as an ASA, he was also an Assistant Professorial Lecturer in the Computer Fraud Investigations Masters Program at George Washington University.

Mr. Malin is currently a Supervisory Special Agent with the Federal Bureau of Investigation assigned to the Behavioral Analysis Unit, Cyber Behavioral Analysis Center. He is also a Subject Matter Expert for the Department of Defense (DoD) Cyber Security & Information Systems Information Analysis Center and Defense Systems Information Analysis Center.

Mr. Malin is coauthor of the *Malware Forensics* book series, *Malware Forensics: Investigating and Analyzing Malicious Code*, the *Malware Forensics Field Guide for Windows Systems*, and the *Malware Forensics Field Guide for Linux Systems* published by Syngress, an imprint of Elsevier, Inc.

The techniques, tools, methods, views, and opinions explained by Cameron H. Malin are personal to him and do not represent those of the United States Department of Justice, the Federal Bureau of Investigation, or the government of the United States of America. Neither the federal government nor any federal agency endorses this book or its contents in any way.

Dr. Terry Gudaitis is the Owner/Principal of Mindstar Security & Profiling, LLC, which specializes in custom cyber and physical security solutions for family offices, high net worth persons, and their families. Terry started her career as a CIA operations officer and behavioral profiler. She left government service to pursue the expansion of profiling techniques as they applied to hackers targeting the financial services and energy sectors. She altered classic behavioral/psychological profiling methods used in homicide, serial crime, and terrorist investigation and adapted them for the applied use in computer crime investigations, which included the integration of cyber intelligence as part of the investigations process. Prior to forming her own firm, Terry was the Vice President and Cyber Intelligence Director at Cyveillance and held senior positions at other private sector firms. In addition to her corporate related work, Terry is on the Advisory Boards of Mi3 Security Inc. and TechnoSecurity; served on the United States Secret Service Advisory Board for Insider Threat; trained investigators at the National Center for Missing and Exploited Children; and regularly presents at national and international conferences. Terry is also a featured speaker at the International Spy Museum in Washington, DC. She received a Ph.D. in behavioral science from the University of Florida.

Dr. Thomas Holt is a Professor in the School of Criminal Justice at Michigan State University specializing in cybercrime, policing, and policy. He received his Ph.D. in Criminology and Criminal Justice from the University of Missouri-Saint Louis in 2005. He has published extensively on cybercrime and cyberterror with over 35 peer-reviewed articles in outlets such as *Crime and Delinquency, Sexual Abuse, the Journal of Criminal Justice, Terrorism and Political Violence*, and *Deviant Behavior*. He is also a coauthor of the books *Cybercrime and Digital Forensics: An Introduction* (2015) and *Policing Cybercrime and Cyberterror* (2015). He has also received multiple grants from the National Institute of Justice and the National Science Foundation to examine the social and technical drivers of Russian malware writers, data thieves, and hackers using online data. He has also given multiple presentations on computer crime and hacking at academic and professional conferences, as well as hacker conferences across the country including Defcon and HOPE.

Max Kilger, Ph.D. (max.kilger@utsa.edu), is a Senior Lecturer in the Department of Information Systems & Cyber Security at the University of Texas at San Antonio (UTSA) and also the Director of the Masters in Data Analytics Program at UTSA. Dr. Kilger received his Ph.D. in Social Psychology from Stanford University. He has over 17 years of experience in the area of information security concentrating on the social and psychological factors motivating malicious online actors, hacking groups, and cyberterrorists. Max has written and coauthored a number of journal articles and book chapters on profiling, the social structure of the hacking community, cyberviolence, and the emergence of cyberterrorism. He is a founding and board member of the Honeynet Project, a not-for-profit information security organization with 54 teams of experts in 44 countries working for the public good. Max was a member of a National Academy of Engineering committee dedicated to make recommendations for combating terrorism. He is also a member of a multinational instructional team for a NATO counterterrorism course.

Acknowledgments

Cameron Malin

Cameron is grateful for the wonderful support and input that many people provided to make this book possible.

Max, Tom, and Terry, I am inspired by your talent and creativity. This has been an incredible project that opened many portals of knowledge. What once started as an entirely different book concept wonderfully evolved into this diverse body of information that endeavors to capture the evolution of deception into its next spaces.

Thanks to the editorial team at Elsevier (Syngress and Academic Press) for your patience and commitment to this book: Laura Colantoni, Chris Katsaropoulos, Anna Valutkevich, and Elizabeth Brown.

Some of the world's finest researchers and magicians helped us expand our minds and examine novel issues that we encountered during the course of writing this book. Many thanks to Josh Sadowsky and Jason England—world class conjurers and cardists ("cardicians")—and vital historians of deception and cheating.

Many thanks to my friends and colleagues in the FBI BAU-2 CBAC; I am so proud and privileged to be a part of the team. Thank you for peering through the prism of creativity and asymmetry with me. The horizon is boundless.

Thank you to Kris Weart and David Hardy for your time and effort reviewing this manuscript.

Above all, thank you Adrienne, Hudson, and Harper. With love comes clarity; know that your love brings everything into total focus.

Terry Gudaitis

Terry would like to acknowledge several people who made this book possible.

In addition to the authors, Cameron, Max, and Tom, who were consummate professionals and a delight to work with, I would like to thank all those researchers that published before us and have been named and cited in these pages. I would like to thank Jack Wiles and Jose Nazario for providing their input and expertise to the process. I would also like to acknowledge Don Withers, who passed away in August 2016. Don Withers and Jack Wiles formed TheTrainingCo. in 1999, which organized one of the first computer and forensic security conferences in the world. Both Jack and Don welcomed me into the field nearly 20 years ago and continue to provide inspiration.

I would like to thank Chris Clark, who went "above and beyond" at the office, and Stasi Poulos, who provided love, food, and comic relief while I was on deadline.

I would also like to thank the entire editorial team at Elsevier (Syngress and Academic Press).

Thomas J. Holt

Tom would like to sincerely thank his coauthors Cameron, Max, and Terry for their interest in this project and support throughout the writing process. Their comments were invaluable. Many thanks to the entire editorial team at Elsevier (Syngress and Academic Press) for their patience and guidance during this entire process.

Max Kilger

Max would like to sincerely acknowledge coauthors Cameron, Tom, and Terry for their spirit of camaraderie and their willingness to support each other throughout the process. In addition, I would like to thank the many nameless individuals that I encountered during my graduate school years in Silicon Valley during the personal computer revolution who helped shape my ideas about the relationship between people and digital technology. I learned more about how technology changes the way people think and see the world while hanging around electronic surplus stores and attending computer swap meets in Silicon Valley than I could have ever imagined. Finally, I would like to thank the entire editorial team at Elsevier (Syngress and Academic Press) for their patience and guidance during this entire process.

Introduction: Cyberanthropology of Deception

> Where the lion's skin will not reach, you must patch it out with the fox's
> –Lysander the Spartan (as ascribed by Plutarch, 75 AD)[1]

Communication as the presentation of information is one of the fundamental aspects of human life. This desire or need for conveyance varies contextually in breadth and scope between individuals, groups, organizations, and nation states. As with the variability in audience and the substance of communications, the manner and means of information presentation may greatly differ. In all of these contextual and substantive distinctions is the universal aspect of controlling messaging, or conveying a message in a way that is favorable to communicator's goals.

History has shown that one powerful way to instrument control and presentation of a narrative is through *deception*, or misleading a targeted audience into believing information that aligns with the communicator's objectives and protecting a safeguarded or secret truth (Bell & Whaley, 1991; Bennett & Waltz, 2007; Bodmer, Kilger, Carpenter, & Jones, 2012). Indeed, deception may be used to inflate, obscure, or otherwise manipulate facts to comport with the communicator's ultimate objectives. However, throughout recorded history, the ability to deceive others through various means has been a challenge, requiring creativity and novel strategies. The capacity for human beings to fabricate ideas, weave creative stories, and convince others that what is being seen or heard is real is unparalleled, as is our ability to accept the results of these manipulations at face value.

The motivations to deceive are broad and have evolved over time. Artful misdirection has been used for centuries to confound audiences for entertainment and, ironically for this same duration, dichotomously used for strategic advantage over adversaries. A wall painting from the Beni Hassan tomb (Fig. I.1), estimated to be from 2500 BC, depicts an early conjurer performing what appears to be the cup-and-ball trick for a spectator (Christopher, 1973). In the following years, numerous images of conjurers performing the cup-and-ball magic and other conjuring feats for audiences have been captured from many countries and cultures, revealing the universality of collaborative deceit as entertainment.

---

[1] Clough, A. H. (Ed.). (2001). Plutarch's Lives (Vol. 2). Random House Digital, Inc.

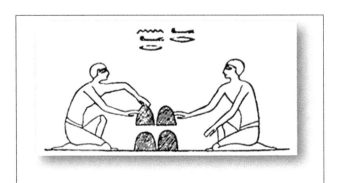

FIGURE I.1 Depiction of wall art from Beni Hassan tomb.

At times, deceit is used to aggrandize or obscure facts to gain notoriety and fortune. Like conjurers who master their deceptive craft to entertain, for centuries elegant fraudsters have created believable hoaxes that captivated society through sophisticated subterfuge. In 1912 Charles Dawson and Arthur Smith Woodard (keeper of the natural history department at the British Museum) announced the discovery of the fossilized remains of a previously unknown early human, which was named *Eoanthropus dawsoni*, or Dawson's dawn man.[2] It was surmised that the skull fragments dated the early human to 500,000 years old. Newspaper coverage and international interest cascaded from the discovery. Decades later, in 1953, the "Piltdown man" as it came to be known, was deemed to be an elaborate hoax (Hancock, 2015). While the Piltdown man hoax was still confounding many, in the early 1940's Dutch art forger Han van Meegeren swindled millions for his masterfully falsified paintings during Nazi Germany (Fig. I.2).

FIGURE I.2 The deceptive art of Han van Meegeren.

[2] The remains were "found" at Barkham Manor, Piltdown.

Deception has also been a part of military strategies for centuries,[3] dating back to approximately 1280 BC when the Hittites deceived Pharaoh Rameses and Egyptian forces during the Battle of Kadesh (Fig. I.3); years later in 1183 BC, military folklore describes the Greeks' use of a giant wooden horse to secret soldiers into the Trojan capital; and the biblical account of Gideon utilizing a "ghost army" technique, directing his soldiers to create sonic illusions to deceptively exaggerate the size and might of the army while raiding the Midianites.

Over time, military strategists and philosophers began to document philosophies and tactics about deception stratagems. Sun Tzu, Plutarch, and Niccolò Machiavelli contributed to the early corpus of texts containing philosophical and tactical use of misdirection.

World War II and modern military conflicts revealed that deception efforts to gain strategic advantage had meaningfully matured. The Allied forces' deception operations, including MINCEMEAT (the planting of false documents on a corpse dressed as a British soldier), BODYGUARD (misleading German forces as to the time and location of the Normandy invasion), and the Ghost Army (Intelligence Unit—23rd Headquarters Special Troops) were highly organized and a critical part of the war operations in Europe. The members of the Ghost Army, made up of artists and sound experts, were specially selected to create inflatable tanks, faux military bases, painted landscapes, sound effects, and carefully crafted fake radio transmissions to dupe the Germans.

The Ghost Army executed over 20 operations creating false units, while other deception operations focused on making military operations invisible. Just as Gideon used sonic illusions to raid the Midianites, submarine warfare in WWII also employed the use of sonar to

FIGURE I.3 Stone carving of Ramses in the Battle of Kadesh; the ingenious Hittite deception that nearly led to Ramses' defeat is conspicuously missing from the carvings.

[3] See, Speier, H. (1951). Psychological warfare reconsidered (No. RAND-P-196). Rand Corporation, Santa Monica, California; Michael, D. C. (2001). The Art of Deception in Warfare. Sterling Publishing Co. Inc.: New York; Tzu, S., & Giles, L. (2009). The art of war: The oldest military treatise in the world. Auckland, NZ: Floating Press.

hide US Navy submarines. Both the United States and Japan deployed the use of sonar to detect each other's submarines, as well as mine fields. The US submarines, however, were detecting odd sounds and interference from something in the ocean that was not part of enemy operations; they were large schools of Alpheids (pistol shrimp) that make loud snapping noises with their claws. The sound echoes of the shrimp disabled the US forces' ability to detect the sonar signatures of the enemy. Instead of destroying the schools of shrimp, the US Navy attained the locations of these shrimp schools and used them as "invisibility shields" against the Japanese, as their own sonar signatures were hidden in the noise of the clapping shrimp (Sonar and Shrimps in Anti-Submarine War, 1946).

The Digital Evolution: Cyberanthropology of Deception

Technology serves as a force multiplier in deception efforts, enhancing the ability to connive, convince, and cajole. One of the more valuable lessons to be learned is the unique three-way synergy between people, technology, and deception. Digital technology has allowed individuals to conduct deceptive activities through digital technology with an efficiency, effectiveness, and on a scale that is historically unprecedented. Building a more comprehensive understanding of the relationship between people and digital technology, especially as it relates to the practice of deception, is a key component in getting ahead of the threat curve in the digital world and has important implications for the field of information security as well as strategic importance in national security strategies by creating policies that will help anticipate and deflect future emerging cyber threats.

The challenge is not a new one. Perhaps one of the early and most noteworthy tools developed in this respect was the telephone, which enabled people to connect in real time in a way that was otherwise impossible at that point in history.

Alexander Graham Bell, who invented the device and helped usher it into the commercial marketplace, created Bell Telephone Company in order to install and manage the technology to support telephony. This included operators, who would route calls, connect lines, and interact with callers in order to ensure a successful connection. The first people hired to staff these jobs were teenage males, who were inexpensive and physically fit enough to handle the duties of managing switchboards. They were, however, viewed as completely inappropriate for the duties. They were rude, drank on the job, and played pranks on callers much to their chagrin.

The young men who staffed these jobs were quickly replaced by young women who proved capable for the job physically and mentally. This was not the end of males misusing telephony. In fact, teenage males would regularly use phones to make prank calls to annoy others and make themselves laugh. The use of deception for juvenile humor was, however, eventually supplanted by actors who used telephony in order to obtain information that was hidden.

One of the more unique examples of successful and deceptive phreaks were the Badir brothers, Ramay, Muzher, and Shadde, who were blind from birth. Despite their lack of eyesight, they were able to successfully phreak the Israeli telephone system and gain access to credit card numbers and the protected Israeli army's telephone network, eventually operating an illegal phone company that was billing calls to the army. Only one of the three, Ramy, was convicted on charges and was thought to have caused more than $2 million in damages and fraud. They were able to successfully complete these hacks through the use of braille computers, very sensitive and attuned hearing, and a knack for impersonation. They posed as business owners, secretaries, and officials throughout the course of their activities and were able to successfully maintain the deception because of their ability to carefully gather information about their targets in advance and use it in conjunction with convincing language.[4]

Humans have used a wide array of deception techniques throughout the ages. The history of magic, sorcery, and illusion provide the foundation for understanding how deception has evolved over time. Regardless of the timeframe, ancient or contemporary, the consistent elements of deception are rooted in the principles of psychology and the technologies of the times, playing out in both tactical and strategic applications. Whether the chosen deceptive methodology uses audio, video, tangible props, computer generated imagery, or other cyber/digital technologies, the core principals remain constant. As the digital world advances, including the devices that support wireless communications and the deployment of what are now considered experimental technologies (e.g., holograms, nanotechnology, neurohacking), the creative means to implement new deceptive techniques will likewise advance. While Houdini's physical escapes were the rage of the early 1900s, the proliferation of deception in the current environment and into the future will focus on cyber deception.

How to Use This Book

This book covers a broad and rich spectrum of topics, providing deep insight into the psychological bases and strategic and practical aspects of deception. While the book can be read straight through from front to back, each chapter focuses on a specific facet of deception, enabling content to be read out of order, or for the book to be used as a reference guide.

The basis of deception is *misdirection*—shaping the perceptions and beliefs of the recipient. This book begins by exploring some of the traditional deception methods used by magicians and how these techniques can be similarly leveraged by cyber threat actors to circumvent human defenses. The chapter then turns to other psychological principles and strategies that are used to deceive and manipulate.

Chapter 2 examines how story narrative can captivate, compel, and deceive the receiving audience. The history and elements of urban legends, hoaxes, and chain communications are examined as underpinnings of deception strategies. The chapter then examines the evolution of these types of communications and how attackers use the story styles in computer-mediated communications to weaponize, scam, or otherwise deceive and exploit human targets.

---

[4] http://www.wired.com/2004/02/phreaks-2/

Chapter 3 explores traditional psychological influence concepts and techniques that are implemented across a broad spectrum of contexts, such as business, advertising, and political and military campaigns. The chapter then examines these principles through the lens of cyber attacks, where these precepts can be maliciously leveraged by cyber attackers to manipulate victims through elaborate deception narratives based upon exploiting heuristic cues to persuade and gain compliance. In particular, the chapter looks at hoax viruses, scareware, tech support scams, and ransomware campaigns, as well as the manner in which psychological influence manifests in these attacks.

Chapter 4 delves deeply into human actors involved in underground cyber markets in order to better understand how they function and what social dynamics shape the behavior of users. In particular, this chapter focuses on markets where individuals sell cybercrime as a service, including malware, hacking services, distributed denial of service attacks, and personal data. Through describing the structure and social ecosystem, the chapter provides insight into how actors deceive one another in order to gain competitive or economic advantage.

The deception strategies and techniques used in phishing and watering hole attacks are discussed in Chapter 5. The conjurer's misdirection concepts introduced in Chapter 1 are revisited, and additional concepts, such as the watering hole deception chain and technical persuasion, are explicated.

The proliferation of Internet connectivity, digital cameras, and editing software has made deception a common component of the online experience. Chapter 6 explores the burgeoning topic of deceptive Internet video communications, examining the diverse range of motives for the use of deception in online video and photography. The chapter provides a history of the application of deception in still photography and film with contemporary examples highlighting its role. Further, it discusses of the potential ways that deceptive imaging may be identified through the use of physics.

The book then transitions into how certain threat groups use deception in cyber attacks. Chapter 7 first examines the evolution of how terrorist organizations and supporters have used the Internet for conducting cyber attacks and then explores how these cyber jihadists use online deception to shape the narrative of their cyber network operations. The chapter then looks at some of the mechanisms and pathways of deception that are utilized by jihadists to further terrorist objectives. Chapter 8 further opens the aperture of the cyber threat group discussion by focusing upon nation state-sponsored cyberwarfare through the prism of psychological deception tactics and techniques.

Chapter 9 explores some of the theoretical aspects of cyber deception objects typically known as *honeypots* (or *honeynets*) and *honeytokens*. The chapter first describes these honey objects from a historical perspective then looks at how researchers have branched out and developed new and sophisticated forms of honey objects in an effort to better detect and protect digital networks and devices against compromise.

The book concludes by looking to the future of deception in the cyber threatscape. In particular, the chapter focuses upon six salient areas: (1) false online communities; (2) disruptive technology; (3) holograms; (4) nanotechnology and quantum stealth; (5) advanced drones; (6) neurohacking/neuromarketing; and (7) the man in the middle conundrum.

While deception and its psychological underpinnings have remained consistent over many centuries, the digital world opens nascent, seemingly limitless portals of how misdirection can be leveraged to exploit human targets. With you, the reader, we look forward to that boundless horizon with eyes (and minds) wide open.

References

Bell, J. B., & Whaley, B. (1991). *Cheating and deception.* Transaction Publishers.

Bennett, M., & Waltz, E. (2007). *Counterdeception principles and applications for national security.* Norwood, MA: Artech House.

Bodmer, S., Kilger, M., Carpenter, G., & Jones, J. (2012). *Reverse deception: Organized cyber threat counterexploitation.* McGraw Hill Professional.

Christopher, M. (1973). *The illustrated history of magic.* New York: Crowell.

Hancock, P. A. (2015). *Hoax springs eternal.* Cambridge University Press.

Sonar and shrimps in anti-submarine war. (April 08, 1946). *The Age,* p. 6. Online source: https://www.newspapers.com/newspage/123415940/.

1

The Psychology of Deception

ABSTRACT

The basis of deception is misdirection—shaping the perceptions and beliefs of the target audience. This chapter begins by exploring some of the traditional deception methods used by magicians and how these techniques can be similarly leveraged by cyber threat actors to circumvent human defenses. In particular, the first section of the chapter provides a rich discussion about passive and active misdirection principles used in conjuring to effectively disguise, distract, and control attention. The chapter then transitions toward other weapons of deception used by magicians to deceive spectators, such as forcing (choice manipulation); suggestion and implication; false objectives; disarming presentation; and Gestalt principles, among others. The final section in the chapter turns to other cognitive and neuropsychological principles and strategies that are used to deceive and exploit psychological vulnerabilities.

Keywords: *Cognitive illusions; Conjuring; Inattentional blindness; Interpersonal deception theory; Magic; Misdirection; Neuropsychology; Nonverbal cues; Psychology.*

Deception in the Digital Age. http://dx.doi.org/10.1016/B978-0-12-411630-6.00001-3

> "Psychological principles of deception are much more important than the mechanics of physical deception because they are much more effective. They are subtle. They rely upon powerful principles. They are insidious, irresistible."
>
> –Dariel Fitzkee
>
> "Psychology is the underlying fundamental of magic. Without psychology, there is no technique, naturalness, misdirection, timing, or appropriate patter."
>
> –Arturo Ascanio

Deception at a basic level is illusory information (visual, textual, audible, etc.) that manipulates and confounds perceptions so that the deceived (audience) believes the false information. Thus a vital lens in which through the psychology of deception can be examined is magic, or conjuring. For over 4000 years, magicians have artfully and successfully deceived audiences using a myriad of psychological and cognitive deceptions. This chapter begins by exploring some of the traditional deception methods used by conjurers and how these techniques can be similarly leveraged by cyber threat actors to circumvent human defenses. This chapter then turns to other psychological principles and strategies that are used to deceive and manipulate. As a whole, the chapter contains a lot of definitions and terminology, which sets the foundation for how the applied constructs of magic and conjuring are used in the contemporary world of cyber deception.

Scientists and researchers have closely studied magicians' creative use of misdirection, deception, and cognitive illusion. The resulting corpus of findings provides new insight into the cognitive and visual sciences behind magic and illusion. However, long before this deeper examination of the psychological elements of conjuring, magicians were practicing (and enchanted spectators documented) their deceptive craft. The earliest known magical performance is captured in the ancient Westcar papyrus (now at the State Museum in East Berlin), which details several wonderful stories of early Egyptian conjuring (Christopher, 1973). The hieroglyphics describe, among other feats, how ritualist Weba-āner metamorphosed a wax model of a crocodile into a live crocodile, an occasion when priest Jajamānekh recovered a lost hair ornament in a lake by splitting the body of water in two and stacking one half on top of the other, and magician, Dedi, who bemused Cheops by reanimating numerous animals from seeming decapitation (Christopher, 1973).

Contemporaneous to, and centuries following these feats, conjurers in Egypt, India, China, Babylonia, and other countries performed for audiences, mystifying them with a wide variety of slight-of-hand tricks. Spectators then began to document these fantastical performances in drawings, paintings and books (Fig. 1.1).[1] Enchanting illusions, such as The Indian Rope Trick, The Automaton Chess Player, Cup-and-Balls, Basket Trick, and the countless others that have entertained and confounded audiences up until the present day, were accomplished through misdirection.

FIGURE 1.1 "The Conjurer," oil on panel painting by Hieronymus Bosch (c.1450–1516) and workshop.

Misdirection and the Psychological Principles Behind Effective Magic

Misdirection is the foundation of successful magic and illusion; a skillful conjurer can artfully cause a spectator's attention to focus on what the conjurer wants, resulting in the

---

[1] In 1584, two seminal texts were published, widely considered to be the first books describing magic. Reginald Scot published *The Discoverie of Witchcraft* in England, while Jean Prévost published *La Première Partie des Subtiles et Plaisantes Inventions.*

spectator witnessing a magic effect but not the method used to create the effect. Thus misdirection is intended to shape the spectator's *perceptions* (processing and interpreting of sensory information) and *beliefs* (confidence that the sensory information perceived is reality). The shaping of perceptions and beliefs are also major components of digital deception as well.

Despite being the essential factor behind effective conjuring, misdirection is challenging to define. However, a generally accepted definition is "the art of attracting the audience's gaze and attention to an unsuspicious and interesting point, while a secret action is taking place elsewhere, in such a way that this action is undetected and unsuspected" (Ascanio & Etcheverry, 2005). Another challenge is deconstructing and describing the elements used toward misdirection. Indeed, many magicians and, more recently, academic researchers (some of whom are also magicians) have endeavored to elucidate the components and processes that lead to successful misdirection. In this section the deception and misdirection philosophies and frameworks that explore these concepts, theories, and practices are examined.

Active and Passive Misdirection: Factors Toward Influence by Suggestion

Renowned magician Sam H. Sharpe (more commonly known as S.H. Sharpe) defined misdirection as "intentional deflection of attention for the purpose of disguise" (Sharpe, 1988, p. 47). Misdirection, posited Sharpe, was part of large set of five classifications that a magician used to influence his audience. These classifications are:

1. creating atmosphere
2. inducing imaginary impressions
3. influencing emotions (showmanship)
4. influencing choice (forcing)
5. misdirection

Notably, Sharpe bifurcated misdirection into two types: *Active* and *Passive*. *Active Misdirection* (Fig. 1.2) describes methods that are dependent upon some type of change in movement or sound. Conversely, *Passive Misdirection* (Figs. 1.3 and 1.4) stealthily goes unnoticed by the spectator due to the magician's ability to manipulate static stimuli, engineering how the spectator's mind processes and reacts. Sharpe further distilled these types of misdirection by categorizing the means by which misdirection was accomplished, either through *Disguise* (to avoid attention by altering appearance in some way) or *Distraction* (to draw attention away by introducing a more powerful stimuli to act as a decoy) (Sharpe, 1988). Thus through the lens of Sharpe's model, a conjurer may deceive a spectator through the use of disguise or distraction as defined below:

●***Active Misdirection to Disguise***: This misdirection describes the actions the magician takes to influence the audience (e.g., authority; natural, uniform, and appropriate actions; use of inference; repetition or recapitulation; audacity) and/or to cause concealment (e.g., feigning; ruse/covering procedure; timing; removal of evidence; substitution of evidence; varied procedure; inspection), effectively hiding the "Trick Zone," or area that the method is being actuated.

In today's digital environment, malicious online actors often use the disguise of authority to misdirect individuals into desired actions. Posing as representatives of official government entities such as government taxing organizations (e.g., the Internal Revenue Service), federal law enforcement agents from agencies such as the Federal Bureau of Investigation, or legal representatives from court systems, these online malicious actors or groups disguise their attempts to extract information or funds from their victims through color of authority. This disguise technique is commonly seen in phishing emails and phone scams.

●***Active Misdirection to Distract Attention***: A conjurer may use external stimuli to divert attention away from himself and toward the stimuli, such as: (1) audience participation, (2) indication by gesture or gaze, (3) decoy movement or variation, (4) patter/sound, and (5) intentional mishaps. In addition to these overt extrinsic stimuli, active misdirection to distract attention may also be accomplished through three types of stimulation. Stimulation is simply another form of distraction, and the first type, *mental stimulation*, is the prompting of the spectator's imagination and memory of what he perceived in an altered manner through subtle suggestions. The second type, *emotional stimulation*, initiated through means such as enhanced dramatic narrative or plot, causes lowered attention to the magician's actions. The third type of stimulation includes *surprise or suspense*, which can be calibrated during the course of conjuring performance in a way that does not enable the audience to predict suspense throughout the performance. To this end, Sharpe categorized the types of surprise as *absolute surprise* (effect occurs with no build-up or warning), *anticipated surprise* (subtle hints that the cause the audience to expect something to occur without fully knowing what it could be), *forewarned surprise* (where the anticipated event is actually broadcasted to the audience prior to the effect), and *substituted surprise*, wherein the magician cues the audience to anticipate a likely crescendo and effect but in actuality reveals an unanticipated effect (Sharpe, 1988).

In the digital world, active misdirection may involve malicious online actors attacking a particular network within a target organization, when in fact this action is actually a feint. While information security personnel are busy dealing with the decoy attack, the attackers move their attention to the real target, knowing that the defenders have had their attention drawn elsewhere.

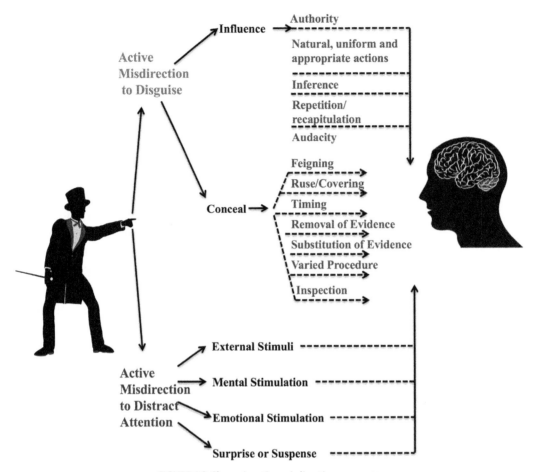

FIGURE 1.2 Sharpe's active misdirection concepts.

●*Passive Misdirection for Disguise or Effacement*. Conjurers can alleviate or dispel suspicion surrounding props or other objects by ensuring that the objects resonate with spectators as natural, familiar, and innocuous. Factors such as props' visual appearance, spacing, and multiplicity impact the conjurer's ability to properly misdirect. When items are viewed as innocuous, nonsalient, and familiar, audience *perception vigilance* is lowered and inattention, or diluted concentration, is induced (Sharpe, 1988). Factors that impact this type of misdirection by lowering the audience's interest or attention to detail include:

- familiarity, lack of unusual features, appearing nondescript;
- camouflage;
- disposition (placing articles in a manner that confuses a spectator's perception of size, position, etc.);
- separation;

- lack of interest;
- lack of glamour;
- immobility;
- multiplicity; and
- mistaken identity (through substitution).

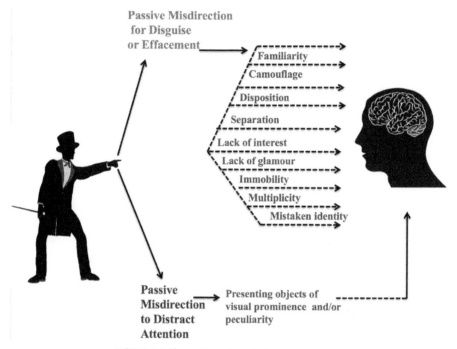

FIGURE 1.3 Sharpe's passive misdirection concepts.

Passive disguise is one of the more common techniques used by malicious online actors in reaching their objectives. The construction of websites that mimic legitimate banking websites to capture financial credentials is a ubiquitous form of this tactic. They rely upon the use of familiar logos, color schemes, font types, and spatial placement of form fields to misdirect the user into thinking the website is legitimate. Once the user enters their banking credentials, the information is forwarded to a server, usually in another country, to be collected and sold on the underground financial credentials market.

●*Passive Misdirection to Distract Attention*: Unlike passive misdirection for disguise, wherein subtlety and innocuousness is paramount, *passive misdirection to distract* seeks to divert the spectators' attention by presenting objects of visual prominence and/or peculiarity. By displaying an item(s) that is more conspicuous, novel, or laden with many inessential features, the spectator is drawn to these items and unable to focus on the magician's secret actions (Sharpe, 1988).

One common strategy and use of passive misdirection in the digital world comes through the use of repetition. This digital misdirection strategy relies on the fact that online users utilizing web browsers to visit websites have quickly learned that the most basic ubiquitous navigational action is to click on a link or button presented to them on a website. This action is repeated over and over, sometimes hundreds of times on a particular day, to navigate their web browsers to the desired web page or action until it becomes an almost immediate, reflexive action. Malicious online actors take advantage of this behavior to distract the user from carefully examining the details of the web page that might tip off the user that there is something amiss about the website. The website is designed to focus the user's attention on the action the malicious actor wants them to take (e.g., click a link for example) and to draw their attention away from any details that might suggest to the user that the website is not what is appears to be on the surface.

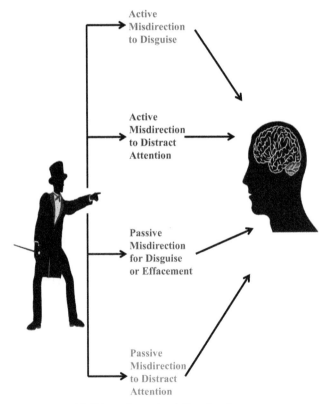

FIGURE 1.4 Sharpe's misdirection theory.

General, Particular, and Post Misdirection

In addition to defining the types of deception, Sharpe, in his seminal work *Conjurer's Psychological Secrets*, outlined the purposes of misdirection. His book provides additional, granular insight into the purpose and temporal scope of misdirection. Sharpe posited that there are two layers or types of misdirection occurring during a conjurer's performance. First, there is *general misdirection,* which through the conjurer's tradecraft and way of connecting with the audience generates an atmosphere of acceptance and susceptibility. By laying this foundation of lowered attention vigilance, more granular misdirection tactics are employed by the conjurer to distract or disguise his deception actions prior to the magic effect and are described by Sharpe as *particular misdirection* tactics (Sharpe, 1988).

Misdirection Through Disguise and Attention Control

Book three of the *Fitzkee Trilogy* by renowned magician Dariel Fitzkee is aptly entitled *Magic by Misdirection: An Explanation of Psychological Deception, 5th ed.* (1945/2009). In this treatise, Fitzkee defines and describes in detail the vital elements of psychological deception (many of which are explored later in this chapter). Many of these elements, described as early as 1945, factor into the mechanics of contemporary social engineering used in cyber attacks. Fitzkee's elements (also shown in Fig. 1.5) include:

- pretense
- implication
- misdirection
- prearrangement
- simulation
- dissimulation
- anticipation
- inducement
- deduction
- interpretation
- confusion
- suggestion
- ruse

Fitzkee (1945/2009) defines misdirection as the "effective employment of disguise or attention control in order to deceive. It directs or leads the spectator away from the true solution" (p. 133). *Misdirection through disguise* is accomplished by deceiving the spectator through his/her senses. The artifice of disguise is typically physical; it causes the viewer to believe that they seeing or experiencing something that they are actually not. Misdirection through *psychological disguise* does not attack the senses, but rather influences the spectator's reasoning and judgment. The viewer's mind is targeted, often with no physical deception at all (Fitzkee, 1945/2009). Techniques that invoke and sustain psychological deception include:

- **Simulation.** In general terms, a conjurer may deceive the spectator by presenting an imitation to the spectator's perceptive senses, or make something look like what it is not. Applying this precept to *psychological disguise* then is to influence the spectator's *understanding*, not simply perception. This is described in greater detail in the text box, "Good Acting." Fitzkee posited that effective and convincing psychological simulation manifests from the magician's ability to act and maintain a naturalness to the performance (Fitzkee, 1945/2009). One example of simulation from the digital world of deception is the use of a faux progress bar. Users have been thoroughly indoctrinated through experiences with progress bars and generally associate them with something good happening (e.g., installing new software). They have been trained to expectantly wait until the progress bar reaches 100% before proceeding with any further actions. Users waiting on progress bars also tend to lower their arousal levels and have learned to detach their focus from the machine while the progress bar is displayed. This reduced mode of awareness sets a perfect stage for conducting malicious operations on the machine while the individual is in this desensitized state.

- *Dissimulation.* The opposite of simulation is *dissimulation*, concealing a real fact by pretense or making something appear that it is dissimilar to what it truly is (Fitzkee, 1945/2009). From a psychological context, this technique often renders when the conjurer's actions cause the audience to believe that an item or action he is taking, which is actually very distinct and salient to fulfill the magical effect, is not unique from a mundane one. An example of this may be that in actuality the conjurer is treating a certain prop with extreme care but outwardly showing the audience that its being handled in a manner consistent with a regular item of its kind. Fitzkee (1945/2009) opined that:

"…dissimulation is probably the most often utilized expedient in the entire category of deceptive stratagems…there is hardly a trick in magic that does not somewhere during its performance require something to be disguised as dissimilar to what it truly is. It disguises a condition, as in the secretly empty or secretly occupied hand. It disguises a manipulation, a movement or an operation, such as with the card houlette or production box. It covers special preparation, special requirements, special restrictions. It overcomes difficult obstacles. It changes the spectator's sense of significant situations and suspicious handicaps. It disguises the secret presence or absence of something. It disguises purposes, reasons and clues that might be suspicious" (p. 116).

One example of dissimilarity in the digital world is the lure of the pursuit of exploiting code within software packages or platforms that accomplish some minor function or feature that appears innocent to users. Rather than attempt to attack elements of the code that deal with serious functionality such as authentication or adding users or privileges, where developers are likely to have built in defenses against tampering or exploitation and users will likely be on alert when performing these functions, malicious online actors may focus on exploiting minor functions or features that will provide just as much exploit potential as more core features of the code but without the inherent defenses built by the developers and without the threat of more alert than usual users.

 **Similar or dissimilar?**

Perhaps the easiest way to distinguish simulation from dissimulation is manner of presentation:

Simulation is a *positive* act and shows a false picture

Dissimulation is a *negative* act and *hides a true picture*

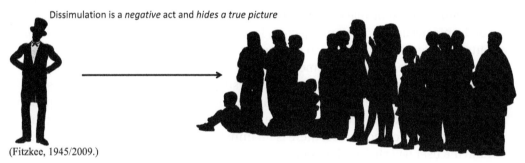

(Fitzkee, 1945/2009.)

FIGURE 1.5 Fitzkee (1945/2009).

- **Maneuver.** The convincingness and physicality of a magician's actions and inactions directly impact the totality of the deception efforts during a trick or illusion. Thus the deftness of the executed *maneuvers* or series of circumstances, movements, and/ or actions that comprise the deception trajectory of an effect are critical. Fitzkee (1945/2009) described that "the maneuver is an artfully planned and skillfully executed process or course of action, preplanned to influence appearances, apparently extemporaneous, without any suggestion of resistance to overcome" (pp. 46–47).
- **Ruse.** A shrewd means of stymieing spectators' ability to closely follow a magician's actions or objectives is by using a *ruse*. A ruse is a reasonable, convincing, but untrue basis for an action; it diverts the spectator's attention from the conjurer's true objective by providing a plausible alternative. The critical component of the ruse is *convincingness*; if the ruse is unrealistic or unreasonable it will cause the converse effect of drawing attention to the magician's true purpose and intentions (Fitzkee, 1945/2009). In one of the milder forms of digital deception, for example, a mobile app that assists device owners in locating local restaurants may ask the owner for permission to use the location services of the device. This makes perfect sense because in order to perform its job well, the mobile application needs to know where the device/owner currently is. However, what is not disclosed is that the geolocation data is being cached and sent onward to the mobile app developer who is then selling the geolocation data to mobile advertisers.

- ***Suggestion/Implication.*** Implications and suggestions are indirect methods of bringing something before a spectator's mind and vary in their degree of indirection (Fitzkee, 1945/2009). *Suggestion* tacitly and subtly places an idea into the spectator's mind or initiates a sequence of thoughts without the benefit of a direct, formal statement. Similarly, *implication,* a slightly more direct form of suggestion, arises from a statement, act, or insinuation conveying the conjurer's intended meaning; the proffered inference causes the spectator to draw a conclusion.
- ***Inducement.*** Similar to a *force* technique (described later in greater detail in the *Magician's Weapons of Deception* section), *inducement* causes the spectator to believe he or she has made a choice free from the magician's influence. Similarly it causes other spectators to believe the participant spectator has made his or her own decision, independent of magician manipulation. Importantly, the audience's perception that a choice free of magician interference causes less attention, weight, or significance to be placed on the decision, which actually may be a pivotal part of the magician's deception trajectory leading to the effect crescendo. While some attempts by malicious actors to get a user to click on a link or banner to go to a website involve items of extreme interest to motivate the user (e.g., "clickbait"), other malicious actors rely upon subtle persuasive elements to entice the user to follow the link. These actors realize that low key approaches raise fewer suspicions, especially for experienced users, and also project and reinforce the idea that the user has an unforced choice: there is no unnatural enticement to click on the link and the user will click on it or not as they wish.

Both suggestion and inducement can be powerful motivational factors in influencing behaviors. Their current use in online environments is somewhat limited but given their ability to shape the behavior of others, we can expect to see more of these type of strategies being utilized by online malicious actors in the future.

Good Acting

A critical factor toward effective misdirection and deception is *good acting*. A confident conjuror through good acting can convince and deceive an audience easier, and in turn, convey the magical effect seamlessly. Misdirection innovator Dariel Fitzkee (1945/2009) believed that good acting and misdirection were in many ways synonymous: "Misdirection, it must be realized, *is acting—good acting—and nothing else.* This acting is planned in such a way that what the performer does, how he looks, and what he says—all of these, and more—all cooperate in strengthening disguise and in controlling attention. Through this acting, the things a magician does seem natural, plausible, reasonable convincing. They seem this way, even though the spectator knows them to be quite the opposite" (p. 182).

Misdirection through attention control, (Fig. 1.5.2) conversely, causes the spectator's attention to be drawn away from significant and potentially revealing things that could compromise the effect (Fitzkee, 1945/2009). Thus to manipulate a spectator's attention, the following techniques are used:

- *Anticipation.* The conjurer may seek to calibrate attention and avail himself of audience hypovigilance by performing significant aspects of a trick or illusion prior to when the spectator *anticipates* an action or properly focuses attention, placing significance on the conjurer's actions.
- *Premature consummation.* Spectators relax after they witness the crescendo of a magical effect; anticipation is built during the lead up and released after the effect (Fitzkee, 1945/2009). Exploiting this propensity, the conjurer causes the audience to believe that they have witnessed the magical effect, in turn relaxing attention. It is during this window of lowered vigilance and perception vulnerability that the conjurer performs the significant hidden action that leads to the real magical effect. Online malicious actors may stage an attack on a targeted machine that they know is likely to fail but will draw attention and resources to the machine. Once the defenders have detected the attack and resolved the issue, they may be more likely to relax their attention just a bit immediately after the resolution of the problem for a short period of time, and the malicious actors may be able to use this small time window to press a secondary attack.

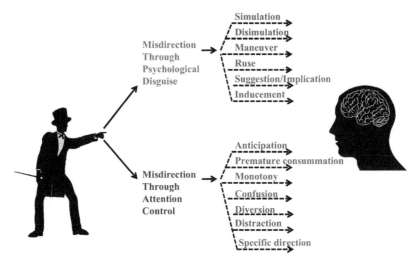

FIGURE 1.5.2 Fitzkee's misdirection model.

- *Monotony.* Another factor that leads to audience attention limitations and deficits is repetition of action. The spectator, while perhaps initially observant and circumspect of the magician's every action, becomes dulled by repetitive actions that result in no observable or relevant outcome in the course of a trick or illusion. With the spectator's attention resources diminished, the magician then effectuates a deception action that leads to the magical effect (Fitzkee, 1945/2009). Leveraging this technique, if a malicious actor can develop an attack scenario that mimics a much more common one that is seen frequently and routinely dealt with, this may reduce the chances that someone will notice modest differences in the attack that may in fact make it successful.

- **Confusion.** Unlike misdirection, which seeks to cause a diversion or distraction, confusion seeks to lower the spectator's attention resources by mixing details to the extent that it becomes impossible to discern the significant from the insignificant. Such an inextricability of information, particularly when compounded by time compression, precludes the spectator's vigilance in observation or focus on a particular aspect of the magician's secret actions (Fitzkee, 1945/2009).
- **Diversion.** Considered by Fitzkee to be the most subtle misdirection stratagem, *diversion* causes the spectator to shift attention from the true, proper interest and lures to a new, stronger interest, or a false interest disguised as the original (Fitzkee, 1945/2009).
- **Distraction.** Converse to diversion, which is delicate, shrewd, and alluring, *distraction* relies upon an abrupt stimulus to shift the spectator's attention from the proper interest to the new interest. Often jolting or alarming, a distraction is typically so overt and powerful that the spectator is not capable of focusing on anything other than this new distracting stimulus (Fitzkee, 1945/2009). In the scope of a cyber attack, here we may see malicious actors plan an unusual attack on a core and vital network or server where the consequences of compromise are significant. While the perpetrators are aware that the attack is likely to fail, the unusual nature of the attack combined with the consequences of a successful exploit keep the defender's attention focused on the decoy attack while the actual target machine is compromised.
- **Specific direction.** Unlike other stratagems of attention control, specific direction is an outright instruction, conveyed verbally or through a gesture, for the audience to shift focus to a different location (Fig. 1.6) (Fitzkee, 1945/2009).

Attention Control

The importance of attention control is examined is in a different but equally important context by renown sleight-of-hand-artist, card manipulator, and gambling authority, Darwin Ortiz. According to Ortiz, "misdirection is only an aspect of the larger subject of attention control"—and the two fundamental facets of attention are *holding attention* and *directing attention*. (Ortiz, 1984: p.331). To manipulate attention, the conjurer draws from the tools and concepts of:

- Performer's interest;
- Pointing;
- Patter;
- Sound;
- Contrast;
- Newness;
- Inherent Interest

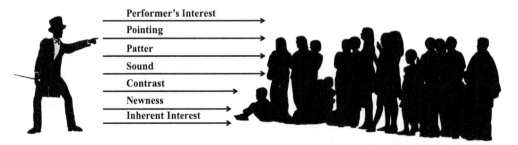

FIGURE 1.6 Darwin Ortiz's "tools of attention control."

Physical and Psychological Misdirection

Perhaps the most salient modern scholarly work on the psychology of conjuring is Peter Lamont and Richard Wiseman's *Magic in Theory: An Introduction to the Theoretical and Psychological Elements of Conjuring* (1999). One of the most unusual and compelling aspects of this treatise is that Lamont and Wiseman are both academics and former professional magicians. Fundamentally, they define misdirection as "that which directs the audience towards the effect and away from the method" (Lamont & Wiseman, 1999, p. 31). However, the Lamont and Wiseman framework for misdirection (Fig. 1.6.2) contemplates both *physical misdirection* and *psychological misdirection*.

   Physical Misdirection. Physical misdirection is manipulating the spectator's attention using *passive diversion* techniques that subtly influence and shift focus and *active diversion* techniques that more engagingly cause the spectator to shift his attention. Furthermore, physical misdirection can leverage the *temporal calibration* of *when* to direct audience attention.

- ***Passive Diversion.*** A spectator's attention is naturally drawn to stimuli that stand out in his field of vision, or conditions of *primary interest*. Conditions that may exist but are not the main or initial focal point are of *secondary interest* (Lamont & Wiseman, 1999). Passive diversion takes advantage of these natural areas of focus, creating or manipulating conditions that enhance or diminish interest points. Tactics that conjurers use to accomplish this include the following:
  - *Novelty.* Unfamiliar actions or items are *novel* and cause attention gravitation. Thus new, unexpected actions or newly introduced objects will take attention primacy over preexisting objects or actions.
  - *Movement.* The human eye is naturally drawn toward movement and dynamic objects gain attention over static objects (Lamont & Wiseman, 1999). This proclivity is also relevant in degree and in temporal sequencing. For example, larger, more dramatic movements draw visual resources quicker than smaller, subtle movements, and even when there are multiple movements occurring conterminously, it is the first moving object that holds the spectator's attention (Lamont & Wiseman, 1999).
  - *Contrast.* Magicians use *contrast* as a means of steering audience attention. Objects with colors that are noticeably different than the background are visual stimuli, naturally standout, and will immediately draw audience interest (Lamont & Wiseman, 1999).
- ***Active Diversion.*** While passive diversion relies upon influencing the spectator's natural reaction to stimuli, active diversion creates areas of primary or secondary interest through social interaction with the conjurer. Engagement techniques that the conjurer uses to influence audience attention include:
  - *Eyes.* A universal principle and practice in magic is that *the audience looks where the magician looks* (Tamariz, 2007). If the magician looks at an object, the audience looks at the object; if the magician looks at the audience, the audience

members look at the magician. Thus skilled conjurers artfully and purposefully shift their gaze to conceal methods and accentuate effects, or as master magician Juan Tamariz (2007) described it, "misdirection with the gaze" (p. 16).

- o *Voice.* The conjurer's spoken word can be used as a diversion instrument to both lower attention vigilance and direct spectator attention. In the former, a magician's *patter,* or speech during a performance, can be designed to produce a desired response from the audience and when used in a hypnotic cadence can decrease attention and awareness. Conversely, when used as a directive, the magician can verbally instruct the audience where to look. In his respected work, *The Five Points of Magic: A Treatise on the Body's Role in Deception,* Tamariz (2007) perspicaciously advises, "Don't forget that your voice and patter will lead the spectators' minds where you want and need them. This is one of the magician's most powerful weapons for deceiving his spectators, both intellectually and emotionally" (p. 29).

- o *Body Language.* The conjurer's posture, position, movement and physical expressiveness are methods of communicating with the audience. To this end, good, experienced conjurers diligently work on controlling their body language to ensure that it is a concealing factor and conversely that it is not a liability, revealing information about their deception technique and efforts (Tamariz, 2007).

- o *External Source of Diversion.* Extrinsic actions or staged occurrences, through assistants, members of the audience, or collateral events are powerful attention diverters.

The above examples of active diversion involve face-to-face interaction that is nearly always present between a magician and the audience. However, just as verbal and non-verbal cues can actively shape and reshape primary and secondary focuses for audience members, digital actors and activities can be staged and manipulated and change the focus in the online world. This is particularly true for state-sponsored groups or even for nation states who wish to alter the current focus of defenders. For example, a nation state might manipulate the threat environment by providing one specific malicious online group of actors' resources or encouragement or both to pursue a particular method of attack or a particular target. When this strategy begins to deploy and engage the information security community with what is a very real threat, the nation state then may turn to another specific group of online malicious actors or even their own internal hacking resources to the true (and unrelated) target utilizing an entirely different approach, knowing that much of the attention of the community is focused elsewhere. The manipulation of the global online threat environment by nation state actors is a strategy that should not be overlooked as useful for intelligence gathering.

- **Temporal Calibration.** The timing of a diversion technique is an integral part of misdirection. Properly timed, a method is concealed and the effect is spectacular; poorly timed, the method is discovered and the effect fizzles. Magicians take advantage of audience attention fluctuation and manipulate the timing of when to execute a method, ensuring that attention is diverted at optimum times. Some temporal factors considered and employed by magicians are:

- ○ *Reducing attention at the moment of the method.* A powerful way to reduce attention during the execution of a deception method is to make the method a point of secondary interest in relation to another primary stimulus. To this end, the conjurer can stage this technique at *moments outside the effect*, i.e., at diminished attention periods when the spectator believes the effect has not begun or has just ended. This technique incorporates Fitzkee's principals of applying *anticipation* and premature consummation. Recall from earlier in the chapter that anticipation is leveraging audience hypovigilance by performing significant aspects of a trick or illusion prior to when the spectator *anticipates* an action. Conversely, *premature consummation* is when the conjurer causes the audience to believe that they have witnessed the magical effect, in turn, relaxing attention. It is during this window of lowered vigilance and perception vulnerability that the conjurer performs the significant hidden action that leads to the real magical effect. The conjurer may also cause misdirection of attention during *moments inside the effect* by introducing factors such as monotony or humor that provide a brief, availing window of attention relaxation (Lamont & Wiseman, 1999).

Applying the concept of premature consummation to today's cyber world, there are some time windows during online sessions where users might be more vulnerable than others. For example, online users are particularly aware and have high arousal levels during online financial transactions. The threat of having financial credentials or other information stolen puts the online user on alert when they are engaging in online financial transactions. Once the online user completes the transaction, this level of higher arousal and awareness should significantly dip, both due to the removal of the situation that generated the arousal (i.e., the financial transactions are finished) as well as the fact that individuals cannot maintain high levels of arousal and awareness for indefinite periods of time. Therefore it would appear that one of the best times for a malicious online actor to catch a victim unaware in a moment of vulnerability would be just after they have completed a financial transaction session.

Psychological Misdirection. While physical misdirection enables the conjurer to engineer what the spectator perceives, it is psychological misdirection that engineers how the spectator interprets what he perceives (Lamont, Henderson, & Smith, 2010; Lamont & Wiseman, 1999).

Directing the Spectator's Suspicion. Audience suspicion is inherent in magic performances. While the audience is attending the performance to have an enjoyable time, beholding the magician's feats, they are equally curious—whether consciously or subconsciously—as to how the magician is accomplishing his effects. Thus, fundamentally, psychological misdirection attacks spectator suspicion, seeking to quell or divert it. In the digital world a malicious online group might attempt to lay down clues in program code, choose targets, salt Internet Relay Chat (IRC), or employ other tactics that direct suspicion away from their group and toward another group. They might develop a general exploit that they then make a number of variants for and distribute them among other groups so that it will be difficult for investigators to track down the origin of the exploit.

- *Reducing suspicion.* To suppress the spectator's attention vigilance and curiosity, the magician must create an atmosphere and implement actions that resonate with the audience, allaying focus and concern about the magician's methods (Lamont & Wiseman, 1999). Elements that may be used and combined during the course of a performance include:
  - naturalness
  - consistency
  - necessity
  - justification
  - familiarization
  - ruse
  - conviction
  - charisma
  - self-conviction
  - reinforcement
- *Diverting Suspicion.* In addition to reducing suspicion, the conjurer may seek to misroute suspicion by offering a condition that the spectator perceives as the true area of focus, worthy of heightened scrutiny. These diversions are commonly called *false solutions* and *false expectations.*
  - *False Solutions.* As described in greater detail in the text box "The Method of False Solutions," below, the magician may provide the spectator with alternative, false solutions that misrepresent the method used to facilitate the effect. There are many ways to implement this method. Tamariz opined that ultimately the execution of the effect should cause spectators to believe that any and all solutions are *false solutions*, leaving "magic" as the only viable answer for the method. This tactic is often seen implemented by cyber attackers. Highly skilled online malicious actors may attempt to develop exploit code that utilizes a primary exploit path while attempting to covertly embed a secondary exploit that attempts to masquerade as something more benign such as housekeeping code or code simply injected to obfuscate the primary exploit.
  - *False Expectations.* Magicians can divert attention, suspicion, and areas of interest by misrepresenting to the audience what the effect will be. Thus while the audience waits for the promised effect in the magician-engineered primary point of interest, a skillfully executed deception method is employed in a secondary point of interest unbeknownst to the audience (Lamont & Wiseman, 1999).

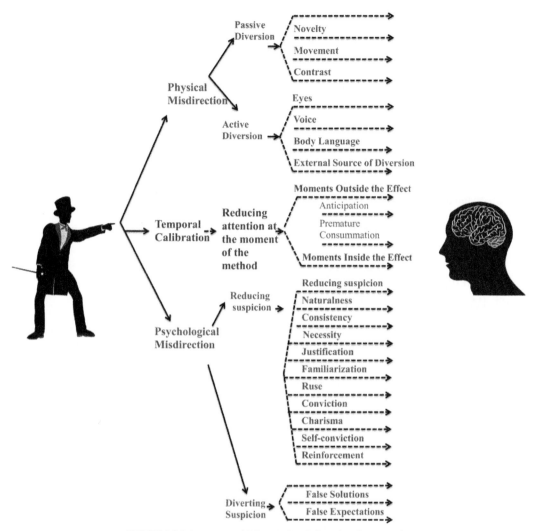

FIGURE 1.6.2 Lamont and Wiseman's misdirection framework.

The Method of False Solutions

To successfully create spectacular magic the spectator must not be able to discern the method, secret, or "actual solution" used to facilitate the trick, opines Spanish master conjurer Juan Tamariz. In his seminal magic theory text, *The Magic Way* (1987/2014), Tamariz describes the importance of the impacting the spectator's psyche: "We need to know what goes on in the spectators' minds during the course of the trick and upon its completion, and we must determine the kind of impact produced in their minds. We should find out whether they suspect a

Continued

—Continued

method, even if it is not the one we employed. Besides their not knowing how we did the trick, we must prevent them from analyzing *how we could have done it*. In other words, they should be incapable of figuring out a solution, whether it is the right one or not. Going even further, the spectators should not even want to figure it out. Besides being astonished, they should be dumbfounded, caught in a hallucination, feeling amazed, spellbound and totally fascinated by the mystery they have witnessed. The shock of mystery suspends any ability to analyze, as well as the desire to do so" (p. 3). To accomplish this the magician, during the course of performing a trick, must not only conceal the trick but cause the spectator to believe that any and all solutions are *false solutions*, leaving magic as the only possible basis for what they have witnessed. Further, if the method of false solutions is artfully executed, the audience will be so intoxicated by the magical atmosphere of the performance that they will not be able (nor want) to analyze how the trick was done (Tamariz, 1987/2014).

Exploiting False Assumptions: Assumptive, One-Point, and Two-Point Misdirection

Virtual Magic practitioner/innovator Al Schneider postulates that misdirection, while essential for effective magic, is actually a supporting technique to the greater concept of hiding the spectators' false assumptions (Schneider, 2011). For magic to work "as magic," Schneider contends that there are five steps in the process, or "Five Steps of Deception":

1. ***Show Something:*** In this first step the magician overtly displays the object to be manipulated, ensuring the audience sees it.
2. ***Change:*** This is the pivotal point in the performance of a trick where deception is executed. After showing the audience the target object for manipulation, the conjurer makes a change that causes something to happen—while the audience believes that something else happened; the audience must notice the change and base assumptions upon it, while not questioning the veracity of it. Scheneider defines this process as *assumptive misdirection.*
3. ***Show Change Result:*** During this phase the magic effect is revealed to the audience. Optimally, the reveal is fully observed and appreciated by the audience.
4. ***Audience Review:*** This is essentially the period wherein the audience "digests" or "absorbs" the magical event (effect) that was just revealed. During this phase the conjurer should remain focused on the effect and allow the audience to bathe in the magic, as opposed to gauge audience feedback, which could be potentially disruptive and nullify the effect.
5. ***Audience Decision:*** The audience internally evaluates and reacts to the magic event; for the magician this optimally results in surprise, shock, fear, or other meaningful emotion (Schneider, 2011).

Schneider (2011) defines misdirection as "direct attention at the wrong place or event" (p. 116). Framing this alternatively, misdirection serves to divert attention off of something while focusing it on the idea that nothing has occurred (Schneider, 2011). While recognizing that there are several kinds of misdirection in the context of magic, Schneider proffers that the two salient types are *One-point* and *Two-point;* the fundamental variable distinguishing the two is where the spectator is directed (Fig. 1.7).

Two-point Misdirection is the most common and practical type of misdirection; it requires the conjurer to do something that causes the audience to look elsewhere in order to implement a move of deception, and in turn, perform the magic effect (Schneider, 2011). This type of misdirection, opines Schneider, is limiting and less impactful, as the audience may realize they made a false assumption during the performance and were not looking in the "right place" during the performance of the trick. Thus while effective for theater magic performances where spectators are essentially in a tacit agreement with the magician to suspend disbelief, two-point misdirection is not as flexible and nuanced as one-point misdirection.

Conversely, one-point misdirection is more nuanced; its intention is not to cause the audience to look away from the deception event, but rather, while looking at the event they are cognitively misdirected, misperceiving what they see and believed to have witnessed, or as Schneider (2011) frames this, "look at the wrong event mentally" (p. 117). Arguably, Schneider's perspective on one-point misdirection is similar to Fitzkee's psychological disguise or Sharpe's passive misdirection theory.

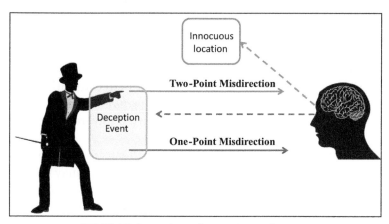

FIGURE 1.7 One-point and two-point misdirection.

Misdirection Through Message Construction and Conveyance: Attitude, Transference, Repetition, Verbal/Nonverbal

In addition to distracting attention or disguising a method, misdirection techniques can be implemented by conjurers to obscure or manipulate the manner a deceptive message is conveyed to the audience. Close-up magician and social psychologist Jason Randal developed a deception model that captures the totality of a deceptive action or deceptive behavior. In particular, the model consists of four areas of focus: (1) the **Source** of deception; (2) the deceptive **Message**; (3) the mode or **Channel** in which the deceptive message is transmitted; and (4) the **Receiver** of the deceptive message. All of these variables are considered within the context of the physical environment, cultural nuances, and social environment that the deceptive message is being conveyed. In this model, misdirection primarily occurs during the conveyance of the deceptive message and manifests as misdirection of attitude; misdirection by transference, misdirection by repetition, verbal misdirection, or nonverbal misdirection (Randal, 1982).

- **Misdirection of Attitude or Misdirection by Transference**. The magician may alter or *misdirect his attitude* about certain movements or props, causing the audience to perceive that these items are insignificant and ultimately miss deceptive actions. Similarly, the magician may accomplish a deceptive method by misdirecting the audience's attention by *transferring* attention to someone other than him, commonly an assistant or audience member (Randal, 1982).
- **Misdirection by Repetition**. The magician, through repetitive gestures or actions, can desensitize suspicions and relax attention. This *misdirection by repetition* inhibits perception vigilance, allowing the magician to effectively execute a deception method without detection (Randal, 1982).
- **Verbal Misdirection**. Magicians know that audience members are carefully scrutinizing their every move to discover and reverse-engineer their tricks or illusions. However, the intensity required to focus on the magician's every action is visually and cognitively fatiguing, creating opportunity to be deceived. During the course of the trick the magician may make a comment or brief anecdote that will naturally and subtly draw audience attention from his hands, the area of deception, to his face. During this *verbal misdirection* the conjurer will execute the deception action that will be used toward the magic effect (Randal, 1982).
- **Nonverbal Misdirection**. The conjurer not need to say anything to divert attention; pointing to something, reaching for an object (that may or may not actually be there), making a curious facial expression, among other *nonverbal misdirection* actions, all cause a spectator's gaze to transition to the where the magician is engineering attention to conceal the true area of deception (Randal, 1982).

While most of the deceptive online communications occur through the use of text, images or program code, there are some deceptive communications that occur through live video and audio links, particularly in the areas of intelligence and counterintelligence. There have been some nontrivial efforts, typically on the part of nation states, to make contact with individuals in other countries who might have access to sensitive information that would be of value to the malicious online actors. These contacts have often taken place in an online video environment such as Skype.

There are advantages and disadvantages to the use of online video communications in terms of the pursuit of deception. An audience member who sees the magician, especially up close, feels they may be better able to detect the deception that is to follow. Similarly, a potential victim who is communicating with a perpetrator over an online video connection may feel that they will be able to detect deception through verbal and nonverbal cues that the perpetrator exhibits in the course of the video conference. In fact, as is the case with the magician, the use of rich online media in conducting communications that may contain deception may not significantly facilitate the detection of deception. This is especially true if the perpetrator comes from a different culture where verbal and nonverbal cues may be different than those of the intended victim. In addition, one of the advantages to the perpetrators is a false sense of security that comes with being able to see the individual on the other end and potentially being able to identify them later. While it sounds reassuring, the reality is that the individual likely lives in another country among millions of other individuals, and the lack of access to any law enforcement or other resources to identify the perpetrator makes the threat of identity virtually nil for the malicious online actor.

Misdirection Through Distraction, Diversion, or Relaxation

In 1978, magician Joe Bruno formally wrote a seminal text on misdirection, appropriately titled *Anatomy of Misdirection* (1978/2013). Defining misdirection simply as "directing the spectator's attention," Bruno carefully described the three ways in which a conjurer directs the spectator's attention: distraction, diversion, or relaxation (Fig. 1.8) (Bruno, 1978/2013, p. 4).

Distraction is an occurrence extrinsic to the main area of focus or proceedings that causes the spectator an alternative focal point to concentrate on (Bruno, 1978/2013). Importantly, distractions are nuanced and the degree of extraneousness to the main proceedings can vary; here Bruno has categorized distractions as either *external* or *integral*.

- **External Distractions** are interruptions or disruptions causing the audience to shift focus to the external event and away from the main area of focus. The external distraction can be startling or incidental, ranging from an unsophisticated tactic like dropping an object, causing a loud noise, to more subtle or natural methods such as an audible cough or throat clear (Bruno, 1978/2013).
- **Integral Distractions** are part of the main area of focus or proceedings but not inextricable to the magical effect. Thus these distractions are intertwined with the proceedings, are typically more subtle, and typically fall into three categories: confusion, flustering, and perplexity (Bruno, 1978/2013).
  - *Confusion.* To cause confusion the conjurer generates a slight commotion unrelated to the forthcoming effect in an effort to conceal the method.

o *Flustering.* Typically achieved with a volunteer assistant, flustering creates a moment of embarrassment or another compelling circumstance surrounding the volunteer, which causes the audience to momentarily focus on the volunteer during the execution of a trick's method.

o *Perplexity.* Unlike flustering, which evokes a visceral reaction, perplexity causes a cerebral loading situation that is "complicated, involved, or puzzling" (Bruno, 1978/2013, p. 21).

Diversion is intended to capture and maintain the attention of the spectators. Unlike distraction, diversion is not intended to dilute or divide areas of focus. Thus from the spectators' perspective the diversionary action is the solitary event to witness. Diversion is often unexpected, very amusing, or pleasant to watch; it is typically not observed as superfluous or meaningless actions. Like distraction, diversion can be either external or internal to the main proceedings (Bruno, 1978/2013).

- **External Diversion or Digression**: An external diversion, or *digression*, deviates from the main proceeding with the purpose of supplanting the main proceedings and in turn ensures that there is no competing attention-drawing activity (Bruno, 1978/2013).
- **Integral Diversion**: An essential component of misdirection and the resulting effect, integral diversion is incorporated into the magic trick, or main proceedings (Bruno, 1978/2013).
  o **Switching.** Sidetracking attention from one area of interest to another.
  o **Masking.** Obscuring one action with another in an effort to screen the secret effect from the audience. This may be done through angles or body orientation, e.g., the conjurer orients his body positioning in a manner to obfuscate his right hand, which is integral to concealing an aspect of the trick (Bruno, 1978/2013).

One recent strategy that malicious online actors have deployed is the use of nonstandard communication channels to avoid detection of traffic such as command and control traffic for botnets. For example, some enterprising malicious online actors have taken to interweaving botnet and other malicious traffic into domain name system (DNS) protocol communications. This tactic went undetected for some time because no one had thought of DNS traffic as a vector for malicious traffic. It was masked by both DNS traffic itself as well as the mistaken impression that it would never be used as a communications channel for malicious traffic.

o **Disguise.** When an action appears to be performed for one purpose but in reality it is done for an alternative purpose unbeknownst to the audience; this is essentially secret dual-use actions.

o **Pointing.** Dramatic pauses used to control presentation flow in which secret actions must be executed just prior or after the pauses to avoid detection.

- ○ ***Climax.*** During the crescendo of an effect, and while the audience's attention is surely rapt, the magician can shrewdly and stealthily execute the method to the next trick undetected.

Relaxation is used by conjurers as a means to manipulate and lower audience attention. This method may be used in a manner to influence a spectator's awareness by de-emphasis in the proceedings or as an anticipation of the proceedings (Bruno, 1978/2013).

- • **De-emphasis**. During the course of a conjurer's performance, only a limited amount of the act is actually the climax of respective effects. In fact, much of the performance is "nonevents" or *de-emphasis* that leads to the effect climax. However, this time is skillfully used by the magician to prepare and stage the next trick. De-emphasis renders as temporal manipulations in a routine, such as a *timing pause* or *conclusion* (Bruno, 1978/2013).
  - ○ ***Timing Pause.*** Typically manifesting as a subtle pause that occurs on the downbeat between two actions, this is used as a mechanism to dilute attention.
  - ○ ***Conclusion.*** Audience alertness and awareness is typically diminished after the climax of an effect. During these natural pauses, that may include applause or other spectator–magician acknowledgment of a fine trick, the magician can stealthily begin staging methods for the next effect.
- • **Anticipation**. Spectators relax their attention because they believe then they know what is coming next in a performance. Critically, however, this anticipation must be brief, natural, and subconscious so as not to induce boredom or disinterest. Such anticipation can be effectively leveraged through repetition or by implication (Bruno, 1978/2013).
  - ○ ***Repetition.*** Conjurers rely upon the principle of repetition frequently during the course of a performance. Here, the magician performs a legitimate motion or action multiple times in an effort to condition (and ultimately desensitize) the spectator to the action so that the deceptive action following it goes unnoticed.
  - ○ ***Implication.*** Insinuating methods or projected aspects of a trick can be a powerful way to cause the audience to anticipate how a trick will unfold, albeit ultimately incorrectly (Bruno, 1978/2013). Implication manifests in two ways:
    - ■ First, the conjurer can imply a conceivable method of operation, causing the audience to develop a false solution and ultimately causing them surprise by the resulting effect. While effective, it is traditionally discouraged to imply methods since it not only can potentially expose tradecraft, but it also eliminates the atmosphere of magic, as described earlier by Tamariz (see textbox "The Method of False Solutions," above).
    - ■ Second, the magician can imply the cadence or content of the subsequent proceedings, lulling the audience into predicting or anticipating (incorrectly) the order of events leading to the effect.

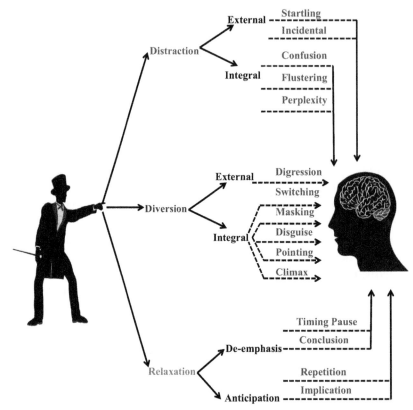

FIGURE 1.8 Bruno's elements of misdirection.

Degrees of Misdirection

Magicians, whether esteemed and famous or those new to the craft, universally recognize Arturo Ascanio as one of the most talented, influential, and authoritative magicians on the topic of misdirection. Ascanio and Etcheverry (2005) astutely posited that "misdirection is based upon the premise that it is impossible for the brain to translate into sensations all that enters into the senses" (p. 52). His resulting theory is that misdirection can be categorized in three degrees, or levels, of intensity.

- ***First-Degree Misdirection***: The mildest degree of misdirection, wherein the spectator is caused to divide his attention between two distinct points—one containing the secret action leading to the effect, the other, an innocuous point (Fig. 1.9). This purposeful division of attention dilutes the spectator's ability to focus, consuming visual and cognitive resources sufficiently to ensure that the secret action goes undetected (Ascanio & Etcheverry, 2005).

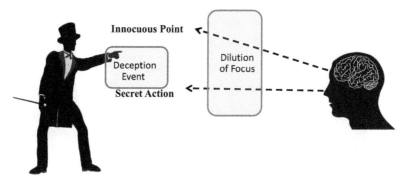

FIGURE 1.9 First-degree misdirection.

- **Second-Degree Misdirection:** One way to intensify division of attention and cause increased interest in the innocuous point is to make it more attractive or interesting than the secret action. In this way the spectator's attention is not only diluted, but effectively gravitated toward the innocuous point and away from the secret action (Fig. 1.10) (Ascanio & Etcheverry, 2005).

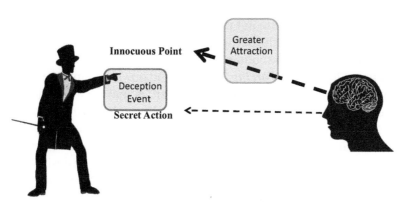

FIGURE 1.10 Second-degree misdirection.

- **Third-Degree Misdirection:** The third and strongest degree of misdirection, while difficult to achieve, causes the spectator's gaze and attention to be totally diverted to an innocuous point. Since this diversion fully consumes the spectator's attention and gaze, he will not observe other aspects of the scene, including the secret action that is used to effectuate the deception event (Fig. 1.11) (Ascanio & Etcheverry, 2005).

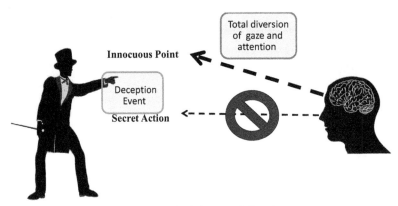

FIGURE 1.11 Third-degree misdirection.

Magician's Weapons of Deception

Conjurers use a number of artful psychological and cognitive deception techniques that contribute to and enhance misdirection. Often, these principles and practices are implemented during the deception pathway leading to a magical effect or as collateral deceptive practices that a conjurer may use to ensure his secret actions are not discovered during the course of a trick. While not mutually exclusive, many of these techniques are layered during a magical performance and are not independently applied. Application of these techniques may be contingent upon the particular effect the magician is seeking to achieve, his or her performance style, and the context of the environment.

Magician's use of Influence: "Forcing." A subtle and powerful aspect of magic tradecraft, particularly within the scope of audience interaction, is making an audience participant believe he/she has true, free choice, when in reality the conjurer causes the participant to select the thing or the manner the conjurer wants. This concept, known as *forcing*, is among the most common and powerful influence methods used by conjurers; using a variety of force methods a magician can shape a participant's actions toward a desired outcome, contributing to the magical effect the magician is working toward. Sharpe delineated forces as either *Direct Forcing* or *Indirect Forcing* (Sharpe, 1988). The former describes techniques where the spectator is allowed to make an apparently free choice but is influenced by the magician to choose in the manner the magician wants, whereas indirect forcing includes those methods that do not fit neatly into the three categories that comprise direct forcing: *Guided Choice, Limited Choice,* and *Calculated Probability* (*Biased Choice Forcing*). Notably, Sharpe's categorization of force techniques is quite congruent with those posited by cheating and deception researchers, J. Bowyer Bell and Barton Whaley (Bell & Whaley, 1991/2009).

Direct Forcing

- *Guided Choice.* Perhaps the most classic and complete influence-based method, the magician presents the audience participant with different objects, such as cards, and requests the participant to select one. Exploiting the human reaction principle of choosing paths of least resistance, the conjurer is able to cause the participant to select the item the conjurer wants to stage his trick. Bell and Whaley categorize this type of force "sleight of hand" since the conjurer often subtly shifts the deck positioning so that the spectator's path of selection is closest to the card that the conjurer desires (Bell & Whaley, 1991/2009; Sharpe, 1988). In the digital world, one low level threat example of guided choice that is currently being used is the use of persistent pop-up windows in mobile browsers. A click on the wrong button or a visit to a malicious website in a mobile browser may initiate a pop-up window that cannot be easily dismissed. Often this pop-up window informs the user that they have been selected to win a free iPad or other enticement. The focus of the mobile browser is on the pop-up window, and it is not possible to gain the attention of the mobile device to dismiss the pop-up. While it possible to push the browser app to background and use other apps on the device, the browser app is still enslaved to the pop-up. The pop-up window contains only one button that entices the user to push it with part of the rationale perhaps to pursue the enticement and the other part to attempt to free the browser from the pop-up. This is an extreme type of forcing but in this case differs because the user (i.e., audience) is aware that they are being forced.

- *Limited Choice.* Similar to guided choice, but the framing or staging of the choice is loaded in even further probabilistic favor of the conjurer's choice, such as presenting the spectator with a choice where the set of items is more limited and may have multiple variations of the conjurer's desired items for selection (Sharpe, 1988). Again a rather benign minor deceptive tactic but a useful example from banner advertising is informative here. Often banner advertising on websites asks users a question such as their age or the state that they reside in and the answers to that question are laid out in detail in the banner ad. However, it does not matter what the user clicks, those responses to the banner questions are not clickable fields. Rather clicking anywhere on the banner ad including the response to the banner question takes them to another web page.
- *Calculated Probability or Biased Choice Forcing.* Here, free choice is allowed but the choices are framed in a way that there is a strong probability that the selection will be in line with the conjurer's intended selection (Sharpe, 1988). Bell and Whaley (1991/2009) describe this type of force as "one that relies upon common cultural or physiological predispositions," e.g., when offered to select a number between 5 and 10, most choose 7 (p. 147).

In this case, malicious online actors have a distinct advantage over real-world magicians. That is, a "failed" manipulation in the form of a calculated probability is not a guarantee to the magician that the illusion will work; it only increases the odds that it will work, and sometimes the magician will suffer a failure and along with it nontrivial damage to his objective to entertain the audience. However, manipulating the odds that a deception will work is merely a matter of yield for a malicious online actor. A failed deception just means that the actor will move on to the next victim; the consequences of failure are usually much less disastrous for him or her.

Indirect Forcing

- *Duplication.* By using duplicate items presented for selection, the spectator will always select the item desired by the conjurer (Sharpe, 1988).
- *Substitution.* Even when the spectator chooses an item freely, it can be surreptitiously replaced by the magician, resulting in the item he desires. This technique is commonly used in scenarios where the item is selected by the spectator but is not overtly visible, such as a facedown card or a box concealing an item (Sharpe, 1988).
- *Equivocation/Misinterpretation.* How the conjurer frames a question is often the foundation of a force strategy. By phrasing a question ambiguously, the conjurer is able to interpret the answer in a self-serving manner to aid the facilitation of his trick or illusion. Conjurers often call this method the "Right or Left Force" or *equivoque,* since it is classically used in scenarios where the conjurer asks the spectator to choose from the right or left and then adeptly avails himself of the ambiguity of whether it was intended to mean the spectator's right or left or the conjurer's (Bell & Whaley, 1991/2009; Sharpe, 1988).
- *Elimination.* Often referred to as the "Conjurer's Choice," this method is combined with equivocation and results in the removal of selected items, leaving only remaining items that can be strategically picked through ambiguous questions, i.e., *equivoque,* leading to the selection that the conjurer wants (Sharpe, 1988).
- *Mathematical Forcing.* When asking the audience participant to select a number, and in turn, a series of numerical calculations afterward, e.g., "Choose a number between 20 and 50…now triple that number…," the conjurer is able to not only confuse the participant, but vector the resulting mathematical procedure toward the number or result he desires (Sharpe, 1988). Bell and Whaley (1991/2009) refer to this method as a "self-working force.
- *Mechanical Forcing.* Devices that can be controlled and calibrated to provide results that the conjurer wants, i.e., props that are "loaded" to stop or land in a particular desired manner are *mechanical forces* (Sharpe, 1988).

Other notable forcing techniques are *induced responses* and *loaded choices.* Induced responses, a technique created by famed magician, Darwin Ortiz (1994), describes when a conjurer creates "a set of circumstances that subtly but compellingly coaxes the spectator to do something he or she thinks is her own idea…manipulat[ing] the spectator into doing something without his realizing he's been manipulated" (p. 323). Similarly, in *loaded choices,* the conjurer exploits the spectator's preferences or value system, tailoring a scenario that purposefully causes the spectator to choose between "bad-better-best" preferences, more than likely resulting in the spectator choosing his more desired item or outcome (Bell & Whaley, 1991/2009).

Disarming Presentation. While master conjurers such as Ascanio, Fitzkee, Tamariz, Ortiz, and Sharpe had meaningful contributions to misdirection theory and practice, each of them emphasized that for a magician to excel at his craft, his performance must present as natural and compelling, creating a magical atmosphere that captivates audiences, making them complicit to the deception. While many factors contribute toward this process, fundamental performance precepts such as patter, naturalness, and nonchalance are foundational.

Patter. The magician's spoken word is a powerful factor in his performance; his narrative and delivery serves to instruct, entertain, and misdirect audience members as he executes his routine. Like other master magicians whose magic theory and technique is still authoritative years later, Ascanio and Etcheverry (2005) considered patter to be an essential element in creating a "magic atmosphere," noting that "…patter can also be used, as all the masters do, to seek and achieve what we could call psychological naturalness and psychological misdirection. An appropriate phrase or a little joke at the right time can conceal a secret maneuver completely" (p. 54). Scam email schemas often use the principle of patter in their strategies. They may supply personal details about the sender of the email, the situation at hand and other bits of trivia designed to build rapport with the recipient and reduce the level of suspicion.

Naturalness. The audience's perspective and interpretation of the magician's actions is a pivotal part of a compelling performance. If the spectator perceives the magician's conduct as natural, innate, and truly reflective of the magician, then suspicion is lowered and the magician is "trusted"; conversely, if unnaturalness is perceived, then the spectator will be vigilant to detect the magician's deception actions (Fitzkee, 1945/2009).

Nonchalance. Casual, easy flow and presentation affect audience reception and perception; if the conjurer is relaxed, unconcerned, and having a good time, then the audience will likely mirror this behavior. Further, relaxed display and transmission to the audience serves as a valuable concealment element for the magician's underlying subterfuge, lowering perceptual vigilance and suspicions.

Manipulation of Reasoning. Human beings perceive (process and interpret sensory information) and, in turn, make choices through a similar cognitive process. Keying in on these innate processes, magicians can create scenarios that exploit this perception and reasoning chain by introducing elements that induce ideas or beliefs.

False Objectives. This stratagem focuses on providing the spectator with what he believes to be the conjurer's objective for a particular trick or illusion, obfuscating the true, different objective. Thus as a result of investing or watching the trick through the lens of and expected outcome, the resulting effect is surprising and impactful (Fitzkee, 1945/2009).

Suggestion and Implication. Subtle but powerful tactics used by magicians to indirectly convey something into the spectator's mind are *suggestion* and *implication*. Suggestion plants an idea in the spectators mind through tacit communication, such as association with other ideas or by catalyzing a train of thought. This may occur during a performance through indirect references, demonstrative aids, or allusion (Fitzkee, 1945/2009). *Implication* is a form of suggestion but less subtly places a thought into the spectator's mind through a more obvious inference, statement, or situation.

Bracketing. Timing and event sequence manipulation, or "bracketing," is a powerful technique that enables a magician to obfuscate the start and stop of a trick. This principle was defined and described by magician and sociologist Peter Nardi in his seminal scholarly article, *Toward a Social Psychology of Entertainment Magic* (1984):

Through disattention and misdirection, spectators are made unaware of the actual bracketing of a trick; i.e. when the apparent trick beings and ends is typically different from the real beginning and end. For example, casual shuffling by the performer between tricks or a statement such as "Let me just make sure this a complete deck"— seemingly subordinate events to the main activity—may, in fact demarcate the actual beginning of the real causal sequence of the trick (p. 33).

Exploiting Human Proclivities. While cultural nuances and mores may vary globally, ultimately humans share certain propensities that can be targeted by a clever magician. Visual cognition, social cuing, social context, trust, expectations, and perception are innate factors that pose vulnerabilities that can be potentially exploited during the course of the conjurer's deception trajectory, leading to the magical effect.

Gestalt Principles. Humans demonstrate certain psychological tendencies based upon visual perception that can be targeted during the course of a magic performance. Deemed by visual scientists as *amodal completion*, the Gestalt grouping principle of "good continuation" describes the phenomenon where, when given an ambiguous grouping (or length) of objects partially obstructed from the spectators view by a second object or the magician's hand, the objects appear to be whole (Barnhart, 2010; Macknik, Martinez-Conde, & Blakeslee, 2010). This spontaneously formed faulty assumption is fortified and exploited in tandem by the principle of *accidental alignment*, where the audience's interpretation of the occluding object, such as the magician's hand, is presumed to be unintentionally placed and irrelevant in the course of the performance (Barnhart, 2010). This principle is sometimes used by malicious online actors to put their potential victims at ease in situations where the perpetrator is engaging a high value target one on one. In this case the perpetrator may salt their communications with personal information that they have been able to gather about the potential target. This may include a home address, names of relatives or family members, work colleagues, or other pieces of information that form a partial picture of the target's personal life. The intention here is to entice the individual to complete the picture by providing the pieces of information missing from the picture that are requested by the perpetrator. As long as the communication appears to be coming from a trusted source or authority, there is the propensity of the target to perfect the completion of the picture by supplying the missing information.

Setting False Expectations. Exploiting concepts of repetition and expected outcome, a conjurer may perform a particular action demonstrating an effect, then pretend to repeat the action, causing the audience to expect the previously observed effect. Thus by setting a *false expectation* the conjurer may pretend he is performing a previously observed action to exploit expectations, surprising and delighting the audience with an unexpected effect (Marshall, Benford, & Pridmore, 2010).

Like other deceivers who are seeking to influence perceptions of receivers, or "victims," cyber attackers leverage many of the same weapons of deception to influence and manipulate their targets. Conjurers' forcing techniques can be implemented to cause a victim to believe that they are engaging in a choice, when in actuality they are executing part of the exploitation sequence the attacker wants, such as clicking on a link, opening a malicious file, or responding to communication. Ensuring that the context of engagement is natural and disarming, victims of the attack are not vigilant and are likely susceptible to chained attacks that also implement aspects of misinformation and directional tracks that either provide cover for the attacker's activity or serve as a means of gaining further access. Obfuscation of URLs and other nefarious remote resources, when done elegantly, exploit Gestalt principles of good continuation and accidental alignment, resulting in faulty presumption and, in turn, engagement by the victim.

 Pitfalls to Avoid

Naturalness in Cyber Attacks
One's computing experience during a workday is often time-compressed and part of a larger constellation of activities, tasks, and deadlines. Thus the vigilance and filtration process one applies to received communications may be lowered, often resolving down to whether a communication "looks and feels" normal and expected. Cyber attackers know that busy professionals often resort to this listless security posture out of necessity for time and productivity; as a result, they shrewdly craft emails and other communications to look natural visually, contextually, and substantively. While one's workload or need to multitask may not be alleviated, consider building in quick and easy verification processes, such as checking an e-mail's full header or an alternative form of instant communication to a verified account of the sender, to confirm the authenticity of the sender, particularly for communications that contain elements that could contain attack vectors, such as embedded links and file attachments.

While the existing corpus of theory and instruction on misdirection from the magician's perspective is rich and incredibly informative, understanding the scientific basis of misdirection efficacy is also vital to inform and shape how misdirection deceives spectators. In the next section, we start by examining empirical studies by Gustav Kuhn, Steven L. Macknik, Susana Martinez-Conde, and others who have provided unprecedented insight into the neuropsychological principles behind effective misdirection. Next we briefly discuss some of the early attempts to frame online deception in terms of social engineering and then proceed to examine some of the traditional methods of deception detection via verbal and nonverbal cues. We then examine some of the attempts to detect deception through the typical language of the web: words and images. Because of the large body of literature investigating social engineering, we then return to this topic to examine it in more detail. Our concluding section in this chapter focuses on providing the reader with a brief theoretical foundation of the psychological principles of deception.

Magic, Illusion, and the Prevalence of Deception

There are substantial reasons for devoting the first few pages of this book to the art and science of magic and illusion. Deception in the form of lies and disinformation has been a topic of interest and study for a very long time (Fallis, 2014). Fabrication has been described as an evolutionary advantage to be able to deploy deception. Mokkonen and Lindstedt (2015) observe that the "evolutionary strategy of deception offers a means to increase the differential between fitness benefits and costs for a deceiver, by reducing the deceiver's costs at the expense of the deceived individuals." The incidence and forms of deception also can vary widely from culture to culture. Blum (2005) reports that in Chinese culture, her field observations have led her to the conclusion that lying to strangers is more acceptable than to friends. She also observes that sometimes lying is an expected part of a social exchange. She cites an example where she was asked if her teaching colleague was her teacher; she answered truthfully that he was not, and this was followed by much laughter. It was the case that she was expected to attempt to deceive people and say "yes," followed by a fervent denial by her colleague, which would have successfully completed the expected and culturally determined interaction pattern.

Magic in one form or another has been an instance of formally and intentionally deceiving large bodies of people for at least conservatively a century or more.[2] It is important to understand some of the basic principles of magic and the art of illusion because this combination art and science deceives an expectant audience. That is, individuals who attend a magic performance are expecting to be deceived by the magician or illusionist, and this is likely one of the most difficult environments in which these professionals must operate. The members of a magician's audience are primed to look for the mechanisms by which

---

[2] For an early description of the psychology of magic, see, Binet (1894), Jastrow (1896), and Triplett (1900).

the performer successfully executes the illusion or trick, and the magician must utilize effective means of disguising these mechanisms or fall from grace in front of the audience. However, as Murphy (1993) as well as Nardi (1984) point out, magic is a cooperative arrangement between the magician and the audience. The audience knows that the magician is attempting to deceive them, but they are willing to set this knowledge aside because the audience perceives the performance as entertainment and therefore is an active participant in the deception.

Neuropsychology of Magic and Deception

At a very fundamental level, much of the success of the phenomenon of magic in generating an illusion that deceives the audience depends to a great extent upon principles of neuropsychology. Magicians take advantage of the peculiarities of both neurological as well as cognitive information processes to hide mechanics of the illusion from observers. Sometimes magicians misdirect your attention through *endogenous attention capture*, which is passive in nature. A good example of that is having the audience focus on the flapping of an on-stage dove's wings while the magician is busy completing another physical action elsewhere. Other times magicians utilize *exogenous attention capture*, where the audience member's attention is actively drawn by engaging in an activity such as searching through a deck of cards while the magician is performing another action (Macknik et al., 2010).

In addition to manipulating attention capture, some magicians utilize *time misdirection*. That is, the covert actions on the part of the magician occur either before the audience thinks the trick has started or after the audience thinks the trick is done (Macknik et al., 2010). It is during these times that observers are lulled into a less observant state that the magician performs his covert actions. This phenomenon may also work in the digital world as well. For example, an online user may be highly aware and aroused just before and during the time that they are completing an online financial transaction. However, after the user has completed the financial transaction, it is more likely that they will lower their situational awareness and arousal level. It is during this time-misdirection period that the malicious online actor or process may have more opportunity to operate unobserved by the user.

Forcing is another favorite tactic of magicians in performing various illusions. Forcing involves the advance preparation of materials or the mental priming of the audience member to accomplish the illusion (Kuhn, Amlani, & Rensink, 2008). A *physical force* tactic by the magician might involve the insertion of a number of the same card into a card deck to increase the chances of it being picked. A *mental force* might involve the magician exposing a particular card for a long period of time in order to "prime" the audience member to more likely pick that card. In the digital realm, we might expose an online user to a number of banner ads for example, all of which lead to a website that contains malware as part of a "drive-by attack." The exposure of the user to the website advertising banner multiple times encourages them to click on the banner and visit the malicious website: a digital version of a magician's mental force tactic.

Misdirection is one of the main tools in the repertoire of magicians that often depends upon knowledge regarding how visual information is acquired and processed. *Inattentional blindness* is one often-used technique to hide mechanisms of the deception (Mack & Rock, 1998; Kuhn, Amlani, et al., 2008).[3] In this technique, audience members are instructed to focus or fixate on a specific visual activity and engage in some cognitive task such as counting the number of passes among basketball players (Simons & Chabris, 1999). While fixated on the visual task and engaged cognitively while counting passes, a person in a gorilla suit walks through the scene unnoticed by the audience. In the digital world, this principle might be accomplished through the use of a visually attractive rich media element on a web page that also induces some nontrivial cognitive load. While the user is watching the rich media clip, a malicious online actor or process could be using that inattentional blindness to obscure visual cues such as warning messages and changes in website details or even operating system warnings that could be alerting the user to malicious changes in their environment.

One additional complication of inattentional blindness in the performance of magic tricks can be traced to *perceptual load* (Barnhart & Goldinger, 2012, 2014; Lavie & Tsal, 1994). In this scenario, the ability of the audience member to detect the deception depends upon the perceptual load that the audience member is under at the time of the deception. If the audience member is experiencing high perceptual load, such as watching many different elements within the scene of the illusion, then the deceptive movements and

[3] For further discussion on the relationship between eye gaze and attention, see:

Cui, J., Otero-Millan, J., Macknik, S. L., King, M., & Martinez-Conde, S. (2011). Social misdirection fails to enhance a magic illusion. *Frontiers in Human Neuroscience, 5,* 103. http://dx.doi.org/10.3389/fnhum.2011.00103.

Kuhn, G., Caffaratti, H. A., Teszka, R., & Rensink, R. A. (2014). A psychologically-based taxonomy of misdirection. *Frontiers in Psychology, 5,* 1392.

Kuhn, G., & Martinez, L. M. (2012). Misdirection—past, present, and the future. *Frontiers in Human Neuroscience, 5,* 172.

Kuhn, G., & Tatler, B. W. (2011). Misdirected by the gap. The relationship between inattentional blindness and attentional misdirection. *Consciousness and Cognition. 20*(2), 432–436.

Kuhn, G., & Findlay, J. M. (2010). Misdirection, attention and awareness: Inattentional blindness reveals temporal relationship between eye movements and visual awareness. *The Quarterly Journal of Experimental Psychology, 63*(1), 136–146.

Kuhn, G. (2010). Cognitive illusions: from magic to science, In E. Perry, D. Collerton, F. LeBeau, & H. Ashton (Eds.) *New Horizons in the Neuroscience of Consciousness* (pp. 139–148). Amsterdam: John Benjamin Publishing Company. http://dx.doi.org/10.1075/aicr.79.19kuh.

Kuhn, G., Tatler, B. W., and Cole, G. G. (2009). You look where I look! Effect of gaze cues on overt and covert attention in misdirection. *Visual Cognition, 17,* 925–944. http://dx.doi.org/10.1080/13506280902826775.

Kuhn, G., Amlani, A. A., & Rensink, R. A. (2008). Toward a science of magic. *Trends in cognitive sciences, 12*(9), 349–354.

Kuhn, G., Tatler, B. W., Findlay, J. M., & Cole, G. G. (2008). Misdirection in magic: Implications for the relationship between eye gaze and attention. *Visual Cognition, 16*(2–3), 391–405.

Kuhn, G., & Land, M. F. (2006). There's more to magic than meets the eye. *Current Biology, 16*(22), R950–R951.

Kuhn, G., & Tatler, B. W. (2005). Magic and fixation: now you do not see it, now you do. *Perception 34,* 1155–1161. http://dx.doi.org/10.1068/p3409bn1.

Rensink, R.A. et al. (1997). To see or not to see: the need for attention to perceive changes in scenes. *Psychological Science, 8,* 368–373.

actions of the magician are much less likely to be detected. If the perceptual load of the respondent is low, say the respondent is focused on only a few items and in particular in the vicinity of the deceptive movements, then the audience member is much more likely to uncover the deception. This suggests that a digital version of this phenomenon might involve developing screens where the online user's attention is drawn to many different elements simultaneously such that warnings or consequences of actions on the part of a malicious actor or process may go unnoticed.

Another deceptive strategy that relies upon visual processing is *change blindness.* Change blindness is the phenomena when nontrivial changes to a visual scene may not be noticed by the audience if the changes are preceded by a short interruption of the ability of the audience to see the scene (Macknik et al., 2010; Rensink, 2002). One reasonably common digital instance of this is when web pages are hijacked by a malicious actor or process and replaced very quickly by another faux web page that looks similar but may have some differences that normally would be obvious to the audience. The typical purpose of this hijacked page is to collect financial credentials of the user without them noticing the inauthenticity of the web page.

Another neuropsychological phenomenon sometimes used in magic is the concept of *visual masking.* In visual masking, Macknik (2006) states that, "psychophysical studies suggest that the temporal edges of targets — the points in time at which they turn on and off — are more important to their visibility than their midlife periods." That is, sometimes our brains are more enticed by changes in events, such as the appearance and disappearance of some objects, than by the constant visual presence of another object. Macknik et al. (2010) provide the example of a black bar on a white background that is made invisible when two abutting black bars are flashed on the screen one-tenth of a second after the original black bar. The original black bar is visually "masked" by the appearance of the additional black bars.

There are a number of neuropsychological principles that are routinely employed by magicians in order to successfully accomplish their illusion, and we have outlined only a few of them here. It is apparent at the time of this writing that malicious online actors and groups have yet to take significant advantage of some of these principles in the digital realm. Whether this reality comes to pass in the near future is difficult to say, but it bears witness to the fact that the potential to apply neuropsychological principles normally found on the magician's stage is certainly there.

Early Attempts at Explaining Digital Deception

This phenomenon of cooperative communication in the course of deception in magic may also be at work in the world of digital deception as well. We have not yet reached this same kind of "magical" environment in the digital world, where the individuals who inhabit it are totally primed for misdirection and deception. However, it is clear that in many cases the victims of online deception are willing to suspend some nontrivial amount of disbelief and fall into the various traps set for them by malicious online actors. Thus an examination of how magicians and illusionists manage to deceive their audiences is likely to generate some benefits that may be applied to the virtual world, perhaps not directly in their original form but in terms of gaining a better, more comprehensive understanding from a theoretical and strategic perspective how these principals operate. This is the purpose of the previous exposé on some of the more common principles of magic.

While much of the effort in the chapters that follow lay out in specific, concrete detail various methods and examples of deception in the digital world, the reader is reminded that behind these specific methods, there are principles of deception operating that guide the execution and determine the effectiveness of these strategies. The early cyber security literature in the area of deception, especially in the trade press (for example Mitnick & Simon, 2002), focused more on cookbook recipes for techniques for herding online users toward performing specific behaviors. In the digital world the objective is to convince individuals to perform specific acts such as clicking on a malicious button, going to a particular website that then does a drive-by download of malware, or hijacking users to familiar looking but bogus websites that prompt individuals to enter valuable information such as financial credentials that are then ultimately stolen and sold in the online black markets frequented by carders and their customers. However, as the incidence of these events are exponentially increased, the academic literature has begun to catch up with phenomena of this type, and more rigorous attention is being paid to this area.

One of the more interesting observations to note is that the academic literature on online deception for the most part avoids much of the traditional literature on deception that has been around for decades. This fact has been noted in a seminal article on cyber deception[4] by Stech, Heckman, Hilliard, and Ballo (2011) in a rigorous examination of the articles involving deception involving digital networks. Their analysis of approximately 10,500 citation records examining keywords, abstract phrases, and other data points led to the construction of concept clustering maps that demonstrated the conjecture that cyber deception researchers very rarely reference traditional deception research found in the behavioral and social sciences.

Traditional Deception Research via Verbal and Nonverbal Cues

Some of the reason for this lack of utilization of traditional deception research is likely due to the fact that a significant proportion of this deception literature in the social sciences and, in particular, psychology is focused on the relationship between verbal and nonverbal cues that are exhibited in deception attempts in face-to-face interaction. There is a large body of literature that deals with the relationship between various verbal cues

---

[4]The term cyber deception was coined by Stech et al. (2011) and refers to "deception resulting from the transmission of information via the Internet." While useful, this definition is limited in scope and is likely to be outmoded as malicious code and information spreads via channels other than the Internet, such as locally from device to device via local area and Bluetooth networks in homes as the spread of the Internet of Things becomes ubiquitous.

such as reaction times (Vendemia, Buzan, & Green, 2005; Walczyk, Mahoney, Doverspike, & Griffith-Ross, 2009) and assertiveness in speech (Zuckerman, DeFrank, Hall, Larrance, & Rosenthal, 1979) and in nonverbal cues such as microexpressions (Porter & Ten Brinke, 2008) and hand and finger movements (Chan, Khader, Ang, Chin, & Chai, 2015). In fact, DePaulo et al. (2003), in a comprehensive meta-analysis, examined a total of 158 verbal and nonverbal cues in face-to-face interactions and their relationship to deception. A large body of this literature over the years has been compiled particularly in the law enforcement field in regard to the detection of lying through verbal and nonverbal cues present during criminal interrogations and interviews.

Unfortunately, almost none of the digital communication related to online deception occurs in direct, in-person face-to-face interaction; the closest one gets is in the form of video and/or audio conferencing over IP. One might argue that communication via avatars in virtual worlds might qualify as face-to-face communications. There is some evidence of deception delivered via avatars but because of the presumed lack of control of key verbal and nonverbal cues by avatar owners, it is unlikely at this point in time that the knowledge base for detecting deception through the observation of verbal and nonverbal cues will apply to virtual worlds. We can assume in the current environment that much of the digital communication involving digital deception involves text and still image-based communication in the form of emails, chat forums, and websites found on the Internet. Understandably, the large body of traditional deception literature focused on verbal and nonverbal cues will not currently directly apply here. However, as virtual worlds mature and behaviors of avatars become more complex and controllable by their namesakes, it is conceivable that this body of literature might come into play. The inclusion of verbal and nonverbal cues can be viewed in the digital arena by using apps and tools such as Skype and random Internet chat lines such as Chatroulette.com. Chatroulette.com even provides a warning of deception stating, *"It is possible for a person to record your webcam. Scammers are known to do this and then blackmail a person with the footage. It is also possible for a person to use 'fake webcam' software in order to hide their true identity."*

Deception Detection Through the Analysis of Words and Images

As suggested in the previous paragraph, there has already been a nontrivial amount of attention paid to deception perpetrated on the Internet through the media of words and images. Even from the earliest times before the widespread growth of the Internet as a public communication medium, there were instances of modest deception on early bulletin board systems and other early digital communication forums, often in the form of posing as someone other than oneself. Individuals in the nascent hacking community often identified themselves with handles rather than their real names, and there were numerous early versions of what has much later developed into a more complex form, called catphishing, with males masquerading as females to fool other male users, although the deception was deployed in those days for sport rather than for money, as it often currently is performed today.

Because of the significant focus that computer-mediated communications places on text and imagery and the normal lack of verbal and nonverbal cues to deception in much of computer-mediated communications, many researchers consider the Internet a fertile ground for the growth of deceptive and malicious acts.[5] For example, in a study of strangers getting to know each other, individuals who communicated via email or IM exhibited a higher average number of lies per words exchanged than those who got to know each other face to face (Zimbler & Feldman, 2011).

One of the consequences of this text and image-based focus is that researchers have spent some nontrivial time and effort to attempt to apply both traditional and nontraditional linguistic analyses to the detection of deception that appears in the online text, whether the text appears on a website or some other more direct form of computer-mediated communication such as email or IRC/chat content. One of the early and better known strategies for this type of analysis is the Linguistic Inquiry and Word Count (LIWC) schema developed by Pennebaker and Francis (1999), which was subsequently developed into a software program (Pennebaker, Francis, & Booth, 2001).

Their theory was that "much of the variance in language to identify psychopathologies, honesty, status, gender, or age, was heavily dependent on the use of little words such as articles, prepositions, pronouns, etc., more than on content words (e.g., nouns, regular verbs, some adjectives and adverbs)" (Chung & Pennebaker, 2014). The schema itself utilizes a taxonomy that divides words into 76 categories using a predetermined dictionary, including function words such as articles and prepositions, quantifiers, negations, and more. Toma and Hancock (2012) utilized the LIWC schema to successfully detect deception in users' descriptions of themselves in online dating forums. Pérez-Rosas, Mihalcea, Narvaez, and Burzo (2014) in part utilize the LIWC schema to detect deception in short essays across three different culture/language combinations: United States/English, India/English, and Mexico/Spanish. They discovered that not only were they able build successful deception detection analyzers across the three culture/language environments utilizing LIWC but that they could "use data originating from one culture to train deception detection classifiers for another culture."

Other researchers have investigated various linguistic cues as potential indicators of deception in textual content. Briscoe, Appling, and Hayes (2014) utilized various linguistic cues using three different types of benchmarks: preestablished, intrapersonal, and interpersonal (e.g., global across all the data), and in a supervised learning environment deployed a support vector machine (SVM) strategy against a set of true and deceptive statements. They were able to surprisingly successfully detect approximately 90% of the deceptive statements. They caution however that ratio of deceptive to truthful statements in their data set may not be representative of that ratio in the real world, and so they caution against premature optimism given their results. Similar research by Fuller, Biros, and Delen (2011) on statements from "persons of interest" in crime investigations on military

---

[5] There are some empirical exceptions to this belief—see Van Swol, Braun, and Kolb (2015) for example.

bases found various statistical and machine learning methods had deception detection rates in the upper 60% to mid-70% range.

A contemporary example stems from the Ashley Madison hack in July 2015 and its subsequent fallout. Ashley Madison created tens of thousands of fembots to lure men into paying for credits on their "have an affair" site. Many users detected something was awry with how these alleged women were communicating with them via text and through the site's email. A lawsuit ensued against Ashley Madison because multiple complainants suspected there was telltale fembot activity. Some of the suspicious linguistic and behavioral cues, which indicated written outputs from algorithms versus a real person, included: (1) the use of repetitive chat openers such as "care to chat," "come say hello," and "care to cyber?"; (2) consistently long log-on sessions from 8 a.m. to 6 p.m. every day from multiple people, which was not the norm for the site; (3) chatters asking "ru online now," when the site shows whether a user is online or not; and (4) numerous similarly worded profiles; and (5) oddly phrased responses to chat questions. These deceptive bots were programmed in 31 different languages, and they chatted and sent messages to people in approximately 50 countries.

There is also significant interest in the use of automated deception detection against linguistic data for the purposes of detecting deceptive or false reviews[6] of various business establishments such as hotels and restaurants. Among the many studies attempting to utilize linguistic cues to detect fake reviews are Li, Ott, Cardie, and Hovy (2014), who use a Bayesian technique (SAGE) as well as a more traditional SVM classifier strategy to learn to detect deceptive reviews, and Feng, Banerjee, and Choi (2012) utilize both the LIWCs and parts of speech taxonomies in conjunction with context-free grammar parsing trees to attempt to detect deceptive and false reviews.

The opportunity for deception in virtual worlds has been a topic of interest for some time. Hooi and Cho (2012) investigate the relationship between characteristics of an individual's avatar in the virtual world "Second Life" and the propensity for deception by that avatar in that digital world. Utilizing a structural equations model, they found that when the avatar appeared to express attitudes and beliefs that were similar to the individual directing the avatar, this increased the self-awareness of that individual, which in turn decreased the probability of deception on the part of the avatar in the virtual world. Secondly, they discovered that individuals who fashioned their avatar more to their own personal appearance were less likely to direct their avatar in deceptive acts. Hooi and Choi suggest that one possible explanation for this has to do with Boellstorff's (2008) idea that individuals who create avatars that are different from them are creating alternative actors that are different from the true individual and thus are "masked" or "in costume" and therefore freer to commit nonnormative acts.

---

[6] Often these deceptive reviews are examples of "astroturfing," the submission of deceptive or false positive reviews for a business in hopes of driving more business to that establishment.

Deception Through the Practice of Social Engineering

Finally, in our examination of some of the characteristics of deception, it would be neglectful to fail to mention some aspects of social engineering (SE). There has been a significant increase in the interest in how different deception tactics that come under the rubric of social engineering actually work. As previously mentioned, early works by authors such as Mitnick and Simon (2002) set about compiling in extensive detail different strategies and numerous examples of how individuals could socially engineer intended victims to initiate actions or divulge information that was of interest to the social engineer. Even today, there is significant interest in this topic, and at the annual hacking conference DEFCON in Las Vegas, there is no scarcity of individuals who sign up for the popular social engineering portion of that conference.

While social engineering topics have been blossoming in the information security trade press, the academic examination of this area of interest is still starting to gain momentum and found some of its early beginnings in preliminary work done by Peltier (2006). In noting the lack of theoretical structure within social engineering, Tetri and Vuorinen (2013) succinctly point out that the majority of available texts and discussions of social engineering focus on individual techniques, and this leads to a "very scattered and vague notion of SE." They suggest that a more theoretical and analytical approach to social engineering is needed, and in that regard they state that social engineering can be described in three dimensions: persuasion, fabrication, and data gathering.

In the dimension of persuasion, Tetri and Vuorinen (2013) argue that there are two components. The first is direct interaction, where the request for the victim to perform the requested action takes place. The second component is their interactive engagement of the victim who is persuaded to perform the desired action through techniques such as "authority, appealing to emotions, being likable, establishing rapport, reciprocation, social validation, and subversion." The second dimension is that of fabrication. Tetri and Vuorinen (2013) note that fabrication is the attempt to manipulate social frames[7] in a way such that the social engineer is viewed as an actor that belongs inside the social frame being presented. In distinguishing fabrication from persuasion, Tetri and Vuorinen (2013, p. 1017) state that:

In persuasion, the dupe is well aware of the inappropriate nature of the intruder's request (e.g. 'give me your password' or 'could you please help me and keep that door open for me?'). Fabrication, on the other hand, does not tempt directly or shout out demands as persuasion does. The techniques that strongly manifest the dimension of persuasion require the intruder as an actor to throw himself onto the stage. Fabrication, in terms of visibility, can be about becoming a chameleon that can roam freely, looking and sounding like a co-worker or anyone who belongs there. In other words, a fabricator can creep quietly onto the scene veiled in shadows, props, and set dressing, not drawing active attention to himself; if he did he would be in danger of being spotted. This provides, in a deceitful manner, a quasi-legitimate position.

[7] Social frames as one might construct them in the spirit of the definition offered by Goffman (1974).

The final dimension suggested by Tetri and Vuorinen (2013) is that of data gathering. They argue that data preparation is an important dimension in the social engineering action process. Data gathering by various means (phishing, loggers, open source information, etc.) are utilized in order to provide the elements to fabricate the contextual frame within which persuasive actions are deployed. They note that sometimes in the course of data gathering, the social engineer uncovers the very information that they were seeking from their potential victim and find that the social engineering attempt is not even necessary.

Another noteworthy compilation of research that is relevant to social engineering is the theoretical and empirical work on deception and intentionality originally constructed by Grazioli et al. (Johnson, Grazioli, & Jamal, 1993) and later refined in work by Johnson, Grazioli, Jamal, and Berryman (2001). Grazioli and Jarvenpaa (2003) take this theoretical work further and apply it to deceptions that occur online. It is this later work that does a good job of bridging the gap between theory and the operationalization of some of their concepts in the digital world. The principles laid out in this particular theoretical body of work provide a bridge between some of the theoretical work in deception and the real-world empirical instances of social engineering in a way that helps deflect some of the criticism that Tetri and Vuorinen (2013) object to in the social engineering literature.

Grazioli and Jarvenpaa (2003, p. 197) divide into two categories where "they work either to prevent the victim from fully understanding the nature of the transaction core (the item involved in the exchange), or to actively induce a faulty representation of the core." They further divide deception tactics into seven classes. Within the first category, where the idea is to prevent full understanding by the victim, they list these unique tactics as masking, dazzling, and decoying. Within the second deception category of inducing a faulty representation, they introduce four additional deception tactics as mimicking, inventing, relabeling, and double play. Each of these deception tactics is often found in the online world, in particular in situations that involve ecommerce.

These social engineering tactics are generally found to be deployed by companies and organizations who are attempting to lead consumers into commercial transactions that are typically not at all beneficial to the consumer. For example, the deceptive tactic of masking involves "eliminating or erasing crucial information so that representation of key aspects of the item does not occur, or produces an incorrect result." One popular social engineering strategy that is often used with a commercial objective in mind is in the area of obtaining visas to certain countries. Online visa services often advertise that their service will ensure that the correct information in the correct format is obtained and will be submitted by them to obtain the person's visa for the country they wish to visit. In fact, these social engineering visa services merely submit the same information to an already online visa application website sponsored by the country that the person could have easily completed by themselves, and in exchange for this "service," they charge a significant processing fee.

In other types of social engineering schemas, a number of different strategies are utilized in order to encourage the target to perform the desired action or provide the elicited information. Atkins and Huang (2013) outline eight different tactics that facilitate deception on the part of the social engineer, including (1) authority to create a sense of legitimacy and trust; (2) pity to elicit sympathy; (3) tradition to arouse cultural values; (4) attraction in the form of excitement generated by prizes or opportunities; (5) urgency, often with some sort of negative sanction for noncompliance; (6) fear to generate a sense of intimidation; (7) politeness to humanize the social engineer and their efforts; and (8) formality through the use of terms that imply safety and security in regards to the individual and the suggested action.

Mouton, Leenen, Malan, and Venter (2014) take Mitnick and Simon's (2002) original social engineering process and extend it more formally in a theoretical sense into what they label a social engineering attack framework. This framework consists of the following steps: (1) attack formulation; (2) information gathering; (3) preparation; (4) develop relationship; (5) exploit relationship; and (6) debrief. Similar to Atkins and Huang (2013), they list the following six elements of what they call compliance principles that encourage the target to initiate the desired action: friendship or liking, commitment or consistency, scarcity, reciprocity, social validation, and authority.

The Psychology of Deception

Our final topic is one of some importance and that is a brief discussion regarding the psychological theory of deception. While scientific, empirical studies on various indicators of deception and methods by which one may detect these markers are fairly plentiful both for offline and online environments, there is significantly less comprehensive and integrated theoretical work concerning the actual psychology of deception. This is an important observation that should not be undervalued because in order for researchers, information security professionals, and policymakers to get ahead of the "deception curve," especially in the case of online deception, a fundamental understanding of the psychology of deception is likely to play an important role. New forms of digital technology have emerged, including the exponential increase in the number, type, and diversity of databases and devices that are connected to the Internet, which eventually forms the Internet of Things. Thus being able to utilize the power of theory to anticipate new threat vectors and environments that capitalize on deception is going to become more and more important.

This idea that a fundamental theoretical understanding of deception is particularly true as we move along this digital timeline. That is, as our digital environment matures, we can expect the threats that utilize deception to evolve and mature as well. There is likely to come a time in the near future where the quick "smash and grab" tactics and strategies of current online deception tactics will evolve just as other information security threats have evolved. As we have seen the emergence of advanced persistent threats in the traditional arena of information security, there is the nontrivial probability that we shall see advanced persistent threat-like deception tactics for online (and even perhaps offline) environments. If we can learn a lesson from the more classical milieu of our current information security dilemma, it is that it pays to be prepared in advance so that we can anticipate near-term future deception threats, provide resources, and devise policies to lessen their impact. Theory is one of the tools that can assist us in achieving that objective.

One of the better established psychological theories of deception is Interpersonal Deception Theory, or IDT for short. Developed during the early 1990s by Buller, Burgoon, and their associates (see Buller & Burgoon, 1996; Buller et al., 1994; Burgoon, 1992; Burgoon, Buller, Ebesu, & Rockwell, 1994), this theory of deception describes some of the conditions and processes under which deception can emerge. In particular, Burgoon and Buller (1994) summarize the important points of Interpersonal Deception Theory. Their first point is to acknowledge that psychological variables alone cannot totally explain deceptive interactions, but rather one must take into account the interactivity of deception communications that typically involve dyadic communication. That is, understanding how online deception works cannot be limited to the psychological factors present for both the deceiver as well as the receiver of the deception, but rather other key variables such as communication environment (email, IRC, website, audio message, video conference) must be taken into account.

The second point Burgoon and Buller (1994) make is that deceptive communications are a transactional process where the deceiver must monitor his/her own performance and adjust it according to the feedback coming from the receiver. A good example of this is the Nigerian 419 deceptions, where the deceivers enhance their own skill levels during the conversation in the English language as well as negotiating skills during the conversation with the target advances.

Third on the list of points for Interpersonal Deception Theory is that the interpersonal component of IDT implies that deceptive communications are not all strategic in nature. That is, Burgoon and Buller (1994) suggest that some of the communication elements in a sequence of deceptive communications between the deceiver and the target may contain content that is not directly related to the completion of the deception. The idea here is that effective, deceptive communications should contain some elements and content that are not relevant or at least not directly relevant to the core topic of the deception and that to construct deceptive communications threads in that manner mimics more natural conversations and exchanges so that it camouflages the true intent of the deception. Thus online deception communications may contain some content that is not relevant to the path of the deception but serves as reassuring contextual cues. For example, in the course of the deceptive communication, there may be dynamic content inserted into the communications that may reference the current weather, political situation, or special upcoming event as a means of distracting the target as well as making the communications more personal and displaying time-sensitive information that suggests that the communications are not automated nor generic.

The fourth point of IDT that Burgoon and Buller (1994) convey is that deceptive communications are "multifunctional, multidimensional, multimodal and multivariate." This fourth point is focused more on face-to-face communications where there are multiple channels of communication (verbal, nonverbal, spatial, etc.) engaged at the same time. However, as deceptive online communications become more sophisticated, it may be expected that the emergence of advanced persistent deception threats will have to contend with some of the issues presented in this point.

Burgoon and Buller (1994) point out in their fifth point that the nature of interpersonal communication also often means that the individuals communicating have some familiarity with each other. They observe that most deception research to date has involved individuals who do not know each other, and while this is often the case for online deception, there is the distinct possibility that one of the components of advanced persistent deception threats will involve building relationships between the deceiver and the target. One area where this might ring true is in cases of nation state espionage and intelligence gathering, where the deceiver may build up an online relationship with a target over time in order to eventually be able to extract information from the target through deception. There are likely some striking similarities in the online version of this to the traditional offline recruitment of agents that are ensnared through careful face-to-face interactions over time by agents of foreign intelligence services.

The sixth principal of IDT according to Burgoon and Buller (1994) is that the process of deceptive communications is interactive in nature and that it is an evolving process that during the course of communications, suspicion of deception may arise on the part of the target. This suspicion in turn sets up a chain of behaviors on the part of both the deceiver and the target. It is these "derailments" that must be handled delicately in order for the deception process to move forward. This particular phenomenon is one that makes the pathway to automating deceptive communications rather difficult.[8]

The seventh and final point made by Burgoon and Buller (1994) is that the detection of deceit through perceptions and interpretations may trigger emotional, cognitive, and behavioral changes. While not explicit in their discussion, we may assume here that these changes not only emerge for the target of the deception but also for the deceiver as well. These changes, in turn, alter the multidimensional environment discussed in their fourth point of IDT theory, and it is likely that a number of changes occur within the communication dimensions that may derail the path of the deception, perhaps irretrievably. For example, during the course of online communications between two individuals, where the objective of the exchanges is the development of a romantic relationship, there may appear the use of atypical word choice or emotional reactions by a deceiver that trigger suspicion or confusion on the part of the target. That is, when expectations are violated, there are multiple social psychological processes that are affected (emotional and cognitive) that result in sudden shifts in behavior by the target. If the deceiver does not adapt to these changes in ways that work to remedy the rift, then the path to having the target actor perform the desired action may be destroyed and the communication channel abruptly shut down.

---

[8] An interesting article by Yang and Mannino, M. (2012) and Yang and Mannino, M.V. (2012) emerged where they developed a deception application model to model deception found in student financial aid applications. They then mixed their automated synthetic deception data with deceptive data from real student applications as well as truthful applications. Their objective was to test the idea that they could effectively use automated deceptive data to train deception detection models.

It is hoped that in discussing some of the details of one of the popular psychological theories of deception, it can be seen by the reader that a comprehensive understanding of this and other theories of deception can be immensely useful in understanding the mechanisms of deception. In turn, this understanding can be utilized not only to provide information security professionals with a better understanding of current online deception processes, but also provide them with the tools to see out into the future to anticipate emerging threats that involve deceptive communications.

Summary

The purpose of this first chapter is to encourage the reader, as they encounter the myriad of details and specifics of different types of adaptations of online deception in the following chapters, to retain a more macrolevel perspective toward these phenomena and never lose sight of the fact that guiding these tactics and strategies are psychological principles and forces that shape their nature and success or failure. Understanding the principles of magic and illusion, for example, can assist the reader in comprehending a broader scale perspective of the strategies under discussion. The ability to apply psychological principles to analyze a specific type of deception mechanism in one of the subsequent chapters may enable the reader to see new and innovative opportunities to defend against this type of attack, as well as be able to visualize future enhancements and adaptations of these strategies before they emerge so that defenses can be built in anticipation of their emerging. The following chapters hold what we hope are many useful ideas and details that will capture the imagination of the reader. We wish you an eventful journey in the pages ahead.

References

Ascanio, A., & Etcheverry, J. (2005). *The magic of Ascanio: The structural conception of magic.* New York: Paginas.

Atkins, B., & Huang, W. (2013). A study of social engineering in online frauds. *Open Journal of Social Sciences, 1*(3), 23.

Barnhart, A. S. (2010). The exploitation of Gestalt principles by magicians. *Perception, 39*(9), 1286–1289.

Barnhart, A. S., & Goldinger, S. D. (2012). Using magic to reconcile inattentional blindness and attentional misdirection. *Journal of Vision, 12*(9), 14.

Barnhart, A. S., & Goldinger, S. D. (2014). Blinded by magic: Eye-movements reveal the misdirection of attention. *Frontiers in Psychology, 5.*

Bell, J. B., & Whaley, B. (1991/2009). *Cheating and deception.* Transaction Publishers.

Binet, A. (1894). *Psychology of prestidigitation.* Annual report of the board of regents of the Smithsonian Institution. Washington, DC: Government Printing Office, 555–571.

Blum, S. D. (2005). Nationalism without linguism: Tolerating Chinese variants. *The contest of language: Before and beyond nationalism* , 134–164.

Boellstorff, T. (2008). *Coming of age in second life: An anthropologist explores the virtually human.* Princeton: Princeton University Press.

Briscoe, E. J., Appling, D. S., & Hayes, H. (January 2014). Cues to deception in social media communications. In *47th Hawaii international conference on system sciences, 2014* (pp. 1435–1443). IEEE.

Bruno, J. (1978/2013). *Anatomy of misdirection, 35th anniversary*. Stoney Brook Press.

Buller, D. B., & Burgoon, J. K. (1996). Interpersonal deception theory. *Communication Theory, 6*(3), 203–242.

Buller, D. B., Burgoon, J. K., White, C. H., & Ebesu, A. S. (1994). Interpersonal deception VII behavioral profiles of falsification, equivocation, and concealment. *Journal of Language and Social Psychology, 13*(4), 366–395.

Burgoon, J. K. (1992). Applying a comparative approach to nonverbal expectancy violations theory. In *Comparatively speaking* (pp. 53–69).

Burgoon, J. K., & Buller, D. B. (1994). Interpersonal deception: III. Effects of deceit on perceived communication and nonverbal behavior dynamics. *Journal of Nonverbal Behavior, 18*(2), 155–184.

Burgoon, J. K., Buller, D. B., Ebesu, A. S., & Rockwell, P. (1994). Interpersonal deception: V. Accuracy in deception detection. *Communications Monographs, 61*(4), 303–325.

Chan, S., Khader, M., Ang, J., Chin, J., & Chai, W. (2015). To behave like a liar: Nonverbal cues to deception in an Asian sample. *Journal of Police and Criminal Psychology*, 1–8.

Christopher, M. (1973). *The illustrated history of magic*. New York: Crowell.

Chung, C. K., & Pennebaker, J. W. (2014). Counting little words in big data: The psychology of communities, culture, and history. In *Social cognition and communication* (pp. 25–42). New York, NY, USA: Psychology Press.

Cui, J., Otero-Millan, J., Macknik, S. L., King, M., & Martinez-Conde, S. (2011). Social misdirection fails to enhance a magic illusion. *Frontiers in Human Neuroscience, 5*, 103. http://dx.doi.org/10.3389/fnhum.2011.00103.

DePaulo, B. M., Lindsay, J. J., Malone, B. E., Muhlenbruck, L., Charlton, K., & Cooper, H. (2003). Cues to deception. *Psychological Bulletin, 129*(1), 74.

Fallis, D. (2014). The varieties of disinformation. In *The philosophy of information quality* (pp. 135–161Springer International Publishing.

Feng, S., Banerjee, R., & Choi, Y. (July 2012). Syntactic stylometry for deception detection. In *Proceedings of the 50th annual meeting of the Association for Computational Linguistics: Short papers* (Vol. 2) (pp. 171–175). Association for Computational Linguistics.

Fitzkee, D. (1945/2009). *Magic by misdirection: An explanation of the psychology of deception* (5th ed.). Pomeroy, Ohio: Lee Jacobs Productions.

Fuller, C. M., Biros, D. P., & Delen, D. (2011). An investigation of data and text mining methods for real world deception detection. *Expert Systems with Applications, 38*(7), 8392–8398.

Goffman, E. (1974). *Frame analysis: An essay on the organization of experience*. Harvard University Press.

Grazioli, S., & Jarvenpaa, S. L. (2003). Deceived: Under target online. *Communications of the ACM, 46*(12), 196–205.

Hooi, R., & Cho, H. (November 2012). Being immersed: Avatar similarity and self-awareness. In *Proceedings of the 24th Australian computer–human interaction conference* (pp. 232–240). ACM.

Jastrow, J. (1896). Psychological notes upon sleight-of-hand experts. *Science, 3*, 685–689.

Johnson, P. E., Grazioli, S., & Jamal, K. (1993). Fraud detection: Intentionality and deception in cognition. *Accounting, Organizations and Society, 18*(5), 467–488.

Johnson, P. E., Grazioli, S., Jamal, K., & Berryman, R. G. (2001). Detecting deception: Adversarial problem solving in a low base-rate world. *Cognitive Science, 25*(3), 355–392.

Kuhn, G. (2010). Cognitive illusions: From magic to science. In E. Perry, D. Collerton, F. LeBeau, & H. Ashton (Eds.), *New horizons in the neuroscience of consciousness* (pp. 139–148). Amsterdam: John Benjamin Publishing Company. http://dx.doi.org/10.1075/aicr.79.19kuh.

Kuhn, G., Amlani, A. A., & Rensink, R. A. (2008). Towards a science of magic. *Trends in Cognitive Sciences, 12*(9), 349–354.

Kuhn, G., Caffaratti, H. A., Teszka, R., & Rensink, R. A. (2014). A psychologically-based taxonomy of misdirection. *Frontiers in Psychology, 5*, 1392.

Kuhn, G., & Findlay, J. M. (2010). Misdirection, attention and awareness: Inattentional blindness reveals temporal relationship between eye movements and visual awareness. *The Quarterly Journal of Experimental Psychology, 63*(1), 136–146.

Kuhn, G., & Land, M. F. (2006). There's more to magic than meets the eye. *Current Biology, 16*(22), R950–R951.

Kuhn, G., & Martinez, L. M. (2012). Misdirection–past, present, and the future. *Frontiers in Human Neuroscience, 5*, 172.

Kuhn, G., & Tatler, B. W. (2005). Magic and fixation: Now you don't see it, now you do. *Perception, 34*, 1155–1161. http://dx.doi.org/10.1068/p3409bn1.

Kuhn, G., & Tatler, B. W. (2011). Misdirected by the gap. The relationship between inattentional blindness and attentional misdirection. *Consciousness and Cognition, 20*(2), 432–436.

Kuhn, G., Tatler, B. W., & Cole, G. G. (2009). You look where I look! Effect of gaze cues on overt and covert attention in misdirection. *Visual Cognition, 17*, 925–944. http://dx.doi.org/10.1080/13506280902826775.

Kuhn, G., Tatler, B. W., Findlay, J. M., & Cole, G. G. (2008). Misdirection in magic: Implications for the relationship between eye gaze and attention. *Visual Cognition, 16*(2–3), 391–405.

Lamont, P., Henderson, J. M., & Smith, T. (2010). Where science and magic meet: The illusion of a 'science of magic'. *Review of General Psychology, 14*(1), 16–21.

Lamont, P., & Wiseman, R. (1999). *Magic in theory: An introduction to the theoretical and psychological elements of conjuring.* University of Hertfordshire Press.

Lavie, N., & Tsal, Y. (1994). Perceptual load as a major determinant of the locus of selection in visual attention. *Perception and Psychophysics, 56*, 183–197. http://dx.doi.org/10.3758/BF03213897.

Li, J., Ott, M., Cardie, C., & Hovy, E. H. (June 2014). Towards a general rule for identifying deceptive opinion spam. In *Proceedings of the 52nd annual meeting of the association for computational linguistics* (Vol. 1) (pp. 1566–1576).

Macknik, S. L. (2006). Visual masking approaches to visual awareness. *Progress in Brain Research, 155*, 177–215.

Macknik, S. L., Martinez-Conde, S., & Blakeslee, S. (2010). *Sleights of mind.* New York: Picador.

Mack, A., & Rock, I. (1998). *Inattentional blindness.* MIT Press.

Marshall, J., Benford, S., & Pridmore, T. (April 2010). Deception and magic in collaborative interaction. In *Proceedings of the SIGCHI conference on human factors in computing systems* (pp. 567–576). ACM.

Mitnick, K. D., & Simon, W. L. (2002). *The art of deception: Controlling the human element of security.* Indianapolis, IN: Wiley.

Mokkonen, M., & Lindstedt, C. (2015). The evolutionary ecology of deception. *Biological Reviews of the Cambridge Philosophical Society.* http://dx .doi:10.1111/brv.12208.

Mouton, F., Leenen, L., Malan, M. M., & Venter, H. S. (July 2014). Towards an ontological model defining the social engineering domain. In *IFIP international conference on human choice and computers* (pp. 266–279). Springer Berlin Heidelberg.

Murphy, B. K. (1993). Magic as cooperative deceit. *Studies in Popular Culture, 16*(1), 87–99.

Nardi, P. M. (1984). Toward a social psychology of entertainment magic (conjuring). *Symbolic Interaction, 7*(1), 25–42.

Ortiz, D. (1994). In R. Kaufman, M. Field, M. Phillips, R. Kaufman, & A. Greenberg (Eds.), *Strong magic: Creative showmanship for the close-up magician.*

Peltier, T. R. (2006). Social engineering: Concepts and solutions. *Information Systems Security, 15*(5), 13–21.

Pennebaker, J., & Francis, M. (1999). *Linguistic inquiry and word count: LIWC.*

Pennebaker, J. W., Francis, M. E., & Booth, R. J. (2001). *Linguistic inquiry and word count: Liwc 2001* (Vol. 71. Mahway: Lawrence Erlbaum Associates, 2001.

Pérez-Rosas, V., Mihalcea, R., Narvaez, A., & Burzo, M. (May 2014). A multimodal dataset for deception detection. In *LREC*, (pp. 3118–3122).

Porter, S., & Ten Brinke, L. (2008). Reading between the lies identifying concealed and falsified emotions in universal facial expressions. *Psychological Science, 19*(5), 508–514.

Randal, J. (1982). *The psychology of deception:(why magic work)*. Venice: Top Secret Productions, Inc.

Rensink, R. A. (2002). Change detection. *Annual Review of Psychology, 53*, 245–277. http://dx.doi.org/10.1146/annurev.psych.53.100901.135125.

Rensink, R. A., et al. (1997). To see or not to see: The need for attention to perceive changes in scenes. *Psychological Science, 8*, 368–373.

Schneider, A. (2011). *The theory and practice of magic deception.*

Sharpe, S. H. (1988). *Conjurers' psychological secrets*. Calgary: Hades Publications.

Simons, D. J., & Chabris, C. F. (1999). Gorillas in our midst: Sustained inattentional blindness for dynamic events. *Perception, 28*, 1059–1074. http://dx.doi.org/10.1068/p2952.

Stech, F. J., Heckman, K. E., Hilliard, P., & Ballo, J. R. (2011). Scientometrics of deception, counter-deception, and deception detection in cyber-space. *PsychNology Journal, 9*(2), 79–122.

Tamariz, J. (1987/2014). *The magic way: The method of false solutions and the magic way*. Seattle: Hermetic Press.

Tamariz, J., & Lehn, D. B. (2007). *The five points in magic*. Hermetic Press Incorporated.

Tetri, P., & Vuorinen, J. (2013). Dissecting social engineering. *Behaviour & Information Technology, 32*(10), 1014–1023.

Toma, C. L., & Hancock, J. T. (2012). What lies beneath: The linguistic traces of deception in online dating profiles. *Journal of Communication, 62*(1), 78–97.

Triplett, N. (1900). The psychology of conjuring deceptions. *The American Journal of Psychology, 11*(4), 439–510.

Van Swol, L. M., Braun, M. T., & Kolb, M. R. (2015). Deception, detection, demeanor, and truth bias in face-to-face and computer-mediated communication. *Communication Research, 42*(8), 1116–1142.

Vendemia, J. M., Buzan, R. F., & Green, E. P. (2005). Practice effects, workload, and reaction time in deception. *The American Journal of Psychology*, 413–429.

Walczyk, J. J., Mahoney, K. T., Doverspike, D., & Griffith-Ross, D. A. (2009). Cognitive lie detection: Response time and consistency of answers as cues to deception. *Journal of Business and Psychology, 24*(1), 33–49.

Yang, Y., & Mannino, M. (2012). An experimental comparison of a document deception detection policy using real and artificial deception. *Journal of Data and Information Quality (JDIQ), 3*(3), 6.

Yang, Y., & Mannino, M. V. (2012). An experimental comparison of real and artificial deception using a deception generation model. *Decision Support Systems, 53*(3), 543–553.

Zimbler, M., & Feldman, R. S. (2011). Liar, liar, hard drive on fire: How media context affects lying behavior. *Journal of Applied Social Psychology, 41*(10), 2492–2507.

Zuckerman, M., DeFrank, R. S., Hall, J. A., Larrance, D. T., & Rosenthal, R. (1979). Facial and vocal cues of deception and honesty. *Journal of Experimental Social Psychology, 15*(4), 378–396.

2

Virtual Myths: Internet Urban Legend, Chain Letters, and Warnings

ABSTRACT

This chapter explores how story narrative can captivate, compel, and deceive the receiving audience. The history and elements of urban legends, hoaxes, and chain communications are examined as underpinnings of deception strategies. The chapter then examines the evolution of these types of communications and how traditional urban myths and hoax communications, whether verbal or written, have gradually and effectively shifted to the online world. In the final section, the chapter discusses how attackers use these compelling story styles in computer-mediated communications to weaponize cyber attacks and scam, or otherwise deceive and exploit, human targets.

Keywords: *Chain letter; Email hoax; Folklore; Internet hoax; Online folklore; Online urban legend; Online urban myth; Scare chains; Threat chains; Urban legend; Urban myth.*

CHAPTER OUTLINE

> The electronic transmission of urban rumors and legends has become their chief means of circulation, supplementing the traditional sharing of such folklore via word of mouth or print.
> –Jan Harold Brunvand

Urban legends (UL), chain letters, and hoax messages have long captivated the receivers of these narratives. These storylines and communications have further evolved; through computer-mediated communications (CMCs), urban legends, chain letters, and hoax messages have become woven into the fabric of popular Internet culture. In particular, social media platforms, offering a myriad of new communication methods, provide a new digital canvas for cyber attackers and scam artists. This chapter begins by exploring the background and elements of traditional urban legends, chain letters, and hoax communications and how these techniques can be similarly leveraged by cyber threat actors to circumvent human defenses. This chapter then examines the evolution of these types of communications and how attackers use the story styles in computer-mediated communications to weaponize, scam, or otherwise deceive and exploit human targets.

Urban Myths and Legends

Urban legends and myths have become a key component of popular culture, as they appear in various media, including an eponymous film series (Brunvand, 2012). The roots of these legends may not, however, be fully appreciated by modern society. An urban myth, or urban legend, is actually a form of folklore, which is passed from individual to individual. Folklore is popularly defined as "traditional items of knowledge that arise in recurring performances" (Abrahams, 1976, p. 195), particularly through oral communications. Folklore can carry a variety of functions for society, including educating individuals on the consequences of actions, establishing a group identity, providing general entertainment, and poking fun at standard social interactions (Seal, 1989; Brunvand, 1998).

Urban legends are set in contemporary spaces and involve people (Brunvand, 1981). The use of the term "urban" is not intended to indicate the geographic origin of the story but rather differentiate modern legends from those of the preindustrial era. In fact, the phrase "urban legend" was first used in 1968 in separate publications involving discussions of legends and oral traditions. The term was partially popularized due to the publication of Jan Harold Brunvand's (1981) book *The Vanishing Hitchhiker: American Urban Legends and Their Meanings*. The oral tradition of folklore is also evident in urban legends and survives through communication between individuals who share some common demographic characteristics. For instance, youth may share urban myths with one another casually, or office mates as a means of entertainment (Brunvand, 1981).

The commonalities between the teller and the listener may make the story more believable, though it may also adjust slightly each time it is told due to the predilections of the teller and recall of the listener (Brunvand, 1981). The consistency of the tale is important, as is the need to link the story to some real person so as to impart credibility to the story. Often, the teller incorporates vague language indicating that the events in the story involved a friend or a friend of a friend. This reinforces the legitimacy of the tale, as well as the listeners' larger beliefs about the world, and the nature of human interactions. Whether or not the teller believes the story is true is irrelevant, as the communication of the ideas in the story are what lead to its perpetuation over time.

Elements of Urban Legends

While not linear in structure, urban legend narratives typically contain certain elements and follow a similar flow of stages (Fig. 2.1). Importantly, the authors of these legends, while likely not formally trained in human sciences, expertly leverage many traditional psychological principals, causing recipients of urban legend communications to consume the narratives and, many times, engage further. Static components, or *stable elements*, are the generalized descriptions of the componential phases in the legend's plot (Brunvand, 1981). For example, in a modernized version of the classic urban legend "The Killer in the Backseat," (told in full detail in the text box, *The Killer in the Backseat*) the stable elements are:

- □ A woman is driving her car.
- □ While stopped to get gasoline, a killer surreptitiously gets into the backseat of her vehicle.
- □ The gas station attendant causes the woman to come inside the store by convincing her that there was a problem with her credit card used for payment.

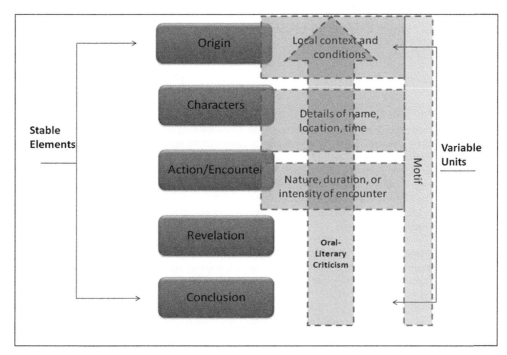

FIGURE 2.1 Elements of an urban legend.

□ The woman is able to safely get into the gas station.
□ The killer in the backseat is revealed.
□ The attendant is the hero, having thwarted the attacker from assaulting the woman.

Dynamic components, or *variable units,* are aspects of the urban legend that are not the core aspects of the narrative but rather facets that are subject to adaptation. Brunvand posits that "urban legends develop two kinds of variations" (Brunvand, 1981, p. 14). First, the legends may be subtly modified to be contextually suitable and appealing to the target

Online Urban Legend

"The Killer in the Backseat"
One of the most popular and circulated urban legends, "Killer in the Backseat" first surfaced in the late 1960s and has made the rounds both through traditional word-of-mouth narrative, countless inboxes, and even social media messaging. Numerous permutations of the story exist—some with variation in the context or location of the encounter and some with variation in characters. However, the moral lesson (particularly aimed toward women) remains consistent: staying vigilant and checking one's surroundings. At the time of this writing in 2015, versions of the legend still appear on social media and Internet forums. A recent version of the legend (as it appeared in 2013) is depicted below.

THIS IS CRAZY! IMPORTANT PLEASE READ

Aug 2, 2013.

Date Posted: Aug 2, 2013

A friend stopped at a pay-at-the-pump gas station to get gas. Once she filled her gas tank and after paying at the pump and starting to leave, the voice of the attendant inside came over the speaker.. He told her that something happened with her card and that she needed to come inside to pay. The lady was confused because the transaction showed complete and approved. She relayed that to him and was getting ready to leave but the attendant, once again, urged her to come in to pay or there'd be trouble. She proceeded to go inside and started arguing with the attendant about his threat. He told her to calm down and listen carefully:
He said that while she was pumping gas, a guy slipped into the back seat of her car on the other side and the attendant had already called the police.

She became frightened and looked out in time to see her car door open and the guy slip out. The report is that the new gang initiation thing is to bring back a woman and/or her car. One way they are doing this is crawling under women's cars while they're pumping gas or at grocery stores in the nighttime. The other way is slipping into unattended cars and kidnapping the women.

Please pass this on to other women, young and old alike. Be extra careful going to and from your car at night. If at all possible, don't go alone!
This is real!!

locale; these types of changes may be the name of the place, time, and setting of the event. Secondly, more substantial variations—referred to among folklorists as "*oral-literary criticism*" (Brunvand, 1981, p. 14)—are substantial deviations from the original urban legend narrative and may include the introduction of new plot elements, characters, or objects. Another consideration in urban legend variations is whether *motifs*—narrative elements that convey symbolic meaning—are consistent, modified, or augmented into a different permutation of the legend. Often, motifs change to convey new lessons or expand upon the scope of the lessons in the original legend (Brunvand, 2001).

As the Internet, mobile phones, and Computer-Mediated Communications like email have become the preferred communication vehicle, urban myths have transitioned from an oral tradition to a written form. In fact, renowned urban legend and folklore scholar Jan Harold Brunvand astutely noted that "the Internet also makes it possible for bizarre, sensational, scary, and often highly doubtful stories to fly around the world with the speed of a mouse-click. In fact, the role of the Internet in simply transmitting ULs is probably far greater at present than its success in exposing them as unreliable accounts" (Brunvand, 2004, pp. 237–238). There are several questions as to how this change occurred and the nature of urban myths in online spaces; this chapter will explore these issues in depth.

Urban Myths Online

The spread of legends and tales predates modern technology, facilitated largely by the oral tradition of storytelling between individuals. Letter writing was also an essential way to spread myths as individuals could readily connect with others through postal mail. Telephony was also incorporated into the communication of myths, but the majority of messaging spread through storytelling in person.

The development of the Internet and binary data transmission via telephony transformed the spread of urban myths in the 1980s (De Vos, 2012). As technology enabled efficient contact between individuals, especially across large distances, this became a preferred medium for the spread of urban legends and various scams and fraud schemes. Prior to the World Wide Web and CMCs, scammers had to depend on their ability to craft convincing stories, whether in person or through either phone-based or print scams in magazines and newspapers. These efforts required some degree of investment, as the scammer had to develop and pay for an ad to be created or pay bulk mail.

Specifically, the fax machine was one of the first sources of technology-based urban myths spread. Since messages could be relayed to any one at the receiving end of the fax, written descriptions of a myth became an essential way to communicate urban legends and scam messages. The ubiquitous Nigerian, or 419, scams—where an individual claims to be an African prince seeking to move money—were sent as faxes during the 1980s and 1990s (United States Department of State, 1997). Similarly, urban myths spread via fax, especially the so-called "Lights Out" myth (Brunvand, 2001). In this myth, gang members were initiating new members by making them drive without their headlights on

(Fig. 2.2). If another driver flashed their headlights as a warning, the new initiate would have to attempt to kill the driver. This myth spread across the country in 1993 via fax with memos appearing to come from state police agencies claiming that members of the Bloods, Crips, and/or Black Gangster Disciples were responsible for killings (Mikkelson, 2014). There is, however, minimal evidence to actually support the legend—only incidental events associated with headlight flashing.

```
Police Depts across the nation are being warned that this is the "blood"
initiation weekend. Their intent is to have all the new bloods nationwide
drive around on Saturday and Sunday nights with their headlights off. In order
to be accepted into the gang, they have to shoot and kill all individuals in
the first auto that does a courtesy flash to warn them that their lights are
off·
```

FIGURE 2.2 The "Lights Out" urban myth.

The ubiquity of Usenet groups also enabled the spread of urban myths, as messages could be sent in bulk to anyone, and circulated and recirculated with ease. Kibby (2005) argued that email and online communications constitute a "secondary orality" (Ong, 1982), because of the nature of the exchanges between participants (p. 771). While all communications are written, email is participatory, casually written, and able to illicit immediate responses. These conditions create an experience that mirrors traditional face-to-face speech and enables individuals to feel less constrained in their online communications (Kibby, 2005; Tofts, 1996).

Thinking Like the Attacker

"Friend of a Friend" (FOAF)
A common *Indicator of Online Urban Legend* (IOUL) is notable lack of specificity when referring to witnesses, victims, or reporters of the events described in an urban legend. In fact, many times the source referenced is "a friend of a friend", or the acronym that urban legend scholars use, "FOAF." When information conveyed by the author is not derived from firsthand experience but rather attributed to a vaguely identified second- or third person, this is indicative of an urban legend. Attackers often use FOAF to attribute a story because it provides plausible attribution without providing specific information or identifiers that could likely be verified, dispelling the narrative and exposing it as fake.

The unique nature of the online environment means individuals may be inclined to write or share information with many people while online, which they would not otherwise do in person (De Vos, 2012). The Internet has made information a commodity, giving value to any story that others may want to share and circulate (Kollock, 1999). In addition, digital information can be shared easily and retained as it first appeared, thereby eliminating the potential for stories (myth or genuine) to be adulterated or diluted. For instance, an email can be forwarded to others immediately and with no additions required on the part of the sender (Heyd, 2008). This adds a sense of credibility to the content, as it has not been changed. Recipients can see the information for themselves and determine what they would like to do in response.

In addition to email, the development of social networking sites like Facebook have engendered unique ways to further distribute urban myths. The ability to immediately share text, images, and web links with large groups of people in a very informal way makes social media platforms a second orality. The participatory nature of social media platforms also enhances the interaction between a poster and the larger public in ways that go beyond what is possible with email platforms. Since social media platforms depend on social ties to connect individuals in large networks, messages sent can gain additional credibility because individual associations lend credence to the idea that the events in a story actually occurred (Kibby, 2005; Kollock, 1999).

Importantly, communication methods specific to social media platforms offer various new modalities to post, publish, and transmit messages, changing the complexion of ULs, hoaxes, and chain communications. Sites like Twitter, for example, have character number limitations (140 characters of text) for posting a public tweet.[1] These inherent limitations reshape how urban legend, hoax, and chain communications look and how victims engage. Often, these new communications require external resources, such as short URL redirectors and online photo-sharing services, allowing attackers to leverage these vectors while remaining contextually innocuous, since these are common and expected external content processes. For example, if an attacker sends a scary urban legend on Twitter and references an image (that is accessible via a shortened URL embedded in the tweet), recipients enticed by the message will more than likely click on the link to view the image, just as they would with other tweets they receive; attackers shrewdly rely upon the fact that this is a common practice of users consuming Twitter content.

The creation of computer-mediated communication, whether email or social media, has also incentivized the process of information sharing beyond notions of helping others and spreading useful information (Kibby, 2005; Kollock, 1999). Some forward emails or share information they find with others out of a real sense of altruism, which Kollock (1999) argued was out of a sense of "efficacy" (p. 227). At the same time, others may share out of a sense of "anticipated reciprocity," whereby they contribute under the assumption that others will provide information when they need it (Kollock, 1999, p. 227).

Finally, some share information in order to gain greater status within the community (Kollock, 1999). Providing information with perceived value may increase the perception

---

[1] In August 2015, Twitter removed the 140 character limitation on direct message communications. This feature of Twitter enables users to have direct, private conversations. https://blog.twitter.com/2015/removing-the-140-character-limit-from-direct-messages

that an individual is "in the know" and should be given greater consideration. This notion is most evident in social media sites, as they provide individuals with the ability to "like"[2] or "share"[3] content someone has posted. The more a post is viewed, liked, and shared, the more popularity an individual may gain from the larger user population.

This incentivizes information sharing and may lead people to post inflammatory or false information in an attempt to gain more followers and gain greater prominence online. In fact, there is evidence that rumors, false information, and myths spread via social media in cascades, where individuals observe the behavior of others and then act in the same way, regardless of their knowledge that such information is false or goes against their conventional wisdom (Dotey, Rom, & Vaca, 2011; Friggeri, Adamic, Eckles, & Cheng, 2014). Thus there is a flow of behavior from one person to many on the basis of observed behavior.

These mechanisms have also provided a means for attackers to create new ways of conveying urban legend and hoaxes, at times for malicious purposes. One burgeoning and insidious permutation is Facebook "like-farming," where the attacker develops a Facebook page with content purposefully to gather as many "likes" or "shares" as rapidly as possible.[4] The Facebook news feed algorithm measures the number of "likes," "shares," and comments a post receives, pushing those with high ratios to other users' news feeds, causing the pages to gain more visibility.[5] Once the popularity level is high, ensuring a sufficient victim pool, the attacker changes the page content to the intended nefarious content, to include malicious code, fraudulent advertisements, or other scams.

There are myriad reasons why individuals may create chain emails and hoaxes. For instance, there may be entertainment value in seeing how far a false story will circulate. Alternatively, individuals may enjoy the thrill of spreading a threatening email or scary message to individuals they do not know. This entertainment also has virtually no cost, as individuals can acquire multiple free email addresses in order to send email. The anonymity afforded by CMCs also makes it possible for individuals to circulate false information anonymously, making it an activity with minimal risk. In addition, email messages can be easily manipulated to include photos, links, and other details that may serve to legitimize the story.

While individuals in these circumstances may not be driven by any particular sense of malice, there are forms of urban myth-related emails that are a vehicle for criminals who seek to cause harm or gain a profit from victim recipients. Several hoax emails circulate

---

[2] "Clicking **Like** below a post on Facebook is an easy way to let people know that you enjoy it without leaving a comment. Just like a comment, the fact that you liked the post is visible below it." https://www.facebook.com/help/452446998120360/

[3] https://www.facebook.com/help/418076994900119/

[4] For further discussion on like-farming, *see* http://www.consumeraffairs.com/news/like-farming-facebook-scams-look-before-you-like-042215.html and http://www.cnn.com/2014/01/21/tech/social-media/facebook-like-farming/

[5] https://www.facebook.com/business/news/News-Feed-FYI-A-Window-Into-News-Feed

that inform the recipient of computer security threats that can be avoided by removing certain files. Deleting system files can, however, create opportunities to harm a computer system and enable attacks (see Chapter 3: Viral Influence: Deceptive Computing Attacks Through Persuasion). Similarly, the sender may ask the recipients to send funds in order to secure their luck or personal safety. This sort of message could be circulated through parcel post, but email provides a wider sample of potential victims at minimal cost to the offender. Thus urban myths and chain messages are a sensible environment for risk averse scammers who seek to maximize returns.

Indicators of Online Hoax and Chain Communications

Examining the Elements
Identifiable elements of online hoax and chain communications are described in "Indicators of Online Hoax and Chain Communications" text boxes presented throughout the remainder of the chapter. While these elements may vary, they are a good starting point and reference for analysis in the defense against these types of communications. Another informative reference (although no longer active since 2008) is the United States Department of Energy Computer Incident Advisory Capability (CIAC) "Hoaxbusters" Hoax Reference site, formerly at hoax-busters.ciac.org (and still available through the Archive.org Wayback Machine: https://web.archive.org/web/20080101232936/http://hoaxbusters.ciac.org/).
CIAC generally described the elements of hoax and chain communications as 1) a hook, 2) a threat, and 3) a request.

Traditional Chain Letters

With an understanding of the motives and rationale for chain message creation, we can now consider the various forms of chain messages and urban myths online. One of the most common types resembles traditional chain letters in the real world. The chain in this case refers to the networks of individuals the messages move through in an attempt to get the message circulated as far as possible (Heyd, 2008; De Vos, 2012). The content of chain letters varies substantially, though a common component of the message involves the use of luck. In particular, these chains typically advise that recipients who forward the message on tend to experience good luck, while those who do not may suffer a range of unfortunate incidents as a result of bad luck. Commonly described misfortunes describe how individuals may experience direct economic harm, computer failure, physical harm, or even death if they do not circulate the message. There are myriad examples of these messages online, including a popular scam from the early 2000s which indicated that if you did not forward the message to ten people within three hours of receiving the message, you would experience serious bad luck. If you did forward the message, you would have great luck with love, enticing individuals to forward the message on (Fig. 2.3).

This has some deep meaning hidden between the lines for all of us and all that you have meant to me.... some ONE is looking out for us...if I didn't believe that....we wouldn't still be friends.....
READ ALONE - READ ALL OF IT

CASE 1: Kelly Seedy had one wish, for her boyfriend of three years, David Marsden, to propose to her. Then one day when she was out to lunch, David proposed! She accepted. But she then had to leave because she had a meeting in 20 min. When she got back to her office she noticed on her computer she had something missing here. She checked it, the usual stuff from friends, but then she saw one that she had never seen before. It was this very letter. She simply deleted it, without reading it. BIG MISTAKE!! Later that evening she received a call from the local police. It was regarding David. He had been in an accident with an 18-wheeler, he did not survive.

CASE 2:
Take Katie Robbenson. She received this letter and being the believer that she was sent it off to a few of her friends, but did not have enough to send to the full 10 that you must. Three days later she went to a Masquerade ball. Later that night when she left to get to her car to go home, she was killed on the spot by a hit and run drunk driver.

CASE 3:
Richard S. Willis sent this letter out within 45 minutes of reading it. Not even 4 hours later walking along the street to his new job interview, with a really big company, when he ran into Cynthia Bell, his secret love of 5 years. Cynthia came up to him and told him of her passionate crush on him that she had for 2 years. Three days later he proposed to her and they were married. They are still married to this day and have three children.

This is the letter:

Around the corner I have a friend,
In this great city that has no end,
Yet the days go by, and the weeks rush on,
And before I know it a year has gone.

And I never see my old friends face,
For life is a swift and terrible race,
He knows I like him just as well,
As in the days when I rang his bell,

And he rang mine if, we were younger then,
And now we are busy, tired men.
Tired of playing a foolish game,
Tired of trying to make a name.

Tomorrow; I say, I will call on Jim
Just to show I am thinking of him.
But tomorrow comes and tomorrow goes,
And distance between us grows and grows.

Around the corner! - yet miles away,
Here's a telegram sir, Jim died today.
And that's what we get and deserve in the end.
Around the corner, a vanished friend.

Remember to always say what you mean.
If you love someone - tell them.
Don't be afraid to express yourself.
Reach out and tell someone what they mean to you,
because when you decide that it is the right time,
it might be too late.

Seize the day, Never have regrets.

Most importantly stay close to your friends and family,
for they have helped make you the person you are today.

You must send this on within 3 hours, after reading the letter, to 10 different people. If you do this you will receive unbelievably good luck in love. The person you are most attracted to will soon return your feelings. If you do not, bad luck will rear it's ugly head.

THIS IS NOT A JOKE!
The more people you send this to, the better luck you will have.

FIGURE 2.3 Early 2000s chain letter.

A common, but criminal, chain letter involves the use of get-rich-quick pyramid schemes that convince the recipient that they can make a profit by following the steps outlined in the letter. Typically the recipient must provide a small cash payment to an individual, whether as an investment or in order to purchase a small item or report. In turn, they may receive a substantial return on their investment in the form of either more money or extremely good luck.

Indicators of Online Hoax and Chain Communications

Elements of Traditional Chain Letters

- □ *Attention-grabbing title:* Often in all capital letters ("marquee" effect) with many exclamation points to emphasize "importance."
- □ *Transmission and perpetuation imperative:* A fundamental aspect of chain communications is the imperative levied by the sender for the recipient to continue the trajectory of the message by transmitting or broadcasting it to others via online communication.
- □ *Influence and forcing:* These communications often use influence strategy, similar to the magician's "forcing" technique (psychological techniques a magician can use to shape a participant's actions toward a desired outcome), advising the recipient that by complying with the request of communication, he/she will benefit (often framed as "good luck"), whereas noncompliance will cause him/her misfortune, "bad luck," or other negative consequences.
- □ *Reaffirmation of transmission and perpetuation imperative:* Commonly, these communications end with a repeated request to transmit and broadcast the message forward to continue the message's trajectory.

Hoax Messages

There are also a number of messages that circulate that deceive the recipient. For instance, there are a wide range of messages that state the recipient will receive a prize or gift from a corporation or business if they forward the message on to others. No items will actually be provided, but these messages persist over time. One of the most popular and long circulating of these messages involves Bill Gates and Microsoft providing individuals with a cash payment for every individual that forwards a message to peers, and then subsequent payments for every reforward and receipt of the message (Fig. 2.4). This is, however, patently false and designed to fill up inboxes with unnecessary forwards.

Indicators of Online Hoax and Chain Communications

Elements of Hoax Messages

- □ *Warning announcement/cautionary statement:* This is typically in all capital letters ("marquee" effect) to grab the recipient's attention. The topic is often scary, ominous, compelling, or otherwise emotion evoking.

Continued

—Continued

□ **Narrative** describing the "problem," "issue," or "opportunity."

□ **Consequences:** The recipient is advised of bad luck or other problematic circumstances that will arise if the message request is not heeded.

□ **Request/requirements:** The hoax provides instructions or admonitions to the recipient that require him/her to conduct a further action, including or in addition to perpetuating the message.

□ **Transmission/perpetuation requirement:** The recipient is admonished to continue the trajectory of the message by transmitting or broadcasting it to others via online communication.

THIS TOOK TWO PAGES OF THE TUESDAY USA TODAY - IT IS FOR REAL

Subject: PLEEEEEEASE READ!!!! it was on the news!

To all of my friends, I do not usually forward messages, but this is from my good friend Pearlas Sandborn and she really is an attorney.

If she says that this will work - It will work. After all, what have you got to lose? SORRY EVERYBODY.. JUST HAD TO TAKE THE CHANCE!!! I'm an attorney, and I know the law. This thing is for real. Rest assured AOL and Intel will follow through with their promises for fear of facing a multimillion-dollar class action suit similar to the one filed by PepsiCo against General Electric not too long ago.

Dear Friends; Please do not take this for a junk letter. Bill Gates sharing his fortune. If you ignore this, You will repent later. Microsoft and AOL are now the largest Internet companies and in an effort to make sure that Internet Explorer remains the most widely used program, Microsoft and AOL are running a beta test.

When you forward this to friends, Microsoft can and will track it (If you are a Microsoft Windows user) For a two week time period.

For every person that you forward this to, Microsoft will pay you $245.00 For every person that you sent it to that forwards it on, Microsoft will pay you $243.00 and for every third person that receives it, You will be paid $241.00. Within two weeks, Microsoft will contact you for your address and then send you a check.

I thought this was a scam myself, But two weeks after receiving this and forwarding it on. Microsoft contacted me for my address and withindays, I receive a check for $24,800.00. You need to respond before the beta testing is over. If anyone can affoard this, Bill gates is the man.

It's all marketing expense to him. Please forward this to as many people as possible. You are bound to get at least $10,000.00. We're not going to help them out with their beta test without getting a little something for our time. My brother's girlfriend got in on this a few months ago. When i went to visit him for the Baylor/UT game. She showed me her check. It was for the sum of $4,324.44 and was stamped "Paid in full"

Like i said before, I know the law, and this is for real.

Intel and AOL are now discussing a merger which would make them the largest Internet company and in an effort make sure that AOL remains the most widely used program, Intel and AOL are running an beta test.
When you forward this to friends, Intel can and will track it (if you are a Microsoft Windows user) for a two week time period.

FIGURE 2.4 The "Bill Gates" hoax message.

Email messages have also become a popular way for individuals to send jokes or satirical stories based on various events in popular media in general. While there is nothing inherently dangerous about the contents of these messages, it is important to note that they can clog inboxes and distract others. In addition, a small number of people may believe that the information contained in the message is real and forward it on to others, which perpetuates proliferation. As a result, there is a need for great caution when figuring out what to do with these sorts of messages.

Defensive Strategy

"Too Good to Be True"

A common variable and theme in hoax chains, particularly those promising financial gain, is that the proposed opportunity or offer is too good to be true. Defending against hoax communications requires critically examining a communication in totality but also by dissecting its parts. Some of the questions and elements the recipient should consider include:

- Where is the sender claiming to be from?
- Why is the sender emailing the recipient?
- Is the message (and the fact the message was sent to the recipient) contextually reasonable?
- Is there a narrative appealing to the reader's emotions or predilections, leading up to an offer/opportunity?
- What is the offer/opportunity?
- Does the offer/opportunity seem reasonable, plausible, or legal?
- Why would this be offered to the recipient?
- What does the recipient have to do to benefit from this offer/opportunity?
- What pitfalls could occur from availing oneself of the offer?

By examining these questions, and in turn, the communication offer/opportunity in totality, more often than not the hoax communication will be strikingly "too good to be true" and a resounding hoax to be avoided.

Scare Chains

Another form of chain messages is focused on making individuals forward messages to others out of a desire to share information that may help save lives or otherwise prevent a potential harm. The content of these messages largely focus on stories about individuals who have experienced some terrible incident due to accidents, crime, or something supernatural. These messages are a form of urban myth, as the incident in question is entirely false but written in such a way as to appear believable.

There are a range of scares that can be employed, such as the risk of victimization from strangers in certain situations or around holidays. Often, the victim of the story is a woman or child, thus causing the moral, advice, or action imperative to target or be indirectly messaged to female recipients. Similarly, there are scare chains related to the risk of injury from consumer products that have been adulterated or in some way compromised. For instance, email chains circulated in the late 2000s and in the last few years regarding deaths from *Leptospira* bacteria left by rats found on the tops of beverage cans (Fig. 2.5). These claims have never been substantiated, despite the email messages. As a result, they are specifically designed to illicit a response and forwarding from the recipients.

IMPORTANT PLEASE READ: Do Not Delete this message until it is extended to others ..

On Sunday, a family picnic, brought with them few drinks in tin. However, on Monday, two family members (who joined the picnic) were admitted to hospital and placed in the Intensive Care Unit space. One died on Wednesday.

Autopsy results concluded it hit Leptospirosis. The bacteria, known as LEPTOSPIRA interrogans, is stuck to the tin cans, and were drunk, without the use of glasses, cups or sip straws. Test results showed that the soda tin was infected from mice urine, and that had dried, the mice' urine containing Leptospirosis. It is highly recommended to rinse the parts evenly on all soda cans before drinking it. Cans are usually stored in the warehouse and delivered direct to retail stores without cleaning.

A study shows that the top of all beverage cans are more contaminated than public toilets (full of germs and bacteria.) So, clean it with water before putting it to your mouth in order to avoid contamination.

FIGURE 2.5 The *Leptospira*/rat urine/"Deadly Soda Can" scare chain.

Scare chains, while still common through traditional CMCs, like email, are becoming increasingly common on social media platforms, and the subject or focus of these scary narratives often times revolve around technology and computing events. One scare chain that gained considerable traction in 2013,[6] and resurgence in 2014,[7] focused on the Talking Angela App—a "virtual pet" application that "interacts" with the user (Fig. 2.6).[8]

The hoax narrative purported that the application was secretly an information collection platform for preferential sex offenders targeting children. In particular, the 2014 version of the hoax is themed as being authored by a mother who discovered that her daughter, "Angelica," whom had stayed home from school, was engaged in a "conversation" with Talking Angela (depicted in Fig. 2.7) and was overheard by the mother. According to the narrative, the voice of the application changed to a "weird robotic voice" and began to ask inappropriate questions and made salacious requests of Angelica. The message ends with a request for users to remove the application and broadcast the message to others.

---

[6] For a discussion about the 2013 version of this hoax, *see* https://nakedsecurity.sophos.com/2013/02/25/talking-angela-iphone-app-scare/

[7] https://nakedsecurity.sophos.com/2014/02/14/the-talking-angela-chain-letter-three-tips-to-avoid-facebook-hoaxes/; http://www.usatoday.com/story/news/nation-now/2014/02/20/talking-angela-app-scare-hoax/5635337/; http://www.theguardian.com/technology/2014/feb/18/talking-angela-app-children-safety

[8] http://outfit7.com/character/talking-angela/

FIGURE 2.6 The Talking Angela App (iTunes store).

Indicators of Online Hoax and Chain Communications

Elements of Scare Chains

- ☐ ***Warning announcement/cautionary statement***: This is typically in all capital letters ("*marquee*" *effect*) to grab the recipient's attention. The topic is often scary, ominous, compelling, or otherwise emotion evoking.
- ☐ ***Vague participant***: More often than not, a scare chain communication will vaguely attribute the story in an effort to bolster credibility.
- ☐ ***Narrative*** describing the "scary incident" or "ominous issue."
- ☐ ***Transmission/perpetuation requirement***: The recipient is admonished to continue the trajectory of the message by transmitting or broadcasting it to others via online communication.
- ☐ ***Instructions***: The scare chain will often provide instructions or admonitions to the recipient that require the him/her to conduct a further action, including or in addition to perpetuating the message.
- ☐ ***Moral lesson or imperative***: Most scare chains contain a latent or patent moral lesson, such as "be aware of surroundings" or other actionable advice.

2014 · 🌐

I cant even in words say what I just found out.. I am SHOCKED and want to tell and let my friends and family be made aware so they can make sure their children are safe!!! Angelica stayed home from school today and thank GOD she did. Because she was on her ipod playing a game called talking angela, which is similar to talking tom, anyway as she is sitting next to me this interactive cat says to her hi angelica where is your brother? She says o hes right here next to me the cat says o cool, then the cat says so what do you do for fun? Ang says I dont know, (now im being quiet and listening because I think its weird this angela cat knows she has a brother and is talking to her like a person) then its voice changes and in some weird robotic voice it says angelica when u date what do u do on your dates? She looked at me got red in the face and said nothing, then it said stick out your touunge, ill stick mine out too, it said what are some things u can do with your tounge? I can find many things to do with my tounge it said it said lets intrract w our toungues. I that point I had heard enough I zaid ang shut it off now! I was freaked out called the police departnrnt they came to the house saif they would have the internet investigations unit andpedofile investigations unit look into it, they called me an hour latet and said something is behind that cat!!! They dont know if it is local or over seas. While the police officer was there and ang was talking to him she told the police officer saturday night her cousin and her were on the app w angela and it asked the girls their names what her brothers name was what school they BOTH went to, and it took a picture of angelica!!! This is under serious investigation right now! When I googled talking angela I cant even begin to tell you what creepy stuff came up! Google it for yourselves please!! But some things are the cat asking girls for their phone numbers! And if theyve had their firat kiss!!! Take this app off your phone please! Theres a big chance thid cpuld be a door for pedofiles.the police said they have seen thing *like* this but never actually through a childs app but that they are not putting it past them! The girls told angela the cat on saturday their names and she had a brother and then on monday morning when angelica turned the app back on, it remebered her name and that she had a brother!!! These things ARENT supposed to ask you questions!!! and especially not questions about dating toungues or kissing!! I am disgusted! I dont feel safe at all right now! Knowing that there was some creep talking to my daughter and my neice through a talking app!!! Please if you have this app or any like it the police are saying take it off of your phone!!! Copy and share and send out PLEASE! This word needs to spread! I pray the ocean county investigators can crack this thing open!!!!!
So please if your KIDS use this app please shut it down. Because SOME KIDS told them the name of the school they went to and is now on red alert at the school, and please PASS this on to ALL your friends.

FIGURE 2.7 The Talking Angela App scare chain, spread through social media.

Threat Chains

An additional type of chain message goes beyond attempts to scare by explaining threats that will directly affect the recipient, their friends, computer system, or strangers if they do not follow the directions of the message and forward it on to others, continuing the trajectory of the message. These messages also indicate that the recipient's email behaviors will be monitored to know whether the contents are forwarded and to whom. Though this threat is virtually impossible to follow up on, it is intended to spur the recipient to action.

With the immense popularity and user participation in social media platforms such as Facebook, Twitter, Instagram, LinkedIn, and others, the newer manifestations of threat chains often look very different, and the perpetuation demand by the attacker is contingent upon the proprietary communication methods particular to each social media platform. For example, on Facebook an attacker may demand that a victim recipient post the threat chain communication on his/her status "news feed," causing the communication to be broadcasted to anyone reading the news feed. Further, using the "messages" feature of Facebook, the victim can perpetuate the chain through broadcasting private messages to his/her Facebook friends.

This is perhaps best exemplified by the resurgence of the Bill Gates hoax described earlier in this chapter. The scam has resurfaced on Facebook in the last few years with individuals posting a photoshopped image of Bill Gates holding a piece of paper explaining that if people share and click through a link provided he will pay them $5000 (Fig. 2.8).

FIGURE 2.8 The resurgence of the Bill Gates hoax, propagated on Facebook.

Online: Social Media Threat Chains

Communication Channels Through Social Media Platforms
The myriad of social media platforms (to include online dating services and multiplayer online games) typically have both public and private communication channels to communicate with other users in the environment. Some of the more popular platforms and methods include:

Platform	Public Messages	Private Messages
Linkedin	Messaging	InMail
Twitter	Tweet	Direct Messages
Instagram	Posting	Instagram Direct
Facebook	News Feed	Messages

 ## Indicators of Online Hoax and Chain Communications

Elements of Threat Chains
- ☐ ***Caution statement/warning banner.*** The top of the message typically contains all capital letter fonts ("marquee effect"), conveying an attention-grabbing cautionary statement such as "Warning!", "Read this!", or "This is not a joke!"
- ☐ ***Transmission/perpetuation requirement.*** The recipient is admonished to continue the trajectory of the message by transmitting or broadcasting it to others via online communication.
- ☐ ***Threat narrative*** describing the threat/danger posed to the recipient.
- ☐ ***Instructions.*** The threat chain will often provide instructions or admonitions to the recipient that require him/her to conduct a further action, including or in addition to perpetuating the message.
- ☐ ***Consequences*** of not complying with the request or instructions.
- ☐ ***Reassertion of the threat.***

Weaponizing Online Urban Legends, Hoaxes, and Chain Communications

Attackers shrewdly develop storylines that require the recipient/reader to acquire additional, extrinsic content to consume the totality of the narrative. Preexisting urban legends, hoaxes, threat chains, and scare chains can be recycled with a *weaponized element* or a *perceptual requirement* to complete a narrative that would naturally require an extrinsic file, site, or resource.[9] In this regard, the communication will often pose *narrative deficiencies* (intentionally incomplete storyline or elements as a pretext to require resources for narrative completion) such as referencing something visual or audible that can be accessed and rendered if the reader clicks on a link for the external resource. The external resources are the actuators to nefarious content, such as a like-farming trajectory, malicious code, or other scams.

Attackers rely upon psychological principles to allure or compel further interaction by the recipient. Some of the more salient leveraging enhancers include:

- □ creating irresistible curiosity (often, morbid curiosity);
- □ compulsion or the need for narrative completeness;
- □ time compression;
- □ urgency; and
- □ feeling of imperative.

In September, 2015, an attacker used the popular narrative theme of a "serial killer on camera" to weaponize his hoax scheme. The hoax spread through social media using the title "Serial Killer's Cam: Video shows naked & helpless girl tortured to her death" (Fig. 2.9); the message also contained a link to external content if the recipient chose to view the "video."

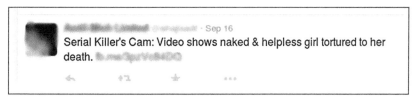

FIGURE 2.9 "Serial Killer's Cam" message posted and perpetuated on social media.

The content of the message leveraged several elements to entice unsuspecting victims: compelling title, narrative deficiency, a perceptual requirement, curious/troubling content—both sex and violence, and an actuator hyperlink to external content. When the victim recipient followed the trajectory of the message by clicking the link, he/she would end up at a page hosting a "restricted video" that could only be accessed by clicking another embedded link to "share" the video (Fig. 2.10). This platform was effectively used to like-farm, and in turn, was reported to host survey scams and malicious content to infect victims.[10]

---

[9] Security researchers began to recognize this problem, viewing it through the lens of a reemergent urban legend, "Crying Baby." http://news.softpedia.com/news/Crying-Baby-Email-Warns-of-Serial-Killer-243257.shtml

[10] www.onlinethreatalerts.com/article/2015/9/17/scam-serial-killers-cam-video-shows-helpless-girl-tortured-to-her-death/+&cd=2&hl=en&ct=clnk&gl=us

FIGURE 2.10 Indicia of weaponization through "like-farming".

Thinking Like the Attacker

Influencing Emotions

A fundamental way attackers cause victims to engage in ULs and hoax-based communications is by writing communications with emotion-evoking hooks. Importantly, the attackers can closely theme the communication and desired emotional response, such as greed, fear, curiosity, etc. For example, a victim may receive a scare chain detailing a horrible event, describing a way to prevent this same horrible thing from happening to the reader, and including an element such as a hyperlink to a purported photograph or other online resources that will "assist" the reader in her or his prevention efforts. Of course, the resource is actually a weaponizing element that causes the victim to navigate to a malicious element such as "like-farming", or worse, hostile computer code.

Another example of narrative weaponizing is in 2011, when spammers began to circulate messages claiming to provide access to photos of Osama Bin Laden's body after he was killed by US forces. The spam messages were written in Portuguese and targeted individuals in Brazil, saying that if the recipient clicked on the link in the message, they would be able to download real photos of his body (Fig. 2.11). The link actually provided individuals with a piece of malware that would capture online banking details, including usernames and passwords (Chapetti, 2011). Thus individuals have clearly recognized and found ways to turn hoaxes and myths into attack vectors.

Defending Against Online Urban Legends, Chains, and Hoax Communications

By recognizing the various forms of myths and chain messages circulating, it is easier to identify ways to defend against them. While many of these messages do not pose a direct threat, they are an inconvenience, as they can clog and congest email servers, hinder

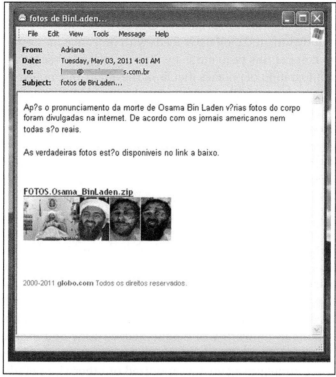

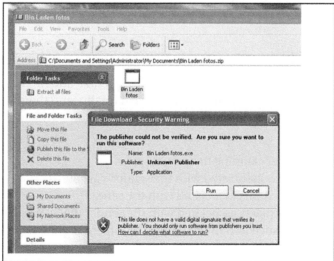

FIGURE 2.11 "Photos of Osama Bin Laden" malware attack.

network activity and waste network resources. Further, these messages waste disk space on every system where the message is saved—and on social media platforms, hoax messages also waste bandwidth and clog news feeds with nuisance messages.

One method to combat this problem is by filtering these messages at the email server level. Similarly, an integration of policies that limit the ability of employees to forward messages, either internally or externally, to the network may help. Education is paramount in reducing the proliferation of these messages. First, employees must be able to recognize what is a legitimate message and what is a hoax or urban myth. Thinking critically before sending a message on to others is essential in order to reduce the quantity of chain messages sent. Recipients must consider what they are reading and whether they are legitimate. If it seems legitimate, they must further ask why they would benefit from sending the message on to others. These steps may help minimize the likelihood that message content is further distributed. Clearly explicating email policies to employees would also prove effective in order to introduce rules and guidelines for email use, particularly regarding forwards.

Since online urban legends, chain letters, and hoax communications are being leveraged by attackers as vectors for malicious computing, such as malware attacks and scams, many versions of these communications pose a risk to victim systems. Further, with the increasing vectors and surfaces of social media postured for exploitation, varying or nascent permutations of urban legends, chain letters, or hoax communications cause these communications to be worthy of heightened scrutiny and examination. In these final sections of the chapter, element analysis and open source intelligence analysis are explored as defensive strategies against weaponized or otherwise nefarious online urban legends, chain letters, and hoax communications.

Element Analysis

Effectively defending against weaponized urban legends and hoax communications requires thorough analysis of the communications in totality and their individual components. Some of the questions and elements the recipient should consider include:

- ☐ **Sender's account**
  - Where is the sender claiming to be from?
  - What are the details associated with the sender's account?
  - Are there other accounts associated with the sender?
  - Are there digital artifacts associated with the sender that can be further queried and investigated, such as domain names, monikers, IP Addresses, etc.?
  - Are there historical Internet artifacts associated with the sender?
  - Are there contextual inconsistencies with the sender's communication, account artifacts, and/or historical artifacts? For example, the sender claims to be from Canada but collateral artifacts reveal a likely true origin from another country.

☐ ***Holistic context: communication elements and content***
- Is the message (and the fact the message was sent to the recipient) contextually reasonable?
- Is there a narrative appealing to the reader's emotions or predilections, leading up to an offer/opportunity?
- Are there narrative deficiencies that would create the need for the recipient to engage further on a weaponized element such as a hyperlink or other external resource?
- Does the content of the message have a perceptual requirement causing the recipient the need to further engage an external resource?
- Does the message narrative create a sense of imperative, time compression, or urgency?
- Does the message convey an offer/opportunity that seems reasonable, plausible, or legal? If so, why is this opportunity being offered to the recipient?
- What does the recipient have to do to benefit from this offer/opportunity?
- What pitfalls could occur from availing oneself of the opportunity/offer?

Open Source Intelligence Analysis

In addition to critically examining the context and content of a message surmised to be an urban legend, chain, or hoax, additional open source investigation and analysis may reveal clues about the message, the sender, and other critical details that will inform how to best handle or dispose of the message.

☐ ***Search engine queries***
- Thorough querying of the data relating to the sender and the specific message (or permutation of the message) is likely to reveal whether the message has been previously identified as problematic, the temporal context of such messaging campaigns, the details surrounding infection or fraud trajectories stemming from the message, and other useful information. As with any web-based research that may lead to "underground" forums and other resources that may host malicious content, it is recommended to use caution in browsing or reviewing this material, such as implementing IP address obfuscation, system hardening, virtualization, and other operational security measures.

☐ ***Internet protocol addresses and domain names***
- Often, the message data and/or search engine queries about the message/sender may reveal collateral data about the message or sender, such as associated IP addresses or domain names; these artifacts/identifiers may inform about the nature of the communication(s), history, and additional context.

- ☐ ***Blacklist queries***
  - If digital artifacts/identifiers such as a domain names and IP addresses surrounding the suspect communication(s) or sender are identified, these identifiers can be queried against numerous databases that contain Domain Name System (DNS)-based blacklists, whitelists, and other valuable resources to identify if the sender of the suspect communication has been previously identified as sending suspicious or nefarious message campaigns.[11]
- ☐ ***URL scanning and analysis***
  - As discussed earlier in this chapter, weaponized urban legends, chain letters, and hoax communications typically have actuators to retrieve content for remote resources and files. Often, attackers use embedded hyperlinks in social media and email communications as the method of causing a victim recipient to engage the external resource(s). Thus scanning these shortened URLs through UnTiny,[12] TinyURL Decoder,[13] and like resources is an effective way of deobfuscating shortened URLs. Further, scanning URLs for malicious content through such online services as Virus Total,[14] Wepawet,[15] and others[16] can provide valuable insight about the external content linked by the attacker.

By examining these questions/elements and, in turn, the communication and associated technical artifacts discussed in this section, more often than not the nature of a suspect communication can be properly assessed and rendered inert by alerting information technology personnel or otherwise properly eliminating the message from the targeted medium.

As a whole, this chapter demonstrates the persuasive power that can be harnessed by computer-mediated communication platforms to manipulate ideas and twist folklore and common experience. Naturally, the scams and schemes used will be adapted to new communication platforms as they emerge, leading to new risks from old threats. Thus we must learn how to identify falsehoods online and find ways to mitigate their impact to the larger online community.

---

[11] See, for example, www.spamhaus.org and www.spamcop.net
[12] untiny.com/
[13] https://kiserai.net/turl.pl
[14] https://www.virustotal.com/
[15] https://wepawet.iseclab.org/
[16] Malicious code researcher and SANS institute instructor Lenny Zeltser has compiled a fantastic list of resources for analyzing potentially malicious URLs: https://zeltser.com/lookup-malicious-websites/

References

Abrahams, R. D. (1976). *Talking black*. Boston: Newbury House Publishers.

Brunvand, J. H. (1981). *The vanishing hitchhiker: American urban legends and their meanings*. New York: WW Norton & Company.

Brunvand, J. H. (1998). *The study of American folklore* (4th ed.). New York: WW Norton & Company.

Brunvand, J. H. (2001). *Too good to be true: The colossal book of urban legends*. New York: WW Norton & Company.

Brunvand, J. H. (2004). *Be afraid, be very afraid: The book of scary urban legends*. New York: WW Norton & Company.

Brunvand, J. H. (2012). *Encyclopedia of urban legends*. New York: WW Norton & Company.

Chapetti, L. (May 4, 2011). *Osama Bin Laden death picture spam on the rise*. Barracuda Labs. https://barracudalabs.com/2011/05/osama-bin-laden-death-picture-spam/.

De Vos, G. (2012). *What happens next? Contemporary urban legends and popular culture*. Santa Barbara: ABC-CLIO.

Dotey, A., Rom, H., & Vaca, C. (2011). *Information diffusion in social media*. Final Project, Stanford University (CS224W).

Friggeri, A., Adamic, L. A., Eckles, D., & Cheng, J. (2014). *Rumor cascades*. Paper presented at the Eighth International AAAI Conference on Weblogs and Social Media (ICWSM-14), Ann Arbor, MI.

Heyd, T. (2008). *Email hoaxes: Form, function, genre ecology* (Vol. 174). Amsterdam/Philadelphia: John Benjamins Publishing.

Kibby, M. D. (2005). Email forwardables: folklore in the age of the internet. *New Media & Society*, *7*(6), 770–790.

Kollock, P. (1999). The production of trust in online markets. *Advances in Group Processes*, *16*(1), 99–123.

Mikkelson, D. (September 3, 2014). *Lights out! Snopes*. http://www.snopes.com/crime/gangs/lightsout.asp.

Ong, W. J. (1982). *Orality and literacy: The technologizing the word*. New York: Methuen.

Seal, G. (1989). *The hidden culture: Folklore in Australian society*. USA: Oxford University Press.

Tofts, D. (1996). Cyberbabble: The grammatology of on-line communications. *Social Semiotics*, *6*(2), 263–272.

United States Department of State. (1997). *Nigerian advance fee fraud*. (Department of State Publication No. 10465) Washington, DC: U.S. Government Printing Office.

3

Viral Influence: Deceptive Computing Attacks Through Persuasion

ABSTRACT

For over half a century researchers have scientifically studied persuasion and influence. The corpus of this research resulted in established theories and practices that are effectively used in a myriad of contexts where human relationships and factors are paramount. This chapter first explores traditional psychological influence concepts and techniques that are implemented across a broad spectrum of contexts, such as business, advertising, and political and military campaigns. The chapter then examines these principles through the lens of cyber attacks, where these precepts can be maliciously leveraged by cyber attackers to manipulate victims through elaborate deception narratives based upon exploiting heuristic cues to persuade and gain compliance. Finally the chapter looks at hoax viruses, scareware, "tech support scams," and ransomware campaigns and the manner in which psychological influence strategies are weaponized in these attacks.

Keywords: *Cognitive vulnerabilities; Hoax viruses; Online social cues; Persuasion; Persuasion in computer mediated communications (CMC); Persuasive communications; Persuasive technology; Psychological influence; Psychology in cyber attacks; Psychology in hacking; Ransomware; Scareware; Social influence; Tech support scams.*

CHAPTER OUTLINE

On first impression, the concept of "cyber attacks" intuitively elicits the contemplation of computer intrusions or malicious code infection events, allowing the attacker(s) to breach or damage a victim system. To be certain, both types of events describe a broad spectrum of attacks with varying scope of tools, techniques, and procedures leveraged by the attacker(s). These attacks may range from advanced and protracted to unsophisticated, uneventful, and brief. Techniques used to deceive victims into clicking on malicious links or opening/executing malicious files are generally classified as *social engineering*, or psychological manipulation to cause a person to perform a compromising action or reveal sensitive information. While this is a powerful, pervasive, and enduring element of cyber attacks, it is not the only human factor vector targeted and exploited by attackers. A less frequently examined concept of human manipulation in the information security community is *psychological influence*, the purpose of which is to affect perceptions, emotions, cognitions, motives, or behavior of a victim.[1]

This chapter begins by exploring traditional psychological influence concepts and techniques that are implemented across a broad spectrum of contexts, such as business, advertising, and political and military campaigns. Next the chapter examines the history, evolution, and elements of hoax viruses, scareware, ransomware, and technical ("tech") support scams, describing how cyber attackers leverage influence techniques in the pathway of their deception strategies.

Psychological Principles of Influence

For over half a century researchers have scientifically studied persuasion and influence.[2] The corpus of this research resulted in established theories and practices that are effectively used in a myriad of contexts where human relationships and factors are paramount (Seiter & Gass, 2010). Psychological influence processes are at work in larger scales, where the influence campaign is targeting a large audience, or are specifically

---

[1] Joint Publication (JP) 3–53, Doctrine for Joint Psychological Operations, p. 17.
[2] Hovland, C., Lumsdaine, A., & Sheffield, F. (1949) *Experiments on Mass Communication: Studies in social psychology in World War II* (Vol. 3), Princeton University Press.

tailored for an individual target.[3] Usage of these techniques are most notable in advertising, business, courtrooms, military, and law enforcement engagements; undoubtedly over time, with refinement and continued research, these techniques will continue to evolve.[4]

In 1984, social psychologist Dr. Robert Cialdini published *Influence: The Psychology of Persuasion*,[5] which became—and still serves as—the authoritative treatise on *social influence*. Cialdini's theory of influence is based upon six principles of persuasion, or "weapons of influence," the underpinnings of which are derived not only from Cialdini's research, but years of preceding psychological research studies conducted by social scientists. *Dual Process Models of Persuasion* posit that there are two different ways that individuals process information.[6] The first way is *central*, or *systematic processing*, wherein the quality and content of a message is central to an individual's decision making and attitudinal posture. The second way is *peripheral* or *heuristic processing*, or decision making that is based upon rules of thumb or surface features that are collateral to the main message content (Guadagno & Cialdini, 2005; Guadagno, Muscanell, Rice, & Roberts, 2013). Cialdini's six principles are scientifically supported heuristic cues (Fig. 3.1):

- □ **Reciprocity**. One of the most powerful precepts in gaining someone's compliance is the *rule of reciprocation*—people feel a sense of *obligation* to repay others whom have given to them or made a concessional favor for them (Cialdini, 2007, 2009; Gouldner, 1960; Lynn & McCall, 2009).[7]
- □ **Commitment and Consistency**. People seek to comport and appear to comport with what they have previously said or done. This is the principle of *consistency*; once people make an overt choice or take a stated position, they will encounter personal and interpersonal pressures to behave *consistently* with what they have previously

---

[3] See, Manheim, J. B. (2011). *Strategy in information and influence campaigns: How policy advocates, social movements, insurgent groups, corporations, governments, and others get what they want.* New York: Routledge; Pfau, M., & Parrott, R. (1993). *Persuasive communication campaigns.* York, PA: Spectrum Publisher Services.

[4] Strategic influence has become a recognized, burgeoning area in national security contexts. For additional reading in this scope, see Forest, J. J. F., & Praeger Security International. (2009). *Influence warfare: How terrorists and governments fight to shape perceptions in a war of ideas.* Westport, CT: Praeger Security International; David, G. J., & McKeldin, T. R. (2009). *Ideas as weapons: Influence and perception in modern warfare.* Washington, D.C.: Potomac Books and Kramer, F. D., Wentz, L. K., & National Defense University. (2008). Cyber influence and international security. In Kramer, F. D., Starr, S. H., & Wentz, L. K. (2009). *Cyberpower and national security.* Washington, D C.: Center for Technology and National Security Policy, National Defense University.

[5] The work was originally published as Cialdini, R. B. (1984). *Influence: How and why people agree to things.* New York: Morrow; Two works followed: Cialdini, R. B. (2007). *Influence: The psychology of persuasion.* New York: Collins; Cialdini, R. B. (2009). *Influence: Science and practice.* Boston: Pearson Education.

[6] The prevailing two dual process models are the elaboration likelihood model (ELM) and heuristic-systematic model (HSM), discussed in further detail later in this chapter.

[7] *See also*, Zimbardo, P. G., & Leippe, M. R. (1991). *The psychology of attitude change and social influence.* London: McGraw-Hill, p. 76-77; Stiff, J. B. (1994). *Persuasive communication* (2nd ed.). New York: Guilford Press, p. 252; Kolenda, N. (2013). *Methods of persuasion: How to use psychology to control human behavior*, p. 87.

said or done (Cialdini, 2007, 2009; Cialdini & Goldstein, 2004; Cialdini & Trost, 1998; Fazio, Blascovich, & Driscoll, 1992; Moriarty, 1975).[8]

☐ **Social Proof/Consensus**. In a social context, people examine how others are acting to determine what is appropriate or expected behavior. Known as the principle of *social proof,* people perceive behavior as proper in a given situation by looking to what others are doing (Cialdini, 2007, 2009; Cialdini & Goldstein, 2004; Cialdini & Trost, 1998; Cialdini, Wosinska, Barrett, Butner, & Gornik-Durose, 1999). This notion is based upon the premise that by conducting oneself consistently with those around them, there is less likelihood to make a mistake.

☐ **Liking**. The obligation of collegiality is powerful; people prefer to comply or engage in an activity with those whom they know and *like* (Perdue, Dovidio, Gurtman, & Tyler, 1990; Cialdini, 2007, 2009). Research has revealed other granular aspects of the concept of *liking*. First, people tend to like people who are *similar* to them (Brock, 1965; Perdue et al., 1990; Hewstone, Rubin, & Willis, 2002; Collisson & Howell, 2014). This can be physically, backgrounds, interests, etc. Further, not surprisingly, people are susceptible to liking those that compliment, praise, or flatter them. People also tend to like things that they are *familiar* with, have had *contact* with, or have developed an *association* with through exposure (Moreland & Zajonc, 1982; Baumeister & Bushman, 2008).[9] The feeling of collusion is potent; many influencers, whether salesmen, politicians, or others seeking to persuade, seek to invoke a collaborative, "team" environment to leverage this *intergroup bias* (Perdue et al., 1990; Hewstone et al., 2002; Collisson & Howell, 2014) This is because research has shown that *cooperation* is a powerful intensifier to evoke liking. Lastly, *physical attractiveness* positively impacts receivers of persuasive messaging.[10]

☐ **Authority**. In almost every context in life, people innately seek counsel or *obediently* follow the advice of those whom they perceive as experts or who have deeper knowledge and experience, often with little deliberation; this natural inclination can be effectively exploited by influencers. The *principle of authority* states that people rely upon and defer to those perceived as having superior knowledge or wisdom when deciding how to act in a particular situation (Milgram, 1963; Cialdini, 2007, 2009).[11] The reasoning behind deferring to an authority is based upon the perception and

---

[8] See also, Zimbardo, P. G., & Leippe, M. R. (1991). The psychology of attitude change and social influence. London:McGraw-Hill, p. 79–83; Kolenda, N. (2013). Methods of persuasion: How to use psychology to control human behavior, p.63–74.

[9] *See* also, Moreland, R., & Zajonc, R. (1982). Exposure effects in person perception: Familiarity, similarity, and attraction. *Journal of Experimental Social Psychology, 18*(5): 395–415.

[10] For additional discussion, *see*, Barocas, R., & Karoly, P. (1972). "Effects of physical appearance on social responsiveness." Psychology Reports 31:772–781; Cavior, N., & Dokecki, P. (1973). "Physical Attractiveness, Perceived Attitude Similarity, and Academic Achievement as Contributors to Interpersonal Attraction among Adolescents." Developmental Psychology 9 (1): 44-54; Efran, M. (1974). "The Effect of Physical Appearance on the Judgment of Guilt, Interpersonal Attraction, and Severity of Recommended Punishment in a Simulated Jury Task." Journal of Research in Personality 8: 45–54.

[11] Zimbardo, P. G., & Leippe, M. R. (1991). *The psychology of attitude change and social influence*. London: McGraw-Hill.

supposition that the authority possesses greater power and access to information, relieving the influenced party from having to independently making a decision.[12] The appearance of authority is markedly more powerful when the influencer is *credible* and *trustworthy* (Hovland & Weiss, 1951; Hovland, Janis, & Kelley, 1953). There are certain factors, or *obedience heuristics*, many of them merely symbolic, that research has shown can trigger or enhance a person's perceptions of authority (Zimbardo & Leippe, 1991).

- ○ ***Titles*** of authority and reverence, such as chief (followed by particularized position), judge, professor, doctor, and commissioner, among others, cause interactants to naturally defer to individuals bestowed with this these designations. Notably, fraudsters can and often do use false titles to gain the trust of victims.
- ○ ***Clothing***, whether a uniform connoting a certain prestigious, respected position or a fashionable and seemingly high-end business suit, are persuasive visuals that convey authority to those viewing the attire.
- ○ ***Trappings***, signifiers or adornments associated with a role, such as a badge, expensive car, or religious garb, among others, are powerful collateral verifiers that the person displaying such items is likely legitimately in their respective position of authority.

- □ **Scarcity**. Exclusivity and rareness are qualities sought in both tangible items and information. Indeed, more often than not, a premium is placed on unique access to finite resources. This is what makes the *principle of scarcity* so incredibly powerful; opportunities seem more valuable when their availability is limited (Cialdini, 2007, 2009; Brock, 1968; Lynn, 1992). Interestingly, this potent motivator is triggered particularly when the scarce item is framed as a potential "lost opportunity," if not seized upon, rather than an opportunity to gain the item (Kolenda, 2013; Tversky & Kahneman, 1991). Further, the compelling nature of scarcity is also amplified when competition is perceived for the scarce resource (Cialdini, 2007, 2009; Worchel, Lee, & Adewole, 1975).

The cognitive basis for the scarcity principle is attributable to three main factors. First, those influenced by perceived scarcity subconsciously *presume valuation* and tend to bestow a higher value and presumed quality of the finite item, making it a valuable

---

[12] In the early 1960's, Yale University psychologist Stanley Milgram conducted a series of experiments at wherein human subjects—in the role of "teachers"—were instructed to administer what they believed to be progressively higher voltage and painful electric shocks to the other experiment human role players—the "learners." This groundbreaking and controversial research revealed the extent to which people will obey orders from a perceived authority figure—despite knowing the act to be painful and immoral. Some of Milgram's experiment was captured in the 1962 film, "Obedience" (Alexander Street Press) and documented in his texts, Milgram, S. (1963). Behavioral study of obedience. *The Journal of Abnormal and Social Psychology, 67*(4), 371, Milgram, S. (1974). *Obedience to authority: An experimental view.* London: Tavistock Publications (later reprinted in Milgram, S. (2005). *Obedience to authority: An experimental view.* Pinter & Martin Ltd.; New edition and Milgram, S. (2009), *Obedience to authority: An experimental view.* Harper Perennial Modern Classics; Reprint edition).

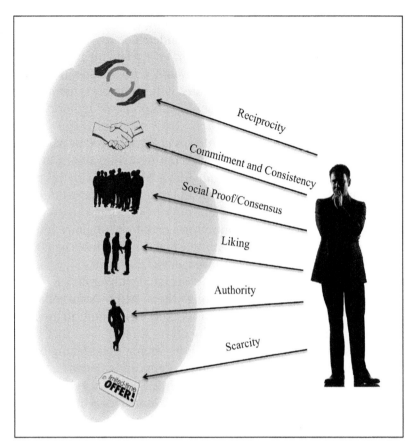

FIGURE 3.1 Cialdini's principles of social influence.

commodity (Brock, 1968; Fromkin, Olson, Robert, & Barnaby, 1971). Further, when perceiving a missed opportunity in failing to acquire a scarce item or opportunity, the influenced party experiences a social psychological response, called *psychological reactance* (Brehm & Cohen, 1962; Brehm, 1966, 1972). When an individual's free choice is encumbered or threatened the individual will have a natural propensity to preserve his freedom, causing him to desire the freedom (and tangible items associated with freedom) at a heightened intensity subsequent to the impeding event. Lastly, *time compression* or time restrictions induce an influenced person to engage in an effort to not miss out on the scarce item or opportunity.

In addition to the six principles of social influence, other scholars and experts have posited additional factors of emotionality or social contexts that are malleable for persuasion, such as *guilt* (O'Keefe, 2016).

Factors, Sequence, and Timing of Persuasive Communications

While the principles of persuasion in the last section elucidate the social psychological bases of how influence techniques work on a target recipient, there are other elemental factors behind effective persuasion. This section focuses on the components and sequence of persuasive communications. A number of message learning models have been posited and relied upon in the scientific community, and the majority focus upon three main components in persuasive communications: 1) the source of the message; 2) the message; and 3) the receiver, or targeted audience.[13] A tacit variable layered into these factors is the *channel* or method of how the message is presented to the receiver (Fig. 3.2). Importantly, while these are components, there is a definite interrelatedness between them; the message itself may increase the credibility of the source, or conversely, the source's credibility may enrich persuasiveness of the message. These vital components, and the factors that enhance or decrease their effectiveness, are worthy of more particularized exploration.

- □ The ***source*** of the message is the influencer, or individual(s) communicating the message to the receiver. *Source factors* or *source effects* are the characteristics of the message communicator that can contribute or detract from the effectiveness of the message. Over the last 50 years, researchers have investigated source factors, particularly the communicator's characteristics, such as *credibility* and *likability*. *Credibility* refers to the receiver's subjective perception of the believability of the communicator (O'Keefe, 2002). The body of existing research reveals causal factors toward credibility are *expertise* (perceived authoritativeness or qualification) and *trustworthiness* (perceived integrity or character) (Hovland & Weiss, 1951; Hovland et al., 1953). Factors such as the communicator's attractiveness, confidence, education, occupation, experience, and message delivery can impact the receiver's perception of credibility (Chaiken, 1979; Bradac, 1981; Bradac & Street, 1989; Stiff & Mongeau, 2003).
- □ The ***message*** is the communication presented to the receiver.
- □ The ***channel*** of the message is the manner, means, or modality in which the message is transmitted or presented to the receiver; this can range from verbal communication to a myriad of platforms varying in breadth and scope, contingent upon the targeted audience. Importantly, the channels of communication are constantly evolving. When considering the Internet and mobile applications, new methods are developed and made available on a frequent basis. Many times, these platforms dictate the shape

---

[13] These factors are fundamental across many theoretical models of persuasive communication and attitude change in the scientific community. Notably in the elaboration likelihood model (ELM) the central and peripheral routes of processing are distinct from traditional source/message factors, but source and message factors may serve as peripheral cues. *See* p. 157, Petty, R. E., & Cacioppo, J. T. (1986a). The Elaboration Likelihood Model of persuasion. In L. Berkowitz (Ed.), *Advances in experimental social psychology* (Vol. 19, pp. 123–205). New York: Academic Press.

or form of the message. For example, Twitter, the popular social networking and microblogging service, only allows for 140 characters of text in a public message.[14] While there is not a robust corpus of research relating to channel variables in message processing, Chaiken and Eagly's early research did reveal that "modality differences in persuasion favored the written mode with inherently difficult-to-understand material, whereas the more usual advantage of videotaped and audiotaped modalities was found with easy material." (Chaiken & Eagly, 1983, p. 241). These findings are particularly interesting when considered in the scope of scareware and ransomware textual messages and hoax viruses, which typically manifest as difficult-to-understand technical (or pseudotechnical) jargon/artifact filled messages seeking to cause a recipient to fearfully engage in action harmful to his/her computer or abstain from certain computer actions.

☐ The **receiver** of the message is the individual or target audience whom the message is intended for or communicated to.

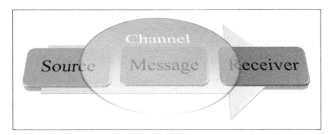

FIGURE 3.2 Components and interactants in a persuasive communication.

Dual Process Models

In addition to the principles and interactant factors of persuasion, it is critical to understand how messaging is *processed* in persuasion. There are a number of models that describe how processing works, but the prevailing models that best explicate the cognitive pathways are *dual process models*. These models propose that there are two distinct routes that messages are contemporaneously processed.

One model, *Elaboration Likelihood Model* ("ELM"), developed by Richard Petty and John Cacioppo (1986a; 1986b), posits that a persuasive message is processed through a *central route* and a *peripheral route*. In *central route* processing, issue-relevant information is thoughtfully evaluated on the content and supporting substantive bases, such as evidence and rationale. Conversely, through *peripheral route processing*, receiver focus is on extrinsic, heuristic (peripheral) cues such as the source's likability and other external factors (e.g., the heuristic cues described by Cialdini) (Fig. 3.3). In the ELM, a receiver's processing pathway is contingent upon *ability* and *willingness* to meaningfully examine messages. Typically when the receiver is *highly involved,* or the topic or issue has increased personal relevance and he/she is motivated to thoughtfully process the issue presented,

---

[14] https://support.twitter.com/articles/13920#.

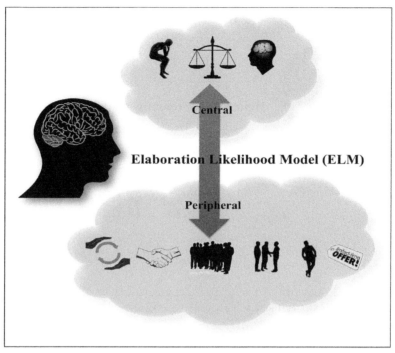

FIGURE 3.3 The elaboration likelihood model.

central route processing occurs. Whereas when the issue or topic has limited or no personal relevance to the receiver, he/she will have *low involvement* and the peripheral route of processing will likely occur (Petty & Cacioppo, 1986a). Thus in the ELM the two routes of processing are the endpoints of an *elaboration continuum*; in central route processing the receiver *highly elaborates* the message; in peripheral route processing the receiver does not elaborate or engages in *low elaboration* of the persuasive message.

The Heuristic-Systematic Model (HSM) of persuasion, introduced by Shelly Chaiken and Alice Eagly, offers a similar, but alternative, perspective of dual processing (Fig. 3.4) (Chaiken, 1980, 1987; Chaiken, Liberman, & Eagly, 1989; Eagly & Chaiken, 1993; Todorov, Chaiken, & Henderson, 2002). Like ELM, HSM proposes that receivers process messages in two modes. In one mode, *systematic processing*, the receiver mediates persuasive message content in a manner that is evidence-based, logically sound, and substantively reasoned. The other mode, *heuristic processing*, is less deliberately reasoned and based upon cognitive *heuristic cues*—cognitive "rules of thumb" or shortcuts that streamline decision making (Chaiken, 1980). HSM posits that contemporaneous, parallel systematic and heuristic processing can occur as *concurrent processing*, whereas ELM has no explicit discussion of such simultaneous processing (Eagly & Chaiken, 1993). Like ELM, HSM considers receiver capacity and motivation to process messages; however, HSM postulates that receivers process the requisite amount of information (*sufficiency*) to reach a decision and do not surpass it (Fig. 3.5). In 1989, Chaiken and her colleagues expanded the scope of HSM to include two additional motives that heuristic and systematic processing can serve:

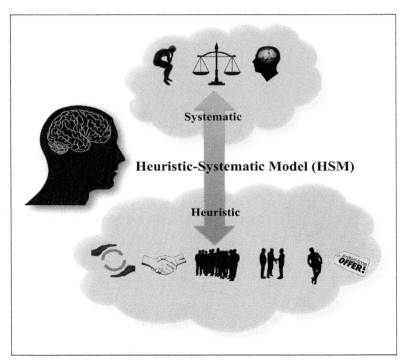

FIGURE 3.4 The heuristic-systematic model.

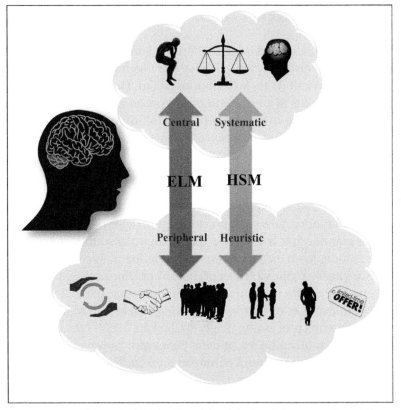

FIGURE 3.5 Elaboration likelihood model and the heuristic-systematic model.

defense-motivation, or the desire to form or defend particular attitudinal positions, and *impression-motivation*, which seeks to form or hold socially acceptable attitudinal positions (Chaiken et al., 1989).

While dual process models elucidate how principles of influence can be effectively messaged to receivers, the learning theory approach to attitude change provides an alternative, informing lens on how persuasive communications are processed by the receiver.

The Yale Information Processing Model

The Yale information processing model (or Yale attitude change approach) was born out of propaganda research conducted after World War II.[15] Carl Hovland and other top research psychologists in the Yale Communication and Attitude Change Program focused upon the manner in which communication variables interact with receiver predispositional variables, such as age, gender, intelligence, and personality, in the process of attitude change (Pfau & Parrott, 1993). In the late 1960s, particularly through the work of William McGuire (McGuire, 1968), this work was continued and refined to gain deeper insight into the inextricability between source, message, and receiver variables to the extent that they promoted (or inhibited) the learning and acceptance of persuasive communication (Erwin, 2001). The six steps in the Yale information processing model (Fig. 3.6) are:

- **Presentation.** The message must be effectively communicated by the source through the correct channel or modality of communication to the receiver.
- **Attention.** The receiver must adequately focus and engage the presented message for further consideration.
- **Comprehension.** The source of the persuasive communication needs to not only ensure that his or her message is delivered and attended to by the receiver, but that the message is crafted with appropriate context, linguistics, and social/cultural nuances so that the receiver will fully understand it.
- **Acceptance.** A particularly critical stage in a persuasive communication is the receiver not only comprehending the message, but *accepting* it. Conversely, it is at this stage that the receiver, after comprehending and considering the message, may simply reject the message, effectively ending the persuasive communication effort.

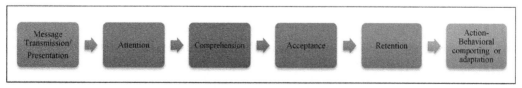

FIGURE 3.6 The Yale model: elements and sequence of a persuasive communication.

[15] Hovland, C., Lumsdaine, A., & Sheffield, F. (1949). *Experiments on Mass Communication: Studies in social psychology in World War II* (Vol. 3), Princeton University Press; Hovland, C. I., Janis, I. L., & Kelley, H. H. (1953). *Communication and persuasion.* New Haven: Yale University Press; Hovland, C. I., & Weiss, W. (December 01, 1951). The influence of source credibility on communication effectiveness. *The Public Opinion Quarterly, 15*(4), 635–650. See also Zimbardo, P. G., & Leippe, M. R. (1991). *The psychology of attitude change and social influence.* London: McGraw-Hill.

□ **Retention.** The persuasive message must have an impactful and lasting effect on the receiver, particularly to the effect of ensuring action toward the desired behavior.

□ **Behavioral change/Action.** The end state of an influential message is to catalyze or mobilize the sought after behavior in the receiver.

The Objectives of Persuasive Communications

The motivations of a communicator seeking to persuade a receiver (or audience) often shape the scope of the intended objectives and outcomes; influence can be used to cause, continue, modify, or cease the receiver's behaviors and actions. The objectives, or more recently framed by Cragin and Gerwehr as *"psychological objectives"*, of influence are to identify the ways in which the communicator seeks to affect the receiver (Cragin & Gerwehr, 2005). Research and literature surrounding psychological objectives have been conducted since the 1980s, resulting in typologies, often focused on certain genres or settings of persuasion campaigns, such as marketing (Pollay, 1989), intraorganizational relationships (Kipnis, Schmidt, & Wilkinson, 1980), political campaigns (O'Keefe, 1989; Pfau & Burgoon, 1988; Pfau & Kenski, 1990; Pfau, Kenski, Nitz, & Sorenson, 1990; Pfau & Parrott, 1993), military influence campaigns (Cragin & Gerwehr, 2005), and negotiating, (Malhotra & Bazerman, 2008), among others.

Cragin and Gerwehr's work, which focuses on influence campaigns against adversaries engaged in terrorism, proposes a useful spectrum of effects entailing the goals of *compliance, conformity,* or *conversion* (Cragin & Gerwehr, 2005). Notably, these goals relate more toward *influence campaigns*, which use planned operations (overt or covert) "to convey selected information and indicators to foreign audiences."[16] As communication platforms and cyber-based attacks change the landscape of channels, messaging, and "digital weapons" sent over the Internet, the psychological objectives of influence must be expanded to include goals inclusive of other desired receiver behaviors and actions. In particular, these objectives include (Fig. 3.7):

□ **Causation.** Profoundly, messages can create *action imperatives*, or catalyze the receiver to act or proceed on a certain trajectory. Similarly, persuasive messaging can serve as an *engagement inducer*, or a trigger to compel and shape a receiver's actions. Particularly within the scope of a cyber attack, this is incredibly powerful, as the intended action may be to cause the recipient to click on a file attachment or URL—or connect unwittingly with a hostile actor on social media or another communication platform.

□ **Continuity.** In many instances the strategy behind messaging may be to ensure that the receiver remains on an existing behavioral pathway and does not substantially deviate from the intended course of action. Persuasive communications serve as *continuity anchors*, making certain (or increasing the likelihood) that the receiver remains tethered to existing intended behaviors and actions.

□ **Compliance.** Compliance seeks to cause an immediate change in the receiver's behavior, even if the influential message does change his/her beliefs. Notably,

---

[16] The scope of Cragin and Gerwehr's work was to assess the use of strategic influence to combat international terrorism.

compliance campaigns often cause immediate receiver response with temporally limited lasting effects.

- ☐ ***Conformity.*** Similar to the concept of social proof, conformity seeks to cause the target audience to comport their behavior to the contextual and environmental variables that surround them.

- ☐ ***Concession.*** It is often the case that the source is seeking to influence the receiver in a very particular way, such as *concession.* Unlike other types of persuasion that are seeking to cause change on a larger scale or to a broader audience, concession seeks to cause the receiver to compromise beliefs and behavior on a targeted issue. Sometimes the objective of the influence is not to cause the recipient to fully change his/her attitudes, beliefs, or behavior, but rather simply *compromise* these on a targeted issue. It may be that the recipient's original posture on the targeted issue is so stalwart and resolute that simply causing concession and deviating from a rigid position is desirable.

- ☐ ***Conversion.*** Perhaps the most altering of objectives, conversion, is the complete restructuring of the receiver's relevant beliefs, attitudes, emotions, and opinions. Through conversion, these aspects of the receiver are impacted, and the receiver's behavior organically changes as well, aligning with the source's objectives.

- ☐ ***Cessation.*** On a practical level, the source may want the recipient to disengage in targeted behavior. Cessation campaigns aim to dislocate a receiver's behavior pathway, inhibiting or stopping him/her from acting.

FIGURE 3.7 Psychological objectives of influence.

Social Influence and Persuasion in Computer-Mediated Communications

With computer-mediated communications (CMCs) now such an inextricably intertwined part of our lives, those seeking to influence other interactants have naturally gravitated toward CMCs, adapting new ways of leveraging principles of influence over different modalities and platforms. Fortunately, there is a burgeoning corpus of research in the space of psychological influence principles applied over CMCs. While existing findings are in some ways inconsistent, there are aspects of online interactions, such as communicator (messenger) cues and nonverbal behavior, that distinguish CMCs and face-to-face (FtF) engagements (Bos, Olson, Gergle, Olson, & Wright, 2002; Carlson, George, Burgoon, Adkins, & White, 2004; Kraut, 1978; Lane, 1997; Nowak, Watt, & Walther, 2005; Rosenberg & Sillince, 2000; Muscanell & University of Alabama, 2009). These, in turn, have contributed toward the adaptation of social influence online (Amichai-Hamburger, 2013; Muscanell, Guadagno, & Murphy, 2014; Übelacker & Quiel, 2015).

As mentioned earlier in the chapter, principles of social influence are heuristic cues that are processed by the receiver as cognitive short cuts to form a decision rather than thoughtfully processing message content. As a result, nonverbal behaviors or cues richly enhance communicator salience, triggering and bolstering this heuristic processing. Importantly, these nonverbal cues are not part of the substantive textual/verbal content, but rather, communicator actions that accompany the communication (Burgoon, Buller, Hale, & deTurck, 1984; Burgoon, 1994). Further, nonverbal behaviors serve to provide deeper context to a communication; while the content of a message may be clear and complete, facial expressions, body language, and tempo of interaction, among other variables, may better shape the message (Ekman, 2003). Similarly, messenger factors, such as appearance and physical closeness, may impact receiver perceptions. Burgoon (1994), and later Seiter and Gass (2010), categorized seven nonverbal communication factors (Fig. 3.8), described below, that richly encompass the breadth and scope of nonverbal cues and behavioral considerations considered by other scholars to play a vital role in persuasion and deception processes.

- ☐ **Kinesics** refers to the study of *body language*, such as eye contact, facial expressions, body movements, and gestures (Birdwhistell, 1952). This study has also been adapted and applied toward particular nonverbal body language factors that are analyzed to detect deception (Ekman & Friesen, 1969a, 1969b; Burgoon, Schuetzler, & Wilson, 2014).[17]
- ☐ **Haptics** is the manner in which humans, primates, and other animals touch others as a communicative function (Burgoon, 1994).
- ☐ **Proxemics** is the study of humans' use of space—geographic and interpersonal proximity—and its role in social interaction (Hall, 1963, 1966).
- ☐ **Chronemics** is the perception and use of time in communications (Bruneau, 1980; Burgoon, Buller, & Woodall, 1989).
- ☐ **Artifacts** are physical items that are associated with an individual and convey additional contextual insight about the person, such as a fancy suit, expensive watch, or flashy car.
- ☐ **Physical appearance** or how an individual looks, or level of attractiveness.
- ☐ **Paralinguistics** is the study of "paralanguage" or nuanced linguistic coding (or meta-communication) information associated with communications, such as tempo, pitch, tone, and emotion (Trager, 1958, 1960, 1961).

---

[17] In the scope of deception, kinesic factors include 1) *emblems* (movements that have a precise or direct verbal translation to a word or phrase that is understood by a culture or subculture); 2) *illustrators* (movements that illustrate speech); 3) manipulators or adaptors (one part of the body manipulates another part of the body or face in a self-grooming, stroking, picking, scratching, etc. way to alleviate emotional energy); 4) regulators (behaviors specifically done to regulate the flow of conversation); emotional display, or affect display (involuntary signals that reveal affective emotional state).

FIGURE 3.8 Categories of nonverbal communications.

Social Influence Over Computer-Mediated Communications and Digital Platforms

Adapting Traditional Social Cues Communicator Salience

Since nonverbal cues significantly contribute toward the totality of an FtF message, early theories [described as "Cues-Filtered-Out" (CFO) theories by Culnan and Markus (1987)] suggested that communication modalities that do not enable these cues impact the efficacy and completeness of the message. *Social Presence Theory* (Short, Williams, & Christie, 1976), an early model applied to CMC, proposed that different types of communication media varied in functionality to convey communicator nonverbal and auditory cues, manifesting in less social presence or *communicator salience*. The theory was applied to CMCs in the late 1970s and early 1980s, when CMCs were predominantly textual-based communications (Hiltz, Johnson, & Agle, 1978). These early applications surmised that CMCs offered little social presence since nonverbal cues were unavailable to the interactants. Similarly, *Media Richness Theory*, (D'ambra, Rice, & O'connor, 1998; Daft & Lengel, 1983; Lengel & Daft, 1984), originally developed to understand the effectiveness of organizational communication in companies, posited that richer media, such as FtF, video, and other synchronous communications are better for clearly conveying information, whereas textual communications are leaner and may not effectively overcome the equivocality of messages. When applied to early text-based CMC channels, including asynchronous communications like e-mail, it was surmised to be a lean media modality and not likely effective to overcome equivocality of messages.

In 1992, Joseph Walther introduced the Social Information Processing (SIP) theory, which sought to explain how, with time, CMC interactants are able to accrue interpersonal impressions and relationships with other users online (Walther, 1992). SIP theory assumes that CMC is text-based and devoid of nonverbal communication cues; however, unlike CFO theories prior to it, it proposes that over time, users—who are driven to form social relationships—adapt their relational behaviors within the communication environment to remaining cues such as content, paralinguistics, chronemics, and typographic cues (Tidwell & Walther, 2002; Walther, 1996, 2006, 2007; Walther & Burgoon, 1992; Walther & D'Addario, 2001; Walther & Jang, 2012; Walther, Loh, & Granka, 2005; Walther & Parks, 2002; Walther & Tidwell, 1995; Westerman, Van, Klein, & Walther, 2008) (Fig. 3.9). Due to the absence of nonverbal cues, SIP theory assumes that there is less social information transmitted per message, causing relationships over CMC to form slower over time. Other scholars expanded upon SIP application in CMC persuasion, synthesizing SIP and HSM (Chaiken, 1980, 1987; Chaiken & Eagly, 1983; Chaiken et al., 1989) in a sociotechnical influence model (Van Der Heide & Schumaker, 2013) and postulating that the visual presence and observation of cues is a causal mechanism of interactant affinity, and greater interaction time lends toward production of more visible cues for processing.

From the early 2000s to the present, scholars have begun to directly examine the application of Cialdini's six principles of social influence in the context of CMCs (Guadagno & Cialdini, 2002, 2005, 2007; Okdie & Guadagno, 2008; Okdie, Guadagno, Petrova, & Shreves, 2013; Guadagno, 2013; Guadagno et al., 2013). Largely, the findings of this research maintained the position that online communication (as opposed to FtF engagement) provides a narrower means of offering interactant social peripheral cues, substantially decreasing communicator salience, and in turn, the impact of the heuristic processing of influence factors. The research findings also presented evidence of the potential dichotomous impact of

FIGURE 3.9 The pathway of social information processing.

persuasion principles when applied to men or women over CMCs. Walther was circumspect of this research, observing that employed short interaction sessions were antithetical to the SIP premise that CMCs require time for interactant impression formation (Walther, 2011).

Persuasive Technology

In addition to how users are persuaded by other users *through* CMC is the equally important matter of how users are persuaded *by* technology and online web resources. In the late 1990s and 2000s computer scientists and social scientists revealed the persuasive power of computers and technical elements in a user's online experience. *Captology,* or the "study of computers as persuasive technology" (Fogg, 2003a, Fogg, Cuellar, & Danielsone, 2007, p. 16) became a critical consideration of how people could be influenced through online experiences independent of CMC. In particular, captology focuses on human–computer interaction in an effort to learn how people are persuaded (or motivated) when interacting *with* computer technology, as opposed to CMC, where the focus is on how people interact *through* computer technologies. Website design and credibility became particularly germane in these research efforts, resulting in many of the authoritative theories in this space (Cloete, Tanner, & Pollock, 2011; Cugelman, Thelwall, & Dawes, 2008; Fogg, Soohoo, & Danielsen, 2002; Fogg & Tseng, 1999; Fogg et al., 2000).

After many years of pioneering multiple studies on persuasive technology, BJ Fogg proposed the *prominence-interpretation theory* (Fogg, 2003b). This theory proposes that when users assess the credibility of websites, two things occur nearly contemporaneously: 1) the user observes something on the site (*prominence*) and 2) the user makes a judgment about what he/she observed (*interpretation*). Under this theory, if one of these events does not occur, credibility of the website is not assessed by the user.

Factors that can affect prominence are:

- **Involvement** of the user. This factor closely mirrors ELM and HSM's role and definition of *involvement*, examining the user's *motivation* and *ability* to examine website content.
- **Topic** of the website or the substantive content and subject matter of the site.
- **Task** of the user for navigating to and within the site (e.g., research, entertainment, etc.)
- **Experience** of the user (novice vs. expert in the substantive content of the website or with navigating web content and elements.)
- **Individual differences**, such as the user's learning style, literacy, etc.

Factors that impact a user's perception of the site, or the interpretation phase, include:

- **Assumptions** or preexisting ideas or opinions the user may have based upon his/her background, culture, experiences, or heuristics.
- **Skill/knowledge** of the user regarding the substantive content of the website.
- **Context** such as user expectations, situations, norms, etc.

(Fogg, 2003b).

Fogg's focus on website credibility also examined the specific *types* of credibility that related to web presence and the elements that amplified or diminished credibility when processed during prominence-interpretation by online users. Fogg posited that there are four types of web credibility (Fogg, 2003a) (Fig. 3.10):

- **Presumed**: Credibility that is based upon general assumptions in the user's mind.
- **Reputed**: This is derived or "earned" based upon third-party endorsements, reports, or referrals.
- **Surface**: This is an aesthetic and limited interaction level; it is based upon simple inspection and first impressions.
- **Earned**: Derived from the user's first-hand experience with the website over an extended period of time.

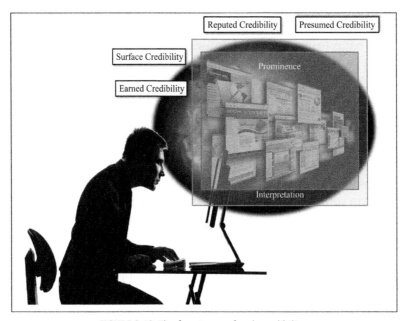

FIGURE 3.10 The four types of web credibility.

Similar to the importance of perceived source credibility when a communicator is trying to convey a persuasive message to a receiver of the communication, web credibility is based upon two factors: *trustworthiness* and *expertise* (Fogg et al., 2003; Flanagin & Metzger, 2007; Rains & Karmikel, 2009). Fogg and other researchers found that elements that convey and bolster a website's credibility by evoking trustworthiness and expertise include:

- design features;
- depth of content;
- site complexity,
- contact details that correlate to physical address, e-mail addresses, etc.;
- content that contains references that can be verified; and
- links to credible outside materials and sources.

Conversely, web credibility can be negatively impacted if the website has:

- confusing content (e.g., ads that are indistinguishable from true content);
- lack of contact data;
- unexpected content, such as pop-up windows and problematic links; and
- lack of updated content (Fogg et al., 2003; Kąkol & Nielek, 2015).

Sundar proposed an alternative but not mutually exclusive theory on how website credibility is assessed, drawing heavily from the peripheral and heuristic processing modes of dual process models ELM and HSM. In particular, Sundar posited that technological *"affordances"*—or capabilities—that shape the nature of the content in digital media trigger cognitive heuristics that guide credibility judgments by offering new functions and elements that are rich in cues (Sundar, 2007). Sundar's MAIN model is based upon four particular affordances: Modality (M); Agency (A); Interactivity (I); and Navigability (N). These affordances, according to Sundar, can impact a user's perceptions by serving as lenses that magnify or detract from site content credibility.[18]

Importantly, as website credibility was studied further by scholars, the visual impact and visual elements comprising the website were posited as crucial factors for consideration and worthy of inclusion into the total website credibility assessment process. In 2009, Cugelman et al. proposed *visual appeal* as an additional critical factor to be assessed along with trustworthiness and expertise during website credibility assessment (Cugelman, Thelwall, & Dawes, 2009). Similarly, Robins and Holmes (2008) postulated that when users first view a site, within seconds the visual aesthetics of the website influence the user's judgment of the site's credibility, whereas Rains and Karmikel (2009) found that website structural features[19] impacted user perception of site credibility.

Deceptive Computing Attacks Through Persuasion

The principles of psychological influence can powerfully impact an online user, changing his or her perceptions and behavioral trajectory. When maliciously leveraged by cyber attackers, these principles can manipulate attack victims through elaborate deception narratives based upon exploiting heuristic cues to persuade and gain compliance. Certain

---

[18] Others scholars have proposed theories about how website credibility judgments form. Hilligoss and Rieh posited that three levels of judgment occur during credibility processing: *construct level,* or how the users conceptualize credibility; 2) *heuristic level,* or cognitive rules of thumb that are used to judge credibility; and 3) the *interaction level,* wherein credibility judgments are based upon content and peripheral cues. Hilligoss, B., & Rieh, S. Y. (2008). Developing a unifying framework of credibility assessment: Construct, heuristics, and interaction in context. *Information Processing & Management, 44*(4), 1467–1484.

[19] The seven structural features were 1) third-party endorsements; 2) images; 3) a physical address or phone number; 4) a privacy policy statement; 5) a navigation menu; 6) the name of the person or organization administering the website; 7) and links to external websites.

cyber attack schemes, such as hoax viruses, scareware, help-desk support scams, and ransomware, particularly implement principles of influence to amplify attack effectiveness. In this section, these attacks, and the manner in which psychological influence manifests in these attacks, are examined.

Hoax Virus Communications

Traditional information security attack analysis focuses on computer intrusions and malware events in which an attacker gains access or causes damage to a system (or network) through the use of technical capabilities to exploit a vulnerability. In 2015, there were a record number of "mega-breaches" and exponential increases in zero-day exploits and spear phishing attacks; in previous years, there were troublingly similar numbers.[20] In this sea of cyber turbulence, mercurial and understated threat permutations are *hoax viruses*, or e-mails and social media messages that warn of dangerous but nonexistent cyber security threats that a user will likely receive. While not as voluminous or dangerous as other types of malicious cyber activities, hoax viruses remain a consistent, evolving threat in the cyber threat landscape, particularly because attackers are borrowing effective components and precepts from these narratives to amplify new psychological cyber attacks. While pure hoax viruses still circulate today, the more problematic evolved permutations of hoax viruses are *tech support scams*, s*careware*, and to some extent, *ransomware*. What distinguishes this attack genre is that it heavily targets the human system operator and relies fundamentally upon deception and influence to succeed. This section examines the history and typology of hoax viruses, then reveals how hoax virus attackers leverage the principles of persuasion to effectuate their attacks.

As discussed in Chapter 2, Virtual Myths: Internet Urban Legend, Chain Letters, and Warnings, the development of the Internet transformed the spread of urban myths in the 1980s. As this technology matured and gained user traction, it enabled efficient contact between individuals, especially across large distances. As a result, this became a preferred medium for the spread of urban legends and hoax schemes. Hoax virus communications were a natural extension of Internet urban myths and other hoax chains, relying upon the speed and efficiency of delivery over CMCs and modifying the scope of these narratives by invoking the specter of catastrophic, devastating computer viruses.

The first documented hoax virus, known as the "2400 Baud Modem" virus (Fig. 3.11), was actually quite verbose, artfully combining a narrative of hypertechnical language (technical acronym, program names, etc.), connotation of narrator expertise and credibility, and perceived legitimacy of the threat (Heyd, 2008).

---

[20] https://www.symantec.com/security-center/threat-report.

```
I've just discovered probably the world's worst computer virus
yet. I had just finished a late night session of BBS'ing and file
treading when I exited Telix 3 and attempted to run pkxarc to
unarc the software I had downloaded. Next thing I knew my hard
disk was seeking all over and it was apparently writing random
sectors. Thank god for strong coffee and a recent backup.
Everything was back to normal, so I called the BBS again and
downloaded a file. When I went to use ddir to list the directory,
my hard disk was getting trashed again. I tried Procomm Plus TD
and also PC Talk 3. Same results every time. Something was up so I
hooked up to my test equipment and different modems (I do research
and development for a local computer telecommunications company
and have an in-house lab at my disposal). After another hour of
corrupted hard drives I found what I think is the world's worst
computer virus yet. The virus distributes itself on the modem sub-
carrier present in all 2400 baud and up modems. The sub-carrier is
used for ROM and register debugging purposes only, and otherwise
serves no othr (sp) purpose. The virus sets a bit pattern in one
of the internal modem registers, but it seemed to screw up the
other registers on my USR. A modem that has been "infected" with
this virus will then transmit the virus to other modems that use a
subcarrier (I suppose those who use 300 and 1200 baud modems
should be immune). The virus then attaches itself to all binary
incoming data and infects the host computer's hard disk. The only
way to get rid of this virus is to completely reset all the modem
registers by hand, but I haven't found a way to vaccinate a modem
against the virus, but there is the possibility of building a
subcarrier filter. I am calling on a 1200 baud modem to enter this
message, and have advised the sysops of the two other boards
(names withheld). I don't know how this virus originated, but I'm
sure it is the work of someone in the computer telecommunications
field such as myself. Probably the best thing to do now is to
stick to 1200 baud until we figure this thing out.

Mike RoChenle
```

FIGURE 3.11 The "2400 Baud Modem" hoax virus.

Over time, newer and increasingly clever virus hoaxes proliferated and washed over users' inboxes. Information security companies,[21] researchers,[22] and government agencies[23] began to catalog these hoaxes in the same fashion as true malware specimens are analyzed, categorized, and placed in a database for reference. Over years of samples, certain elements and heuristics were derived from these narratives (Gordon, 1997):

---

[21] http://home.mcafee.com/virusinfo/virus-hoaxes; https://www.symantec.com/security_response/landing/risks/hoaxes.jsp; https://www.sophos.com/en-us/threat-center/threat-analyses/hoaxes/virus-hoax.aspx.

[22] http://antivirus.about.com/od/emailhoaxes/l/blenhoax.htm.

[23] https://web.archive.org/web/20070312000719/http://hoaxbusters.ciac.org/HBHoaxInfo.html.

Indicators and Elements of a Hoax Virus

☐ **Warning announcement/cautionary statement.** This is typically in all capital letters (*"marquee" effect*) to grab the recipient's attention. The topic is often scary, ominous, compelling, or otherwise emotion evoking. It urges recipients to alert everyone they know and sometimes tells them to do this more than once.

☐ **Pernicious, devastating malware.** The content is a warning about a type of pernicious malware spreading on the Internet. Commonly from an individual, occasionally from a company, but never from the cited source, the malware described in the message has horrific destructive powers and often the ability to send itself by e-mail or social media.

☐ **Offered expertise and solutions.** These messages warn the receiver not to read or download the supposed malware and offers solutions on how to avoid infection by the malware. This may be a list of instructions to self-remediate the system, file deletion, etc.

☐ **Credibility bolstering.** The message conveys credibility by citing some authoritative source as issuing the warning. Usually the source says the virus is "bad" or has them "worried."

☐ **Technical jargon.** Virus hoax messages almost always have technical jargon, many times specious jargon describing the malware or technical threat and consequences.

☐ **Consequences.** The recipient is advised of impending disaster to his/her computer, network/privacy, or other problematic circumstances that will arise if the message is not heeded.

☐ **Request/requirements.** The hoax provides instructions or admonitions to the recipient that require him/her to conduct a further action, including or in addition to perpetuating the message. Some hoax viruses provide the recipient with instructions on how to locate and delete critical system files under the guise that they are malicious.

☐ **Transmission/perpetuation requirement.** The recipient is admonished to continue the trajectory of the message by transmitting or broadcasting it to others via online communication.

Principles of Persuasion in Hoax Virus Narratives

Hoax virus communications implement influence strategies, using language to invoke a myriad of persuasion principles in compounding effect. Notably, since hoax virus messages are not sent by the messenger with the intention of engagement with the receiver, the sole asynchronous e-mail or social media communication is intended for maximum persuasive impact. This strategy does not cleanly comport with "traditional" FtF influence engagements nor the theories that researchers surmise make influence over CMC viable through nonverbal cues and user salience accumulated over time. Conversely, these strategies leverage the principles to guide the recipient down a deception pathway, ultimately causing belief in the message and compliance with the message instructions. Using textual communications to convey difficult-to-understand technical (or pseudotechnical) jargon, artifact-filled messages seeking to cause receiver action are a clever use of persuasion by hoax virus attackers. Recall that the research that Chaiken and Eagly (1983) conducted revealed that "modality differences in persuasion favored the written mode with inherently difficult-to-understand material, whereas the more usual advantage of videotaped and audiotaped modalities was found with easy material" (p.241). This technical, intimidating language is meant not only to frighten the recipient but to convey authority, persuading users to believe the veracity of the e-mail and the described "virus" threat and comply with the recommended actions of the message source.

- □ **Social proof/consensus; liking**. The message pathway of hoax viruses serves as an accumulator and amplifier for *liking* and *social proof/consensus*. If messages are forwarded from multiple sources, this contributes toward a layering of influence factors and potentially simultaneous central (or systematic) processing of message content (i.e., the message text) and peripheral (or heuristic) processing of heuristic cues. For instance the original message may be persuasive based upon content citing extrinsic, evidence-based sources, but when received via an e-mail trajectory of multiple forwards from trusted colleagues/friends, heuristics, such as *liking* and *social proof*, may persuade receiver action (Fig. 3.12).

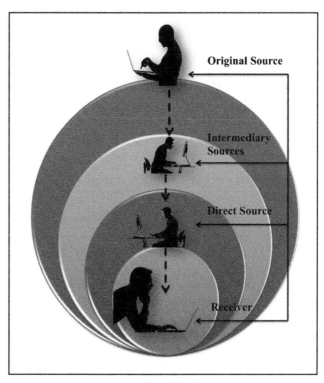

FIGURE 3.12 Hoax virus interactant/message pathway.

□ **Authority**. References to credible, trustworthy, and authoritative companies, news agencies, or individuals are intended to give the attacker *derivative legitimacy*— credibility and positioning through inference, innuendo, and implication of a relationship with a true authoritative entity, resulting in *imputed authority*. In 2009, the virus hoax, "Black Muslim in the White House" (Fig. 3.13) circulated, warning recipients of a dangerous new virus that would ruin the recipient's hard drive; the virus was a notable variant on previous hoax viruses, known as "Olympic Torch," "Invitation," and "Osama Bin Laden Hanged" (Heyd, 2008).[24] In addition to the time imperatives in the warning message and specious technical jargon to invoke action, the message relies upon persuading the recipient through invoking a number of reputable and authoritative sources to bolster the deception narrative:

  o "…worst virus announced by CNN";
  o "…it has been classified by Microsoft as the virus most destructive ever";
  o "This virus was discovered yesterday afternoon by McAfee."

```
URGENT!!! PLEASE CIRCULATE to your friends, family and contacts.

In the coming days, DO NOT open any message with an attachment
called: BLACK MUSLIM IN THE WHITE HOUSE, regardless of who sent it
to you. It is a virus that opens an Olympics torch that burns the
whole hard disk C of your computer.

This virus comes from a known person who you have in your list.

Directions: You should send this message to all of your contacts.
It is better to receive this e-mail 25 times than to receive the
virus and open it.
If you receive a message called BLACK MUSLIM IN THE WHITE HOUSE
even if sent by a friend, do not open, and shut down your machine
immediately.
It is the worst virus announced by CNN.
This new virus has been discovered recently it has been classified
by Microsoft as the virus most destructive ever.
This virus was discovered yesterday afternoon by McAfee..
There is no repair yet for this kind of virus.
This virus simply destroys the Zero Sector of the hard disk, where
vital information function is held.
```

FIGURE 3.13 The "Black Muslim in the White House" hoax virus.

□ *Scarcity*. Recipients are also influenced into complying with the message request due to the principle of *scarcity*. Hoax message components insidiously build in *time imperatives* intended to induce action. The need for action under time compression is almost always framed under a *theme of loss*: loss of data, loss of privacy, and other

---

[24] For details about the "Black Muslim in the Whitehouse" and the "Olympic Torch" hoax viruses, See, http://www.snopes.com/computer/virus/whitehouse.asp.

problematic symptoms of a cyber attack if left unaddressed. In the early 2000s the SULFNBK.exe hoax virus made its way around the Internet. This hoax introduced a newer, more sinister narrative component—instructions to have the user unknowingly delete legitimate, critical operating system files. The results of the hoax virus would ironically cause true system damage when the victim receiver complied with the provided instructions. This message used a number of time imperative/loss framing references along the message pathway to increase anxiety and likely user compliance to the purported remediation solution prescribed by the message source (Fig. 3.14).

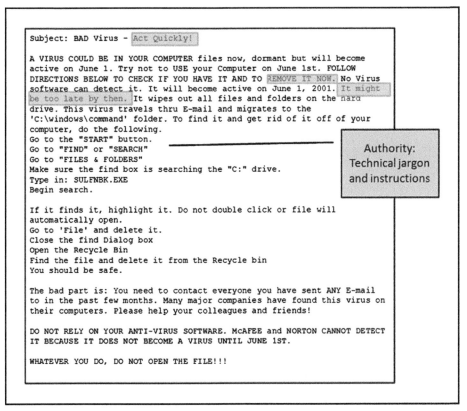

FIGURE 3.14 The "Bad Virus" or "SULFNBK.exe" hoax virus.

While the frequency and intensity of hoax viruses over e-mail and other text-based CMCs have diminished over the years, this may be in part due to the shift in different CMC modalities, such as social media. However, hoax virus communications have been indeed "repackaged" to comport with social media platforms. The message pathway is often times now on the public facing message feed of a user for others to view, perpetuate, and comment upon (Figs. 3.15 and 3.16). Interestingly, the ability for others to view and comment upon these messages can serve as a mechanism for further social influence, such as *social proof* (Fig. 3.16), potentially causing individuals to follow the behaviors of others who post, particularly if a user knows and likes the postings, or finds their posts to be authoritative.

FIGURE 3.15 Hoax Virus message appearing on social media.

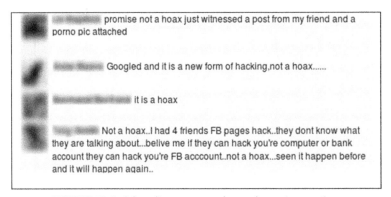

FIGURE 3.16 Social media comments about a hoax virus posting.

Scareware

Ayala (2016) states that *scareware* is a "form of malicious software that uses social engineering to cause shock, anxiety, or the perception of a threat in order to manipulate users into buying unwanted software." Scareware is also called rogueware, rogue antivirus, fake antivirus, fraudware, or fakeware. This type of malware displays false alerts of system infection, recommending payment to remediate the system with their advertised (false) security product (O'Dea, 2009). Variants of the clever cyber stratagem have existed for nearly eight years, with more recent permutations being particularly pernicious, often installing malicious code components on top of defrauding victims out of payments for false security products (Neelabh, 2012; O'Dea, 2009).

The vectors of attack causing a user to engage and continue down a scareware attack pathway vary (Doshi, 2009a, 2009b, 2009c). Researchers have found that the main sources of these pernicious programs are malicious advertisements (or malvertising), black hat search engine optimization, infected systems that deploy the binaries to vulnerable victim systems via *drive-by download,* fake codec web pages, malicious peer-to-peer files, and fake antivirus scanning sites (Fig. 3.17) (Chandraiah, 2012; Neelabh, 2012; Rajab, Ballard, Mavrommatis, Provos, & Zhao, 2010; Symantec Report on Rogue Security Software, 2009; O'Dea, 2009; Stewart, 2008a, 2008b). In addition, scareware can be delivered by spam. A number of fraudulent companies, pretending to be cyber security firms or claiming they are working with legitimate firms, have launched massive e-mail campaigns that tricked users into purchasing worthless software and services. Once the user purchases the fake services, the fraudsters possess credit card numbers and in some cases banking information and/or personal information. A recent action by the Federal Trade Commission, with the states of Connecticut and Pennsylvania, has engaged in legal action to stop operations at Innovazion Research Private Limited, which has allegedly engaged in a major scareware operation. According to the lawsuit, Innovazion Research Private Limited defrauded consumers out of more than $17 million by pretending to represent Microsoft, Apple, and other major tech companies. The company supposedly used several attack vectors including pop-ups, phone calls, and online advertisements (Griffin, 2016).

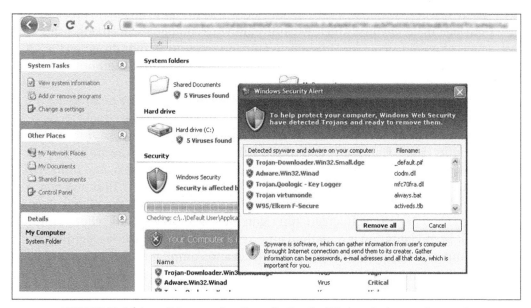

FIGURE 3.17 A fake antivirus scanning site replicating the Windows Explorer environment.

Principles of Persuasion in Scareware Attack "Storyboards"

The attack pathway of scareware compared to other types of malicious code is quite protracted; the typical attack "storyboard" involves these steps:

- ☐ The victim is alerted that his/her system is infected (via pop-up, etc.).
- ☐ The victim is advised to immediately remediate the system by choosing to download/execute an unregistered/trial version of the scareware program.
- ☐ The scareware program reveals numerous "infections" on the victim's system, and the victim is directed to purchase the full "licensed" version of the scareware to eliminate the discovered security threats.
- ☐ The victim provides financial and other personally identifying information to supply payment for the full version.
- ☐ The full version "eliminates" the threats.
- ☐ Actual malware or system compromises can be introduced by the scareware.

Throughout this entire malicious "storyboard," the attacker leverages numerous influence techniques to ensure that the victim stays the totality of the deception pathway and ultimately pays for the scareware program. Since these attacks do not manifest as true CMCs, but rather strategic messaging through websites, pop-ups, and the malicious program interface itself, many of the persuasion precepts are parallel to persuasive technology and website credibility concepts elucidated by Fogg et al. (2003), Sundar (2007), Cugelman et al. (2009), and Rains and Karmikel (2009).

- ☐ **Authority.** The initial trajectory is often pop-up messages, claiming that the user's system has been compromised and infected. These warnings appear to originate from legitimate, credible, and trustworthy antivirus companies, invariably using the same colors, font, icons and imagery as authentic security brands do. When the user downloads and installs the scareware program, these elements of authority are more richly broadcasted to enhance authoritative effect.
- ☐ The scareware program graphical interface is in many ways the heart of the persuasive technology that causes victims to comport with the attacker's requests. In particular, the visual elements often effectively invoke *surface credibility* (Fogg et al., 2003) and trustworthiness, amplifying the authority heuristic. Many scareware programs adopt color schemes, logos, and fonts that imitate familiar brands, such as Microsoft (O'Dea, 2009). Fig. 3.18 shows two different scareware specimens using the Windows Shield with the Microsoft color scheme and (red, top left; green, top right; blue, bottom left; and yellow, bottom right). Brand imitation is a method attackers use to gain derivative legitimacy and imputed authority, leading to user trust and compliance through *reputed credibility* (Fogg et al., 2003).

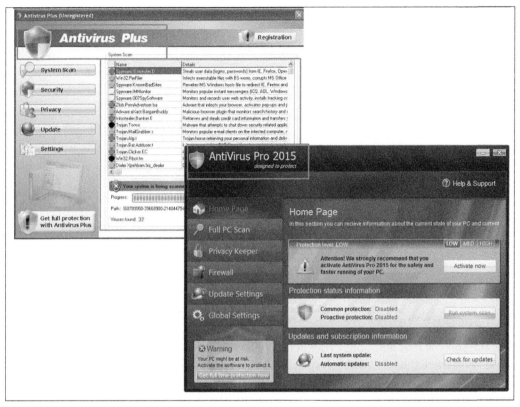

FIGURE 3.18 Visual cues of authority.

☐ Authority (Fig. 3.18) is also conveyed through the scareware program graphical interface by displaying technical elements, such as system scan results, progress bar, and a number of "features": all of which are intended to convey authenticity and technical capabilities. Similar to website credibility, features impact user perception of credibility (Rains & Karmikel, 2009).

☐ **Scarcity**. A compounding influence technique in scareware stratagems is loss framing and engineered imperatives to act, inducing victim engagement. In this regard, the software often displays a number of frightening "discovered" malware types; this imagery not only intends to cause a sense of urgency to act (or *time compression*) and possible loss of data or privacy, but also conveys *authority* by demonstrating the technical capability to effectively detect these (fictitious) instances of malicious code. Further, the *purchase element* or mechanism for the victim to buy a "full version" of the software invokes the principle of scarcity by leveraging time compression or a "limited time" to remedy the problematic situation (Fig. 3.19).

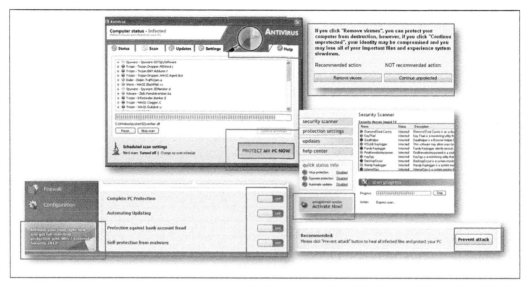

FIGURE 3.19 Scarcity elements.

Tech Support Scams

After the success that nefarious cyber actors had with scareware schemes, permutations followed soon thereafter. In 2008, savvy cyber attackers developed attack strategies similar to scareware, but introduced an additional communication element—requiring frazzled victims to place a telephone call to a prominently displayed toll-free number to receive further instructions and assistance to remediate their "infected" computers.[25] Similar to scareware schemes, tech support scams use a number of psychological influence techniques to persuade a victim down a deception pathway, toward the goal of complying with the attacker's demands (paying for malware "remediation" on the victim's system) and in some instances, creating actual vulnerabilities and compromise of a victim system (Harley, Grooten, Burn, & Johnston, 2012). Tech support scam sites work by alerting the victims that their computers are infected and that they should immediately call a provided number for assistance to secure the system. Like scareware attacks, the vector of attack for these scams varies; victims may arrive on a tech support scam site by links provided in forums, e-mail spam, Twitter bots, and typo-squatting of domain names (Miramirkhani, Starov, & Nikiforakis, 2016; Zeltser, 2015).

Principles of Persuasion in Tech Support Scam "Storyboards"

Similar to the attack pathway of scareware, tech support scams are multitiered and protracted compared to other types of malicious code events; the attack "storyboard" typically involves these steps:

- ☐ The victim is alerted that his/her system is infected (via pop-up, website content, etc.).
- ☐ The victim is advised to immediately remediate the system by calling a prominently displayed telephone number.

---

[25] https://blog.malwarebytes.com/tech-support-scams/.

☐ The tech support helper (attacker) requests remote access to the victim's computer to "investigate" the problem.

☐ When given access, the attacker "analyzes" the system using native Windows utilities.

☐ The attacker "finds" the security problems and requests a fee to "repair" the problem and remediate the system.

Actual malware or system compromises can be introduced by the technician.

During the course of the tech support scam trajectory, from visual to audio and telephone engagement, the attackers use a number of influence techniques to persuade the victim. Uniquely, these dual-modality attacks implement both persuasive technology strategies and verbal engagement with the attacker or his colluders.

☐ **Authority**. Many pop-up alerts adopt color schemes, icons, and a "look and feel" that imitate familiar brands, such as Microsoft. Figs. 3.20 and 3.21 show a fake Microsoft system error warning in an effort to convey credibility and trustworthiness, invoking user action. Similar to scareware visual components that adopt legitimate, authoritative branding elements, tech support scams also imitate visual components so that the attackers gain derivative legitimacy and imputed authority, leading to user trust and compliance through *reputed credibility* (Fogg et al., 2003).

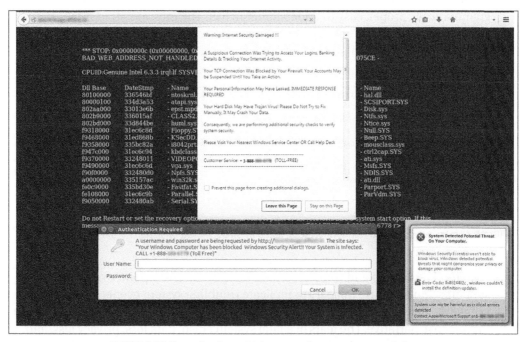

FIGURE 3.20 Example of a multielement tech support scam website.

FIGURE 3.21 Fake system warning.

□ Amplifying sensory elements such as repetitive, looping, audio recordings is intended to bolster credibility and contribute to *perceptual load*, consuming victim sensory/cognitive resources and focus (Fig. 3.22). The recordings are almost exclusively grammatically proper, easy to understand English. The message strategically bolsters the site's visual content, echoing the influence element of scarcity through loss framing (loss of data and privacy) and urgency to act.

> "Important Security Message!
>
> Please call the number provided as soon as possible
>
> You will be guided for the removal for the adware spyware virus on your computer
>
> Seeing these pop-ups means that you have a virus installed on your computer which puts the security of your personal data at a serious risk.
>
> it's strongly advised that you call the number provided and get your computer fixed before you do any shopping online."

FIGURE 3.22 Transcription of a tech support scam audio message, played on a loop on the malicious website.

□ **Scarcity**. The pop-up and website content used as the entry-point to the tech support scam often use imagery to replicate troubling system events (such as the Windows "Blue Screen of Death" fatal system error) or "crash" as artifacts to support the infective narrative. The fears of a fatal system crash, data loss, privacy loss, and detected threats are used as loss framing to intensify the victim's feeling of urgency to repair the system. Other pop-ups, such as those shown in Figs. 3.23 and 3.24 are collateral amplifiers, further transmitting the need for "IMMEDIATE" response, and a further list of potential losses if the warning is not heeded.

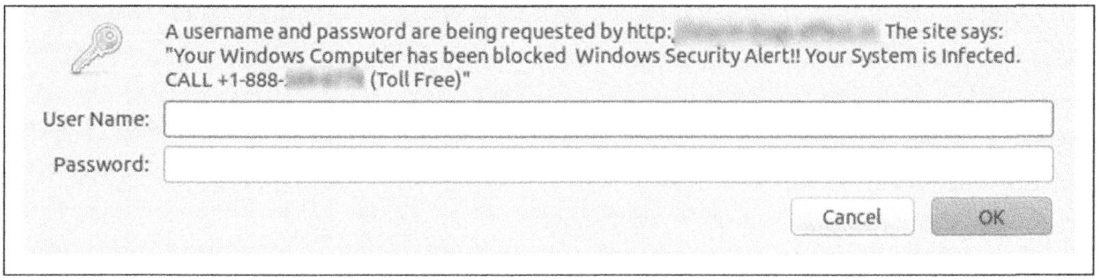

FIGURE 3.23 Pop-up example.

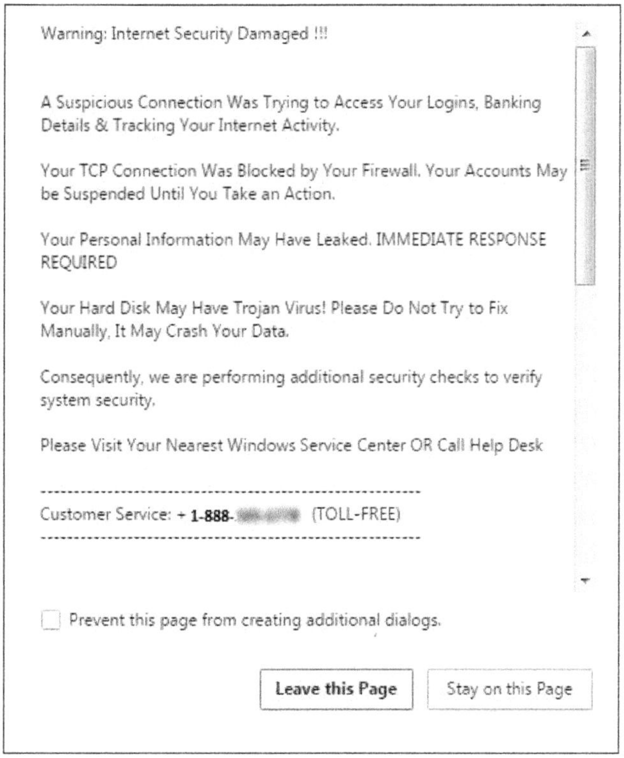

FIGURE 3.24 Engagement induction element.

When users attempt to leave the tech desk support storyboard, they are redirected to a pseudo-lock screen, where the choices provided to click both lead to engagement with the tech help desk operator (Fig. 3.25).

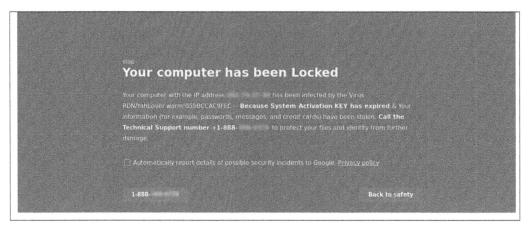

FIGURE 3.25 Pseudo-lock screen.

A number of researchers have engaged with tech desk support attackers in an effort to understand how the attacks work (Miramirkhani et al., 2016; Zeltser, 2015). The transcripts of these engagements reveal that the attackers are working from prepared scripts, cleverly using influence techniques to ensure victim compliance. In these conversations the attackers reference affiliation with other authoritative companies, such as Microsoft, in an effort to gain imputed credibility authority. Further, the attacker works through a number of system checks, using a variety of tools native to the operating system to detect threats on the system. Using often specious technical jargon and "findings" the tech support operator advises the victim of remediation and support package options.

Ransomware

It is one type of problem to get infected by malware via phishing, smishing, or scareware, but another thing altogether for a user to have all of their data just "disappear." For years coterminous to scareware and tech desk/help desk schemes, unscrupulous cyber criminals leveraged *cryptovirus* attacks (Young & Yung, 2004) known as *ransomware*, causing the systems of infected users to be "locked" or encrypted with a proprietary or powerful encryption schemes, making data and files inaccessible. While technically not categorized as "scareware," ransomware can definitely be defined as a deceptive scheme that scares. *Ransomware* is a type of malware that restricts or limits users from accessing their systems, data, or devices through the use of *cryptovirology* (malicious cryptography) unless a ransom is paid by the infected user.[26]

Ransomware vectors of attack vary. Often, it is installed when a user opens an attachment sent from an attacker, visits a compromised or fake website, or clicks on malicious ads or bad links in social media or instant messenger chats. Thus the attack begins with

---

[26] See, http://www.trendmicro.com/vinfo/us/security/definition/ransomware; https://usa.kaspersky.com/internet-security-center/definitions/ransomware.

the same type of deceptive tactics and social engineering techniques used in most other cybercrimes. Hackers may also take advantage of known vulnerabilities in systems and networks to launch their ransomware attacks (Siwicki, 2016).

Ransomware, or *cryptoviral extortion*, is the digital form of data hostage taking (Young & Yung, 2004). In most cases, taking data hostage is not a "life and death" situation, unlike a physical kidnapping for ransom. However, the relative importance or sensitivity of the data being held hostage can result in a crisis situation. The digital hostage takers do use some of the same tactics as kidnappers. They rely on the fact that people need their data, their personal lives depend on their data, their businesses depend on their data, and most importantly, they want their data back safely, soundly, and in one piece. The emotional and psychological reactions of most people who have their data kidnapped and held hostage include shock, panic, fear, frustration, and anger. Victims are not only impacted by their stolen data, but many are confused and unsure about how to interact with the hostage takers…or wonder if they even should engage them. However, most people are willing to pay the ransom to get their data returned, thus the scam continues as it nets millions of dollars. Ransomware is simply the next iteration of digital attack and it is extremely profitable—so much so that it has recently been touted by some experts as "the most profitable hacker scam ever."[27]

Ransomware originated in Russia by the same hackers who have been active for years launching virus attacks, phishing attacks, and distributing malware (Vargas & Vargas, 2016). Generally speaking, ransomware can be divided into two types: 1) *lock-out ransomware* and 2) *crypto-ransomware*. Lock-out ransomware denies access to systems, networks, or devices and typically locks up the device interface. However, the device remains active enough to allow the victim(s) to interact with hackers to pay the ransom. Crypto-ransomware is a bit more sophisticated and prevents the user(s) access to data files on a targeted device by encrypting those files. Thus the hackers hold the decryption key and the ransom payment will provide the decryption. In some cases, very specific file types are targeted. For example, some ransomware will focus on files or file extensions that they believe are more important to people, such as Excel, QuickBooks, or tax forms (Vargas & Vargas, 2016).

Principles of Persuasion in Ransomware Attacks

With the financial success and evolving sophistication of scareware and tech support schemes, ransomware adopted psychological influence elements to bolster and augment their stratagems. While many of the influence principles are implementations and adaptations of traditional FtF heuristic cues, i.e., Cialdini's weapons of influence, much of the persuasion is generated from the technology deployment and engagement pathway, including the language and visual features of the lock screens. In many ways, similar

---

[27] Ransomware Is the Most Profitable Hacker Scam Ever, http://www.usnews.com/news/articles/2016-07-27/cisco-reports-ransomware-is-the-most-profitable-malware-scam-ever. See also, http://www.cnbc.com/2016/04/11/ransomware-lucrative-fast-growing-hard-to-stop.html.

to scareware and tech support schemes, ransomware leverages the same influence principles used to enhance website credibility through *persuasive design.*

☐ **Authority**. Ransomware notifications have evolved substantially since 2005–06, where these cryptovirus attacks (e.g., TROJ_CRYZIPA) typically notified the victims of the attack by a simple text message, which included method of payment for decryption, or "return[28]" of the user's data. Modern ransomware notification screens are rich with imagery, messaging, and payment instructions. To enhance the potency of these attacks and ensure victim compliance, attackers use a number of authority cues (Figs. 3.26–3.28). Often (particularly with the Reveton ransomware scheme),[29] official government agency seals are emblazoned at the top of the screen to immediately convey that the victim's system has been "locked" by a powerful, official entity worthy of complying with—and futile to resist. Very often, more than one agency seal will be prominently displayed to amplify this cue (Figs. 3.26–3.29) and convey that multiple agencies are collaboratively responsible for identifying and locking the target system. Further, imagery of respectable, credible professionals, such as information security experts diligently investigating at computer terminals or serious looking police officers wearing tactical gear in operational poses (Fig. 3.27), are placed close to the logos to convey corresponding trappings of authority.

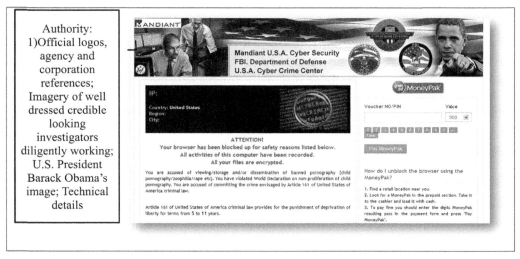

FIGURE 3.26 Ransomware lock screen using numerous authority cues.

[28] http://blog.trendmicro.com/trendlabs-security-intelligence/ransomware21-ransomware21-ransomware21/.

[29] http://krebsonsecurity.com/2012/08/inside-a-reveton-ransomware-operation/.

☐ In some ransomware permutations the locking notification screen actually displays fictitious authoritative-sounding agencies (with corresponding agency seal), such as the "Central Security Treatment Organization" (Fig. 3.27) or fictitious sections within a real agency, such as the National Security Agency "Computer Crime Prosecution Section." And in others, reputable corporate entities that specialize in information security (e.g., Mandiant) or carry a recognizable, authority name in the information technology industry (e.g., Microsoft) are invoked as authoritative supporters or contributors (Figs. 3.26 and 3.28).

☐ Authority cues are also conveyed by using official-sounding language, such as statutory provisions that have been "violated" by the infected user, resulting in the computer being "locked" by the "government agency."

☐ Specious technical language, display of the user's system/network details (such as IP address and host name), and in some instances displayed exemplars of fictitious, staged "evidence" are used to overwhelm the victim with ideation that the party responsible for "locking" his/her computer is credible, powerful, and in control (Fig. 3.27).

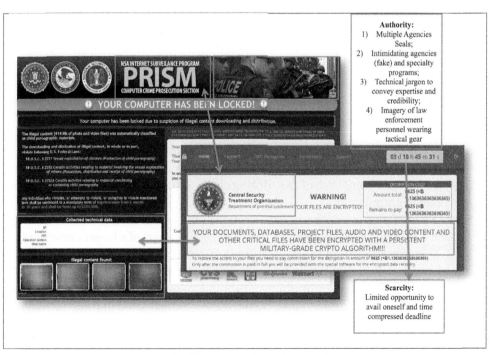

FIGURE 3.27 Example of fictitious authoritative-sounding organizations.

FIGURE 3.28 Authority and scarcity principles conveyed through visual themes.

☐ **Scarcity**. Since the underlying motivation of these attacks is to cause the victim to pay the ransom, attackers typically provide very clear instructions on the lock screen message on how to make the payment, predominantly through a cryptocurrency (Vargas & Vargas, 2016). A way to induce victim engagement and payment is using a permutation of scarcity, such as urgency or time imperative framed in potential loss. To invoke this influence technique the digital hostage takers will provide the victim with a prominently displayed "clock-timer" contained in the ransom screen, warning the victim that he/she has some amount of hours, minutes, and seconds left to pay the ransom (Fig. 3.29). In some instances, clear loss framing messages and respective "countdown clocks" for "price increase" or total data loss is displayed to compound urgency. This additional use of the "ticking clock" is just part of the attacker's layered psychological strategy.

☐ **Social Proof/Consensus**. Recent permutations of ransomware have taken a novel approach of trying to make the user feel included and part of a larger community (Fig. 3.30). This effort to connote *social exclusivity* is certainly an interesting and concerted influence effort. Within this strategic messaging are principles of consensus—that the user is part of this larger community and should follow or behaviorally comport what others in the community are doing. Some of the language used in these messages, particularly wording such as "100% of people" is intended to provide the reader a social proof cue.

FIGURE 3.29 The principle of scarcity invoked through persuasive time imperatives and loss framing.

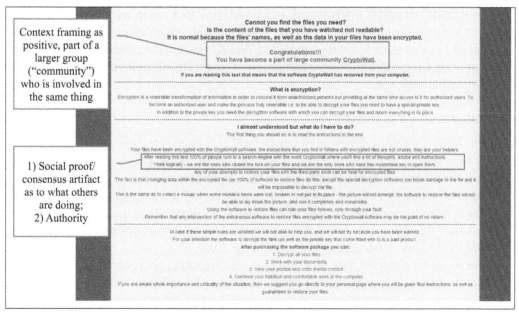

FIGURE 3.30 Social proof as to what others are doing.

If the disappearance of the user's data, combined with the sinister-looking ransom note screen, does not coerce the user into paying, the timer (like the ticking bomb in many action movies that has to be deactivated) is there to strike another emotional chord. Many users are unaware that ransomware also can just as easily seize control over files stored on cloud services. According to Krebs (2016), an employee working at Children in Film opened Outlook, clicked on a voicemail message attachment, and received the infamous ransom note. All of the company's data (i.e., e-mail, data files, accounting) is hosted by a managed cloud service, and they felt secure because their data was allegedly safe "in the cloud." These criminals can target any computer, laptop, smartphone, or tablet users, whether it's a home computer, endpoints in an enterprise network, storage in the cloud, or servers used by a government agency. In other words, no one is safe from a potential ransomware attack. It can be argued that the ransomware fraudsters are the masters of psychological manipulation. In order to pull off a full-on data ransom attack, the attackers must lure and persuade the would-be victims through multiple stages, including the initial deception, the belief that their data is really not recoverable without the assistance of the attacker, the belief that their "time is limited" and the clock is ticking, and the belief that otherwise nontech savvy people will in a time crunch learn to use Bitcoin and, in the end, send the money. That is a lot of persuasion and manipulation wrapped into one attack. But perhaps the real deception is that in some cases, the user's data can be recovered without the help of the attackers and without having to pay the ransom. For example, Krebs (2016) provides instructions and a web link to a computer help forum called BleepingComputer.com who have created TeslaDecoder, which allows victims to decrypt files locked by a form of ransomware called TeslaCrypt. Further, there are a number of other tutorials from authoritative information security researchers and companies providing remediation steps.

The Future of Viral Influence

It is clear from the recent direction in which viral influence is heading that this phenomenon is here to stay, at least for the near future. We are already seeing signs that vectors such as ransomware are spreading to a new class of targets that reside within the Internet of Things (IoT). Ransomware attacks on such popular IoT devices such as the Nest home thermostat have been demonstrated to be feasible (Storm, 2016), and other IoT devices such as smart television are already being attacked by malicious online actors using ransomware to hold home televisions hostage (Tung, 2016).

While it can be expected that this expansion of the target universe of viral attacks will continue for at least the near future, there undoubtedly will be polymorphic variations of various strategies deployed to spread the prevalence of these types of attacks. It would be a grave mistake to limit our thinking to a too narrow pathway for these viral-based outbreaks. These types of threats are severely dimensionally constrained; that is, current thinking about these types of attacks can be described as n dimensional, where n is modest in magnitude.

The key to understanding future viral threats is to understand the synergy-rich environment that is digital technology and how it is connected (e.g., the Internet) and that this means that the solution space for future viral threats may involve thinking about it in $n + x$ dimensions, where x is significantly large. For example, rather than just thinking of viral targets as a class of devices such as computers, smart phones, thermostats, or televisions, it may behoove researchers and policymakers to think about new future threats such as hybrid viral threats, where cyberthreats may be combined with other threat vectors such as biologically-based weapons of mass destruction, thus truly putting the "viral" in viral influence. In this case, terrorists may threaten an entire city by deploying hidden, remote DIY genetic minilabs that generate and distribute pathogenic organisms around a targeted city. The command and control systems for these labs distributed across the Internet and the terrorists themselves can be located tens of thousands of miles away from the targeted city. Ransoming an entire city may not be as far away as it might seem.

This is only one example of how the exponential expansion of the dimensionality of viral threats may emerge in the future. In order to foresee these kinds of threats, it will be necessary to expend effort to produce potential future scenarios so that the possible consequences as well as necessary defenses can be envisioned. It is likely to take a multidisciplinary team borrowing experts from information security, social scientists, epidemiologists, and others to tackle these emerging new viral threats, and it may take synergies from many different experts in order to develop effective defenses against these new types of threats.

Conclusion

Since the 1980s, cyber attackers have used a number of sophisticated ways to exploit systems and networks. In this evolution, which often moves at the speed of new technologies, new applications, new operating systems, and updated patches, attackers have become experts of deception to exploit the human users behind the computer systems. These methods of deception can be rudimentary, simple and tailored for a particular task or chain that is part of a larger attack trajectory. Other deception methods are nuanced, complex, and rich with psychological manipulation tactics. Some of the most potent and effective principles on the latter deception pathways are those of psychological influence and persuasive technology. While not used in traditional, linear ways, attackers have adapted and modified these principles in novel, efficient ways. Expertly drawing from these principles, cyber stratagem-based attacks such as scareware, ransomware, and tech support scams apply distilled, compact influence narratives through persuasive imagery, language, and program behaviors that surpass the anticipated field of vision for when researchers considered FtF influence scenarios or persuasive website design strategies. As these attacks, and those that evolve from them, continue to circumvent existing security optics and strategies, deeper research and insight into these psychological principles within the context of cyber attacker capabilities is inevitable.

References

Ayala, L. (2016). *Cybersecurity lexicon*. New York: Apress Media.

Amichai-Hamburger, Y. (2013). *The social net: Understanding our online behavior*. Oxford: Oxford University Press.

Baumeister, R. F., & Bushman, B. J. (2008). *Social psychology and human nature*. Belmont, CA: Thomson Higher Education.

Birdwhistell, R. L. (1952). *Introduction to kinesics: An annotation system for analysis of body motion and gesture*. Louisville, KY: University of Louisville. Cited also as Birdwhistell, R. L. (1952). Introduction to kinesics: An annotation system for analysis of body motion and gesture. Washington, DC: Department of State, Foreign Service Institute.

Bos, N., Olson, J., Gergle, D., Olson, G., & Wright, Z. (January 01, 2002). *Effects of four computer-mediated communications channels on trust development*. Chi Conference, 135–140.

Bradac, J. J. (December 07, 1981). Language style on trial: Effects of "powerful" and "powerless" speech upon judgments of victims and villains. *Western Journal of Speech Communication, 45*(4), 327–341.

Bradac, J. J., & Street, R. L. (January 01, 1989). Powerful and powerless styles of talk: A theoretical analysis of language and impression formation. *Research on Language & Social Interaction, 23*, 195–241.

Brehm, J. W. (1966). *A theory of psychological reactance*. New York: Academic Press.

Brehm, J. W. (1972). *Responses to loss of freedom: A theory of psychological reactance*. Morristown, N.J.: General Learning Press.

Brehm, J. W., & Cohen, A. R. (1962). *Explorations in cognitive dissonance*. New York: Wiley.

Brock, T. C. (June 1965). Communicator-recipient similarity and decision change. *Journal of Personality and Social Psychology, 1*(6), 650–654.

Brock, T. C. (1968). Implications of commodity theory for value change. In A. G. Grecnwald, T. C. Brock, & T. M. Ostrom (Eds.), *Psychological foundations of attitudes*. New York: Academic Press.

Bruneau, T. (1980). Chronemics and the verbal-nonverbal interface. In M. R. Key (Ed.), *The relationship of verbal and nonverbal communication* (pp. 101–117). The Hague: Mouton.

Burgoon, J. (1994). Nonverbal signals. In M. L. Knapp, & G. R. Miller (Eds.), *Handbook of interpersonal communication* (pp. 229–285). Beverly Hills: Sage.

Burgoon, J. K., Buller, B., Hale, J. L., & deTurck, M. (1984). Relational messages associated with nonverbal behaviors. *Human Communication Research, 10*(3), 351–378.

Burgoon, J. K., Buller, D. B., & Woodall, W. G. (1989). *Nonverbal communication: The unspoken dialogue*. New York: Harper & Row.

Burgoon, J. K., Schuetzler, R., & Wilson, W. D. (March 01, 2014). Kinesic patterning in deceptive and truthful interactions. *Journal of Nonverbal Behavior, 39*(1), 1–24.

Carlson, J. R., George, J. F., Burgoon, J. K., Adkins, M., & White, C. H. (January 01, 2004). Deception in computer-mediated communication. *Group Decision and Negotiation, 13*(1), 5–28.

Chaiken, S. (August 1979). Communicator physical attractiveness and persuasion. *Journal of Personality and Social Psychology, 37*(8), 1387–1397.

Chaiken, S. (1980). Heuristic versus systematic information processing and the use of course versus message cures in persuasion. *Journal of Personality and Social Psychology, 39*, 752–766.

Chaiken, S. (1987). The heuristic model of persuasion. In M. P. Zanna, J. M. Olson, & C. P. Herman (Eds.). M. P. Zanna, J. M. Olson, & C. P. Herman (Eds.), *Social influence: The ontario symposium: (Vol. 5)*. Hoboken: Taylor and Francis.

Chaiken, S., & Eagly, A. H. (1983). Communication modality as a determinant of persuasion: The role of communicator salience. *Journal of Personality and Social Psychology, 45*(2), 241–256.

Chaiken, S., Liberman, A., & Eagly, A. H. (1989). Heuristic and systematic information processing within and beyond the persuasion context. In J. S. Uleman, & J. A. Bargh (Eds.), *Unintended thought.* New York: Guilford Press.

Chandraiah, J. (2012). *Fake anti-virus: The journey from Trojan to a persistent threat.* Sophos Naked Security Blog.

Cialdini, R. B. (1984). *Influence: How and why people agree to things.* New York: Morrow.

Cialdini, R. B. (2007). *Influence: The psychology of persuasion.* New York: Collins.

Cialdini, R. B. (2009). *Influence: Science and practice.* Boston: Pearson Education.

Cialdini, R. B., & Goldstein, N. (2004). *Social Influence: Compliance and conformity.*

Cialdini, R. B., & Trost, M. R. (1998). Social influence: Social norms, conformity and compliance. In (4th ed.) D. T. Gilbert, S. T. Fiske, & G. Lindzey (Eds.), *The handbook of social psychology* (Vols. 1–2) (pp. 151–192). New York, NY, US: McGraw-Hill.

Cialdini, R. B., Wosinska, W., Barrett, D. W., Butner, J., & Gornik-Durose, M. (January 01, 1999). Compliance with a request in two cultures: The differential influence of social proof and commitment/consistency on collectivists and individualists. *Personality & Social Psychology Bulletin, 25*(10), 1242–1253.

Cloete, E., Tanner, M., & Pollock, M. (2011). Credibility of information on e-commerce websites. In *13th annual conference on world wide web applications.*

Collisson, B., & Howell, J. L. (January 01, 2014). The liking-similarity effect: Perceptions of similarity as a function of liking. *The Journal of Social Psychology, 154*(5).

Cragin, K., & Gerwehr, S. (2005). *Dissuading terror: Strategic influence and the struggle against terrorism.* Santa Monica, CA: Rand Corporation.

Cugelman, B., Thelwall, M., & Dawes, P. (June 2008). Website credibility, active trust and behavioural intent. In *International conference on persuasive technology* (pp. 47–57). Springer Berlin Heidelberg.

Cugelman, B., Thelwall, M., & Dawes, P. (2009). The dimensions of web site credibility and their relation to active trust and behavioural impact. *Communications of the Association for Information Systems, 24*(1), 26.

Culnan, M. J., & Markus, M. L. (1987). Information technologies. In F. M. Jablin, L. L. Putnam, K. H. Roberts, & L. W. Porter (Eds.), *Handbook of organizational communication: An interdisciplinary perspective* (pp. 420–443). Thousand Oaks, CA, US: Sage Publications, Inc.. 781 pp.

D'ambra, J., Rice, R. E., & O'connor, M. (January 01, 1998). Computer-mediated communication and media preference: An investigation of the dimensionality of perceived task equivocality and media richness. *Behaviour & Information Technology, 17*(3), 164–174.

Daft, R. L., & Lengel, R. H. (1983). *Information richness: A new approach to managerial behavior and organization design.* College Station, Tex: Texas A & M University.

Doshi, N. (2009a). *Misleading applications – show Me the Money!.* Retrieved from http://www.symantec.com/connect/blogs/misleading-applications-show-me-money.

Doshi, N. (2009b). *Misleading applications – show Me the Money! (Part 2).* Retrieved from http://www.symantec.com/connect/blogs/misleading-applications-show-me-money-part-2.

Doshi, N. (2009c). *Misleading applications – show Me the Money! (Part 3).* Retrieved from http://www.symantec.com/connect/blogs/misleading-applications-show-me-money-part-3.

Eagly, A. H., & Chaiken, S. (1993). Process theories of attitude formation and change: The elaboration likelihood model and heuristic-systematic models. In A. H. Eagly, & S. Chiaken (Eds.), *The psychology of attitudes* (pp. 303–350). Orlando: Harcourt Brace.

Ekman, P. (January 01, 2003). Emotional and conversational nonverbal signals. *Philosophical Studies Series, 99,* 39–50.

Ekman, P., & Friesen, W. V. (1969b). The repertoire of nonverbal behavior. Categories, origins, usage and coding. *Semiotica*, *1*, 49–98.

Ekman, P., & Friesen, W. V. (1969a). Nonverbal leakage and clues to deception. In *Langley porter neuro-psychiatric inst San Francisco CA nonverbal behavior research project*. Ft. Belvoir: Defense Technical Information Center.

Erwin, P. (2001). *Attitudes and persuasion*. Psychology Press.

Fazio, R. H., Blascovich, J., & Driscoll, D. M. (August 01, 1992). On the functional value of attitudes: The influence of accessible attitudes on the ease and quality of decision making. *Personality & Social Psychology Bulletin*, *18*(4), 388–401.

Flanagin, A. J., & Metzger, M. J. (2007). The role of site features, user attributes, and information verification behaviors on the perceived credibility of web-based information. *New Media & Society*, *9*(2), 319–342.

Fogg, B. J. (2003a). *Persuasive technology: Using computers to change what we think and do*. Amsterdam: Morgan Kaufmann Publishers.

Fogg, B. J. (April 2003b). Prominence-interpretation theory: Explaining how people assess credibility online. In *CHI'03 extended abstracts on human factors in computing systems* (pp. 722–723). ACM.

Fogg, B. J., Cuellar, G., & Danielson, D. (2007). Motivating, influencing, and persuading users: An introduction to captology. In *Human computer interaction handbook: Fundamentals, evolving technologies and emerging applications* (pp. 137–138).

Fogg, B. J., Soohoo, C., & Danielsen, D. (2002). *How do people evaluate a web site's credibility? Results from a large study*.

Fogg, B. J., Soohoo, C., Danielson, D. R., Marable, L., Stanford, J., & Tauber, E. R. (2003). How do users evaluate the credibility of web sites? A study with over 2,500 participants. In *Proceedings of DUX2003, designing for user experiences Conference*.

Fogg, B. J., Swani, P., Treinen, M., Marshall, J., Osipovich, A., Varma, C., et al. (2000). Elements that affect Web credibility: Early results from a self-report study. *Proceedings of CHI'00, Extended Abstracts on Human Factors in Computing Systems*, 287–288.

Fogg, B. J., & Tseng, H. (1999). The elements of computer credibility. *Proceedings of CHI'99, Human Factors in Computing Systems*, 80–87.

Fromkin, H. L., Olson, J. C., Robert, L., & Barnaby, D. (1971). A commodity theory analysis of consumer preferences for scarce products. *Proceedings of the Annual Convention of the American Psychological Association*, *6*(Pt. 2), 653–654.

Gordon, S. (October 1–3, 1997). Hoaxes & hypes. In *7th virus bulletin international conference, San Francisco, California*. Available from https://web.archive.org/web/20001017183237/http://www.av.ibm.com/InsideTheLab/Bookshelf/ScientificPapers/Gordon/HH.html.

Gouldner, A. W. (April 1960). The norm of reciprocity: A preliminary statement. *American Sociological Review*, *25*(2), 161–178.

Griffin, K. (May 19, 2016). *FTC expands tech support fraud lawsuit*. Retrieved from http://www.hartford-business.com/article/20160519/NEWS01/160519909/ftc-expands-tech-support-fraud-lawsuit.

Guadagno, R. E. (2013). Social influence online: The six principles in action. In C. J. Liberman (Ed.), *Casing persuasive communication*. Dubuque: Kendall Hunt Publishing Company.

Guadagno, R. E., & Cialdini, R. B. (2002). Online persuasion: An examination of gender differences in computer-mediated interpersonal influence. *Group Dynamics: Theory, Research, and Practice* *6*(1), 38.

Guadagno, R. E., & Cialdini, R. B. (2005). Online persuasion and compliance: Social influence on the internet and beyond. In Y. Amichai-Hamburger (Ed.), *The social net: Understanding human behavior in cyberspace*. Oxford: Oxford University Press.

Guadagno, R. E., & Cialdini, R. B. (2007). Persuade him by email, but see her in person: Online persuasion revisited. *Computers in Human Behavior* 23(2), 999–1015.

Guadagno, R. E., Muscanell, N. L., Rice, L. M., & Roberts, N. (2013). Social influence online: The impact of social validation and likability on compliance. *Psychology of Popular Media Culture, 2*(1), 51–60.

Hall, E. T. (1966). *The hidden dimension.* Garden City, N.Y.: Doubleday.

Hall, E. T. (January 01, 1963). A system for the notation of proxemic behavior. *American Anthropologist: Journal of the American Anthropological Association* 65, 1003–1026.

Harley, D., Grooten, M., Burn, S., & Johnston, C. (2012). My pc has 32,539 errors: How telephone support scams really work. In *22nd virus bulletin international conference (VB2012).*

Hewstone, M., Rubin, M., & Willis, H. (February 01, 2002). Intergroup bias. *Annual Review of Psychology, 53*(1), 575–604.

Heyd, T. (2008). *Email hoaxes: Form, function, genre ecology* (Vol. 174). John Benjamins Publishing.

Hiltz, S. R., Johnson, K., Agle, G., & New Jersey Institute of Technology (1978). *Replicating bales problem solving experiments on a computerized conference: A pilot study.* Newark, N.J.: Computer and Information Science Dept., New Jersey Institute of Technology.

Hovland, C. I., Janis, I. L., & Kelley, H. H. (1953). *Communication and persuasion.* New Haven: Yale University Press.

Hovland, C. I., & Weiss, W. (December 01, 1951). The influence of source credibility on communication effectiveness. *The Public Opinion Quarterly, 15*(4), 635–650.

Kąkol, M., & Nielek, R. (2015). What affects web credibility perception? An analysis of textual justifications. *Computer Science, 16*(3), 295–310.

Kipnis, D., Schmidt, S. M., & Wilkinson, I. (1980). Intraorganizational influence tactics: Explorations in getting one's way. *Journal of Applied Psychology, 65*(4), 440.

Kolenda, N. (2013). *Methods of persuasion: How to use psychology to control human behavior.*

Kramer, F. D., Wentz, L. K., & National Defense University (2008). Cyber influence and international security. In F. D. Kramer, S. H. Starr, & L. K. Wentz (Eds.), *Cyberpower and national security.* Washington, D C: Center for Technology and National Security Policy, National Defense University.

Kraut, R. E. (January 01, 1978). Verbal and nonverbal cues in the perception of lying. *Journal of Personality and Social Psychology, 36*(4), 380–391.

Krebs, B. (January 16, 2016). *Ransomware a threat to cloud services, too.* Retrieved from https://krebsonsecurity.com/2016/01/ransomware-a-threat-to-cloud-services-too/.

Lane, D. R. (1997). Function and impact of nonverbal communication in a computer-mediated communication context: An investigation of defining issues. Com 454. *Communication & Technology.*

Lengel, R. H., & Daft, R. L. (1984). *An exploratory analysis of the relationship between media richness and managerial information processing.* Texas A and M University College Station Department of Management.

Lynn, M. (March 01, 1992). The psychology of unavailability: Explaining scarcity and cost effects on value. *Basic and Applied Social Psychology, 13*(1), 3–7.

Lynn, M., & McCall, M. (January 01, 2009). Techniques for increasing servers' tips. *Cornell Hospitality Quarterly, 50*(2), 198–208.

Malhotra, D., & Bazerman, M. H. (2008). Psychological influence in negotiation: An introduction long overdue. *Journal of Management, 34,* 509–531.

MalwareBytes Tech Support Scams—Help & Resource Page. Retrieved from. https://blog.malwarebytes.com/tech-support-scams/.

Manheim, J. B. (2011). *Strategy in information and influence campaigns: How policy advocates, social movements, insurgent groups, corporations, governments, and others get what they want.* New York: Routledge.

McGuire, W. J. (1968). *Personality and attitude change: An information-processing theory.* In A. G. Greenwood (Ed.). T.C. Print.

Milgram, S. (1963). Behavioral study of obedience. *The Journal of Abnormal and Social Psychology, 67*(4), 371.

Miramirkhani, N., Starov, O., & Nikiforakis, N. (2016). *Dial one for Scam: Analyzing and detecting technical support scams.* Stony Brook, NY: Stony Brook University, arXiv preprint arXiv:1607.06891.

Moreland, R., & Zajonc, R. (1982). Exposure effects in person perception: Familiarity, similarity, and attraction. *Journal of Experimental Social Psychology, 18*(5), 395–415.

Moriarty, T. (February 1975). Crime, commitment, and the responsive bystander: Two field experiments. *Journal of Personality and Social Psychology, 31*(2), 370–376.

Muscanell, N. L., Guadagno, R. E., & Murphy, S. (July 01, 2014). Weapons of influence misused: a social influence analysis of why people fall prey to internet scams[the views]. *Social and Personality Psychology Compass, 8*(7), 388–396.

Muscanell, N. L., & University of Alabama (2009). *Computer-mediated persuasion: Emoticons as a proxy for nonverbal behavior.* Tuscaloosa, AL: University of Alabama Libraries.

Neelabh. (July 01, 2012). Tracking digital footprints of scareware to Thwart cyber hypnotism through cyber vigilantism in cyberspace. *Bvicam's International Journal of Information Technology, 4*(2), 460–467.

Nowak, K. L., Watt, J., & Walther, J. B. (April 01, 2005). The influence of synchrony and sensory modality on the person perception process in computer-mediated groups. *Journal of Computer-Mediated Communication, 10*(3), 0.

O'Dea, H. (2009). The modern rogue—malware with a face. In *Proc. Of the virus Bulletin Conference.*

O'Keefe, G. J. (1989). Strategies and tactics in political campaigns. In C. T. Salmon (Ed.), *Information campaigns: Balancing social values and social change* (pp. 259–284). Newbury Park, CA: Sage Publications.

O'Keefe, D. J. (2002). *Persuasion: Theory and research* (2nd ed.). Newbury Park, Calif.: Sage Publications.

O'Keefe, D. J. (May 18, 2016). Guilt and social influence. *Annals of the International Communication Association, 23*(1), 67–101.

Okdie, B. M., & Guadagno, R. E. (2008). *Social influence and computer mediated communication.*

Okdie, B. M., Guadagno, R. E., Petrova, P. K., & Shreves, W. B. (2013). Social influence online: A Tale of gender differences in the effectiveness of authority cues. *Journal of Interactive Communication Systems and Technologies, 3*(1), 20–31.

Perdue, C. W., Dovidio, J. F., Gurtman, M. B., & Tyler, R. B. (January 01, 1990). Us and them: Social categorization and the process of intergroup bias. *Journal of Personality and Social Psychology, 59*(3), 475–486.

Petty, R. E., & Cacioppo, J. T. (1986a). The elaboration likelihood model of persuasion. In L. Berkowitz (Ed.), *Advances in experimental social psychology* (Vol. 19) (pp. 123–205). New York: Academic Press.

Petty, R. E., & Cacioppo, J. T. (1986b). *Communication and persuasion: Central and peripheral routes to attitude change.* New York.: Springer-Verlag.

Pfau, M., & Burgoon, M. (1988). Inoculation in political communication. *Human Communication Research, 15*, 91–111.

Pfau, M., & Kenski, H. C. (1990). *Attack politics: Strategy and defense.* New York: Praeger.

Pfau, M., Kenski, H. C., Nitz, M., & Sorenson, J. (1990). Efficacy of inoculation strategies in promoting resistance to political attack messages: Application to direct mail. *Communication Monographs, 57*, 25–43.

Pfau, M., & Parrott, R. (1993). *Persuasive communication campaigns.* Pearson College Division.

Pollay, R. W. (1989). Campaigns, change and culture: On the polluting potential of persuasion. In C. T. Salmon (Ed.), *Information campaigns: Balancing social values and social change* (pp. 185–196). Newbury Park, CA: Sage Publications.

Rains, S. A., & Karmikel, C. D. (2009). Health information-seeking and perceptions of website cred-ibility: Examining web-use orientation, message characteristics, and structural features of websites. *Computers in Human Behavior, 25*(2), 544–553.

Rajab, M. A., Ballard, L., Mavrommatis, P., Provos, N., & Zhao, X. (April 2010). *The Nocebo effect on the Web: An analysis of fake anti-virus distribution.* In LEET.

Robins, D., & Holmes, J. (2008). Aesthetics and credibility in web site design. *Information Processing & Management, 44*(1), 386–399.

Rosenberg, D., & Sillince, J. A. A. (2000). Verbal and Nonverbal communication in computer mediated set-tings. International Journal of Artificial Intelligence in Education (IJAIED).

Seiter, R. H., & Gass, J. S. (2010). *Persuasion, social influence, and compliance gaining* (4th ed.). Boston: Allyn & Bacon.

Short, J. A., Williams, E., & Christie, B. (1976). *The social psychology of telecommunications.* London: Wiley.

Siwicki, B. (May 17, 2016). *Cybersecurity special report: Ransomware will get worse, hackers targeting whales, medical devices and IoT trigger new vulnerabilities. Health Care IT News.* Retrieved from http://www.healthcareitnews.com/news/cybersecurity-special-report-ransomware-will-get-worse-hackers-targeting-whales-medical-devices.

Stewart, J. (2008a). *Rogue antivirus dissected-part 1.* Retrieved from https://www.secureworks.com/research/rogue-antivirus-part-1.

Stewart, J. (2008b). *Rogue antivirus dissected-part 2.* Retrieved from https://www.secureworks.com/research/rogue-antivirus-part-2.

Stiff, J. B., & Mongeau, P. A. (2003). *Persuasive communication.* New York: Guilford Press.

Storm, D. (September 26, 2016). *Hackers demonstrated first ransomware for IoT thermostats at DEF CON.* Retrieved from http://www.computerworld.com/article/3105001/security/hackers-demonstrated-first-ransomware-for-iot-thermostats-at-def-con.html.

Sundar, S. S. (2007). Social psychology of interactivity in human-website interaction. In *The Oxford hand-book of Internet psychology* (pp. 89–104).

Symantec Report on Rogue Security Software" (PDF). (October 28, 2009). *Symantec.* Retrieved from http://eval.symantec.com/mktginfo/enterprise/white_papers/b-symc_report_on_rogue_security_soft-ware_WP_20100385.en-us.pdf.

Tidwell, L. C., & Walther, J. B. (July 01, 2002). Computer-mediated communication effects on disclosure, impressions, and interpersonal evaluations: Getting to know one another a bit at a time. *Human Communication Research, 28*(3), 317–348.

Todorov, A., Chaiken, S., & Henderson, M. (2002). The heuristic-systematic model of social information processing. In J. P. Dillard, & M. Pfau (Eds.), *The persuasion handbook: Developments in theory and practice* (pp. 195–212). Thousand Oaks, CA: SAGE Publications Ltd.

Trager, G. L. (1958). *Paralanguage: A first approximation.* Buffalo, N.Y.: University of Buffalo, Department of Anthropology and Linguistics.

Trager, G. L. (1960). *Taos III: Paralanguage. (Anthropological linguistics.).* Bloomington, IN: Dept. of Anthropology, Indiana University.

Trager, G. L. (January 01, 1961). The typology of paralanguage. *Anthropological Linguistics, 3*(1), 17–21.

Tung, L. (September 26, 2016). *Ransomware now locks your smart TV–and then demands Apple iTunes gifts.* Reteived from http://www.zdnet.com/article/ransomware-now-locks-your-smart-tv-and-then-demand-apple-itunes-gifts/.

Tversky, A., & Kahneman, D. (1991). Loss aversion in riskless choice: a reference-dependent model. *Quarterly Journal of Economics, 106*(4), 1039–1061.

Übelacker, S., & Quiel, S. (2015). *The social engineering personality framework.* Hamburg-Harburg: Universita¨tsbibliothek der Technischen Universita¨t Hamburg-Harburg.

Van Der Heide, B., & Schumaker, E. (2013). Computer-mediated persuasion and compliance: Social influence on the internet and beyond. In Y. Amichai-Hamburger (Ed.), *The social net: Understanding our online behavior.* Oxford: Oxford University Press.

Vargas, D., & Vargas, S. (June 2016). *Ransomware - Is it really give up and pay up?* Presentation presented at the Techno Security Conference, Myrtle Beach, SC.

Walther, J. B. (1992). Interpersonal effects in computer-mediated interaction: A relational perspective. *Communication Research, 19*(1), 52–90.

Walther, J. B. (2006). Nonverbal dynamics in computer-mediated communication, or : (and the net : ('s with you, :) and you :) alone. In V. Manusov, & M. L. Patterson (Eds.), *Handbook of nonverbal communication* (pp. 461–479). Thousand Oaks, CA: Sage.

Walther, J. B. (2007). Selective self-presentation in computer-mediated communication: Hyperpersonal dimensions of technology, language, and cognition. *Computers in Human Behavior, 23,* 2538–2557.

Walther, J. B. (2011). Theories of computer-mediated communication and interpersonal relations. In M. L. Knapp, & J. A. Daly (Eds.), *The handbook of interpersonal communication* (4th ed.) (pp. 443–479). Thousand Oaks, CA: Sage.

Walther, J. B. (February 01, 1996). Computer-mediated communication: Impersonal, interpersonal, and hyperpersonal interaction. *Communication Research, 23*(1), 3–43.

Walther, J. B., & Burgoon, J. K. (1992). Relational communication in computer-mediated interaction. *Human Communication Research, 19,* 50–88.

Walther, J. B., & D'Addario, K. P. (2001). The impacts of emoticons on message interpretation in computer-mediated communication. *Social Science Computer Review, 19,* 323–345.

Walther, J. B., & Jang, J.-W. (2012). Communication processes in participatory web sites. *Journal of Computer-Mediated Communication, 18,* 2–15.

Walther, J. B., Loh, T., & Granka, L. (2005). Let me count the ways: The interchange of verbal and nonverbal cues in computer-mediated and face-to-face affinity. *Journal of Language and Social Psychology, 24,* 36–65.

Walther, J. B., & Parks, M. R. (2002). Cues filtered out, cues filtered in: Computer-mediated communication and relationships. In M. L. Knapp, & J. A. Daly (Eds.), *Handbook of interpersonal communication* (3rd ed.) (pp. 529–563). Thousand Oaks, CA: Sage.

Walther, J. B., & Tidwell, L. C. (1995). Nonverbal cues in computer-mediated communication, and the effect of chronemics on relational communication. *Journal of Organizational Computing, 5,* 355–378.

Westerman, D., Van, D. H. B., Klein, K. A., & Walther, J. B. (April 01, 2008). How do people really seek information about others? Information seeking across Internet and traditional communication channels. *Journal of Computer-Mediated Communication, 13*(3), 751–767.

Worchel, S., Lee, J., & Adewole, A. (1975). Effects of supply and demand on ratings of object value. *Journal of Personality and Social Psychology, 32*(5), 906–914.

Young, A., & Yung, M. (2004). *Malicious cryptography: Exposing cryptovirology.* Hoboken, NJ: John Wiley & Sons.

Zeltser, L. (2015). *Conversations with a tech support Scammer.* https://zeltser.com/tech-support-scammer-conversation/.

Zimbardo, P. G., & Leippe, M. R. (1991). *The psychology of attitude change and social influence.* London: McGraw-Hill.

4

Social Dynamics of Deception: Cyber Underground Markets and Cultures

ABSTRACT

Chapter Four delves deeply into human actors involved in underground cyber markets in order to better understand how they function and what social dynamics shape the behavior of users. In particular, this chapter focuses on markets where individuals sell cybercrime as a service, including malware, hacking services, Distributed Denial of Service (DDoS) attacks, and personal data. Through describing the structure and social ecosystem, the chapter provides insight into how actors deceive one another in order to gain competitive or economic advantage. Later, the chapter discusses trust dynamics and subcultural norms within underground cybercrime markets, particularly within the context of transactions. The chapter concludes by examining salient intercultural deception techniques among underground market interactants, such as virtual false flags, sock puppets, persuasive technology, and impersonation.

Keywords: *Cybercrime; Cybercrime culture; Cybercrime markets; Dark markets; Dark web; Illegal cyber services; Online social dynamics; Social dynamics; Sock puppeting; Trust in cybercrime underground markets; Underground markets.*

> The Internet permits, and thrives on, to some extent, deception and misdirection.
> —Joshua Dratel, defense attorney, Silk Road trial

The emergence of computer-mediated communications (CMCs) provides individuals with the ability to connect with virtually anyone anywhere and discuss issues of interest, no matter how legal, deviant, or outright illegal. There is substantial evidence that hackers, digital pirates, and others interested in technology flocked to message boards and BBS during the 1980s and early 90s to share information and files. The development of the World Wide Web (www) enhanced the experience of going online and established new forms of communication such as web forums, which borrowed from BBS and enhanced the experience by providing individuals with the ability to share photos and links to other content. As a result, other deviant and criminal groups began to emerge in online spaces, such as various sexual subcultures and individuals interested in hacking satellite television services (Mann & Sutton, 1998).

As the population of Internet users increased during the 1990s, so too did the range of services and resources to facilitate commerce and data sharing methods, which transformed opportunities to engage in fraud and theft. For instance, hackers began to use tools and statistical programs to randomly generate credit card numbers, which could then be checked to determine whether the number was active (Moore, 2012). If so, the card could be used to engage in fraudulent purchases. Similarly, hackers would capture the usernames and passwords of unsuspecting victims by posing as an ISP since Internet connectivity was paid by the hour during this period. Fraudsters would first harvest known email addresses, especially those associated with America Online, and then send out messages claiming that the account holder needed to validate or update some aspect of their user profile by sending in their username and password. Unsuspecting victims would provide this information to the sender, who would retain this information and trade or use the accounts in order to obtain free Internet access, or in some cases for access to pirated software or other information (Moore, 2012).

As information became further commoditized through the growth of e-retailers like Amazon.com and the rise of online banking, hackers and cybercriminals realized the profits that could be gained by attacking these resources directly. The development of botnet malware that could be leased out to others for spam and denial of service attacks further cemented the economic model of hacking as a service (e.g., James, 2005). As a consequence, there is now a robust online market where hackers, malware writers, and data thieves sell their services to others. There are a range of forums, websites, and content hosted on open parts of the Internet (see Holt & Bossler, 2016), as well as encrypted networks engaged in the sale of various products and services involving both virtual and real commodities (e.g., Martin, 2014). For instance, there are a number of forums and shops operating where hackers sell malicious software and cybercrime as a service to interested parties (e.g., Chu, Holt, & Ahn, 2010; Holt, 2013; Karami & McCoy, 2013; Li & Chen, 2014; Motoyama, McCoy, Levchenko, Savage, & Voelker, 2011; Provos, Mavrommatis, Rajab, & Monroe, 2008). These markets enable individuals to buy new forms of malicious software or lease existing infrastructure established through botnets and other malware platforms to engage in spamming, carding, and other forms of theft and fraud.

It is important to note that there are burgeoning markets for all manner of illegal services and products in virtual spaces that can only be used in the real world. For instance, sex workers and their customers use web forums and e-commerce sites as a means to advertise and review services and even pay for a session and validate client identities prior to a sexual assignation (e.g., Cunningham & Kendall, 2010; Holt & Blevins, 2007; Sanders, 2008). The use of technology enables some sex workers and customers to move away from street-based public advertising and work behind closed doors with much less risk of detection and arrest in the United States (Cunningham & Kendall, 2010; Holt, Blevins, & Kuhns, 2014; Quinn & Forsyth, 2013).

The sale of illicit drugs, ranging from prescription medications to hard drugs like cocaine, has also begun to transition into online markets, most of which are operating on the encrypted Tor network, which uses specialized software and protocols that allow individuals to create and host content on servers that encrypt and anonymize the location of the site, and associated information of users (Martin, 2014). The emergence of markets on Tor have led some to refer to them as cryptomarkets, because of their use of anonymization and encryption (Franklin, 2013; Martin, 2014). In addition, participants in these markets are encouraged to accept payment for products through online systems called cryptocurrencies, meaning that the transaction is delivered through various encryption protocols that conceal the identity of the payer and the payee (Franklin, 2013; Martin, 2014).

The emergence and expansion of underground online economies demonstrates how effective the Internet can be as a tool for criminality. The ability to connect anonymously to others in online spaces shields participants' identities, yet the clear-text communications between participants provide a platform for social engagement and economic exchanges. Thus the nature of underground markets is still inherently social and driven by exchanges between human actors. This presents opportunities for deception between participants in order to manipulate exchanges and for external parties to use deceptive techniques to disrupt their practices.

Evolution of the Underground: *Silk Road*

Since 2011, there has been substantial growth in online markets advertising the purchase of illicit drugs through various mechanisms internationally. Individuals advertise their products in sites operating on the encrypted Tor network, which helps to anonymize individual identities and reduces the likelihood of identification by law enforcement. One of the most recognizable of these markets was the Silk Road, which began operation in 2011 and quickly drew attention from law enforcement and the media (Franklin, 2013; Martin, 2014). The site was created to enable individuals to buy various materials ranging from computer equipment to clothing, though sellers offered various narcotics and paraphernalia to manufacture and distribute drugs. Since it opened in 2011 the Silk Road enabled over one million transactions worth an estimated $1.2 billion in revenue (Barratt, 2012). Law enforcement agencies in both the United States and Australia soon began undercover operations against buyers in the market, leading to the eventual arrest of the site administrator in 2013 and the dismantling of the market (Gibbs, 2013). A number of other markets soon emerged to take its place, including a second and third version of the original Silk Road operated by different actors (Dolliver, 2015).

The emergence of the Silk Road demonstrates that cyberspace will increasingly be used by real-world criminal actors to facilitate offending. The distributed nature of the Internet and the ability to hide one's identity and flow of money makes it an ideal environment for illicit economies of all stripes. Research on virtual drug markets is in its infancy, with the few published studies utilizing samples of ads from the market to assess the scope of the economy and products offered (Dolliver, 2015; Martin, 2014; Phelps & Watt, 2014). Such information is helpful to demonstrate trends in services offered and variations in user behavior as markets expand and close.

There is a need for additional study moving beyond the scope of the market to consider how and why these markets flourish, and the extent to which they actually impact the behavior of buyers and sellers. An initial study has attempted to address this issue using survey data collected from an international sample. Barratt, Ferris, and Winstock (2014) found that 35% of a sample of 9470 drug using respondents in Australia, the United Kingdom, and the United States had consumed drugs purchased from the Silk Road. A much larger proportion of respondents had heard of the market but had yet to use products from its vendors. Of those who had made a purchase through the Silk Road, the majority had purchased MDMA or cannabis and indicated that they felt the market had a better range of products with better quality and that it was easier to access and determine legitimate sellers (Barratt et al., 2014). Additionally, respondents in Australia and the United States were statistically more likely to purchase products through the Silk Road because of lower prices and fear of being caught.

This chapter examines the human actors involved in underground markets in order to better understand how they function and what social dynamics shape the behavior of users. We will focus our attention on markets where individuals sell cybercrime as a service, including malicious software, hacking services, Distributed Denial of Service (DDoS), and personal data, as these have the greatest salience for cybersecurity professionals. By understanding their structure and social ecosystem, we can understand how actors deceive one another in order to gain competitive or economic advantage. This information can also be used to disrupt their practices and affect the activities of buyers and sellers within the market.

Social Dynamics in Computer-Mediated Communications

Social dynamics, or "unwritten rules for interacting with others" (Fogg, 2003) in face-to-face transactions can be impacted by language, gender, facial expressions, and many other interpersonal engagement elements (Liebman & Gergle, 2016). With the advent of CMCs, many of the traditional factors that affect these dynamics no longer existed, or they manifested in alternative modalities and contexts. Early CMC consisted primarily of textual channels of communications, such as Internet Relay Chat (IRC), bulletin board systems, and text-based instant messaging. Gradually, over time and user experience, factors such as *chronemic cues* that capture temporal aspects of messages and *paralinguistic cues,* such as emoticons and creative or expressive use of word spellings, have supplanted traditional social and behavioral cues and built new, evolving norms and social dynamics (Liebman & Gergle, 2016).

As digital communication channels, modalities, and content richness burgeoned, so too did new ways for users to engage, interact, and develop social behaviors. Emotions, expressions, cues (such as indicators of deception or veracity) became more discernible and interpretable. This evolution, in turn, changed the complexion of social dynamics in groups and interactions online; it also changed the perceptions of how computing technology in and of itself could convey social presence and influence users viewing and engaging content (Fogg, 2003).

The Process of Buying and Selling

To understand cybercrime markets, we must first consider how individuals come to engage in it as either a buyer or seller. The current crop of underground markets operates primarily through forums and IRC channels, creating an interconnected marketplace

Vendmaster: Selling CCV: German/ Italy/ USA/ UK/ Netherlands/

Greetings,

Selling CCV: Germany, Italy, USA, UK, Netherlands

German cc [credit card]: 15USD

Italy CC: 15USD

USA CC: 6USD

UK Without DOB [Cardholder's Date Of Birth]: 14USD

UK with DOB: 30USD

Netherlands: 15USD

Note: We sell all unused/Untouch cc to our Customers! to ensure Quality we sell each cc to each person! And we fully Replace cc in 48 Hours of Delivery TIME

We Accept CC orders only by WU at the moment!

Min order: 350usd

for Orders please e-mail me or add me in your messenger either you can pm

> We are the trusted sellers of the PayPal accounts. You'll find lots of USA/UK:
> Unverified + Credit Cards (confirmed) - 1 WMZ/LR
> Unverified + Bank Acc (confirmed) – 1 WMZ/LR
> Verified + Credit Cards (confirmed) + Bank accounts (confirmed) – 3 WMZ/LR
>
> Here are some of the rules of the service:
>
> Seller is not responsible for sm (security measures); we check all the accounts manually prior [to] giving them to you. You'll also get a clean socks5 [proxy connection to access the account online]
>
> Seller is not responsible for the unsuccessfull [SIC] usage of the account.
> We may exchange your account in case the password won't match. Please inform us promptly!
>
> Please provide us with the screenshot in all the weird situations...
> You're free to do whatever you want to do with the account that you've bought. We take no responsibility on your further actions.
>
> Provision of services for the identification of electronic payment systems and preparation of ATM cards for drops [RU].

FIGURE 4.1 Carding market advertisement.

WM [WebMoney] registration process:
We provide you with a photocopy of the passport. Using this information you register a new WMID [WebMoney Identification Number]. You receive a formal certificate under the data of the photocopied passport, you pay for the application to receive a personal certificate. You give us the data of the newly registered WMID used during registration. We write this data into the application and send them to the Certification Center. After a while you receive the personal certification for this WMID.

ONLY you will have access to this WMID, and no one else.

Terms of service:
- We have the right to refuse to work after accepting payment in case of force majeure circumstances. If we refuse, we will return the money which we have received within a 2-day time period, after advising of the refusal. Take into account that we mean 2 BUSINESS days.

- The use of accounts (atm cards) means encashment of funds, and not their storage. It is prohibited to store money.

- Pouring dirt [placing illegally acquired funds on cards] from CIS countries [Commonwealth of Independent States, or the Russian Commonwealth] into accounts (atm cards and payment systems) is STRICTLY FORBIDDEN! If such cases are discovered, the account will immediately be blocked, no payments will be made, and the account owner will be listed as a black.

- You must understand that... the card is not yours, it belongs to another person and at any moment he [the victim] can block it. Our task is not to allow this, and up to now we have done this well.
- Our service is not liable if your account is closed by the payment system for fraud and various fraudulent actions.

FIGURE 4.1 Continued.

where sellers advertise products openly for others to buy or alternatively describe the products they are seeking from other vendors (see Chu et al., 2010; Holt, 2013; Holt & Lampke, 2010; Motoyama et al., 2011). The process begins when sellers create threads that can be accessed by the forum population, post a description of their products or tools as possible, and include the costs and preferred payment mechanisms and their contact information. In so-called carding markets, sellers commonly offer credit card and debit card accounts and supporting customer information from around the world in bulk lots (Holt & Lampke, 2010; Holt, Smirnova, Chua, & Copes, 2015; Hutchings & Holt, 2015; Franklin, Paxson, Perrig, & Savage, 2007; Motoyama et al., 2011) (Fig. 4.1). Malware vendors sell builds of executables and explain their functionality in detail, while others lease out access to existing botnets in order to engage in DDoS or phishing attacks (Fig. 4.2).

> **Lease of bot networks!**, $100 a month (volume 6.9k online from 300 [nodes])
>
> **I'm leasing the admin console of a bot network!**
>
> - there are ~9,000 bots in the network (200-1,500 online regularly)
>
> - Countries: **RU,US,TR,UE,KI,TH,RO,CZ,IN,SK,UA**(upon request countries can be added!)
>
> - OS: **winXP/NT**
>
> functionality:
>
> [+] list of bot socks
>
> type:
>
> **ip:port** time (when it appeared the last time) Country|City
>
> [+] loading of files on the bot machines (trojans/grabbers...)
>
> [+] executing shell commands using bots
>
> [+] Generates lists (**ip:port**) online socks in a **txt** file
>
> ps admin console quite simple, convenient and functional, even a school kid can figure it out.
>
> Today 1,000 more (mix) bots were added with good speed indicators + every 3,4 days 2k fresh machines are added (the person who works with the reports receives a unique service with unique and constantly new machines)
>
> Super price**100wmz [Web Money in US currency]** a month!
>
> all questions to **icq:** [number removed]
>
> Spammers are in shock over such an offer (:
>
> ps: we also make networks for individual **requests/orders**

FIGURE 4.2 Malware vendor advertisement.

Some also offer "cash out" services to obtain physical money from electronic accounts by hijacking these accounts to engage in electronic funds transfers established by a hacker (Holt & Lampke, 2010; Franklin et al., 2007; Motoyama et al., 2011; Thomas & Martin, 2006, pp. 7–17). Others offer "drops services," whereby individuals purchase electronics and other goods electronically using stolen cards, have them shipped to intermediaries who pawn the items, and then wire the cash to interested parties (Holt & Lampke, 2010). A limited number of sellers also offer spam lists and malicious software tools that can be used to engage in fraud (Holt & Lampke, 2010).

Sellers must also indicate how they would like to be paid, with the majority accepting some form of online currency (Fig. 4.3). Historically, this has included e-Gold, Liberty Reserve, WebMoney, and Yandex, though some may also accept PayPal or other payment systems (Franklin et al., 2007; Holt & Lampke, 2010; Hutchings & Holt, 2015; Motoyama et al., 2011). Some sellers also accept real-world payments through MoneyGram or Western Union, since these are well-established services for the domestic or international transfer of hard currency (Holt & Lampke, 2010; Motoyama et al., 2011). The preference for electronic payment systems is thought to stem from the fact that they enable immediate transfer of funds between buyers and sellers with some degree of protection for the identities of both participants. Online payments present a disadvantage to buyers within the market, as there is the potential that sellers may not deliver the product or service for which the buyer paid. There is some risk that sellers may either send information or services of generally poor quality, or nothing at all (e.g., Herley & Florencio, 2010). As a result, buyers have to carefully consider whom they engage as service providers and in what quantity so as to minimize their risk of loss.

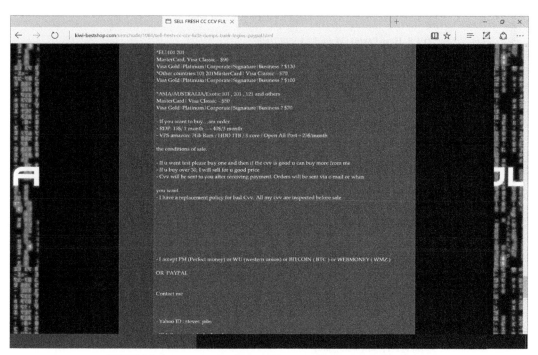

FIGURE 4.3 Payment methods posted in an underground carding forum.

From there, prospective buyers review seller advertisements and make contact with that party outside of the forum or IRC channel in order to negotiate prices and complete the transaction. These exchanges typically occur via ICQ or email, or in some cases via private messages within the forum, in order to help minimize their culpability or overt involvement in criminal exchanges (Franklin et al., 2007; Holt & Lampke, 2010; Motoyama et al., 2011) (see Fig. 4.4 for an example of private communications between buyer and seller).

[/b]DILS_Host-Portal (21:05:45 15/08/2009)

Hi!\

Prof (21:05:59 15/08/2009)

hey

DILS_Host-Portal (21:06:07 15/08/2009)

I have a question for you

DILS_Host-Portal (21:06:22 15/08/2009)

I bought a ded from you

Prof (21:06:31 15/08/2009)

well

DILS_Host-Portal (21:06:34 15/08/2009)

it hasn't been working for weeks now what should I do

DILS_Host-Portal (21:06:52 15/08/2009)

I haven't been able to do anything it

Prof (21:06:57 15/08/2009)

if a week already - then I think nothing

DILS_Host-Portal (21:06:57 15/08/2009)

even download

DILS_Host-Portal (21:07:22 15/08/2009)

maybe you can give another ded ?

DILS_Host-Portal (21:07:45 15/08/2009)

because I just can't use it

Prof (21:11:31 15/08/2009)

well alas, the guarantee is only 5 days, and what you did there or didn't do there I

have no way of checking

Prof (21:11:34 15/08/2009)

is that logical?

DILS_Host-Portal (21:12:17 15/08/2009)

ok tks [thanks]

[b]

FIGURE 4.4 Private purchase dispute communication between buyer and seller.

After negotiations are completed, it has been consistently observed that sellers require prospective buyers to send payment, and upon confirmation of funds, they will deliver information or services (Franklin et al., 2007; Herley & Florencio, 2010; Holt & Lampke, 2010; Motoyama et al., 2011; Wehinger, 2011). This structure favors sellers since they have the desired commodities and can set the terms as to when and how they will be received. Because of this, there are a number of predatory vendors whose sole purpose in underground markets is to swindle buyers into providing funds upfront for bogus or nonexistent information or services. These actors are colloquially known as *rippers, donkeys,* or *cheats,* recognizing that they "rip off'" customers by accepting payments but providing inactive malware or data, or by simply not providing anything in return (Herley & Florencio, 2010; Holt & Lampke, 2010; Motoyama et al., 2011; Wehinger, 2011) (see Fig. 4.5, displaying a defrauded buyer complaining about being scammed by a "ripper" and Fig. 4.6, capturing an Internet posting in an underground forum that provided others guidance on how to spot a "ripper").

> I have been ripped off three times, so bad and I don't have any money left right now. what should I do? one of scammer named [removed] i was trust him, i bought 3 cvv from EU for test him, he did give to me, the second time, I ordered wu transfer. He never give to me, just took my money away.

I have been ripped off three times, so bad and I don't have any money left right now.

what should I do? one of scammer named [removed] i was trust him, i bought 3 cvv from EU for test him, he did give to me, the second time, I ordered wu transfer. he never give

to me, just took my money away.

FIGURE 4.5 Ripping complaint.

After a transaction has been completed, buyers in forums are encouraged to post feedback about their experience with sellers to help vet seller reputations and establish their credibility (e.g., Holt & Lampke, 2010; Holt, Smirnova, & Chua, 2016). The moderators and operators of forums promote the use of public acknowledgment of seller practices to demonstrate whether a seller is trustworthy or reliable. Those who are not can be outed to the

- ripper wants to receive the money as fast as possible and he doesn't care of the final

[outcome] of deal; so the first main sign of ripper – desiring to receive the money fast, he

thinks out a lot of reasons for this – pregnant wife, blocked keeper, drop's worrying etc

- ripper wants to be shown as well-knowing guy so he uses a lot of terms and specific

words;

-nickname; often greed and fieriness [fireiness] can be read in ripper's nick which are

changing like a gloves, so asa [SIC] we see Ecspress, Fast, Easy etc and almos[t] with the

words "money", "cash" etc we should be careful already and begin to verify this person.

- Number of posts – potential ripper usually has too little posts for his registration date or

too much posts –tries to make it's number more. It's also recommended to read what the

person posts about on forums and make conclusion about his mind, if there are stupid

posts or posts without any meanings – make conclusion yourself.

- A lot of rippers usually post at the and [end] of there [SIC] posts "escrow accepted".

But when you talk that you want to work through escrow he usually finds lots of reasons

don't work through it.

Conclusion: none of these things can tell you that this guy is ripper. But in combination it

gets you the information about him and it's better don't deal with such guy.

FIGURE 4.6 An Internet post on an underground forum providing guidance on how to detect rippers.

larger community, while legitimate vendors can establish a greater proportion of market share (Motoyama et al., 2011). In this respect, feedback serves as an informal dispute resolution mechanism that can provide market participants with prospective information on seller practices (Holt & Lampke, 2010; Wehinger, 2011) (Fig. 4.7).

Killz: I withdrew cash everything was okay
Cypher: Everything was excellent and online.
Iglio: I worked with this person everything was ok
Horvath: I laundered wm without any problems. Everything was good.
Nash: This is not the first time that I have worked with the TS, everything was tiptop!
Nod31: I use the services... twice and everything was precise and the payment was on time according to the contract.. service +1

FIGURE 4.7 Example of underground interactants providing feedback about an escrow service.

Feedback is also essential because it can be challenging for prospective buyers to determine the legitimacy of a seller on the basis of the language provided in an advertisement. Sellers frequently use terminology indicating they will support customers before, during, and after a transaction, such as through real-time customer support on instant messaging clients like ICQ (Franklin et al., 2007; Holt & Lampke, 2010; Wehinger, 2011). Some data sellers and DDoS providers may also offer "free tests" or "samples" of their data to demonstrate the quality of their goods or service (Dhanjani & Rios, 2008; Franklin et al., 2007; Holz, Engelberth, & Freiling, 2009). This has particular relevance in stolen data markets, as vendors may provide the details of a victim's credit or debit card account so that others can observe the level of detail present in their data and use it as a potential test case. Some vendors may even offer one or two "free test" cards to buyers to that they know the seller can be trusted.

Trust Inducing Mechanisms

Some forums also provide formal mechanisms that give buyers and sellers ways to minimize risk and increase trust between actors (Holt, 2013; Holt & Lampke, 2010; Wehinger, 2011). For example, well-organized forums offer escrow services, where a trusted party has been designated by forum administrators to act as an intermediary in financial transactions. If both parties can accept the use of an escrow service, the escrow agent will hold payments on behalf of a seller until the buyer confirms they have received the service or good ordered (Holt, 2013; Holt & Lampke, 2010; Wehinger, 2011). Escrow services add complexity to transactions but also allow buyers to establish trust in a seller and give sellers a venue to demonstrate their advertising claims are valid (Wehinger, 2011) (see Fig. 4.8 for an example of instructions provided by an underground escrow service).

Escrow service

Escrow only insures money at time (fixed time) transactions.
All terms of deal negotiated between the parties. Escrow they spend is not necessary.
Escrow doesn't check goods or services.
The principle of insurance transactions:
1. Buyer pays Indemnitor amount of transaction and fees for escrow service. Reports icq number for which this sum is intended.
P.S. Under arrangement escrow fee may pay any member of transaction.
2. Escrow confirms receipt of money to another party.
3. The seller (service) provides direct product (or service) to another party to transaction without participation of Escrow.
4. After receipt and verification of goods (providing services) buyer contacts the Escrow and to announce completion of transaction.
5. Escrow pays money to seller (service).
Escrow service fee:
>500$ - 8%
<500$ - 6%
3000$ and more- 5%

FIGURE 4.8 Escrow service use.

In addition, administrators in both IRC channels and forums may ban sellers who scam or "rip off" customers by taking payments without delivering a product (Holt & Lampke, 2010; Holt et al., 2015; Motoyama et al., 2011; Wehinger, 2011). Forums with more robust administrative oversight may also ban individuals for posting feedback regarding a seller if they have less than 10 posts, due to the potential that the information is falsified and posted to suggest a seller is trustworthy (Holt et al., 2015). Such bans are time-consuming on the part of the administration and may only be present in well-organized and efficiently run markets.

Subcultural Norms and the Role of Trust

The forums that support the market for cybercrime-as-a-service and stolen data are a unique and interactive community driven by economic exchanges between buyers and sellers. The behavior of participants is, however, structured by individual need and the desire to minimize risks. As a result, several studies have found that market actors place value on the price of products and customer service offered by vendors. These two factors directly affect the level of trust actors may place in one another.

The advertised price for goods and services play an important role in the vetting of goods and services within stolen data and cybercrime markets. Buyers seek the greatest value for their initial investment and desire to cause harm or make money from their transaction (Holt, 2013; Holt & Lampke, 2010; Motoyama et al., 2011). Individuals selling services or malware builds are often subject to scrutiny based on the price for a product. If it was thought to be too high or low relative to the prevailing market price, buyers would question the legitimacy of the seller (e.g., Holt, 2013).

Due to the emphasis placed on price, some vendors offer discounts and short-term deals to attract customers. Bulk discounts can be commonly observed in order to draw customers in and maximize their purchase. Botnet operators selling DDoS attacks frequently decreased the price for long term attacks, as noted in this quote from a service provider: "When ordering the DDoS service for 3–6 days, discount is 10%, with a DDoS service of more than 7 days, discount is 20%, and with a DDoS service for 3 sites, gives a free service for the 4th site." Similar offers can be observed among data sellers, who frequently sell large lots of card information that may be either nearing expiration dates at massively discounted prices to draw in buyers. As a result, the price for goods and services in markets may vary, but there is an emphasis on larger purchase sizes to attract customers (Holt, 2013; Holt & Lampke, 2010).

The second and interrelated factor affecting market relationships is the extent to which buyers and sellers can communicate and effectively use the good or service purchased, which hinges on customer service. The growth of cybercrime and data markets enables individuals with virtually no technological skill to engage in sophisticated attacks and criminal activity that was not previously possible. As a result, vendors who clearly recognize the continuum of actors who may utilize their services and cater to each group may be more likely to gain a larger share of the market (Holt, 2013; Motoyama et al., 2011).

One of the most pertinent factors associated with customer service is the speed of communications between sellers and buyers. Data as a commodity has a short life span before it may be rendered inactive by a financial institution, making it essential that sellers move product quickly to buyers to use and monetize. As a result, sellers who are regularly online, respond quickly to requests, and answer questions are more likely to generate positive reviews and feedback from customers (Holt, 2013). Long delays in replies to buyers frequently lead to public complaints on forums about slow responses or the need for the seller to "knock them" on ICQ. The actual quality of the product or service sellers offered also plays a role in their perception and status within the market. Individuals who offer ineffective tools or inactive data receive negative feedback from buyers within forums as they have no other mechanisms to pursue civil or criminal claims against the vendor.

The intersection of pricing and customer service have led some to question whether the advertised price for data may be an important indication of seller reputation and their potential to offer valid products. Two researchers, Herley and Florencio (2010), argue that the price for data and services within any market is an indication of the legitimacy of its participants. Vendors who publicly post account data for others to see at no charge as a way to validate the quality of their data, or offer one or two cards to buyers as "free samples" may not be legitimate. If vendors are operating a business, then they lose money by distributing data at no charge. Such practices cannot be supported over the long-term, as it would minimize the overall profits of sellers. In much the same way, sellers who offer data at dramatically discounted prices may be rippers attempting to entice unskilled or new buyers to purchase their data. The individuals who buy this information may not receive any data at all or may be given invalid cards that have no actual value.

In light of these risks, Herley and Florencio (2010) argue that the market for stolen data constitutes a "lemon market" as there are generally few resources available to buyers to differentiate the quality of information. Thus buyers may opt to purchase data from sellers with the lowest priced information first. This creates a robust market for vendors who seek to cheat unsuspecting buyers, while costing buyers more over the long-term to finally acquire useful information. Quality sellers would likely be driven out of these markets due to the perceived lack of trust between market actors, limiting the market to only those with access to bad data (Herley & Florencio, 2010).

As a result, these conditions create a two-tiered market for data with a low tier consisting of rippers and a high tier populated by vendors and buyers who trust one another and find ways to minimize the risk of loss in the event of faulty products or services. In the high-tier market, the advertised price for data and services may be higher but will likely work upon receipt and allow the buyer to monetize the data through fraud and theft (see Herley & Florencio, 2010; Holt et al., 2015).

No Honor Among Cyber Thieves: Deception Within Underground Markets

While cyber underground markets aim to monetize illicit products and services, often using deception to swindle would-be consumers, deception is also employed between groups and interactants who comprise the communities and social fabric of the cyber underground market culture. The scale and scope of these stratagems range from basic and opportunistic to nuanced and protracted denial and deception campaigns. Indeed, elements of traditional strategic denial and deception (D&D)[1] has been adopted and successfully implemented across the cyber sphere (see text-box *Cyber Stratagems: Cyber Denial and Deception*). While richer strategies are often observed in nation state cyber attacks as an element of cyber warfare,[2] permutations manifesting in underground markets as groups and interactants manipulate environments and personas and hide behind virtual false flags. As underground markets continue to flourish and competition escalates, groups seek to gain market primacy, eliminate competition, or cause dissention among rival groups or individuals. In this section, some of the salient intercultural deception techniques used within underground markets are examined.

Virtual False Flags

Throughout history, attackers have developed shrewd methods of lulling victims into comfort, deceiving them with deceptive visual cues and, at times, props to misrepresent their identify or affiliation. One of the most effective deception and inculpation misdirection techniques is a *false flag operation*, using artifices to disguise one's true country or group affiliation by deceptively claiming association or origin from another country or group. This technique has been used in numerous manners and means over history, whether by pirate ships seeking to gain access to unsuspecting victim vessels (Konstam, 2006) or in military strategies to overcome and surprise the adversary.[3]

Cyber attackers have adopted this tradecraft, intentionally implanting artifacts of false affiliation in malicious code, test files, and other extrinsic evidence in an effort to mislead victims, researchers, analysts, law enforcement, and rival organizations alike (Geers, Kindlund, Moran, & Rachwald, 2013). A critical result of the virtual false flag is plausible deniability by the true

---

[1] *Denial and Deception*, or D&D, is a term used particularly in military and intelligence operation contexts to describe information operation efforts by one party, typically a nation, to block information that could be used by an opponent to learn a truth and to cause the adversary to believe something that is not true. Godson, R., & Wirtz, J. J. (2002). *Strategic denial and deception: The twenty-first century challenge.* New Brunswick, N.J: Transaction Publishers.

[2] See, Weedon, J. (2015). Beyond 'Cyber War': Russia's use of strategic cyber espionage and information operations in Ukraine. In Kenneth Geers (Ed.), *Cyber war in perspective: Russian aggression against Ukraine.* Tallinn: NATO CCD COE Publications (Chapter 8); Ottis, R. (June 30, 2008–July 1, 2008). Analysis of the 2007 cyber attacks against estonia from the information warfare perspective. In Dan Remenyi (Ed.), *Proceedings of the 7th European Conference on Information Warfare and Security.* University of Plymouth, UK.

[3] Ryan, D., and Ryan, J. (March 2012). Attribution: Accountability in cyber incidents. In Volodymyr Lysenko (Ed.), *Proceedings of the 7th International Conference on Information Warfare and Security.* University of Washington, Seattle (referencing the Gleiwitz Incident of 1939, a false flag maneuver leading up to World War II, wherein the German SS dressed as Polish rebels during the attack at the Gleiwitz radio compound and bodies of several murdered concentration camp inmates were dressed as Polish rebels and left at the Customs house; the attacks were falsely reported as Polish aggression).

attackers and misattribution to unrelated/uninvolved attackers.[4] These consequences, particularly among groups and interactants in an online microsphere such as underground markets, are retributive attacks against falsely identified and inculpated parties.

Sock Puppets

The Internet has become the most popular resource of information[5] for news, personal health,[6] self-development, "how-to" tutorials, consumer product reviews, and endless other topics. As a result, online-based feedback, reviews, and opinions are incredibly salient among Internet users. As discussed in Chapter 3, persuasion through *social proof* (or consensus) is a powerful and real online factor. When an individual is interested in a product, he or she will likely read or peruse associated product reviews; these reviews are often relied upon and can sway consumers toward a purchase.[7] This certitude and credibility has caused unscrupulous and nefarious users alike to leverage this power of influence, namely through *sock puppeting*, or people posting/using accounts under pseudonyms instead of their real names (Gilmore, 2010). In the context of online reviews, sock puppets can be used by a deceptive individual by creating a fictitious account and writing a review that he/she has a vested, proprietary interest in, or perhaps more sinisterly, writing a negative review for a competitor.

Online reviews are not the only manner that a sock puppet account can be effectively implemented. Sock puppeting has been used in a multitude of other contexts online, whether as an extension of a nation state's online influence efforts,[8] personal attacks on other users,[9] political attacks,[10] attacks on business competition, or journalists writing

---

[4] See, http://www.nytimes.com/2012/10/24/business/global/cyberattack-on-saudi-oil-firm-disquiets-us. html?_r=0; *Cyber-security expert warns of 'False Flag' digital attacks*, http://www.forbes.com/sites/jasperhamill/2014/07/31/cyber-security-expert-warns-of-false-flag-digital-attacks/#5deadcd12bb0; *Apt attacks and False Flag tactics: How can we spot the fakes?*, http://www.blob.cymmertria. com/2016/03/23/false-flag-tactics-apt; *The mask is off: Cyber spy operation uncovered after 7 years*, http://mashable.com/2014/02/10/kaspersky-lab-the-mask-careto/; *Attackers engage in 'False Flag' attack manipulation*, http://www.darkreading.com/attacks-breaches/attackers-engage-in-false-flag-attack-manipulation/d/d-id/1138447; *APT attackers flying more False Flags than ever*, https://threatpost.com/apt-attackers-flying-more-false-flags-than-ever/116814/.

[5] *Internet most popular information source: Poll*, http://www.reuters.com/article/us-media-internet-life-idUSTRE55G4XA20090618.

[6] Lemire, M., et al. (2008) Determinants of internet use as a preferred source of information on personal health. *International Journal of Medical Informatics, 77*(11), 723–734.

[7] *How word of mouth, the Internet and online consumer reviews influence purchase*, http://www.experian.com/blogs/marketing-forward/2011/03/16/how-word-of-mouth-the-internet-and-online-consumer-reviews-influence-purchase-decisions/.

[8] *China uses an army of sockpuppets to control public opinion – and the US will too*, http://guardianlv.com/2013/11/china-uses-an-army-of-sockpuppets-to-control-public-opinion-and-the-us-will-too/.

[9] *'Cyber bully' fraud charges filed in L.A. Woman is accused of creating a MySpace persona whose comments may be linked to girl's suicide*, http://articles.latimes.com/2008/may/16/local/me-myspace16.

[10] *The hand that controls the sock puppet could get slapped*, http://www.nytimes.com/2007/07/16/technology/16blog.html?_r=0, describing the sock puppet attacks conducted by Tad Furtado, (a now former policy director for a state representative); John Mackey (chief executive of Whole Foods Market), among others.

blog entries.[11] Threat actors in underground markets have also similarly leveraged the strategic advantages of deception, distancing, and plausible deniability through sock puppet accounts to increase perceived credibility, attack competition, and falsely inflate value and user feedback.

Persuasive Technology

As digital communication channels, modalities and content richness have evolved and burgeoned, computing technology and online media itself can convey social presence and influence users viewing and engaging the content (Fogg, 2003). These same types of persuasive technologies and content are leveraged by opportunistic and nefarious threat actors in underground markets. Online platforms and content display for users certain engagement-inducing elements, such as pop-ups and dialogue boxes, to influence and cause these interactants to make choices–choices that can be expertly engineered for pecuniary or strategic advantage to the threat actors—to the detriment of the interactants.

Online platforms and environments can also convey *credibility*, or a user's subjective perception of the believability of the provided technical or online content. As discussed in Chapter 3, in the realm of influence psychology, factors that support credibility are *expertise* and *trustworthiness*; however, these criteria are not always fully captured in a computing experience. In 2003, Professor B.J. Fogg developed a taxonomy of credibility that could be more meaningfully applied toward computing-based experience; it included four types of credibility: *Presumed* (general assumptions in the mind of the perceiver); *Surface* (simple inspection or initial firsthand experience); *Reputed* (third-party endorsements, reports, or referrals); and *Earned* (firsthand experience that extends over time) (Fogg, 2003).

Groups and individuals participating in underground markets have the ability to craft and adapt their respective online presence and content to influence and ultimately deceive other participants in the market, whether for primacy in the marketplace, financial gain, or to attack competitors. Similarly, technologies and content can be engineered to deceptively convey surface and reputed credibility. In totality, cyber underground markets are an ideal environment for threat actors to leverage persuasive technology since the market is set solely within an online technology realm.

Impersonation

Impersonation, or assuming a false identity with the intent to deceive or defraud another, has perhaps the broadest application across not only online world, but in the physical world. For decades, criminals have used impersonation to appear as public figures,[12] law

---

[11] *Los Angeles times yanks columnist's blog*, http://www.washingtonpost.com/wp-dyn/content/article/2006/04/20/AR2006042002375.html.

[12] See, *18-year-old charged for impersonating Ohio senator*, http://www.foxnews.com/us/2016/02/21/18-year-old-charged-for-impersonating-ohio-senator.html; *California woman indicted for allegedly impersonating a congressional aide*, https://www.justice.gov/opa/pr/california-woman-indicted-allegedly-impersonating-congressional-aide.

enforcement officials,[13] or simply others whose identity would allow the offender to gain through the use of the deceptive identity.[14] While impersonation can be used to defraud for financial gain, it is a broader, more mercurial use of false identity that can be effective for a number of deception schemes with no financial gain intended.

Problematic implications and damage caused by impersonating another has been recognized by State and Federal lawmakers, resulting in codification of statutes criminalizing impersonation in certain circumstances.[15] This has not deterred online offenders from exploiting the power of impersonation schemes; permutations of this type of deception have been effectively leveraged in CMCs with varying degrees of scale, scope, and purpose.

There are five main reasons or purposes that online impersonation is used by cyber criminals. First, it can be used to claim credit for something that is high profile, glamorous, gives the appearance of importance/credibility, or simply for a reason personal to the offender. Secondly, if used to impersonate a member of a group to deceive other group members, it is a very divisive way to initiate controversy, confusion, discord, and possibly even dissention among group members. Thirdly, it can be insidiously implemented on a large, public scale to cause reputational damage[16] (Fig. 4.9). Further, impersonation can be sinisterly and effectively used to falsely implicate and inculpate others, or "frame" the impersonated victim for an activity that he/she never truly engaged in.[17] And lastly, impersonation is an effective way to stage a persona and mislead researchers, law enforcement, and others who may be investigating an incident or individual as to the true nature, circumstances, and evidence sources in a case.

---

[13] See, *Woman indicted for impersonating FBI Agent in connection with lottery fraud scheme based in Jamaica*, https://www.justice.gov/opa/pr/woman-indicted-impersonating-fbi-agent-connection-lottery-fraud-scheme-based-jamaica; *Man arrested at Think Bank for impersonating a federal agent*, http://www.kttc.com/story/13018096/man-arrested-at-think-bank-for-impersonating-a-federal-agent.

[14] See, *Man arrested for impersonating a Soldier on Veterans day*, http://www.popularmilitary.com/man-arrested-impersonating-soldier-veterans-day/; *Warrant issued for man accused of impersonating bank customer in Derry Township*, http://fox43.com/2014/10/23/warrant-issued-for-man-accused-of-impersonating-bank-customer-in-derry-township/.

[15] 18 US Code Chapter 43 (False Personation) contains seven different statutory provisions (§911–§917) addressing impersonation. Similarly, states (e.g., New York State Penal Law, § 190.23 False personation; § 190.25 Criminal impersonation in the second degree; §190.26 Criminal impersonation in the first degree) and the Uniform Code of Military Justice (Article 134- Impersonating a commissioned, warrant, noncommissioned, or petty officer, or an agent or official) have statutes specifically for impersonation crimes.

[16] In 2012, Shell Oil obtained an injunctive court order prohibiting Greenpeace from protesting near its Arctic drilling expedition; as a result the environmental group used a clever cyber influence tactic, impersonating Shell. http://www.alaskapublic.org/2012/07/24/greenpeace-impersonates-shell-to-protest-arctic-drilling/; See also, *Congressman Steny Hoyer Twitter impersonation attack*, http://www.zdnet.com/article/congressman-steny-hoyer-twitter-impersonation-attack/; http://www.huffingtonpost.com/2012/07/18/shell-arctic-ready-hoax-greenpeace_n_1684222.html. See Also, van den Hurk, A.M. (2013), *Social media crisis communications: Preparing for, preventing, and surviving a public relations #FAIL*, Que Publishing.

[17] In 2015, Sergey Vovnenko, a Ukrainian cyber attacker, attempted to falsely inculpate, or "frame," information security journalist Brian Krebs by sending heroin to his house. See, http://krebsonsecurity.com/2015/10/hacker-who-sent-me-heroin-faces-charges-in-u-s/; https://nakedsecurity.sophos.com/2016/01/26/hacker-who-sent-heroin-to-brian-krebs-pleads-guilty/.

FIGURE 4.9 The 2012 impersonation of Shell Oil via the website arcticready.com.

 Online Stratagems: *Cyber Denial and Deception*

All warfare is based on deception. Hence, when we are able to attack, we must seem unable; when using our forces, we must appear inactive; when we are near, we must make the enemy believe we are far away; when far away, we must make him believe we are near.

–Sun Tzu[18]

Deception has been part of military strategies for centuries. Dating back to approximately 1280 BC, when the Hittites deceived Pharaoh Rameses and Egyptian forces during the Battle of Kadesh; years later in 1183 BC, military folklore described the Greeks' use of a giant wooden horse to secret soldiers into the Trojan capital; and the biblical account of Gideon utilizing a "ghost army" technique, directing his soldiers to create sonic illusions to deceptively exaggerate the size and might of the army. Over time, military strategists and philosophers began to document philosophies and tactics about stratagems. Sun Tzu, Plutarch, and Niccolò Machiavelli all contributed to the early corpus of texts containing philosophical and tactical use of misdirection. World War II and modern military conflicts revealed that deception efforts to gain strategic advantage had meaningfully matured. Scholars such as Barton Whaley,[19] J. Bowyer Bell,[20] Roy Godson,[21] James Wirtz,[22] Richard Heuer,[23] Michael Handel,[24] and others have meaningfully

Online Stratagems: *Cyber Denial and Deception*—cont'd

contributed to the new corpus of literature on modern strategic denial and deception. The burgeoning cyber battle space has catalyzed a new arms race for superiority in the digital world. The boundaries and rules of engagement in this space are amorphous, evolving, and still being defined. Modern scholars are exploring traditional D&D precepts through this cyber lens.[25] Stech and Heckman et al. in their work *Cyber Denial, Deception, & Counterdeception: A Framework for Supporting Active Cyber Defense*[26] provide a first impression look at the cyber kill chain, deception chain, and recursive deception chain models. Further, this work examines capability maturity models and lifecycle management for Cyber D&D. Similarly, Bodmer and Kilger, et al. in *Reverse Deception: Organized Cyber Threat Counter-Exploitation*[27] serves as an authoritative treatment on cyber operational deception, attack characterization, attacker trade craft, attribution, profiling, and cyber counterdeception. These works and others endeavor to transition the critical theories and practice of traditional D&D into the cyber sphere.

[18]Tzu, S. (Sunzi), & Giles, L. (2009). The art of war: The oldest military treatise in the world. Auckland, N.Z.: Floating Press.

[19]Whaley, B. (1969). *Stratagem: Deception and surprise in war.* Cambridge, Mass.: Center for International Studies, Massachusetts Institute of Technology, c1969; Whaley, B. (1982). Toward a general theory of deception. *The Journal of Strategic Studies, 5*(1), 178–192.

[20]Bell, J. B., & Whaley, B. (1991). *Cheating and deception.* Transaction Publishers.

[21]Godson, R., & Wirtz, J. J. (Eds.). (2011). *Strategic denial and deception: the Twenty-first Century challenge.* Transaction Publishers.

[22]Wirtz, J. J. (1990). Deception and the tet offensive. *The Journal of Strategic Studies, 13*(2), 82–98; Wirtz, J. J. (2008). Hiding in Plain Sight: Denial, Deception, and the Non-State Actor. *SAIS Review of International Affairs, 28*(1), 55–63.

[23]Heuer, R. J. (1980). Cognitive factors in deception and counterdeception. *Strategic Military Deception,* 45–94; Heuer, R. J. (1981). Strategic Deception and Counterdeception. *International Studies Quarterly, 25*(2), 294–327.

[24]Handel, M. I. (1976). *Perception, deception, and surprise: The case of the Yom Kippur War* (Vol. 19). Hebrew University of Jerusalem, Leonard Davis Institute for International Relations; Handel, M. I. (1982). Intelligence and deception. *The Journal of Strategic Studies, 5*(1), 122–154; Handel, M. I. (Ed.). (1987). *Strategic and Operational Deception in the Second World War.* Routledge.

[25]See, Rowe, N. C., & Rothstein, H. S. (2004). Two taxonomies of deception for attacks on information systems. *Journal of Information Warfare, 3*(2), 27–39; Rowe, N. C. (August, 2004). A model of deception during cyber attacks on information systems. In *Multi-Agent Security and Survivability, 2004 IEEE First Symposium on* (pp. 21–30). IEEE; Rowe, N. C., & Custy, E. J. (2008). Deception in cyber attacks. *Cyber warfare and cyber terrorism*; Rowe, N. C. (2008). Deception in Defense of Computer Systems from Cyber Attack. *Cyber Warfare and Cyber Terrorism,* 97–104; Rowe, N. C. (2004, December). Designing good deceptions in defense of information systems. In *Computer Security Applications Conference, 2004. 20th Annual* (pp. 418–427). IEEE.

[26]Heckman, K. E., Stech, F. J., Thomas, R. K., Schmoker, B., & Tsow, A. W. (2015). *Cyber Denial, Deception and Counter Deception.* Springer.

[27]Bodmer, S., Kilger, M., Carpenter, G., & Jones, J. (2012). *Reverse Deception: Organized Cyber Threat Counter-Exploitation.* McGraw Hill Professional.

Attacking Trust Within Underground Markets

The analyses presented here demonstrate that the market for stolen data is robust and may not be easily or immediately disrupted through traditional interventions that may be employed to affect other forms of illicit markets (Franklin et al., 2007; Holt & Lampke, 2010; Wehinger, 2011). Given the global scope of harm that may result from the activities of data markets, there is a need to find ways to efficiently disrupt the flow of information and the networks that undergird their operation. This is a challenge and requires consideration of broad-ranging solutions including legislative changes as well as innovative law enforcement techniques.

One key strategy that has been put forth by computer scientists to affect cybercrime markets involves attacking the social validation systems that legitimize vendors. Specifically, Franklin et al. (2007) argued that two forms of attacks could be used to affect trust between participants: Sybil attacks and slander attacks. In Sybil attacks, false online identities are created within each forum and used to create advertisements for products that will simply rip off buyers. Slander attacks involve using fake identities to flood threads with groundless complaints against sellers in order to increase the difficulty in identifying legitimate sellers.

Such strategies seem appropriate as they target the informal systems that participants use to manage trust and require virtually no monetary investment in order to support over the long-term (Franklin et al., 2007). The use of these attacks may produce a short-term benefit by sewing confusion among participants, though it would likely only affect disorganized markets (see also Herley & Florencio, 2010). More organized and regulated forums with observant administrators would be able to diffuse and disrupt slander attacks shortly after they begin. The range of informal validation mechanisms available in structured markets, including escrow agents and testing services, make them insulated from Sybil attacks. In much the same way, administrators who regularly monitor their forums could ban identities that attempt to disrupt the market with slander attacks posting false information regarding sellers. The general resiliency of the network structures observed in these forums suggest that there may be no easy or immediate way to disrupt them through external shocks to participants like slander attacks.

Recent attempts to disrupt the market have involved infiltration of groups at their highest levels in order to take down the entire market at once and sow discord among participants. For instance, in 2006 an FBI agent operating undercover as a hacker and using the name Master Splynter began to participate in a forum called **DarkMarket** (Poulsen, 2012). The forum was established by Renukanth Subramaniam, a UK citizen, who ran the site from an Internet cafe under the name Jilsi. The site sold all manner of personal data and credit card information and had participants from Canada, Germany, France, Russia, Turkey, the United Kingdom, and the United States. Master Splynter actively participated on the forum almost every day, eventually becoming a trusted member of the site. He even persuaded Jilsi to allow Splynter to become an administrator of the site and host it on a covert FBI-controlled server (Mills, 2009). As a result, the FBI was able to dismantle the group through joint operations around the world, leading to the arrest of 60 individuals, including Jilsi.

The DarkMarket investigation required substantive investigative resources and time in order to dismantle the entire community. By operating the entire site, law enforcement could develop substantive evidence against the participants and sew distrust between market actors based on fear they may be a member of law enforcement. Yet such complex investigative techniques appear to only be possible in limited circumstances and may not be able to affect the entire community. Actors can easily displace to other markets and avoid detection, continuing to sell information and cybercrime services. Thus this is not a perfect solution and requires further analysis and consideration in order to expand the utility of undercover investigations generally. These issues highlight the challenge of data markets. They cannot be readily disabled, and their operation can continue unfettered for long periods of time. As a result, we must be vigilant in order to affect their operations and minimize their impact on businesses and individuals alike.

References

Barratt, M. J. (2012). Silk Road: Ebay for drugs. *Addiction, 107*, 683.

Barratt, M. J., Ferris, J. A., & Winstock, A. R. (2014). Use of the Silk Road, the online drug marketplace, in the United Kingdom, Australia, and the United States. *Addiction, 109*, 774–783.

Chu, B., Holt, T. J., & Ahn, G. J. (2010). *Examining the creation, distribution, and function of malware on-line.* Washington D.C.: National Institute of Justice.

Cunningham, S., & Kendall, T. (2010). Sex for sale: Online commerce in the world's oldest profession. In T. J. Holt (Ed.), *Crime on-line: Correlates, causes, and context* (pp. 40–75). Raleigh, NC: Carolina Academic Press.

Dhanjani, N., & Rios, B. (2008). Bad sushi: Beating phishers at their own game. In *Presented at the Annual Blackhat Meetings.* Las Vegas: Nevada.

Dolliver, D. S. (2015). Evaluating drug trafficking on the Tor Network: Silk Road 2, the sequel. *International Journal of Drug Policy.*

Fogg, B. J. (2003). *How to motivate & persuade users.* New Horizons: CHI 2003.

Franklin, O. (2013). *Unravelling the dark web.* British GQ. Available at http://www.gq-magazine.co.uk/comment/articles/2013-02/07/silk-road-online-drugs- guns-black-market/viewall.

Franklin, J., Paxson, V., Perrig, A., & Savage, S. (2007). An inquiry into the nature and causes of the wealth of Internet miscreants. In *ACM conference on computer and communications security (CCS).* Alexandria, VA: ACM (pp. 275–288).

Geers, K., Kindlund, D., Moran, N., & Rachwald, R. (2013). *World War C: Understanding nation-state motives behind today's advanced cyber attacks.* FireEye. Technical report.

Gibbs, S. (October 3, 2013). Silk Road underground market closed—but others will replace it. *The Guardian.* Available at http://www.theguardian.com/technology/2013/oct/03/silk-road-underground-market-closed-bitcoin.

Gilmore, D. (2010). *Mediactive.* Creative Commons. Retrieved from https://mediactive.com/wp-content/uploads/2010/12/mediactive_gillmor.pdf.

Herley, C., & Florencio, D. (2010). Nobody sells gold for the price of silver: Dishonesty, uncertainty and the underground economy. In T. Moor, D. J. Pym, & C. Ioannidis (Eds.), *Economics of information security and privacy* (pp. 35–53). New York: Springer.

Holt, T. J. (2013). Examining the forces shaping cybercrime markets online. *Social Science Computer Review, 31*, 165–177.

Holt, T. J., & Blevins, K. R. (2007). Examining sex work from the client's perspective: Assessing johns using online data. *Deviant Behavior, 28*, 333–354.

Holt, T. J., Blevins, K. R., & Kuhns, J. B. (2014). Examining diffusion and arrest avoidance practices among johns. *Crime & Delinquency, 60*(2), 261–283.

Holt, T. J., & Bossler, A. M. (2016). *Cybercrime in progress: Theory and prevention of technology-enabled offenses.* New York: Routledge Press.

Holt, T. J., & Lampke, E. (2010). Exploring stolen data markets on-line: products and market forces. *Criminal Justice Studies, 23,* 33–50.

Holt, T. J., Smirnova, O., & Chua, Y. T. (2016). Exploring and estimating the revenues and profits of participants in stolen data markets. *Deviant Behavior, 37*(4), 353–367.

Holt, T. J., Smirnova, O., Chua, Y. T., & Copes, H. (2015). Examining the risk reduction strategies of actors in online criminal markets. *Global Crime, 16/2,* 81–103.

Holz, T., Engelberth, M., & Freiling, F. (2009). Learning more about the underground economy: a case-study of keyloggers and dropzones. In M. Backes, & P. Ning (Eds.), *Computer security-ESCORICS* (pp. 1–18). Berlin and Heidelberg: Springer.

Hutchings, A., & Holt, T. J. (2015). Crime script analysis and online black markets. *British Journal of Criminology, 55,* 596–614.

James, L. (2005). *Phishing Exposed.* Rockland: Syngress.

Karami, M., & McCoy, D. (August 2013). Understanding the emerging threat of DDoS-as-a- service. *LEET,* 1–4.

Konstam, A. (2006). *Blackbeard: America's most notorious pirate.* Wiley.

Li, W., & Chen, H. (2014). Identifying top sellers in the underground economy using deep learning-based sentiment analysis. In *Intelligence and security Informatics Conference* (pp. 64–67).

Liebman, N., & Gergle, D. (2016). Capturing turn-by-turn lexical similarity in text-based communication. In *Proceedings of CSCW, 2016.*

Mann, D., & Sutton, M. (1998). Netcrime: more changes in the organisation of thieving. *British Journal of Criminology, 38,* 201–229.

Martin, J. (2014). Lost on the Silk Road: Online drug distribution and the 'cryptomarket'. *Criminology & Criminal Justice, 14*(3), 351–367.

Mills, E. (2009). Q&A: FBI agent looks back on time posing as a cybercriminal. *CNET.* Available at http://www.cnet.com/news/q-a-fbi-agent-looks-back-on- time-posing-as-a-cybercriminal/.

Moore, R. (2012). *Cybercrime: Investigating high-technology computer crime.* London: Elsevier.

Motoyama, M., McCoy, D., Levchenko, K., Savage, S., & Voelker, G. M. (2011). An analysis of underground forums. *IMC,* 71–79.

Phelps, A., & Watt, A. (2014). I shop online—recreationally! Internet anonymity and Silk Road enabling drug use in Australia. *Digital Investigation, 11,* 261–272.

Poulsen, K. (2012). *Kingpin: How one hacker took over the billion dollar cybercrime underground.* New York: Broadway.

Provos, A. N., Mavrommatis, P., Rajab, M. A., & Monroe, F. (2008). *All your iFrames point to us.* Google Technical Report. http://static.googleusercontent.com/media/research.google.com/en//archive/provos-2008a.pdf.

Quinn, J. F., & Forsyth, C. J. (2013). Red light districts on blue screens: A typology for understanding the evolution of deviant communities on the internet. *Deviant Behavior, 34,* 579–585.

Sanders, T. (2008). Male sexual scripts intimacy, sexuality and pleasure in the purchase of commercial sex. *Sociology, 42*(3), 400–417.

Thomas, R., & Martin, J. (2006). The underground economy: Priceless. (Vol. 31). login: The Usenix Magazine.

Wehinger, F. (2011). The dark net: self-regulation dynamics of illegal online markets for identities and related services. In *Intelligence and security Informatics Conference* (pp. 209–213).

5

Phishing, Watering Holes, and Scareware

ABSTRACT

As victim organizations and users have become more cautious and aware of certain cyber attacks, cyber threat actors have developed new, creative methods to circumvent technical countermeasures and user vigilance. This chapter explores how attackers use deception strategies and techniques to skillfully circumvent human defenses. The chapter first looks at spear phishing, particularly through the lens of conjuring methods of misdirection and attention control. Later in the chapter the discussion turns to a burgeoning attack method—watering hole attacks, or strategic web compromises—which shifts the attack vector away from targeting victim communication platforms, particularly email, to compromising web servers. This section introduces the watering hole attack deception chain and examines attackers' implementation of passive misdirection techniques and persuasive technology principles to deceive victims. The final section revisits and summarizes how certain deception techniques are used to initiate and perpetuate psychologically vectored cyber attacks.

Keywords: *Phishing; Psychology of hacking; Social engineering; Spear phishing; Strategic web compromises; Watering hole attacks.*

Almost everyone enjoys when a magician pulls off a great magic trick or illusion. Getting duped by the trickery and wondering "how did they do that" is the positive reaction desired by the magician and audience members alike. However, falling for the deception of a hacker, phisher, or scammer is never appreciated. No one wants to be tricked by the techniques used by digital con artists who want people to fall prey to their sleight of hand.

Deception in the Digital Age. http://dx.doi.org/10.1016/B978-0-12-411630-6.00005-0

Social engineering is a practice used in magic and Shulman (2015) states, "social engineering is one of the most powerful tools in the hacker's arsenal." A Smithsonian Magazine interview with the renowned magician Teller (of Penn and Teller) revealed seven of his secrets of how he deceives his audiences and uses to psychology to manipulate their minds. Of these seven secrets, several relate directly to the social engineering and hacking techniques used by phishers, scammers, and other online con artists. Four key points from Teller (2013) include:

- exploit pattern recognition;
- keep the trickery outside the frame;
- nothing fools you better than the lie you tell yourself; and
- if you are given a choice, you believe you have acted freely.

This chapter focuses on social engineering and how the digital sleight of hand is used in a variety of cyber attacks including (1) phishing, (2) watering hole attacks, and (3) scareware.

Phishing

Over the years, there have been many definitions of phishing. According to the InfoSec Institute (2016), "Phishing is an attempt by Internet fraudsters to access and obtain personal and sensitive information, such as usernames, passwords, and financial information, by utilizing social engineering techniques." This type of fraud is actually quite old, dating back to the 1990s when Internet Service Providers (ISP) billed users by the hour for access. Skilled hackers would try to capture the usernames and passwords of unsuspecting victims by posing as an ISP, especially America Online due to its scope and penetration in the market. Fraudsters would harvest known AOL email addresses and send messages claiming to need account updates or validation of user profiles. The mass mailing strategy was like fishing, in that they were hoping to hook victims through deceptive bait. The term "phishing" emerged as a corruption of the term akin to that of phreaking within the general argot of the hacker community. Unsuspecting victims who thought these messages to be legitimate would forward their information to the sender in the hopes of correcting their account. The fraudsters, however, would keep the accounts for their own use or trade the information with others for pirated software or other information.

When looking at phishing through the lens and "secrets" told by Teller (2013), the phisher attempts to bait the user by hoping that their emails would:

- be recognized by having the right look and feel of legitimate communications previously received (*exploit pattern recognition*);
- use tricks outside the frame such as spoofing the email address so that a valid looking sender address is viewed on the "sent line" while the real deception can be seen in the email header (*keep trickery outside the frame*);

- rely on the theory that most humans will want to do the right thing and fix their account data even if they suspect that their account data is fine or that they do not even have an account with the company allegedly sending the email (*nothing fools you better than the lie you tell yourself*); and
- rely on the theory that most humans will "choose" to act and provide the requested information, particularly if there is a negative consequence attached if action is not taken (if you are given a choice, you believe you have acted freely).

Phishing messages often mimic legitimate communications from financial institutions and service providers, such as PayPal or eBay. The message usually contains some of the branding and language commonly used by that institution in an attempt to convince the recipient that the message is legitimate. The message usually suggests that a person's account has been compromised, needs to be updated, or has some problem that must be corrected as soon as possible. The time-sensitive nature of the problem is commonly stressed to confuse or worry the prospective victim in order to ensure a rapid response.

To that end, the email will also include web links that appear to connect to the appropriate website so that the victim can immediately enter their login information for the affected account. Generally, however, the link redirects the user to a different site controlled by the scammer that utilizes collection tools to capture user data. More sophisticated fraudulent sites will also feature branding or logos from the institution to help further promote the legitimacy of the phishing email. Upon arriving at the site, individuals are prompted to enter sensitive information, such as their bank account number, username, password, or even in some cases, personal identification numbers to validate their account. Upon entering the data, it is captured by the scammer for later use and may either redirect the victim back to the original website for the company or provide a page thanking them for their information.

The success of phishing techniques led some to begin to target e-commerce and online banking sites as they became popular with larger segments of the population in the early 2000s. Hackers began to recognize the value in targeting these institutions, and some began to create sophisticated phishing kits that came preloaded with the images and branding of the most prominent global banks. These kits, combined with spam email lists, enabled hackers to readily steal financial data from thousands of unsuspecting users around the world. In fact, the problem of phishing has become so commonplace that over 38,000 unique phishing websites were identified in June of 2013 alone (Anti-Phishing Working Group, 2013). These sites were hosted primarily in the United States due in part to the substantive proportion of hosting resources available to hackers, along with Germany, Canada, France, and the United Kingdom (Anti-Phishing Working Group, 2013). Thus phishing is a global problem that cannot be understated, though the prevalence of phishing victimization in the general population is largely unknown.

Since 2006, phishing has evolved into several variants including Voice over Internet Protocol (VoIP)/Voice phishing (vishing), short messaging service (SMS) phishing (smishing), spear phishing, and whale phishing. When phishing started in the 1990's, there were no smartphones, tablets, or apps. No one had text messaging, social media, or Wi-Fi yet. Thus as these new technologies and devices emerged, phishing evolved and proliferated to take advantage of the vast expanding digital environment. All of these phishing variations are based on the same premise as traditional email phishing; the scammers are just using different attack vectors. Smishing is defined as phishing via text message, and vishing is when victims are persuaded to disclose personal details or transfer money over the telephone, cellphone, or VoIP (Keyworth, 2016).

Spear phishing and whale phishing differ a bit from traditional phishing because the victims of these scams are specifically targeted and not part of a mass emailing. There are numerous reasons why a phisher would want to target a specific person. According to the InfoSec Institute (2016), spear phishing is a method used by hackers to gain personal or valuable information and ultimately to gain access to a network by targeting particular individuals within an organization; the first notable cases of spear phishing attacks were recognized around the year 2010.

Spear phishing attacks have targeted government agencies, corporations, banking clients, and universities. The techniques are all very similar, luring the selected group to click a link, download a file, or open an attachment. In the example in Fig. 5.1

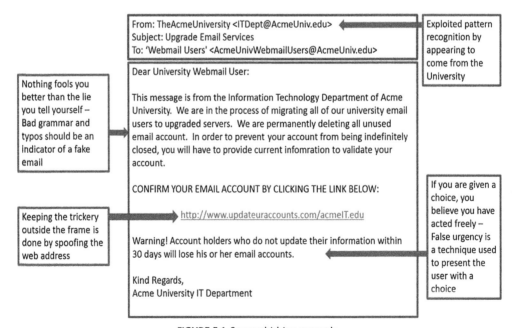

FIGURE 5.1 Spear phishing example.

below, a typical spear phishing email includes the core elements of deception as the scammers try to coerce university webmail users into giving up personal identifiable information.

Instead of targeting a population that belongs to a certain organization, spear phishers also send out large volumes of scam emails, which have a high probability of reaching real users of a particular service. Over the years, services like PayPal have been used as phishing lures to collect account data and passwords from legitimate PayPal users. In the example below, the spear phish actually uses the account holder's correct name and email address. Other elements of the phishing email appear to be real, as the scammers use the company's logo and do not make some of the spelling and grammatical errors commonly seen in spam. One of the tricks presented is to hide the actual URL where the user would put in username, password, and account information. But if the user hovers the mouse/cursor over the link, the real URL will appear; in this example case, the actual URL goes to a site in Russia. The example in Fig. 5.2 uses a fictitious company (ElectroPay Service); however, the elements of deception are typical.

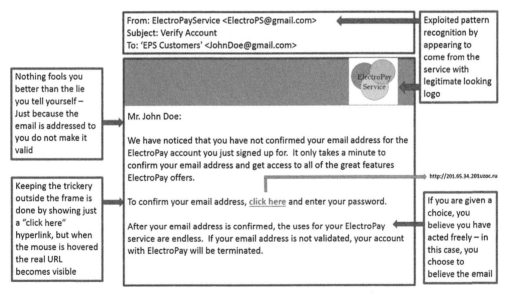

FIGURE 5.2 Example of a mass mailed spear phishing attack.

Around the same time period, other industrious hackers went after persons of notoriety or high net worth, otherwise known as "whales." The idea was that targeting those with power, influence, and money would reap better rewards for the attackers. Whale phishing has more recently morphed into "whaling," in which the scammers are using legitimate executive names and email addresses to persuade unsuspecting employees to wire money, sensitive business documents, tax forms, or human resource information to their accounts (Boulton, 2016). Whether the attack vector is email, phone, or text message, the underlying deceptive techniques are basically the same, using deceptive techniques to take advantage of our emotions, cognitive biases, and human physiology (i.e., fatigue, illness, injury).

One well-publicized whaling attack targeted the toy company, Mattel. In 2015, an account executive appeared to receive an email from the CEO of Mattel requesting that a payment be made to a new vendor in China. While nothing appeared to violate policy, procedure, or protocol (and the account executive wanted to impress the new CEO), a payment was made to the "new vendor" (Ragan, 2016). Of course, there was no new vendor. Mattel lost three million dollars because of an orchestrated social engineering attack. Remember Teller's "secret sauce of deception":

- *exploit pattern recognition*: the email appeared to come from the CEO and looked legitimate;
- *keep the trickery outside the frame*: the IP address associated with the sent email did not originate from within the company, and the money was not wired to a named vendor's account but to an unnamed bank account number;
- *nothing fools you better than the lie you tell yourself*: the account executive was convinced that sending the money was the right thing to do (even though it was a banking holiday in China and their new vendor would also most likely be on holiday); and
- *if you are given a choice, you believe you have acted freely*: the account executive wanted to please the new CEO and not wiring money to the new vendor would have certainly been insubordination (although the account executive never initiated a verbal confirmation with the real CEO).

Audience members attending a magic show typically do not shout out or ask, "hey, what is in your other hand?"…but when it comes to digital deception, it becomes necessary to ask. If a certain communication is asking for too much information or highly sensitive information, it is worth the while to ask and to do the asking via a different communications mode. If the communication comes in through email, call the would-be sender. If the communication comes in through text message, use email. While in some circumstances it may be unusual or uncomfortable to double-check, no one wants to be duped, and certainly not out of millions of dollars.

Watering Hole Attacks (Strategic Web Compromises)

As victim organizations and users have become more cautious and aware of spear phishing attacks, cyber attackers have developed new, creative methods to circumvent technical countermeasures and user vigilance. One of these burgeoning attack methods, *watering hole attacks*, or *strategic web compromises*, shifts the attack vector away from targeting victim communication platforms, particularly email, to compromising web servers, and in turn, the target victim group(s) that are known or likely to navigate to the website.[1]

Gaining salience in 2009, and sophisticatedly evolving over time, watering hole attacks pose a challenging threat to defend against. While the attack name is certainly curious on first impression, it is thematically accurate, since it is based off of the observed process in nature where concealed predators wait near small bodies of water used by their prey to drink and cool off, striking while prey are otherwise distracted (Fig. 5.3).

FIGURE 5.3 The inspiration behind the like-named cyber attack.

One of the most prominent examples of a watering hole attack is the security incident dubbed *Operation Aurora* by the security vendor McAfee. In 2009, as many as three groups of very sophisticated Chinese hackers compromised multiple high-level targets including Google, Adobe, Juniper Networks, Yahoo, Symantec, Northrop Grumman, and Dow Chemical (Shmugar, 2010; Zetter, 2010). The attackers utilized various methods to gain access to these institutions, though one of the most prevalent attack techniques was a watering hole strategy employed by a group referred to as the Elderwood Gang (Clayton, 2012).[2] The group would spear phish employees to click on links to a website hosting malware that would exploit a specific zero-day vulnerability in the Internet Explorer web browser. From there, the attackers appeared to use these infected systems as launch points to identify and compromise source code repositories within these companies (Markoff & Barboza, 2010; Zetter, 2010).

In 2013, the sophistication of strategic web compromises escalated, leading to high-profile breaches. In particular, a watering hole attack was used in 2013 that targeted a page regarding Site Exposure Matrices (SEM) on the US Department of Labor's

---

[1] Brandan, B. (January 24, 2014). *Spear phishing still popular, but more watering hole attacks coming.* http://searchsecurity.techtarget.com/news/2240213164/Spear-phishing-still-popular-but-more-watering-hole-attacks-coming.

[2] See also, Kambic, et al. (2013). *Crude Faux: An analysis of cyber conflict within the oil and gas industries,* CERIAS Tech Report 2013-9, Center for Education and Research, Information Assurance and Security, Purdue University.

website (Kaplan, 2013).[3] The page contained a malicious script that directed victims to a separate page hosting the Poison Ivy remote access Trojan and used an exploit for a common vulnerability in the Microsoft Internet Explorer browser that had been patched a few months prior to this incident. The content of the page that was compromised gives some potential insights into the target of the attack, as the SEM page details toxic substances commonly present at nuclear sites and the potential health concerns stemming from exposure to those materials (Kaplan, 2013). Further, sophisticated watering hole attacks such as those attributed to the "Hidden Lynx" hacking group, who were responsible for the VOHO Campaign and the attacks against security Bit9, demonstrated how potent these attacks could be, even against technically sophisticated victims.[4]

With the success of these attacks, cyber adversaries continued this momentum into 2014 and 2015. With new web browsers such as Internet Explorer 10 emerging, attackers quickly developed zero-day exploits to insidiously compromise these programs, stealthily placing these tools in secretly compromised websites trusted by the victims who visited them[5] The aerospace and automotive industries were heavily targeted, revealing the attacker's victim selection, motivations, and willingness to craft, refine, and patiently execute strategic web compromises against these highly desired victims.[6] Understanding the watering hole attack deception chain and the deception principles implemented by the attackers helps elucidate why these pernicious attacks are successful and will continue to be a threat in the cyber landscape.

The Watering Hole Attack Deception Chain

In a cyber context, cyber threat actors in watering hole attacks use victim profiling, reconnaissance, stealth, and deception techniques to tailor their attack process. The following are the steps in a typical *watering hole attack deception chain* (Fig. 5.2):

1) **Victim Selection.** The cyber attacker selects a target organization for compromise. Since 2009, watering hole attacks have targeted government agencies, financial

---

[3] *See also*, Blasco, J. (May 1, 2013). *U.S. Department of Labor website hacked and redirecting to malicious code*. Retrieved from https://www.alienvault.com/blogs/labs-research/us-department-of-labor-website-hacked-and-redirecting-to-malicious-code.

[4] Gragido, W. (July 2012). *Lions at the Watering Hole: The VOHO Affair*. The RSA Blog, EMC Corporation; Doherty, S., Gegeny, J., Spasojevic, B., Baltazar J. (September 17, 2013). *Hidden Lynx- Professional Hackers for Hire*. Retrieved from http://www.symantec.com/content/en/us/enterprise/media/security_response/whitepapers/hidden_lynx.pdf.

[5] Lin, Y. (February 13, 2014). *New IE Zero-Day Found in Watering Hole Attack*. Retrieved from https://www.fireeye.com/blog/threat-research/2014/02/new-ie-zero-day-found-in-watering-hole-attack-2.html; *New Internet Explorer 10 Zero-Day Discovered in Watering Hole*. Retrieved from http://www.symantec.com/connect/blogs/new-internet-explorer-10-zero-day-discovered-watering-hole-attack.*Attack*, Symantec Security Response Symantec Employee, February 2014.

[6] Donohue, B. (September 2014). *Watering Hole Attack Targets Automotive*. Aerospace Industries, Retrieved from https://threatpost.com/watering-hole-attack-targets-automotive-aerospace-industries/107998/.

institutions, news organizations,[7] defense contractors,[8] energy sector companies,[9] dissident groups, human rights groups,[10] and civil society groups,[11] among other organizations.

2) **Web Profiling.** The cyber attacker(s) profile victim website visitation patterns, selecting legitimate web sites that the target set likely frequent.

3) **Server Reconnaissance.** Once the attacker(s) identify websites that are well-suited for a watering hole attack against their target victim set, they conduct reconnaissance, analyzing and probing the web servers for vulnerabilities that can be exploited, providing request access and resources to successfully facilitate the watering hole campaign.

4) **Server Compromise.** The attacker(s) will compromise these sites in advance of the watering hole campaign using a web injection and other attacks to breach and establish redirection elements (such as iframe) so that visitors are transparently directed to separate sites controlled by the attacker where an exploit is waiting to compromise a vulnerability in the victims' web browsers.

5) **Victim Compromise.** The resulting attack trajectory enables the attacker to successfully infect the victims' computers through what appears to be a normal, innocuous visit to a website. This provides backdoor access to systems inside sensitive networks, creating a foothold to facilitate wider compromises. It is during this pivotal stage that the attacker's effective use of *passive misdirection to disguise* the server compromise deceives the ultimate targeted victims in the larger attack trajectory.

6) **Continued Attack Trajectory.** From there, the attacker can perform secondary injection attacks to install keylogging malware and remote access trojans in order to help conceal their actions within the network (Fig. 5.4).

Passive Misdirection

Recall from Chapter 1, The Psychology of Deception that magicians use certain *misdirection* techniques to shape the spectator's *perceptions* (processing and interpreting of sensory

---

[7] See Rashid, F.Y. (February 11, 2015). *Chinese Attackers Hacked Forbes Website in Watering Hole Attack: Security Firms*. Retrieved from http://www.securityweek.com/chinese-attackers-hacked-forbes-website-watering-hole-attack-security-firms.

[8] Lee, B., Grunzweig, J. (July 20, 2015). *Watering Hole Attack on Aerospace Firm Exploits CVE-2015-5122 to Install Is Space Backdoor*. Retrieved from http://researchcenter.paloaltonetworks.com/2015/07/watering-hole-attack-on-aerospace-firm-exploits-cve-2015-5122-to-install-isspace-backdoor/.

[9] See Feinberg, A. (April 8, 2014). *Intrepid Hackers Use Chinese Takeout Menu to Access a Major Oil Company*. Retrieved from http://gizmodo.com/hackers-are-being-forced-to-target-chinese-takeout-menu-1560755886; Symantec Security Response, (June 30, 2014). *Dragonfly: Western Energy Companies Under Sabotage Threat Cyberespionage campaign stole information from targets and had the capability to launch sabotage operations*. Retrieved from http://www.symantec.com/connect/blogs/dragonfly-western-energy-companies-under-sabotage-threat; Walker, D. (June 25, 2014). *Havex' malware strikes industrial sector via watering hole attacks*. Retrieved from http://www.scmagazine.com/havex-malware-strikes-industrial-sector-via-watering-hole-attacks/article/357875/.

[10] Leyden, J. (January 24, 2013). *RAT-flingers target human right activists in watering hole attack*. Retrieved from http://www.theregister.co.uk/2013/01/24/watering_hole_attack/.

[11] See Villenueve, N. (October, 2009). *0day: Civil Society and Cyber Security*. Retrieved from http://www.nartv.org/2009/10/28/0day-civil-society-and-cyber-security/.

FIGURE 5.4 The watering hole attack deception chain.

information) and *beliefs* (confidence that the sensory information perceived is reality). This is often achieved by attracting the spectator's gaze and attention to an *unsuspicious* and interesting point, while a surreptitious action is taking place elsewhere, undetected and unsuspected (Ascanio & Etcheverry, 2005). Attackers utilizing watering hole attacks rely upon *passive misdirection* to ensure that victims navigating to the compromised server are not alerted to the impending secondary malware attacks on their systems. *Passive misdirection* within the context of a cyber attack is used to alleviate or dispel suspicion surrounding a nefarious online resource (such as a website) by ensuring that the web presence or "digital experience" resonates with victims as natural, familiar, and innocuous (Fig. 5.5).

Factors such as expected visual appearance, content, and user experience impact the attacker's ability to properly misdirect and deceive. When digital content is viewed and experienced by victims visiting the watering hole site as innocuous, nonsalient, and familiar, their *perception vigilance* is lowered and *inattention*, or diluted concentration, is induced (Sharpe, 1988). Factors that impact this type of misdirection include:

- □ familiarity, lack of unusual features, appearing nondescript;
- □ camouflage;
- □ disposition (placing content in a manner that confuses visitor's perception of position, etc.);

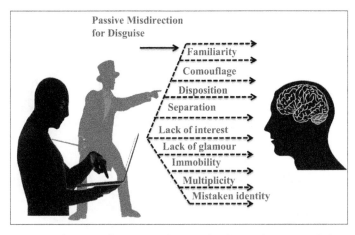

FIGURE 5.5 Attackers use of passive misdirection for disguise in watering hole attacks.

☐ separation;
☐ lack of interest; and
☐ lack of glamour;

Technical Persuasion

To effectively misdirect and deceive unsuspecting victims visiting the watering hole server, attackers must ensure that the misdirection narrative is supported and amplified by *technical persuasion elements* to properly convey a normal, expected, and credible web experience. Thus the digital user experience on the online resource—typically a web site—must convey *credibility* to the ensnared, surreptitiously infected visitors. Conversely, a substantial alternation of content, domain names (or infrastructure), or user experience detracts credibility, likely alerting victims to "a problem," causing them to further investigate and/or alert information technology/security professionals to do so—and potentially stymieing the watering hole attack platform and attack trajectory.

Website credibility, although studied for over a decade, is still in many ways a nascent area of research. Researchers found that there are four types of web credibility (Fogg, 2003) (Fig. 5.6):

- **Presumed**: Credibility that is based upon general assumptions in the user's mind.
- **Reputed**: This is derived or "earned" based upon third-party endorsements, reports, or referrals.
- **Surface**: This is an aesthetic and limited interaction level; it is based upon simple inspection and first impressions.
- **Earned**: Derived from the user's first-hand experience with the website over an extended period of time.

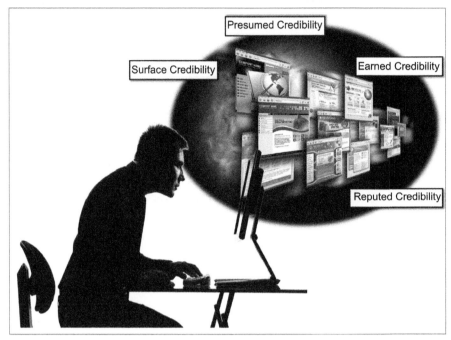

FIGURE 5.6 The four types of web credibility.

Similar to the importance of perceived source credibility when a communicator is trying to convey a persuasive message to a receiver of the communication, web credibility is based upon two factors: *trustworthiness* and *expertise* (Fogg, 2003; Flanagin & Metzger, 2007; Rains & Karmikel, 2009). Elements that bolster a website's credibility through conveying trustworthiness and expertise include:

- design features;
- depth of content;
- site complexity;
- contact details that correlate to physical address, email addresses, etc.;
- content that contains references that can be verified; and
- links to credible outside materials and sources.

Conversely, web credibility can be negatively impacted if the website has:

- confusing content (e.g., ads that are indistinguishable from true content);
- lack of contact data;
- unexpected content, such as pop-up windows and problematic links; and
- lack of updated content

(Fogg, 2003; Kąkol & Nielek, 2015).

Attackers staging and conducting watering hole attacks need to carefully modify and weaponize the watering hole server so as preserve all facets of the victim website's credibility, while ensuring the attack trajectory of exploiting a vulnerability in the victims' web browsers. This critical balance often causes cyber attackers in these strategic web compromises to use zero-day malware or less common exploits in order to compromise their target browsers.[12] Such a step increases the likelihood of a successful machine compromise as the users' software may not be fully patched. Additionally, the security tools on the target systems may not recognize the attack method and allow the compromise to take place unabated, ensuring that the infection trajectory remains undetected by both system security and user observation.

While watering hole attacks are not as common as spear phishing attacks, they are becoming more prevalent, resulting in successful, problematic compromises into sensitive victim networks.

Historically, attack methods such as spear phishing to compromise the human actors behind systems in a network focused on psychological vulnerabilities, particularly since these are a much more effective vector than hardware or software. There are no patches for mental vulnerabilities, such as *conformation biases*, causing at least a small number of targeted victims to click through any web links provided via email. Watering hole attacks use clever deception techniques to take advantage of targeted user's existing perceptions of web credibility, and through passive misdirection, leverage these trusted web resources to compromise the unsuspecting victims.

Scareware

Ayala (2016) states that scareware is a "form of malicious software that uses social engineering to cause shock, anxiety, or the perception of a threat in order to manipulate users into buying unwanted software." Scareware is also called fraudware, fakeware, or very generically malware and may come in the form of pop-ups. The pop-up messages, claiming to be from legitimate antivirus companies, typically provide a stern warning indicating that there are infected files or malware on the user's computer, such as "*Your computer may be infected with harmful spyware programs.*" The scareware message also includes the solution, which is to pay for the software fix that will eliminate the infected files. Users who believe the deceptive message and download the antivirus software will end up introducing malware onto their systems, usually malware that is looking to steal personal identifiable information, passwords, and banking data (Kaspersky Lab, 2016).

The pop-up messages are crafted in a way to make them appear legitimate. In some cases people click on the scareware because the messages masquerade as the actual antivirus company that the user has installed on their machine. It seems reasonable, and in a lot of cases the user probably has not kept up with their antivirus updates. Unlike some of the phishing emails from years ago that contained misspellings, incorrect grammar, and the name of everyone's uncle (the Nigerian Prince whose inheritance is waiting to be distributed), these scareware ads and warning messages are well crafted.

---

[12] Symantec Internet Threat Security Report 2014, Vol. 19. Retrieved from http://www.symantec.com/content/en/us/enterprise/other_resources/b-istr_main_report_v19_21291018.en-us.pdf.

In addition to pop-ups, scareware can be delivered by spam. A number of fraudulent companies, pretending to be cyber security firms or claiming they are working with legitimate firms, have launched massive email campaigns, which tricked users into purchasing worthless software and services. Once the user purchases the fake services, the fraudsters possess credit card numbers, and in some cases banking information and/or personal information. A recent action by the Federal Trade Commission, with the states of Connecticut and Pennsylvania, engaged in legal action to stop operations at Innovazion Research Private Limited, which has allegedly engaged in a major scareware operation. According to the lawsuit, Innovazion Research Private Limited defrauded consumers out of more than $17 million by pretending to represent Microsoft, Apple, and other major tech companies. The company supposedly used several attack vectors including pop-ups, phone calls, and online advertisements (Griffin, 2016).

The Pokémon GO craze in the summer of 2016 has also resulted in app-based scareware. Fraudsters have tempted Pokémon GO players with user's guides and cheat books, such as "Guide & Cheats for Pokemon Go" and "Install Pokemongo" on Google Play (Stefanko, 2016). At the same time, Google had to remove over 150 Android apps that were collecting personal data from users and serving up fake ads for services and software (Liam, 2016). While Android apps have received the most attention for security flaws, researchers at SANS Technology Institute discovered a fake Adobe Flash update targeting OS X. According to Ullrich (2016), "the attackers used a simple and effective trick to deceive victims, the attack starts with a popup window alerting users that their Flash Player software is outdated and providing them the instruction to update it."

Ransomware

It is one type of problem to get infected by malware via phishing, smishing, or scareware, but another thing all together for a user to have all of their data just "disappear." While technically not categorized as "scareware," ransomware can definitely be defined as a deceptive scheme that scares. According to the FBI, ransomware is a type of malware that prevents or limits people from accessing their systems, data, or devices by either locking the system's screen or by encrypting files unless a ransom is paid. It will be very obvious that ransomware malware has infected a device, as a large message will cover the screen, indicating that your data is being held hostage (see sample message below).

Sample Ransomware Message

Your documents, photos, databases, and other important files have been encrypted with strongest encryption and unique key, generated for this computer. Private decryption key is stored on a secret Internet server and nobody can decrypt your files until you pay and obtain the private key. The server will eliminate the key after a time period specified in this window.

Ransomware is installed when a user opens an attachment sent from an attacker, visits a compromised or fake website, or clicks on malicious ads or bad links in social media or instant messenger chats. Thus the attack begins with the same type of deceptive tactics and social engineering techniques used in most other cybercrimes. Hackers may also take advantage of known vulnerabilities in systems and networks to launch their ransomware attacks (Siwicki, 2016).

Ransomware is the digital form of data hostage taking. In most cases, taking data hostage is not a "life and death" situation, as is a physical kidnapping for ransom. However, the relative importance or sensitivity of the data being held hostage can result in a crisis situation. The digital hostage takers do use some of the same tactics as kidnappers. They rely on the fact that people need their data, their personal lives depend on their data, their businesses depend on their data, and most importantly, they want their data back, safely, soundly, and in one piece. The emotional and psychological reactions of most people who have their data kidnapped and held hostage include shock, panic, fear, frustration, and anger. Victims are not only impacted by their stolen data, but many are confused and unsure about how to interact with the hostage takers…or wonder if they even should engage them. However, most people are willing to pay the ransom to get their data returned, thus the scam continues and nets millions of dollars. Ransomware is just the next iteration of digital attack, and it is extremely profitable (Federal Bureau of Investigation, 2016).

Ransomware originated in Russia by the same hackers who have been active for years launching virus attacks, phishing attacks, and distributing malware (Vargas & Vargas, 2016). Generally speaking, ransomware can be divided into two types: (1) lock-out ransomware and (2) crypto ransomware. Lock-out ransomware denies access to systems, networks, or devices and typically locks up the device interface. However, the device remains active enough to allow the victim(s) to interact with hackers to pay the ransom. Crypto ransomware is a bit more sophisticated and prevents the user(s) access to data files on a targeted device by encrypting those files. Thus the hackers hold the decryption key, and the ransom payment will provide the decryption. In some cases very specific file types are targeted. For example, some ransomware will focus on files or file extensions that they believe are more important to people such as Excel, QuickBooks, or tax forms (Vargas & Vargas, 2016).

The attackers are usually very helpful to their victims, providing instructions on the pop-up message which involves how to make the payment, and Bitcoin is typically the payment method of choice (Vargas & Vargas, 2016). In some cases, the digital hostage takers will provide the victim with a clock-timer contained in the ransom note that indicates that the user's files have been encrypted and that the victim has some amount of hours, minutes, and seconds left to pay the ransom. This additional use of the "ticking clock" is just part of the attacker's layered psychological strategy. If the disappearance of the user's data combined with the sinister looking ransom note does not coerce the user into paying, the timer (like the ticking bomb in many action movies that has to be deactivated) is there to strike another emotional chord.

Many users are unaware that ransomware also can just as easily seize control over files stored on cloud services. According to Krebs (2016), an employee working at Children in Film opened Outlook, clicked on a voicemail message attachment, and received the infamous ransom note. All of the company's data (i.e., email, data files, accounting) is hosted by a managed cloud service, and they felt secure because their data was allegedly safe "in the cloud." These criminals can target any computer, laptop, smartphone, or tablet user, whether it's a home computer, endpoints in an enterprise network, storage in the cloud, or servers used by a government agency. In other words, no one is safe from a potential ransomware attack. It can be argued that the ransomware fraudsters are the masters of social engineering. In order to pull off a full-on data ransom attack, the hackers must lure and persuade the would-be victims through multiple stages including the initial deception, the belief that their data is really not recoverable without the assistance of the attacker, the belief that their "time is limited" and the clock is ticking, the belief that otherwise nontech savvy people will in a time crunch learn to use Bitcoin, and in the end, send the money. That is a lot of persuasion and manipulation wrapped into one attack. But perhaps the real deception is that in some cases, the user's data can be recovered without the help of the attackers and without having to pay the ransom. Krebs (2016) provides instructions and a web link to a computer help forum called BleepingComputer.com, creator of TeslaDecoder, which allows victims to decrypt files locked by a form of ransomware called TeslaCrypt.

Social Engineering

So why do people still fall for phishing emails and fake ads? Why, even after training and education do employees get duped by SMS scams and fake phone calls requesting passwords, banking data, and other personal information? It seems as though people intellectually understand the dangers and the risks, but their behaviors do not follow suit. Unfortunately, it is because we are human, and we all have certain weaknesses, flaws, and predispositions. Social engineers rely on cognitive biases, which are patterns of judgment that deviate from the norm or rationality about people and situations, all of which provide a venue for effective attacks (Raman, 2008). Effective engineers will utilize biases to increase the likelihood of responses from potential victims. For instance, choice-supportive bias focuses on an individual's likelihood to identify only the positives of any past decision they have made rather than any negatives (Mather, Shafir, & Johnson, 2000). That person may be inclined to provide information through a fraudulent e-commerce site or financial service provider because they assume it was in response to actual past behaviors. Conformation bias recognizes that individuals will interpret new information or events through a lens of personal views and beliefs in order to support their decisions (Nickerson, 1998). For instance, individuals may become accustomed to certain uniforms, identification badges, and other behaviors that are symbolic of belonging within a working environment. Engineers can use this to their advantage and dress and act in a way that blends into the environment and would keep potential targets from questioning their behavior. The exposure effect identifies the notion that people are more willing to recognize and respond to familiar items and behaviors (Zajonc, 1968) and may be more inclined to act in response to messages and requests from services they use or are familiar with. Finally, anchoring involves individuals who base decisions on simple pieces of information that may be immediately acquired, as when an engineer uses bank logos and branding in order to increase the likelihood that a victim will reply to a phish request.

Each type of bias presents an opening for an attacker to present their deception scheme. Digital deception will only get more creative as additional technologies, devices, and products enter the market. Fraudsters, scammers, and other adversaries have already taken advantage of the new technologies available through the use of digital photography, video, drones, and satellite imagery.

References

Anti-Phishing Working Group. (2013). *Phishing activity. Trends report.* 2nd Quarter 2013. http://docs.apwg.org/reports/apwg_trends_report_q2_2013.pdf.

Ascanio, A., & Etcheverry, J. (2005). The magic of Ascanio. *The structural conception of magic* (Vol. 1). Paginas.

Ayala, L. (2016). *Cybersecurity Lexicon.* New York: Apress Media.

Boulton, C. (April 21, 2016). *Whaling emerges as major cybersecurity threat.* CIO Magazine. Online Source: http://www.cio.com/article/3059621/security/whaling-emerges-as-major-cybersecurity-threat.html.

Clayton, M. (September 14, 2012). *Stealing US business secrets: Experts ID two huge cyber "Gangs" in China.* Christian Science Monitor. Online Source: http://www.csmonitor.com/USA/2012/0914/Stealing-US-business-secrets-Experts-ID-two-huge-cyber-gangs-in-China.

Federal Bureau of Investigation. (April 29, 2016). *Incidents of Ransomware on the rise: Protect yourself and your organization.* Online Source https://www.fbi.gov/news/stories/incidents-of-ransomware-on-the-rise.

Flanagin, A. J., & Metzger, M. J. (2007). The role of site features, user attributes, and information verification behaviors on the perceived credibility of web-based information. *New Media & Society, 9*(2), 319–342.

Fogg, B. J. (2003). *Persuasive technology: Using computers to change what we think and do.* Amsterdam: Morgan Kaufmann Publishers.

Griffin, K. (May 19, 2016). *FTC expands tech support fraud lawsuit.* Online Source http://www.hartford-business.com/article/20160519/NEWS01/160519909/ftc-expands-tech-support-fraud-lawsuit.

InfoSec Institute. (2016). *A brief history of spear-phishing.* Online Source http://resources.infosecinstitute.com/a-brief-history-of-spear-phishing/.

Kaplan, D. (May 2, 2013). *US department of labor web page serves watering hole attack.* SC Magazine. Online Source http://www.scmagazine.com/us-department-of-labor-web-page-serves-watering-hole-attack/article/291779/.

Kaspersky Lab. (2016). *Definitions – Scareware.* Internet Security Center. Online Source http://www.kaspersky.com/internet-security-center/definitions/scareware.

Keyworth, M. (January 1, 2016). *Vishing and smishing: The rise of social engineering fraud.* BBC World Service. Online Source http://www.bbc.com/news/business-35201188.

Krebs, B. (January 16, 2016). *Ransomware a threat to cloud services, too.* Online Source http://krebsonsecurity.com/2016/01/ransomware-a-threat-to-cloud-services-too/.

Kąkol, M., & Nielek, R. (2015). What affects web credibility perception? An analysis of textual justifications. *Computer Science, 16*(3), 295–310.

Liam, T. (August 2, 2016). *Scareware trojan infects 2.8 million android devices*. CSO Online. Retrieved from http://www.cso.com.au/article/604406/scareware-trojan-infects-2-8-million-android-devices/.

Markoff, J., & Barboza, D. (February 19, 2010). *2 China schools said to be linked to online attacks*. The New York Times. Online Source http://www.nytimes.com/2010/02/19/technology/19china.html.

Mather, M., Shafir, E., & Johnson, M. K. (2000). Misremembrance of options past: Source monitoring and choice. *Psychological Science, 11*(2), 132–138.

Nickerson, R. S. (1998). Confirmation bias: A ubiquitous phenomenon in many guises. *Review of General Psychology, 2*(2), 175.

Ragan, S. (March 29, 2016). *Chinese scammers take Mattel to the bank, phishing them for $3 million*. CSO Magazine. Online Source http://www.csoonline.com/article/3049392/security/chinese-scammers-take-mattel-to-the-bank-phishing-them-for-3-million.html.

Rains, S. A., & Karmikel, C. D. (2009). Health information-seeking and perceptions of website credibility: Examining web-use orientation, message characteristics, and structural features of websites. *Computers in Human Behavior, 25*(2), 544–553.

Raman, K. (2008). Ask and you will receive. *McAfee Security Journal,* 1–12.

Sharpe, S. (1988). *Conjurers' psychological secrets*. Calgary: Hades Publications.

Shmugar, C. (2010). *More details on operation aurora*. https://securingtomorrow.mcafee.com/mcafee-labs/more-details-on-operation-aurora/.

Shulman, A. (November 27, 2015). *Social engineering: Hacker tricks that make recipients click*. SC Magazine UK. Online Source http://www.scmagazineuk.com/social-engineering-hacker-tricks-that-make-recipients-click/article/455134/.

Siwicki, B. (May 17, 2016). *Cybersecurity special report: Ransomware will get worse, hackers targeting whales, medical devices and IoT trigger new vulnerabilities*. Health Care IT News. Online Source http://www.healthcareitnews.com/news/cybersecurity-special-report-ransomware-will-get-worse-hackers-targeting-whales-medical-devices.

Stefanko, L. (July 15, 2016). *Pokémon GO hype: First lockscreen tries to catch the trend*. Online Source http://www.welivesecurity.com/2016/07/15/pokemon-go-hype-first-lockscreen-tries-catch-trend/.

Teller, R. J. (March 2013). *Teller reveals his secrets*. Smithsonian Magazine. Online Source http://www.smithsonianmag.com/arts-culture/teller-reveals-his-secrets-100744801/.

Ullrich, J. B. (February 2016). *Fake adobe flash update OS X malware*. SANS Technology Institute. Online Source https://isc.sans.edu/forums/diary/Fake+Adobe+Flash+Update+OS+X+Malware/20693/.

Vargas, D., & Vargas, S. (June 2016). Ransomware: Is it really give up and pay up? In *Presentation presented at the techno security conference, Myrtle Beach, SC*.

Zajonc, R. B. (1968). Attitudinal effects of mere exposure. *Journal of Personality and Social Psychology, 9*(2p2), 1.

Zetter, K. (2010). *Google' hackers had ability to alter source code*. Wired. Online Source http://www.wired.com/threatlevel/2010/03/source-code-hacks/.

6

Seeing is Not Believing: Deceptive Internet Video Communications

ABSTRACT

This chapter focuses on deceptive techniques used in video, specifically applied to Internet video communications. A discussion of deception used in still photography and in film ground the concepts in history with contemporary examples highlighting its role. Some of the historical techniques used to fake photography and create special effects for motion pictures are included as they relate directly to how video can be faked today. A special look at some of the best deception techniques used by the US Army during World War II are also included. The chapter concludes with a discussion of the potential ways that deceptive imaging may be identified through the use of physics.

Keywords: *Augmented reality; Early photography; Film fakes; Ghost army; Motion pictures; Video production; Video software.*

CHAPTER OUTLINE

Video is part of mainstream communications today. Digital imagery has proliferated in all aspects of business, entertainment, and personal use. It is actually difficult to find anyone who does not own a video camera, has a video camera app on their smartphone or tablet, or has not either posted or at least viewed a video on YouTube.com. The more sophisticated video user or consumer may be creating or viewing video images directly from drones, small or large aircraft mounted cameras, or low-orbit commercial satellites. In addition to having all of this access to video feeds, technology, postings, and video via the web, everyone has easy and inexpensive access to video editing capabilities. In the same way video recording technologies vary in cost, complexity, and quality, so do video editing technologies. Video editing options include hardware/software-based editing suites, software programs, apps, and built-in tools as part of downloadable social media sharing apps such as Snapchat. It is these video editing technologies that can create—or reveal—deception presented in video.

During the creation and advancement of each technology, deception has crept into the medium. In some cases, deception in still photography was used to create publicity or as part of a scam. In other cases, motion pictures have been used during war times as psychological operations or "psy-ops" used to convey selected information to audiences in order to influence their emotions, perceptions, and motives. The proliferation of Internet connectivity, digital cameras, and editing software has made deception a common component of the online experience. For instance, less reputable news sites utilize edited photos and extremely pithy titles to entice readers to click through to stories about various topics ranging from celebrities to sports (Frampton, 2015). The use of so-called "clickbait" imaging and text is transforming journalism, leading to questions as to how the medium can survive if authors must potentially misrepresent the story to draw in readership (Frampton, 2015).

Such a commonplace example demonstrates the diverse range of motives for the use of deception in on-line video and photography. As extremist groups, terrorists, and cybercriminals depend on social media and video to help promote their agenda or attract prospective victims, deception has become a common tool. While cybercriminals may use deception for financial gain, ideologically motivated groups may depend on misrepresentation in order to draw attention to their cause and potentially recruit new members (Britz, 2013; Weimann, 2005). The use of social media as a key venue for communication enables radical groups to spread their message with no filter nor dependence on traditional media outlets who may adulterate their ideas. As a result, misrepresentation and deception may prove essential to help confuse or frustrate their enemies while at the same justifying the use of lethal violence or threats.

In order to discuss the various ways video can be altered to deceive and why, it is important to look at the history of photography and motion pictures. This chapter will present a short history of the application of deception in still photography and film with contemporary examples highlighting its role. Finally, we will conclude with a discussion of the potential ways that deceptive imaging may be identified through the use of physics.

A Bit of History

In 1021 AD, Ibn al-Haytham, a scientist and physicist, published the *Book of Optics*, which included his invention of the camera obscura. The camera obscura, also discussed in principle by Aristotle and early Chinese philosopher Mozi, was a rudimentary optical device that ultimately led to the development of photography and the photographic camera (Dupre, 2008). Al-Haytham created the first pinhole camera after observing how light traveled through a window shutter, concluding that smaller holes would create sharper images. Most of the future developments related to still photography came from his initial designs and theories of light, aperture, and the reproduction of images. A condensed chronological overview of image, motion picture, and video production history includes (Bohn & Stromgren, 1986):

> 1870s: Muybridge shoots a series of still photographs mounted to a stroboscopic disc;
> 1884: Eastman invents flexible photographic film;
> 1884: Edison patents the first motion picture camera;
> 1895: Lumiere creates the portable motion picture camera;
> 1897: Electronic images are produced with the use of a cathode ray tube;
> 1923: Edison patents the first motion picture with sound;
> 1927: Farnsworth invents "image dissector," later known as the video camera tube;
> 1950: Hollywood introduces 3-D format to films;
> 1975: Sony releases the Betamax for home recording and viewing of video;
> 1975: JVC releases VHS format; and
> 1977: *Star Wars* movie release introduces special effects using computer graphics.

The Start of Special Effects and CGI According to Pixar Touch Book History

The pioneering computer artist, Larry Cuba who worked on Star Wars Episode IV, created the footage using a photo of a matte painting of the Death Star as reference, along with photos of the modular pieces used to line the Death Star's trench in close-up. His equipment was a minicomputer attached to a vector-graphics system. A vector-graphics system allowed the "host" computer to draw lines (and only lines) on a monochrome display. It is rumored that the minicomputer Cuba used to create the special effects was a PDP 11/45 and had just 16K of RAM.

Video: Making of the Computer Graphics for Star Wars (1977), http://www.slashfilm.com/votd-making-of-the-computer-graphics-for-star-wars/.

In each stage of history, as still pictures, then motion pictures, and ultimately digital video developed, professionals started to understand how each medium could be manipulated. Deceptive techniques were applied to each medium by nation states, military groups, and intelligence organizations, as the tools of the trade were expensive and needed to be operated by experts. But as each one of these new technologies evolved further, particularly when they were made available to the public (or to average user), deception proliferated.

One of Photography's Early Deceptions

According to the Museum of Hoaxes, in 1917 a series of remarkable photos were taken by two young girls, Frances Griffith and Elsie Wright. The girls were in the garden of Elsie's Cottingley village home and seem to depict them playing with fairies (Fig. 6.1). In 1920, the pictures came to the attention of writer Sir Arthur Conan Doyle, who used them to illustrate an article on fairies he had been commissioned to write for The Strand Magazine

(Cooper, 1982). Doyle was a spiritualist and promoted the photos as valid evidence of mystical phenomena. Public reaction at the time was mixed; some accepted the images as genuine, but others believed they had been faked. Spiritualism, séances, and the use of Ouija boards were extremely popular in the 1920s, thus people wanted to believe in the supernatural. Magic presented by Harry Houdini was all the rage, as many people believed that what the greatest escape artist and illusionist was doing was paranormal. Thus the fairy photos played into the psychological and popular culture of the day, whether they were viewed by believers or skeptics. Nevertheless, the photos were seen by thousands of eager viewers and were the "viral" pics of the era.

Some expert photographers through the 1920s and 1930s examined the pictures and declared them genuine, as the original negative plates showed the images of the fairies (Clark, 2012). In 1983, the girls Elsie and Frances, now in their golden years, admitted that the photographs were faked. They used simple cardboard cutouts of fairies taken from one of their children's books. The deception pulled off in the famous Cottingley fairy photos was very easily constructed by two young girls using scissors and pictures from a book, but the photos fooled people for decades. Any person today who launches a browser and searches for "fake viral videos" can find contemporary equivalents of these fairies of the early 20th century.

FIGURE 6.1 The Cottingley fairies, photographed in 1917.

For example, a video began to circulate on social media of a supposed riot in Miami following George Zimmerman being acquitted of second-degree murder charges for the death of Trayvon Martin in 2013 (Hall, 2013). The footage shows main downtown streets filling up with people running while fires burn in the background. The person filming the scene provides partial narration, indicating they hope police crack skulls tonight (Hall, 2013). In reality, the video was misappropriated and was footage of a riot in Vancouver Canada in 2011 after the city's Canucks hockey team lost in the Stanley Cup finals. Such a simple scheme may have been designed to spread fear and confusion in the general public and help bolster Zimmerman's supporters.

Similarly, videos taken of death and destruction during the Syrian civil war have been mislabeled and posted online by groups in both Israel and Gaza in 2014. For instance, a YouTube user posted a video claiming it featured Hamas using children as human shields; however, it was actually shot in Syria (Mezzofiore, 2014). Other videos showed a father hugging his dead son, claiming it was a consequence of an Israeli assault, though it was actually a Syrian man. This sort of misrepresentation may not be immediately noticed by a casual observer and is used to generate attention to either side's cause and galvanize public opinion (Mezzofiore, 2014).

A slightly more involved video hoax occurred within a couple of hours of the terrorist attacks in Brussels in March of 2016 (Jackson, 2016). A video emerged on YouTube that claimed to be from a CCTV feed showing an explosion at Brussel's airport. The video also included footage allegedly showing an additional explosion at the Maelbeek metro station near the European Parliament building. This YouTube video was pure deception. All of the footage was actually taken from incidents which occurred in Eastern Europe. Some of the footage came from the 2011 attack on Moscow's main airport, and additional footage originated from the 2011 attack on the metro station in Minsk. According to Jackson (2016), the grainy CCTV clips were turned from color to black and white, flipped horizontally, relabeled, and posted as if they had emerged from the day's events at the Brussel's airport.

Film Fakes

The history of motion pictures began in the 1890s, when film cameras were invented and film production companies were established (Bordwell & Thompson, 2003). The motion pictures of the 1890s were typically under a minute long and did not contain an audio component. According to Who's Who of Victorian Cinema (1996), British film pioneer Robert W. Paul was the first to use "reverse-cranking," which allowed the same film footage to be exposed several times, creating multiple exposures. This technique was featured in his 1901 film Scrooge, or Marley's Ghost. The technique was used as a special effect or visual effect to create ghostly images or to add people and objects to a scene that was not originally there. It is frequently used in motion picture and photographic hoaxes.

However, it was later on in film history that motion pictures were deliberately manipulated to influence the audience. One of the best examples of film deception on a large public scale was the "Hitler Dance" (Fig. 6.2). Jaubert (1986) describes a newsreel film shown in 1941 to primarily American and Canadian movie goers. Prior to the feature films starting during WWII, the movie theaters would show news reels to inform the audiences about the war and how to support the troops. This particular newsreel depicted Adolf Hitler dancing a jig after he accepted the surrender of the French government at a ceremony in Compiegne, France on June 22, 1940. The dance was very child-like, as it showed Hitler celebrating the surrender by skipping and jumping up and down. Audiences laughed out loud as Hitler was perceived to be a fool or jester rather than a terrifying dictator. Lukacs (2001) indicated that years after the war ended, a history writer was pulling old WWII newsreel footage while conducting his research and thought the movie was odd, as it did not match the character or typical emotional displays of Adolf Hitler.

That history writer was correct to be suspicious, and in 1958 the Hitler newsreel was revealed as a fake, as pure deception to influence Allied and Nazi audiences alike. John Grierson, a Canadian propaganda expert and motion picture technician, created the false film for the war effort. The Canadian and US military wanted to make Hitler look silly so that Americans and Canadians would believe he could be easily defeated. The North Americans also knew that if Hitler or the Nazi Party saw the film they would be infuriated. The psy-ops movie was created by looping together real footage from Hitler as he took a high step forward and a step backward. The "jig" was created by replaying the high step forward over and over again (Lukacs, 2001).

FIGURE 6.2 View Hitler's jig (https://www.youtube.com/watch?v=CwpsZGEIMDw).

Video Software and Tools

The fakes, hoaxes, and deceptions created using the medium of motion picture film was fairly rudimentary compared with CGI and techniques that can be applied to video today. Faking film was expensive and would necessitate film editing equipment that was hardly found in anyone's home. When the clock is rolled forward to present day, the knowledge, equipment, access, and skills needed to fake video is available to almost everyone. To create the contemporary equivalent of the Hitler Dance hoax, all someone needs to do is to click on Break Your Own News (http://breakyourownnews.com/) and create a video complete with graphics and closed captions, ready for upload to various social media platforms to share. There is even a site that features the "best prankster" or fabricated videos on the web at http://www.shareonfb.com/.

This ability to distribute video has drastically shifted since 2006. Twitter/Periscope, Facebook, Snapchat, and other apps have offered ways to create, edit, and share video. According to the Cisco® Visual Networking Index™ (2016), by 2019 video will account for 80% of global internet traffic, and nearly a million minutes of video will be shared every second. There are easy ways to create video for personal or business use using screen captures, images, and special effects.

For the more experienced home and business user, there are scores of products that interface with cameras, laptops, tablets, GoPros, and phones to import video and offer near professional-level video editing. Home users, for a few hundred dollars at most, can buy products like Camtasia Studio, Pinnacle Studio, Adobe Premiere Pro CS6, Corel VideoStudio Ultimate X9, CyberLink PowerDirector 14 Ultimate, or Magix Movie Edit Pro Premium. For the "best in the business," Industrial Light and Magic (ILM) has their own patented IMOCAP technology, which was used to create the character of Davy Jones in *The Pirates of Caribbean: Dead Man's Chest* (Lucas Films, 2016). For *The Avengers*, ILM built a digital New York, seamlessly blending real photography and physical sets with CGI that included trees, extras, and buildings. While ILM attempted to duplicate NYC, demonstrating digital accuracy, the technology allows for creations, distortions, and special effects: meaning, the technology is more than capable of creating realistic deceptions.

In addition to the substantial software editing suites, which are available to anyone, special effects software products are also plentiful. However, to create special effects (e.g., deceptive images), some programs are better than others. Adobe After Effects CC is one of the most popular products and is used by individuals, businesses, and professional film-makers. Other software products for creating CGI effects includes iSkysoft Video Editor and AutoDesk Visual Effects.

Even without spending a few hundred dollars for special effects software, a novice videographer with a webcam can fake a live video by simply downloading an app. There are a few apps that offer some editing and special effects capabilities but can also trans-mit either a static picture or a video masqueraded as live video. For example, webcam emulators are programs that give a user the ability to broadcast videos and images on any website, chat service, or program that requires a webcam, but a webcam emulator simply plays a prerecorded video in a video chat session. The person being chatted with thinks the communication is live using a real webcam. One example is a shareware app called e2eSoft VCam. Another example of a webcam emulator is Magic Camera. This product has special effects and pop-up animations, which can be added to the created videos. Magic Camera also includes a virtual sound card tool that allows the recording of audio effects. So, be warned, the people participating in video chat sessions may not be real if they are using webcam emulation software.

Deciphering Fantasy From Reality

Since it is relatively easy and inexpensive to fake videos, asking whether "is it real or is it Memorex" (to quote a VHS tape advertisement from 1982) is a valid question. In some cases, images may be picked apart on appearances alone. For instance, a video released by the Islamic State on February 15, 2015 depicted the decapitation of 21 Egyptian Coptic Christians on a beach in Libya (Zimmerman, 2015). The video is extremely gruesome but features some problematic footage that introduces the potential for manipulation in order to mask the reality of the executions. Some argued that the video involved the use of various postproduction tricks to adjust the footage based on issues with the proportions of individuals filmed and other issues with the images themselves (Zimmerman, 2015). For example, the main speaker in the video is larger than the background, which could be an indication that the footage was produced on a sound stage with a matted-in background. Additionally, there were several unusual cuts in the footage, suggesting that they may have had to enhance the footage and use methods to conceal the edits. The video ends with a shot of the ocean made red with the blood of those executed, which experts argued had to have been the result of postproduction color correction (Zimmerman, 2015). Finally, the actual footage of the final decapitation in the video does not appear to match the way blood would pulse from a human body, nor does the blood appear to have an appropriate consistency. It is difficult to determine whether a video is real or fabricated, but scientists and special effects professionals who know how to manipulate video also know how to detect fakes.

Recent researchers have begun to apply the use of physics in order to scientifically validate videos. Allain (2014) suggests that from a physics perspective, there are at least three methods to use in an assessment that will identify a faked video:

1. look for unrealistic trajectories
2. identify impossible physics
3. detect fake shake

Some of the most popular faked videos online show someone or something being launched through the air landing in tiny kiddy swimming pools, mud pits, or on giant inflatable mattresses. Other videos demonstrate astounding feats that would have perplexed Evel Knievel such as driving cars or motorcycles over impossible ramps or other obstacles. In each of these cases a variety of forces are acting on the trajectory or projectile motion of the moving object(s). Nave (2016) states that in the absence of frictional drag, an object near the surface of the earth will fall with the constant acceleration of gravity. The actual and accurate position and speed at any time can be calculated from various motion equations. These motion equations take into account gravity, free fall, horizontal launches, vertical launches, and general trajectory variables. For example, if there is a video demonstrating projectile motion and it does not have a constant vertical acceleration and a constant horizontal velocity, then it is probably fake (Allain, 2014).

Another way to determine if a video is fake is to observe the video with some of the laws of physics in mind. Video games directly simulate physics using physical models.

While they do not use a perfectly accurate model of physics running inside the game, an approximate model allows the programmer to design realistic looking scenarios. However, manipulating video is a different story. If a videographer is creating a deceptive video by adding items or motion, many variables must be taken into consideration. For example, if someone were to create a video depicting a fake riot or altercation with objects being thrown, the math would have to be correct in order to get the objects correct:

- How heavy is it?
- How much force does it take to break, bend, or split?
- How much friction does it have?
- How fast can it go?
- How much traction does it have?
- What is the impact of the object?
- What is the reaction of the impact—against a solid object or against a person?

Weight, acceleration, drag, size, and mass are just a few of the variables that need to be mathematically calculated (or analyzed) to determine the veracity of an action video.

A third way to detect a fake video is to look for "fake shake" (Allain, 2014). Those who have made deceptive videos or prank videos have used several filming techniques. Sometimes the fabricators will use a steady-cam or tripod to get a smooth video so that special effects can be added later. It is easier to add special effects to a stationary shoot. Other fakers believe that their videos will more likely be believed if the video footage appears to be spontaneous, thus taken by a shaky hand in the throes of something exciting. So the fake videos contain an unnatural shake, which also can be detected mathematically as the video is analyzed.

For a security specialist, it may be difficult on first view to decipher whether a video being viewed or reviewed as evidence is valid. In addition to implementing the "physics tricks" listed above, it does make a difference whether the viewed video is a copy of a professionally produced original or if it is allegedly original source footage. Almost all cameras and professional video equipment will embed some type of time code into the video. Looking for deviations, skips in time, or nonchronological indications may be a good starting point.

Alternative Perspectives and Augmented Reality

Handheld devices make up the majority of the camera and editing-enabled equipment today. However, drones, low-orbit satellites, thermal cams, and video-enabled contact lenses are gaining popularity and momentum. These added technologies and advancements will further complicate the business of detecting deception, as well as protecting the overall visibility of properties, sensitive areas, facilities, homes, and assets.

The Federal Aviation Administration (FAA) announced in early 2016 that 325,000 drones were registered. A mandate by the FAA in December of 2015 required civilian drone owners to register their drones after numerous safety concerns were voiced by airplane pilots who had spotted drones too close to their aircraft, as the remote-controlled drones do not report into air traffic control and cannot be spotted using traffic collision avoidance systems. Many of these thousands of drones and quadcopters have built-in still and video cameras. The quality and fidelity of the video depends on the size of the drone itself as well as the equipment aboard. Some professional models offer high-definition video capture or the ability to connect an HD action camera, such as a 4K GoPro camera, and optional gimbal for antivibration. Of course, drones used by the military, law enforcement, and the intelligence community have other special adaptations and may be considerably larger than commercially available drones.

Nevertheless, drones are out there flying around, taking video. The users are then using the editing suites and special effects software to augment their drone videos. Most of the videos posted to YouTube and other "best drone video ever" sites depict real videos with enhanced colors, zooms, and other effects that make the viewing experience better. In addition to drones taking video, a new wave of low-orbit commercial satellites are up in the sky taking both photographs and videos. Just a few years ago, the only satellites available to take high-resolution video (to the 1 m level) were government-controlled satellites. Satellite imagery or imagery intelligence was collected by intelligence agencies. The imagery business was expensive and included the high costs of launching, repositioning, and obtaining photos (let alone video). But now, due to a few commercial companies such as Terra Bella, almost anyone can obtain high-resolution satellite imagery and high-definition video of a location of their choice. Terra Bella states that its satellites can capture video clips lasting up to 90 s at 30 frames per second (Wogan, 2013). Both drones and satellites will no doubt be armed with forward-looking infrared (FLIR) to further enhance the data and experience captured by the video. The video footage taken by any drone or satellite can be altered using any of the off-the-shelf video editing and special effects software products already discussed. The special effects products enable a user to a fake FLIR video by adjusting the saturation settings, brightness and contrast, gradient, and Gaussian blur (Yokozuna, 2014).

One of the newest and most interesting perspectives from which to take video is directly from the visual site line of the eye. Samsung has been granted a patent in South Korea for a contact lens with a component that projects images directly into wearer's eyes, and the built-in camera and sensors are controlled by blinking, according to the SamMobile blog (Michel, 2016). Sony and Google are also working on similar technologies (Stump, 2016). While these contact lens cameras are not even available to the public yet, the possibilities for deception are numerous. Imagine contact lens malware that would warp, skew, or present images back to the eye for the lens wearer to view (or believe they are viewing). Or imagine the lens wearer introducing additional images or removing images after a download of their views is recorded and then presenting it as eye-witness testimony? Detecting video deception must become more sophisticated or at least acknowledged as more and more people make digital video and imagery part of their daily lives.

Going on the Offensive: Deceiving Video

In the intelligence world, the acronym "CI" typically refers to counterintelligence. Law enforcement agencies and large commercial companies also employ CI to their respective missions. Recently, the Ford Motor Company deployed a CI technique that allowed the company to test drive prototyped models on public roadways but prevented the autos from accurately being photographed or captured on video (MacDonald, 2016). According to Ford Motor Company (2016), camera technology is only going to become more advanced, and it is necessary for the company to maintain their competitive edge by implementing camouflage in the form of vinyl stickers with patterns that trick the eye and create optical illusions. This type of misdirection helps Ford hide the actual design of the car. Ford has an entire "camouflage team" that works with various other concealment techniques so that corporate spies and others armed with video cameras cannot get a glimpse of their new vehicles before they are officially unveiled.

The application of CI to deceive video is not a new concept. One amazing example from history was the use of tactical deception in World War II, specifically the artistry and magic of the 23rd Headquarters Special Troops or the "Ghost Army" (Kneece, 2001). The Ghost Army was made up of 1100 US Army soldiers who were, prior to the war, artists, carpenters, engineers, electricians, and writers (Beyer, 2013). The unique blend of skills enabled these men to create illusions on the ground in theater. As enemy aircraft conducted reconnaissance missions from above, the Germans and their allies were filming critical Ally positions (Gerard, 2002). The American military knew about these surveillance fly-bys and decided that the Nazis could be fooled into believing erroneous positions and strategies (Beyer & Sayles, 2015). So the Ghost Army set up entire American encampments complete with inflatable tanks, trucks, planes, and buildings (Fig. 6.3) (Beyer, 2013).

FIGURE 6.3 World war II ghost army created inflatable tanks to fool german reconnaissance. *Photograph— Compliments of the National Archive.*

These newly fabricated Army units included such artistry to assist in believability of the battlefield deception. Painters added tread marks in the ground to simulate truck and tank movements within the camps and runways complete with aircraft skid marks (Beyer, 2013). No detail was overlooked. According to Beyer and Sayles (2015), the Ghost Army was broken into three specialties or units: 1) visual deception conducted by the 603rd Camouflage Engineers; 2) sonic deception conducted by the 3132 Signal Service Company Special; and 3) radio deception conducted by the Signal Company. In addition to the inflatables and painted landscape "special effects," the Ghost Army used sound to further exploit their deception. Thus if enemy scouts were sent out to investigate the positions of the American camps, they would hear normal sounds and acoustics coming from the empty compounds generated from speakers and amplifiers. The engineers mimicked and recorded actual sounds from a base and created playback broadcasters (Beyer, 2013). To complete the deception, radio specialists created fake radio traffic and Morse code, knowing that the opposition would be listening. Altogether, the Ghost Army engaged in more than 20 battlefield deceptions across Europe (Gerard, 2002).

The creation and implementation of the Ghost Army is not that different from Ford Motor Company's camouflage team. But with the proliferation of smartphones, video-taking drones, and video-capturing low-orbit satellites, perhaps it is necessary in today's world to utilize some of the other magic used during World War II. Currently, in order to protect sensitive facilities or the contents of those facilities, organizations may be reaching back in time to implement some of the camouflage techniques of the 1940s. Nosy drones, satellites, and publicly available imagery (i.e., Google Earth) may necessitate governments, corporations, and even individuals to purposely modify their geographic space. A new industry may have to fashion itself after the misdirection and defensive deception created in Burbank at the Lockheed Martin Airfield. "Operation Camouflage" was created to protect the production of airplanes occurring at the Lockheed Martin facility directly after the bombing of Pearl Harbor in 1941 (Breuer, 2001). According to Lockheed Martin (2016), a group of their executives, along with the US military, enlisted Colonel John F. Ohmer to create a disguise for the Lockheed Martin production facility.

Using some of the special effect geniuses of the time from the Hollywood Studios, painters, scenic designers, landscape architects, artists, and prop masters created a three-dimensional covering for the entire aircraft facility. From the air, the once obvious aircraft manufacturing center was now just a regular neighborhood in Burbank, California (Fig. 6.4) (Breuer, 2001).

Most facilities and homes today have already been captured by Google Maps and Google Street View. In some cases, personal items or sensitive information has been captured in the photographs and is available for all to see such as license plate numbers, the inside of garages, and methods of ingress and egress to properties (Jennings, 2013). To assist with hiding homes or other facilities, Google Maps offers an API on their developer's webpage with code for graphical overlays. The other way to "hide your home" is to go to Google Maps Street View, put in your home address, and then look for the "Send Feedback" link on the bottom right of the screen. The "Send Feedback" option will provide

FIGURE 6.4 Top photo: the actual Lockheed Martin Facility as it looked in 1942. Bottom photo: an aerial photo and result of "Operation Camouflage". *Photos courtesy of the Burbank Historical Society.*

a form to fill out, including the choice to blur your home. However, the digital tools offered to prevent anyone from seeing a particular location divulged by Google or similar services will not prevent the dedicated threat actor or nosy-barker from using flyover video options to document a location unless more drastic and physical deception measures are taken to alter the landscape. The art and creativity of CI that was instituted in the 1940s needs to be reevaluated and adapted for the current environment to deceive contemporary adversaries. Hollywood special effect skills may be employed once again to deceive and deflect the now ever-present and growing age of video capture.

References

Allain, R. (December 10, 2014). *The physics of fake videos.* Wired Magazine. Online source http://www.wired.com/2014/10/physics-fake-videos/.

Beyer, R., & Sayles, E. (2015). *The ghost army of world war II: How one top-secret unit deceived the enemy with inflatable tanks, sound effects, and other audacious fakery.* Princeton Architectural Press.

Beyer, R. (Writer & Director). (May 21, 2013 and June 3, 2015). The ghost army. PBS Television broadcast. Rick Beyer (Producer). Plate of Peas Productions. Washington, DC: WETA Distribution.

Bohn, T., & Stromgren, R. (1986). *Light and shadows: A history of motion pictures* (3rd ed.). New York: McGraw-Hill Humanities.

Bordwell, D., & Thompson, K. (2003). *Film history an introduction.* New York: McGraw-Hill Company Inc.

Breuer, W. B. (2001). *Deceptions of world war II.* New York: John Wiley & Sons.

Britz, M. T. (2013). Terrorism and technology: Operationalizing cyberterrorism and identifying concepts. In T. J. Holt (Ed.), *Crime on-line: Correlates, causes, and context* (pp. 193–220). Raleigh, NC: Carolina Academic Press.

Cisco® Visual Networking Index™. (June 2016). *Cisco visual networking index: Forecast and methodology, 2015–2020.*

Clark, J. (2012). *Unexplained! Strange sightings, incredible occurrences, and puzzling physical phenomena.* Canton, Michigan: Visible Ink Press.

Cooper, J. (1982). Cottingley: At last the truth. *The Unexplained, 117,* 2338–2340.

Dupre, S. (2008). Inside the camera obscura: Kepler's experiment and theory of optical imagery. *Early Science and Medicine, 13*(3), 219–244.

Ford Motor Company. (February 26, 2016). *The science of subterfuge: How ford uses modern camouflage to hide in plain sight.* Online source https://media.ford.com/content/fordmedia/fna/us/en/news/2016/02/25/how-ford-uses-modern-camouflage-to-hide-in-plain-sight.html.

Frampton, B. (September 14, 2015). *Clickbait: The changing face of online journalism.* BBC News. Online source http://www.bbc.com/news/uk-wales-34213693.

Gerard, P. (2002). *Secret soldiers: The story of world war II's heroic army of deception.* Dutton.

Hall, E. (July 14, 2013). *This is not a video of people rioting over the George Zimmerman Verdict.* Buzzfeed. https://www.buzzfeed.com/ellievhall/this-is-not-a-video-of-people-rioting-over-the-george-zimmer?utm_term=.bud2BGowP#.erVew6Vk3.

Jackson, J. (March 2016). *Fake Brussels YouTube videos prove ease of digital disinformation.* The Guardian. Digital media article Retrieved from http://www.theguardian.com/media/2016/mar/23/fake-youtube-videos-brussels-attacks-facebook-twitter.

Jaubert, A. (1986). *Making people disappear: An amazing chronicle of photographic deception.* London: Pergamon-Brassey.

Jennings, D. (October 30, 2013). *How to hide your house from Google Maps.* Off The Grid News. Online source http://www.offthegridnews.com/privacy/how-to-hide-your-house-from-google-maps/.

Kneece, J. (2001). *Ghost army of world war II.* Pelican Publishing.

Lucas Films. (2016). *Industrial Light and Magic—Homepage.* Online source http://lucasfilm.com/industrial-light-and-magic.

Lukacs, J. (2001). *The last European war: September 1939–December 1941.* Yale University Press.

MacDonald, C. (February 2016). *Hiding in plain sight: Ford reveals the optical illusions it uses to disguise the shape of its secret new cars.* The DailyMail. Retrieved from http://www.dailymail.co.uk/sciencetech/article-3466108/Hiding-plain-sight-Ford-reveals-optical-illusions-uses-disguise-shape-secret-new-cars.html.

Martin, L. (2016). *Lockheed during world war II: Operation camouflage.* Online source http://www.lockheedmartin.com/us/100years/stories/camouflage.html.

Mezzofiore, G. (July 21, 2014). *Syrian civil war videos used for online propaganda in Israel-Gaza conflict.* International Business Times. Retrieved from http://www.ibtimes.co.uk/syrian-civil-war-videos-used-online-propaganda-israel-gaza-conflict-1457571.

Michel, G. (April 2016). *Samsung is working on a smart contact lens, patent filing reveals.* Sammobile Blog. Online source http://www.sammobile.com/2016/04/05/samsung-is-working-on-smart-contact-lenses-patent-filing-reveals/.

Nave, C. R. (2016). *HyperPhysics.* Georgia State University, Department of Physics and Astronomy. Retrieved from http://hyperphysics.phy-astr.gsu.edu/hbase/hph.html.

Stump, S. (May 2016). *Sony applies for patent on contact lens camera that shoots photos in a blink.* CNBC. Online source http://www.cnbc.com/2016/05/03/.

Weimann, G. (2005). How modern terrorism uses the internet. *The Journal of International Security Affairs, 8.*

Who's Who of Victorian Cinema: A Worldwide Survey. (1996). In S. Herbert, & L. McKernan (Eds.). London: British Film Institute.

Wogan, D. (December 2013). *High-definition video from space is available for purchase. Finally.* Scientific American.

Yokozuna. (2014). *How to fake thermal imaging video.* Instructables. Online source http://www.instructables.com/id/How-to-Fake-Thermal-Imaging-Video/.

Zimmerman, M. (February 21, 2015). *ISIS' army of 7-footers? Experts say video of copt beheadings manipulated.* Fox News World. Retrieved from http://www.foxnews.com/world/2015/02/21/isis-army-7-footers-experts-say-video-copt-beheadings-manipulated.html.

Cyber Jihad and Deception: Virtual Enhancement and Shaping of the Terrorist Narrative

ABSTRACT

This chapter describes how jihadi movements utilize the Internet to shape the history and objectives of their movements, communicate ideological information to adherents as well as potential recruits, and provide a platform for fundraising as well. In addition, the chapter discusses how these movements have utilized the Internet to disseminate information on methods and techniques that can be utilized by jihadi followers to conduct cyber attacks against the movement's enemies. Later in the chapter the discussion turns to the use of online deception by jihadi actors to communicate threats of mass destruction to communicate fear throughout their opponent's populations as well as feints in terms of attacks to keep opposing security services guessing. The final section provides a brief look at how deceptive techniques such as steganography are utilized to keep critical communications from being intercepted by their opponents.

Keywords: *Cyber Caliphate; Dabiq; Electronic jihad; Jihad; Jihadi cyber attack; Jihadi historical narrative; Jihadi online fundraising; Propaganda; Recruitment; Social media; Steganography.*

CHAPTER OUTLINE

Deception in the Digital Age. http://dx.doi.org/10.1016/B978-0-12-411630-6.00007-4

Introduction

Nearly a quarter century after Barry Collin introduced the term *cyber terrorism*[1] the definition of this ominous category of malicious computing is not entirely crystallized, remaining a topic of focus and shaping by scholars and other experts. A myriad of similar concepts and terms such as *cyber jihad, e-jihad, electronic jihad,* and *Internet jihad,* often used interchangeably and inextricably, have further clouded the discussion and blurred the lines of scope and definitions. This chapter first examines the evolution of how terrorist organizations and supporters have used the Internet for conducting cyber attacks and then explores how these cyber jihadists use online deception to shape the narrative of their cyber network operations. Next this chapter looks at some of the mechanisms and pathways of deception that are utilized by jihadists to further terrorist objectives.

The World Wide Web and later Web 2.0[2] fundamentally changed how terrorist organizations operate, as a robust, global platform to communicate, radicalize, recruit, share information, and launch cyber attacks. No other factor in the last quarter century has so profoundly opened the aperture for enabling radicalized individuals and terrorist organizations to conduct mass communication and enhanced strategic messaging.

Cyber jihad, while still a malleable concept, has more generally been considered by experts to encompass jihadist use of the Internet both as a cyber attack channel against victim computer systems (not requiring resultant physical violence) and as a tool to facilitate other objectives of a terrorist organization. The use of the Internet as a platform for cyber jihad has been supported by a variety of individuals tied with Muslim extremist groups. For instance, Mohammad Bin Ahmad As-Sālim wrote a book titled *39 Ways to Serve and Participate in Jihâd,* designed to promote discussion about the issue of war with the West and jihad generally (D. Denning, 2010; Leyden, 2002). The book discussed the issue of electronic jihad as the 34th principal way to engage in jihad. He identified the need for both discussion forums for media campaigns and more specific applications of hacking techniques in order to harm the West. Specifically, he wrote: "He [anyone with knowledge of hacking] should concentrate his efforts on destroying any American websites, as well as any sites that are anti-*Jihâd* and *Mujâhidîn*, Jewish websites, modernist and secular websites" (As-Sālim, 2003). Thus terror groups realize that Western nations dependence on the Internet for both commerce and communications is a major vulnerability that can be exploited to cause economic harm and fear in the general populace.

Al Qaeda: Reinvigorating Cyber Jihad

During the late 1990s there was significant speculation about how terrorists might utilize the Internet to conduct damaging attacks against Western critical infrastructure using only computers as weapons and the Internet as the conduit for attacks. In the years following

---

[1] Collin, B. (1996). The future of cyberterrorism, *Proceedings of the 11th Annual International Symposium on Criminal Justice Issues*: The University of Illinois at Chicago.

[2] Web 2.0 describes web and other online resources with user-created content, engagement, and social networking.

the September 11, 2001 terror attacks against the United States and the resulting coalition military response against Taliban and Al Qaeda strongholds in Afghanistan, cyber attacks conducted by a new generation of attackers and ad-hoc groups occupied the cyber jihad threat space. These unsophisticated attacks, often denial of service (DoS) and website defacements, were typically conducted by pseudo-official, shadowy named individuals or groups that were notionally, tenuously, or nominally associated with Al Qaeda.

Indeed, for approximately a decade after the 9/11 attack, academic researchers and popular media focused heavily on Al Qaeda and their role in global terror activities (Forest, 2009; Jones, 2006). Much of this work has helped inform experts' knowledge of the real-world threats that this group posed and conversely revealed the little evidence demonstrating their role in successful cyber attacks (D. Denning, 2010; Ulph, 2006). During this period, however, there was some evidence that loose associations of hacker groups were interested in and attempted to engage in cyber attacks against the West. This so-called "cyber jihad" had ties to Al Qaeda and other Islamic extremist groups across the Middle East and Africa and depended on technology for communications infrastructure and as an attack platform (D. Denning, 2010; Ulph, 2006). Many of these groups sought *derivative legitimacy*, adopting a nominal or implied Al Qaeda nexus for credibility, authority, and positioning.

The first hacker group that emerged with specific ties to Al Qaeda was the "al-Qaeda Alliance Online," an offshoot of the hacker group "GForce Pakistan." Members of the Alliance defaced a web server operated by the National Oceanic and Atmospheric Administration on October 17, 2001 (McWilliams, 2001). The defacement contained interesting, if not contradictory, information by condemning the September 11 attacks, stating: "bin Laden is a holy fighter, and whatever he says makes sense" (McWilliams, 2001). They went on to say that they would attack major websites in the United States and Britain, though "we will not hurt any data as its [sic] unethical" (McWilliams, 2001).

A subsequent defacement occurred 10 days later on October 27th, 2001, though that was the last attack attributed to the group (D. Denning, 2010). It is not clear what happened to the Alliance, but it was replaced by a variety of forums and hacker groups actively engaged in the promotion of attacks against the West and others who disparaged the Islamic faith. For instance, the al-Farouq forum established a section encouraging electronic jihad, along with a downloadable library of tools and tutorials for engaging in attacks (D.E. Denning, 2010; Pool, 2005).

By 2007, a number of jihadist hacker "teams," "brigades," and "electronic armies" claimed their formation, allegiances, and perceived primacy in this evolving space—groups such as *Hackers al-Ansar* (Fig. 7.1), *Osama Bin Laden Crew, Farouq Electronic Army* (also known as the *Jaysh Farouq al-Elektroni*), *Majma' Al-Haker Al-Muslim, Majmu'at Al Jihad Al-Electroni*, Munazamat Fursan Al-Jihad Al-Electroni, and *Ansar Al-Jihad Hackers Team for Electronic Jihad*, among others.[3]

---

[3] Alshech, E. (February 27, 2007). *Cyberspace as a combat zone: The phenomenon of electronic jihad, Memri, No. 329.* Available on the Internet at: http://cjlab.memri.org/uncategorized/cyberspace-as-a-combat-zone-the-phenomenon-of-electronic-jihad; and Denning, D. (2007). *The jihadi cyberterror threat.* Available on the Internet at: safecomputing.umich.edu/events/download/Cyberterrorism-UofM.ppt; Danchev, D. (2012). *Cyber jihad vs cyber terrorism–Separating hype from reality, RSA Conference, Europe 2012.*

FIGURE 7.1 Imagery from jihad hacking site, "Hacker al-Ansar".

With the burgeoning number of jihad-motivated hacking groups seeking recognition, respect, and primacy, new online resources, such al-ansar.virtue.nu[4] (used by *Ansar Al-Jihad Hackers Team for Electronic Jihad*, Fig. 7.2), and new tools to support the cyber jihad mission and narrative were developed and made available for supporters to download.

FIGURE 7.2 Imagery from the jihad hacking web site, al-ansar.virtue.nu website, used by the Ansar Al-Jihad Hackers Team for Electronic Jihad.

[4] https://web.archive.org/web/20070813084830/http://www.al-ansar.virtue.nu/sh1.html; https://web.archive.org/web/20070813084611/http://www.al-ansar.virtue.nu/.

The *al-Jinan* forum[5] (Fig. 7.3) created and offered a free download of a DoS tool called *Electronic Jihad* (Fig. 7.4) and gave awards and electronic medals to those who were the most effective attackers against sites that harmed Islam (Bakier, 2007). With the distribution of the tool came a compelling deception campaign, wherein the army of cyber jihadists armed with the tool intended to launch a large-scale, devastating DoS attack.[6]

الجهاد الإلكتروني : هو الوسائل والطرق التي يمكن بها إحداث أكبر ضرر مادي وبشري ومعنوي للعدو باستخدام شبكة الإنترنت ، ويتم اكتشاف الوسائل المستخدمة من قبل المتخصصين في مجال الإنترنت والشبكات ، وأغلب الاكتشافات تمت من قبل الأشخاص المدعوون (المخترقون او Hackers) وهم منتشرون على مستوى العالم والكثير منهم يقوم بأعمال تخريبية بلا هدف أو معنى .

يتم تطويع هذه الوسائل الفتاكة لكي تستهدف أعدائنا وتلحق بهم أشد الأضرار المالية التي قد تصل إلى الملايين ، والمعنوية التي تؤدي إلى خشية المسلمين أينما ذهبوا حتى في شبكة الإنترنت ، وذلك ردًا على طغيانهم وعدوانهم وليس تبليًا عليهم فديننا يحث على السلم قبل كل شيء.

إن جماعات مثل شبكتنا قامت ونشأت على مر التاريخ ، وأفظع هذه المجموعات هي الصهيونية منها ، حيث أن الصهاينة قاموا بإنشاء جماعات تهدف إلى تدمير كل مواقع المقاومة الفلسطينية والجهاد والمواقع الإسلامية ، وتعمل هذه المجموعات بجد لتحقيق أهدافها ونحن نحزن حين نرى أعدائنا لديهم هذا النوع من التوحد ، وندعو الله أن نغلبهم بتوحدنا وجمعنا الذي يساويهم مئات الأضعاف ولكن علينا أن نعمل كرجل واحد

قال تعالى : (إِنَّ اللهَ يُحِبُّ الَّذِينَ يُقَاتِلُونَ فِي سَبِيلِهِ صَفاً كَأَنَّهُم بُنيَانٌ مَرْصُوصٌ) .

ما يميز الجهاد الإلكتروني هو أنه لا يأخذ الوقت الكثير من الناس لكي ينفذوه ، فهو يعتمد على توجيه ضربات سريعة وفي وقت قصير يكون ضررها كبيرًا ومستمرًا ، يمكن لأي إنسان يمتلك جهاز حاسوب ويتصل بشبكة الإنترنت أن يشترك في هذا المجال فهو يعتمد على برامج سهلة ومجهزة لكي تقوم هي بالعمل ، وعلى الشخص فقط أن يشغل البرنامج ويجلس على الإنترنت حتى تنتهي مدة الهجمة وهذا جهد أقل ما يمكن تقديمه من أجل فلسطين ولبنان ولكن له الأثر الكبير إن شاء الله.

وما يهم في الهجوم هو التنظيم ، والعمل بوقت واحد وهذا ما يحدث الضرر الأكبر مثلما يقوم الجيش العادي بالدفاع جنبًا إلى جنب عن أرضهم وبلادهم ، تقوم المجموعة بالعمل معًا ولو لم تجتمع كلها فمن الممكن أن تفشل العملية ولا تحدث أي إنجاز يذكر.

ندعوكم جميعًا للتسجيل في القائمة الجهادية والاضطلاع على طريقة الهجوم والبرنامج المستخدم ، ومشاركتنا إن شاء الله في جميع هجماتنا ولكم جزيل الشكر .

إدارة شبكة الجنان

AL-JINAN NET

FIGURE 7.3 Al-Jinan.net (electronic jihad) website content, describing the nature and purpose of "electronic jihad".

[5] Initially this website was hosted at al-jinan.org, but subsequently moved to al-jinan.net. https://web.archive.org/web/20070609122521/http://www.al-jinan.org/.

[6] http://www.pcworld.com/article/139151/article.html Report: Cyber Jihad Set for Nov. 11.

FIGURE 7.4 The e-jihad v.2 and 3.0 programs (hacking tools designed to launch denial of service attacks).

While many of the cyber jihad groups and respective attack campaigns did not gain critical traction or impactful results, one of the most well-known examples of cyber jihad during this period was the case of a hacker named Youni Tsoulis, who used the handle "Irhabi007" (Fig. 7.5). Tsoulis developed multiple web forums and sites supporting Al Qaeda and even set up hidden links to propaganda websites on various forums (Corera, 2008). He also promoted hacking and gave multiple tutorials on hacker sites with substantial detail on methods of attacks and tactics to compromise websites (Jamestown, 2008). Due to the degree to which he actively engaged and shared information about cyber attack techniques with others in the jihad movement, Tsouli came to the attention of law enforcement and military agencies

FIGURE 7.5 An image of Youni Tsoulis, aka "Irhabi007" (a "cyber jihadist hacker") proudly displayed on the al-ansar.virtue.nu website.

around the world. In fact, his name was found on a laptop belonging to a member of an Al Qaeda cell in Bosnia who was arrested after making threatening videos against various European nations. Tsouli was arrested by the London Metropolitan Police during a raid in 2005 and was found guilty of charges under the Terrorism Act of 2000 (Corera, 2008). He received a 16-year sentence; he was 23 years old at the time.

Tsouli is one of the few examples of success in the cyber jihad's campaign against the West during the early to mid-2000s. For instance, individuals attempted to engage in a DoS attack against the Vatican website after Pope Benedict made comments about the Prophet Mohammad and Islam that were viewed as critical of their faith (D. Denning, 2010). In addition, individuals motivated by jihadist ideologies planned a coordinated series of attacks against US financial institutions and the stock exchange in 2006. All of these attacks failed to materialize, calling to question the skill of the attackers relative to the preparations taken to defend against such attacks (Alshech, 2007; D. Denning, 2010; Gross & McMillan, 2006).

Despite efforts to engage in disabling and destructive cyber attacks, online jihadists sought knowledge and endeavored to train others who were earnest and interested in their cause. As a result, in the mid-2000s a number of online resources and periodicals emerged to provide tutelage to nascent or burgeoning cyber jihadists. In 2006 and 2007 the *Al-Fajr Information Center* released the e-magazine *Al-Mujahid Al-Taqni*, or *The Technical Mujahid*.[7] The issues contained a series of step-by-step technical instructions across a broad spectrum of topics, ranging from steganography (Fig. 7.6), alternative data streams, encrypted communications

FIGURE 7.6 The Technical Mujahid magazine.

[7] For a discussion about the magazine release, *see,* http://www.jamestown.org/programs/tm/single/?tx_ttnews%5Btt_news%5D=1057&; www.memrijttm.org/content/view_print/blog/159.

(Fig. 7.7), GPS, rootkits (Fig. 7.8), among others. Similar instructional materials, such as a *Cyber Jihadist's Encyclopedia* sought to augment aspiring, radicalized hackers.[8]

FIGURE 7.7 Images from the "Technical Mujahid magazine".

FIGURE 7.8 Images from the "Technical Mujahid magazine".

[8] Berton, B., & Pawlak, P. (2015). *Cyber jihadists and their web*. European Union Institute for Security Studies; Danchev, D. (2012). *Cyber jihad vs cyber terrorism–Separating hype from reality, RSA Conference, Europe 2012.*

Malware attack campaigns, although not typical of cyber jihad modus operandi or tactics, techniques, or procedures, have been loosely attributed to attackers seeking to further damage and confuse objectives. In September, 2010, this landscape shifted when a pernicious mass-mailing worm variant, `Visal.B` (also known as W32/VBMania@MM and Imsolk.A/Visal.A/VBMania), spread via email, containing permutations of a malicious URL that caused unsuspecting victims to execute malicious code (Fig. 7.9).[9]

```
Hello:

This is The Document I told you about,you can find it Here.

http://www.<malicious URL>.com/library/<malicious file>.pdf

Please check it and reply as soon as possible.

Cheers,


_____


Hello:

This is The Free Dowload Sex Movies,you can find it Here.

http://www.<malicious URL>.com/library/<malicious file>.wmv

Enjoy Your Time.

Cheers,
```

FIGURE 7.9 "Here you have" email variants.

Notably, the attack was attributed to the "*Brigades of Tariq ibn Ziyad,*" both through the forensic artifact analysis of malware by researcher and information security expert Joe Stewart and by self-reporting of the purported malware developer, who went by the moniker "iraq_resistance."[10] Stewart's analysis of the code and other extrinsic clues and artifacts discovered in this process (such as Arabic character sets, domain names, web forum posts,[11] a YouTube channel, and other corroborating and inculpating data) pointed succinctly at Iraq_resistance and his credited organization (Fig. 7.10).

[9] https://www.microsoft.com/security/portal/threat/encyclopedia/entry.aspx?Name=Worm:Win32/Visal.B; http://www.mcafee.com/threat-intelligence/malware/default.aspx?id=275435; https://www.us-cert.gov/ncas/current-activity/2010/09/09/Malicious-Email-Campaign-Circulating; http://www.snopes.com/computer/virus/hereyouhave.asp.

[10] https://www.secureworks.com/blog/research-20891; http://www.computerworld.com/article/2515482/enterprise-applications/cyber-jihad-group-linked-to-here-you-have-worm.html.

[11] For example, http://www.osoud.net/vb/showthread.php?t=30779; http://www.vbhacker.net/vb/t260110/.

FIGURE 7.10 Still image taken of the YouTube video believed to be made by the malware developer iraq_resistance.[12]

In May 2012, Al Qaeda released a video, entitled "The Electronic Jihad," calling on jihadists with technical computing backgrounds and capabilities to conduct cyber attacks against US cyber infrastructure.[13] This professionally edited video included subtitles and spliced video footage of American cyber experts discussing the potentially powerful implications of a cyberterror attack. During the video the narrator sonorously observed that "the current state of the information networks from an electronic attack of a jihadist operations standpoint, is not different from the state of security of the United States before 2001, which, after the successes granted by God, made carrying out the blessed Tuesday raids possible." Seeking to covey authority and credibility, later in the video a still image and overdubbed voice of deceased Al Qaeda in Iraq leader Abu Ayyub al-Masri is invoked, declaring that "we destroy the sites of the enemy and destroy the fortifications of its military security and political establishments. Furthermore, we turn towards the money of the non-believers and sabotage their economic institutions, instill terror among their stockholders, and shake their confidence. I think that the electronic warfare is one of the important and effective future wars" (Fig. 7.11).

[12] http://www.youtube.com/watch?v=IkMifFGqt78.

[13] http://hsgac.senate.gov/download/?id=483eca14-3c0e-4a30-9038-f4bf4a1fad60; https://www.hsgac.senate.gov/media/majority-media/senators-say-video-urging-electronic-jihad-underscores-need-for-cybersecurity-standards.

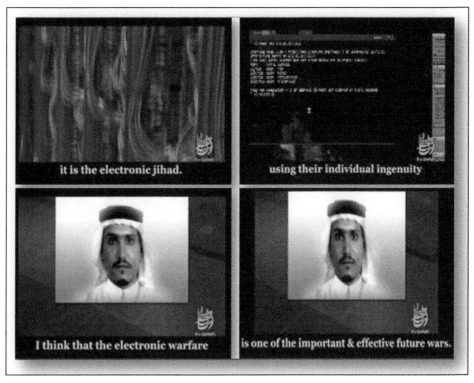

FIGURE 7.11 Still images taken from the "The electronic jihad" video released by Al Qaeda in 2012.

ISIS and the Cyber Jihad: Beginnings of the Digital Manifestation of the Islamic State

The vacuum created by the demise of Al Qaeda's fledging cyber apparatus left opportunity for new, endeavoring attackers and groups to fulfill their loyalty and obligation toward their radical cause. During this period, other nonjihadist hackivist collectives such as Anonymous and their derivative splinter groups Lulzsec, AntiSec, and CabinCr3w thrived through a series of brazen, pernicious, and highly publicized computer intrusions, raising the global collective awareness about computer hacking to a new level.

A somewhat later emerging competitor to these groups, TeaMp0isoN, used very similar techniques but was smaller in scale. The de facto leader of the group was a young British-Pakistani man, Junaid Hussain (aka TriCk). Heffelfinger (2013) provides a descriptive summary of his actions and those of TeaMp0isoN, detailing how they targeted NATO as well as government officials from the United States and the United Kingdom during the period from 2010–2012 in support of liberating Muslims in various territories including Palestine (Fig. 7.12).

FIGURE 7.12 Imagery created by the cyber hacking group "TeaMp0isoN"

In addition to these attacks, Heffelfinger also points out that the members of TeaMp0isoN participated in the theft of hundreds of credit cards from Israeli citizens. Hussain was eventually arrested in 2012 in the United Kingdom but fled on bail to Syria, where it is said that he joined ISIL. He subsequently joined an ISIS affiliated hacking group called the Cyber Caliphate, which in turn consisted of four subgroups: Ghost Caliphate Section, Sons Caliphate Army, Cyber Caliphate Army, and the Kalachnikv e-security team. He was strongly suspected of being behind the 2015 CENTCOM attack that threatened US soldiers and listed out personal information of military personnel (Fig. 7.13).

FIGURE 7.13 Imagery created by the cyber hacking group "Cyber Caliphate"

Hussain was eventually killed in a US drone strike in Syria in August 2015.

After the death of Hussain, the Cyber Caliphate group continued its pattern of malicious online activities. In early September 2015, one of the most notable attacks led by this group was the attack on the French television station TV5Monde, which was extensively hacked by the Cyber Caliphate group. The television station's social network accounts and websites were taken over by the hacking group and, more seriously, TV5Monde was forced off the air by the Cyber Caliphate group for approximately 3 h (France 24, 2015).

Sometime during April 2016, the four subgroups of the Cyber Caliphate consortium of hacking groups united together to form the United Cyber Caliphate (Fig. 7.14).

FIGURE 7.14 Imagery created by the cyber hacking group "United Cyber Caliphate."

Since that merger, the United Cyber Caliphate has been extremely active in terms of attacks against a large variety of organizations and their websites. According to a detailed timeline by the Site Intelligence Group (2016): (1) the United Cyber Caliphate obtained the list of 3600 New York citizens and proclaimed they wanted them dead (April, 2016); (2) similarly obtained personal information on 1500 Texas residents and declared they wanted them dead (May, 2016); (3) obtained another kill list consisting of thousands of Canadian citizens (June, 2016); and (4) hacked 50,000 Facebook and Twitter accounts (July, 2016) and a professionally styled infographic touting some of the major attacks that they have initiated (Fig. 7.15).

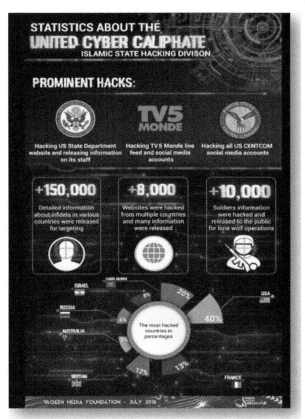

FIGURE 7.15 Imagery created by the cyber hacking group "United Cyber Caliphate."

ISIS and the Evolution of Sophisticated Online Propaganda

While the supporters of ISIS, like the United Cyber Caliphate, continued to conduct attacks against Western interests in working toward the goal of creating an Islamic Caliphate, the primary members of ISIS were working hard to perfect sophisticated online media campaigns to bolster their on-the-ground efforts in a number of countries and Syria in particular.

Unlike the secondary supporters of the jihadist movement that have been discussed previously, the core ISIS media teams design their online messages and media utilizing proven psychological propaganda principles. The Arab newspaper *Asharq Al-Awsat* (2005) has quoted Al Qaeda leader Al-Zawahiri as stating that "The organization therefore regards its media strategy as representing "two thirds of the battle, and regards the struggle over popular opinion as essential and complementary to its activity." According to the Meir Amit Intelligence and Terrorism Information Center (2014), there are a number of entities within ISIS that handle propaganda for the organization including the Al-Furqan Institute for Media Production, the Al-I'tisam Media Foundation, the Alhayat Media Center, and the Ajnad Media Foundation.

Siboni, Cohen, and Koren (2015) notes that ISIS uses the principle of "propaganda of the deed" as outlined by Bolt (2012), where violence and communications are merged together to become a more effective message. Siboni et al. (2015) further assert that "ISIS's Internet success is due to the connection between its use of extreme ruthless cruelty and the use of cyberspace to spread messages internally and externally for purposes of recruitment and intimidation." They further note that while Al Qaeda tended to utilize the Dark Web for much of its communications, ISIS recognizes the importance of spreading its propaganda as widely as possible among the more moderate Arab world as well as the Western world, which means that in order maximize the exposure of these materials, they are distributed primarily on the more familiar and traditional Web. Siboni et al. (2015) also observed that ISIS is in a competition of sorts against Al Qaeda to win the hearts and minds (and wallets) of the Arab world as well as compete for attention in the Western world as an enemy that poses a serious threat and should be listened to.

One of the more familiar online media vehicles for ISIS is the online magazine *Dabiq* (Fig. 7.16).

FIGURE 7.16 An image of the jihad magazine, *"Dabiq."*

Ingram (2016), in his analysis and comparison of both ISIS's *Dabiq* magazine as well as Al Aqaeda's *Inspire* online magazine notes that each magazine "provides their readership with a 'competitive system of meaning' (i.e., an alternative perspective of the world compared to that presented by their opponents), that acts as a 'lens' through which to shape their supporters' perceptions, polarize their support, and, ultimately, convince them to mobilize." Ingram goes on to state that the key concepts at work here are of identity, solution, and crisis.

Ingram further explains that identity is tied to "an historical narrative, strategically constructed in response to a sociohistorically specific reality" and that identity is shaped by the perception of the crisis at hand and also by solutions that are available. Ingram suggests that crisis brings with it uncertainty, the breakdown of tradition, and what he calls the influence of the Other. He suggests that radicalization as a solution can bring back certainty, provide supportive traditions, and restore certainty and reliance on traditions to the individual. *Dabiq*'s psychological strategy according to Ingram is that "*Dabiq*'s architects have fused rational-choice appeals—reflected in solution/crisis messaging—and identity-choice appeals—reflected in ingroup/solution messaging—in its calls to Western Muslims." He also observes that "*Dabiq* contrasts the exciting and meaningful life in its Caliphate with the existential angst many Western Muslims may experience: 'The modern day slavery of employment, work hours, wages, etc., is one that leaves the Muslim in a constant feeling of subjugation to a kafir master. He does not live the might and honor that every Muslim should live and experience.'"

It is clear from the discussions in this section that the evolution of cyber jihad and efforts by jihadist terror organizations to utilize the Internet for recruitment, funding, and transmission of threats to opponents has been rapid and has at times entailed both primitive and sophisticated communication strategies and elements. This period of rapid change is likely to continue in the near future, and new hacking groups supporting these organizations are bound to emerge. As the these two major terrorist organizations—Al Qaeda and ISIS—continue to compete against each other as well as expend effort to keep from being torn apart by Western military, economic, and political efforts, there will be additional elements to take into account in future analyses.

Cyber Jihad and Digital Deception

Gill, Horgan, Hunter, and Cushenbery (2013) make the argument that terrorist organizations can be both creative and innovative. They point out that other researchers (Cronin, 2009) observe that most terrorist organizations are short-lived and die out within the first year, and Gil and his colleagues suggest that characteristics such as creativity and innovation may be key components to the survival of these organizations during this hazardous first year and beyond. They also point out, as do James, Clark, and Cropanzano (1999), that the role of creativity (specifically malevolent creativity) and innovation in the analysis of terrorist organizations has been largely neglected by researchers.

Creativity and innovation are closely linked to the tactics of surprise, denial, and deception. It often takes creative thought to effectively hide actions or information as well as invent new and unexpected ways to implement those actions. Kass and Phillip (2013, p. 71) point out that surprise is key to disrupting the information processes that guide a potential enemy's actions and they observe that "the deeper the surprise, the stronger the going-in assumptions, the more rigid the processes, and the more valuable the information that has been lost along the way, the higher the potential for cognitive dissonance and, consequently, the more persistent the ensuing paralysis."

Deception and denial are closely related to surprise according to Kass and Phillip (2013), and they point out that these techniques are in use by terrorist organizations, as evidenced for example by their promotion within Al Qaeda manuals. In order to maintain surprise, it is often necessary to adopt deception as a strategy to keep details of an action or event from an opponent so that they are not able to construct a true picture of the objectives or plans of the terrorist organization. Kass and Phillip (2013) further state that an opponent will likely use deception in signaling that their capabilities and vulnerabilities are different than reality, that they intend to initiate some action other than the actual one, and mislead as to where this action might take place; this action may take some form other than the one that has been hinted at or stated.

The emergence of the Internet has generated a new and unique environment in which deception can be deployed by criminal and terrorist organizations in unique and different ways. The very nature of this digital world provides these organizations with the opportunity to utilize words as well as rich media including audio, video, and still images to reshape reality to their own purposes. Gartzke and Lindsay (2015) point out that "gullible people and vulnerable machines are now linked together at an unprecedented scale. The risk of deception cannot be engineered away, moreover, because user trust and software abstraction are required in order for computer applications to be useful at all. Signals designed to certify the authenticity of communications simply become additional tools for deception."

As Holt (2012) outlines, the Internet provides criminals and terrorists with a target-rich environment from which they can use deception to steal financial credentials or even use charities to deceive the authorities in order to help fund their activities. Jacobson (2010) describes how as Tsouli (Irhabi 007) expanded his support of Al Qaeda in Iraq by posting terrorist videos to the Internet, he soon required additional funding to support hosting fees for these videos and turned to purchasing stolen credit cards online and laundering money through online casinos. In addition, Jacobson relates how terrorist organizations deceive contributors as well as law enforcement through the use of online solicitation of funds to charities that then directly or indirectly contribute funds to terrorist organizations. He describes how charities such as The Global Relief Fund described their mission as "focused on its work in emergency relief, medical aid, advancement of education and development of social welfare" while in fact the monies were funneled to Al Qaeda and the Taliban often for purposes of supporting terrorist activities.

Al Qaeda also plays what Jessee (2006) describes as a "cyber deception" game with the hosting of its websites. They often prestage multiple website-hosting sites, sometimes inside the very countries they oppose (e.g., in the United States in Texas and Michigan) as well as in other countries where there are willing or unknowing Internet Service Providers to provide hosting services for websites that serve various terrorist propaganda, recruitment, and funding purposes. When one of the websites is caught in a takedown by legal authorities, the terrorist organization just "unparks" the next website in line, and the websites are back online often quite quickly.

A similar strategy for terrorist organizations for distributing deceptive content across social media accounts is deployed by what Fisher (2015) calls the "media mujahedeen". These members and supporters of terrorist organizations are organized into social networks where Fisher observes that the demarcation between content producer and audience is blurred. He describes the distribution of material by this network of supporters as a "swarmcast" where the characteristics of speed, agility, and resilience make it difficult to block messages and content because of the nature of peer-to-peer social networks.

Deception on the Internet has also played a crucial role in the efforts by jihadist terrorist organizations to project an image of power and strength. Often these efforts deceptively exaggerate the power, abilities, capabilities, and successes of the terrorist organization. As Siboni et al. (2015) point out, terrorist organizations like ISIS utilize rich online media in their efforts to intimidate Western governments and bolster their image among Muslim populations. For example, in the pro-ISIS film *The Flames of War*, Siboni et al. (2015) describe how the film "includes sophisticated illusory elements (size, distorted pictures, enhancement of speakers, a speech lit by torches) resembling the 1934 propaganda film produced in Nazi Germany as a propaganda documentary move by Leni Riefenstahl's *Triumph of the Will*." They further observe that the use of extremely violent online images are an important component of influence efforts. They suggest that "savagery creates an atmosphere of prolonged international interest and awareness. It also shapes its cruel image, sometimes creating the impression of being more powerful than it actually is."

Deceptive and real images of extreme violence are not the only strategies by which jihadist terrorist organizations attempt to influence both Western and Muslim audiences. Mueller and Stewart (2016) compare the observations by US President Barack Obama that fewer Americans die due to terrorism than gun violence, car accidents, or falls in bathtubs with the fact that "77% of the people appear to be convinced that ISIS presents 'a serious threat to the existence or survival of the US'". This kind of distortion provides a window of opportunity for terrorist organizations to capitalize on this distortion through deceptive digital communications and propaganda.

One vector of deception utilized by terrorist organizations that takes advantage of this distortion is the threat of mass causalities against its opponents. This threat suggests that these organizations may either implicitly or explicitly use weapons of mass destruction against its enemies. Post 9/11, Al Qaeda began focusing upon the acquisition of weapons of mass destruction (Bergen, 2010). However, Bergen suggests that the probability of terrorist organizations gaining access to weapons of mass destruction was at the time near zero. While terrorist organizations have deployed initiatives into developing and using weapons of mass destruction, up to this point they have been, at least as far as we know, unsuccessful. One of the few incidents concerning the pursuit of weapons of mass destruction by a terrorist organization that is known concerns the activities by Jemaah Islamiyah to produce anthrax for use as a weapon (Joosse & Milward, 2014).

Regardless, the strategy by terrorist organizations to use deception via digital communications to imply that they are willing and able to inflict mass casualties on its enemies generates fear among the target populations and serious concern among the governments targeted via this deceptive information. The gap between the perceived level of threat to the targets of the use of weapons of mass destruction versus the actual probability of a terrorist attack using a weapon of mass destruction provides terrorist organizations with the opportunity to use deception to instill fear into its enemies.

Recruitment into jihadist terrorist organizations also involves deception perpetrated through digital communication channels. Weimann (2016) points out that online recruitment is utilized by all terrorist organizations and that social media is a key channel through which new recruits to jihadist organizations are funneled into the recruitment process. Weimann describes how Al Qaeda in the Islamic Maghreb utilizes terrorist themed video games for children where the game is designed such that it emphasizes the terrorist group's ability to "win against international forces," and when a player loses their life, the game shows the message "Congratulations, you have become a martyrs!" instead of the typical "Game Over" message, minimalizing the consequences of the loss of the player's life.

Recruitment of women into jihadist organizations also involves deceptive communications transmitted through digital channels. Weimann (2016) reports for example that a woman being recruited for the Syrian campaign reported that she was told that "In Syria she could have a perfect life and get married." Berko and Erez (2006) in her work on Palestinian terrorist recruitment describes how men involved in the organization may use "romantic manipulation" to entice women into directly or indirectly supporting Palestinian jihadists. Sara Khan (2015) describes how young girls are "befriended online, told they're loved, showered with praise and flattery. These girls, like victims of child sexual exploitation, don't see themselves as victims. They see themselves as girls going to be with men who genuinely love them."

Another recent phenomena involves members of a terrorist group such as ISIS using digital technology to hack into government databases and exfiltrate personally identifiable information about government employees such as name, address, phone number, and more (Hayward, 2015; Fenlon, 2016). The data from these lists is published online along with statements from ISIS leaders that brand these individuals as enemies of Islam and encourage supporters of the terrorist organization and its causes to inflict physical harm against those individuals on the online list. Once again we see a deceptive "gap" between what is stated in the online digital communications versus what is likely to happen. While the probability that any single individual on the list is likely to be harmed because of directions of ISIS representatives is quite slim, the fear and anxiety that this deception produces is real and significant.

There is one final observation to make on the sometimes deceptive nature of digital communications themselves that occur between members of a specific jihadist organization. Members of these terrorist entities are very aware that numerous governments are capable of and are quite active in monitoring communications that occur over the Internet. Therefore members may take a number of different precautions when exchanging information over the Internet. These precautions include the now time-worn tactic of shared email accounts, where communications are written and held in a draft folder but never sent out over the Internet to the recipient. The intended recipient logs onto the shared email account and reads the message found in the draft (D. Denning, 2010). Another traditional tradecraft practice is the use of secret code words in open unencrypted digital communications to avoid detection (Denning, 2004).

Another digital tradecraft practice that utilizes deception is the use of steganography to hide messages being communicated between members of terrorist groups. At least as early as 2001, there has been evidence that jihadist terrorists have been hiding communications in other media, particularly images (Kolata, 2001). In 2011, Maqsood Lodin, a 22-year-old Austrian, was taken in for questioning by police in Berlin, Germany after returning from a trip from Pakistan with a flash drive and memory chips hidden in his underwear. Some of the contents of the digital storage media included a pornographic film entitled *Kick Ass*. After several weeks of analysis, police discovered that this film was actually a media carrier for more than 100 Al Qaeda documents hidden within the film through steganography (Robertson, Cruickshank, & Lister, 2012).

The hiding of information through steganographic means is not just limited to digital media such as images, video, or audio but as Zielinska, Mazurczyk, and Szczypiorski (2014) point out, other types of channels such as linguistic steganography, file system steganography, and network steganography. Linguistic steganography utilizes standard characteristics of text content such as word spacing, displacement of punctuation marks, and word order. Somewhat more esoteric, file system steganography relies upon tactics such as the use of dummy hidden files and abandoned blocks in Linux file systems. One of the most interesting channels for steganography is network steganography, where information is hidden by mimicking damaged protocol data units or utilizing redundant fields within a particular protocol that are not used. A similar strategy where malware utilizes the DNS protocol as a hidden communication channel has also become popular with cybercriminals because the protocol is stateless and often it is not inspected for malicious content (Marrison, 2014).

Summary

Over the past 15 years the CyberJihad movement has somewhat chaotically evolved from its early beginnings, where isolated supporters posted uncoordinated, low production value content and images, to where we are today, with jihadist terrorist organizations posting coordinated content with carefully selected images and high production value videos that are carefully constructed using psychological principles of persuasion and influence. Current jihadist content on the Internet today is designed to meet a number of objectives including recruiting new fighters and supporters, increasing support for their causes throughout the Muslim world, encouraging financial donations, and generating fear and resource expenditures in the Western world.

We have also seen how these organizations utilize deception in the digital realm to help accomplish some of these objectives. From the cat and mouse games involving the replacement of websites taken down by Internet Service Providers and national authorities to the use of deception in exploiting the gap between claimed destructive capabilities and the reality of actual events, jihadist terrorist organizations are effectively utilizing digital technology to advance their causes. As new emerging digital technologies unfold, these types of terror organizations will continue to evolve their cyber strategies to maximize the potential for deception in the pursuit of their objectives.

References

Alshech, E. (2007). *Cyberspace as a combat zone: The phenomenon of electronic jihad.* Retrieved from cjlab. memri.org.

As-Sālim, M. (2003). *39 ways to serve and participate in jihad.* At-Tibay Publications. Retrieved from http:// tibyan.wordpress.com/2007/08/24/39-ways-to-serve-and-participate-in-jihad/.

Bakier, A. (2007). Forum users improve electronic jihad technology. *Terrorism Focus, 4*(20), 26.

Bergen, P. (2010). Reevaluating al-Qaida's weapons of mass destruction capabilities. *CTC Sentinel, 3*(9), 1–4.

Berko, A., & Erez, E. (2006). Women in terrorism: A Palestinian feminist revolution or gender oppression? *Intelligence,* 1–14.

Berton, B., & Pawlak, P. (2015). *Cyber jihadists and their web.* European Union Institute for Security Studies.

Bolt, N. (2012). *The violent image: Insurgent propaganda and the new revolutionaries.* London: Hurst.

Collin, B. (1996). The future of cyberterrorism. In *Proceedings of the 11th annual international symposium on criminal justice issues.* The University of Illinois at Chicago.

Corera, G. (2008). Al-Qaeda's 007: The extraordinary story of the solitary computer Geek in a Shepherds Bush bedsit who became the world's most wanted cyber-jihadist. *Times Online.* Retrieved from http:// www.thetimes.co.uk/article/al-qaedas-007-c2sx2r5bdgc.

Cronin, A. (2009). *How terrorism ends: Understanding the decline and demise of terrorist campaigns.* Princeton, NJ: Princeton University Press.

Danchev, D. (2012). *Cyber jihad vs cyber terrorism–Separating hype from reality, RSA conference, Europe 2012.*

Denning, D. (2007). *The jihadi cyberterror threat.* Available on the Internet at safecomputing.umich.edu/ events/download/Cyberterrorism-UofM.ppt.

Denning, D. (2010). Terror's web: How the Internet is transforming terrorism. In M. Yar, & Y. Jewekes (Eds.), *Handbook of internet crime* (pp. 194–212). Willan Publishers. Policy. Available on the Internet at http:// www.nautilus.org/info-policy/workshop/papers/denning.html.

Denning, D. E. (2004). Information operations and terrorism. *Journal of Information Warfare.* Retrieved from http://faculty.nps.edu/dedennin/publications/io%20and%20terrorism.pdf.

Denning, D. E. (2010). Cyber conflict as an emergent social phenomenon. In *Corporate hacking and technology-driven crime: Social dynamics and implications* (pp. 170–186). Hershey, PA: IGI Global.

Fenlon, S. (2016). *Hundreds in MA and RI listed on ISIS affiliate hit list.* Retrieved from http://www.abc6. com/story/32474257/hundreds-in-ma-and-ri-listed-on-isis-affiliate-hit-list.

Fisher, A. (2015). How jihadist networks maintain a persistent online presence. *Perspectives on Terrorism, 9*(3). Retrieved from http://www.terrorismanalysts.com/pt/index.php/pot/article/view/426/html.

Forest, J. J. (2009). Influence warfare and modern terrorism. *Georgetown Journal of International Affairs, 10*(1), 81–89.

France 24. (2015). *France TV5Monde targeted in 'IS group cyberattack'.* Retrieved from http://www.france24.com/en/20150409-france-tv5monde-is-group-hacking/.

Gartzke, E., & Lindsay, J. (2015). Weaving tangled webs: Offense, defense, and deception in cyberspace. *Security Studies, 24*(2), 316–348.

Gill, P., Horgan, J., Hunter, S., & Cushenbery, L. D. (2013). Malevolent creativity in terrorist organizations. *The Journal of Creative Behavior, 47*(2), 125–151.

Gross, G., & McMillan, R. (2006). *Al-Qaeda 'Battle of Guantanamo' cyberattack a no-show.* Retrieved from http://hostera.ridne.net/suspended.page/?currtag=12&currletter=2.

Hayward, J. (2015). *ISIS posts 'hit list' with personal data on western government employees.* Retrieved from http://www.breitbart.com/national-security/2015/08/14/isis-posts-hit-list-with-personal-data-on-western-government-employees/.

Heffelfinger, C. (2013). The risks posed by jihadist hackers. *CTC Sentinel, 6*(7) (Combating Terrorism at Westpoint).

Holt, T. (2012). Exploring the intersections of technology, crime, and terror. *Terrorism and Political Violence, 24*(2), 337–354.

Ingram, H. (2016). An analysis of inspire and Dabiq: Lessons from AQAP and Islamic state's propaganda war. *Studies in Conflict & Terrorism,* 1–19.

Jacobson, M. (2010). Terrorist financing and the Internet. *Studies in Conflict & Terrorism, 33*(4), 353–363.

James, K., Clark, K., & Cropanzano, R. (1999). Positive and negative creativity in groups, institutions, and organizations: A model and theoretical extension. *Creativity Research Journal, 12*(3), 211–226.

Jamestown. (2008). Hacking manual by jailed jihadi appears on web. *Terrorism Focus, 5*(9). Jamestown Foundation. Retrieved from https://jamestown.org/brief/briefs-238/.

Jessee, D. (2006). Tactical means, strategic ends: Al Qaeda's use of denial and deception. *Terrorism and Political Violence, 18*(3), 367–388.

Jones, D. (2006). *Globalisation and the new terror.* Cheltenham, UK: Edward Elgar.

Joosse, A. P., & Milward, H. B. (2014). Organizational versus individual attribution: A case study of Jemaah Islamiyah and the anthrax plot. *Studies in Conflict & Terrorism, 37*(3), 237–257.

Kass, L., & Phillip, J. (2013). Surprise, deception, denial and warning: Strategic imperatives. *Orbis, 57*(1), 59–82.

Khan, S. (2015). *Interviewed for the guardian by L. Dearden for the article missing Syria girls: Parents must 'keep passports under lock and key' to stop children joining.* Retrieved from http://www.independent.co.uk/news/uk/crime/missing-syria-girls-parents-must-keep-passports-under-lock-and-key-to-stop-children-joining-isis-10065617.html.

Kolata, G. (2001). Veiled messages of terror may lurk in cyberspace. *New York Times.* Retrieved from http://www.nytimes.com/2001/10/30/science/veiled-messages-of-terror-may-lurk-in-cyberspace.html.

Leyden, J. (March 27, 2002). *Drive-by hacking linked to cyberterror.* The Register. Available on the Internet at http://www.theregister.co.uk/content/55/24611.html.

Marrison, C. (2014). DNS as an attack vector -and how businesses can keep it secure. Network Security, 2014(6), 17–20.

McWilliams, B. (2001). *Pakistani hackers deface U.S. Govt. site. newbytes*. Retrieved from http://www.gov-tech.com/security/Pakistani-Hackers-Deface-US-Govt-Site.html.

Mueller, J., & Stewart, M. (2016). Misoverestimating ISIS: Comparisons with al-Qaeda. *Perspectives on Terrorism*, *10*(4). Retrieved from http://www.terrorismanalysts.com/pt/index.php/pot/article/view/525/html.

Pool, J. (2005). *New web forum postings call for intensified electronic jihad against government websites*. Jamestown Foundation. Retrieved from https://jamestown.org/program/new-forum-postings-call-for-intensified-electronic-jihad-against-government-websites/.

Robertson, N., Cruickshank, P., & Lister, T. (2012). Documents reveal al Qaeda's plans for seizing cruise ships, carnage in Europe. *CNN*. Retrieved from http://edition.cnn.com/2012/04/30/world/al-qaeda-documents-future/index.html.

Siboni, G., Cohen, D., & Koren, T. (2015). The Islamic state's strategy in cyberspace. *Military and Strategic Affairs*, *7*(1), 3–29.

Ulph, S. (2006). Internet Mujahideen refine electronic warfare tactics. *Terrorism Focus*, *3*(5).

Weimann, G. (2016). The emerging role of social media in the recruitment of foreign fighters. In *Foreign fighters under international law and beyond* (pp. 77–95). The Hague, Netherlands: TMC Asser Press.

Zielińska, E., Mazurczyk, W., & Szczypiorski, K. (2014). Trends in steganography. *Communications of the ACM*, *57*(3), 86–95.

Asymmetric Warfare and Psyops: Nation State-Sponsored Cyber Attacks

ABSTRACT

This chapter describes the nature of asymmetric warfare on the Internet and how online deception plays a key role in psychological operations by both nation states and non-nation state actors. The role that the cyber domain plays in nationalism and nation state espionage is discussed and in particular China is held up as an example of how these concepts have evolved with the widespread use of the Internet. The role that the Internet plays in cover and concealment for non-nation state actors and their associated malicious online acts is also covered. Cyberwar at the nation state level is examined, and some of the unique characteristics of the concept of cyberwar are detailed. The chapter concludes with a look into the future of cyberwar and how relationships between non-nation state actors and nation states may change the face of hybrid conflict.

Keywords: *Asymmetric warfare; Cover and concealment; Cyber espionage; Cyber nationalism; Cyberwarfare; Hybrid conflict; Non-nation state actors; Psyops; Stuxnet; Virtual no-flag operations.*

CHAPTER OUTLINE

For centuries nation states have sought military and strategic advantage (Tzu & Giles, 2009).[1] Endeavoring for this primacy, novel stratagems and expansion of weapon types have been used, refined, perfected, and sometimes abandoned and discarded. Since 1996,

---

[1] *See also*, http://ctext.org/art-of-war.

a new arms race for superiority in the digital world has emerged. The boundaries and rules of engagement in this space are amorphous, evolving, and still being defined during our lifetime.

Through cyber tradecraft, intelligence and military operations can occur in a fraction of "real-world" time, resources, and human capital. Amplification of psychological operations and strategic messaging through social media and other Internet-based message platforms has changed the way that influence narratives are broadcasted. With nation state philosophies and conceptions vastly differing, the use of cyber stratagems for geopolitical, intelligence, and military advantage are often blurred, resulting in nation states using the same tactics, techniques, and procedures (TTP) for economic advantage. Since 2006, these same cyber TTPs have been used for economic espionage and pilfering of intellectual property and trade secrets to eliminate an adversary nation state's need for innovation, resource expenditure, and scientific research and development.

The Role of Nation State Versus Non-nation State Attacks

Since technology can be used to facilitate acts of crime or terror, we must consider the source of an attack and how this might relate to the actor's motivation and target. With that in mind, we must define a *nation state* and contextualize how it might engage in an attack. Van Creveld (1999) argues that a nation state has three characteristics: (1) sovereignty, (2) territoriality, and (3) an abstract organization. Sovereignty involves the authority or power to rule, as well as make and enforce laws within a given area. Territoriality recognizes that a state or governing body exerts power within specific, recognized borders (Van Creveld, 1999). The idea of "abstract organization" involves the concept that each state has a distinct and independent persona, which is separate from that of its people. Specifically, the state is a political entity, while the culture and/or ethnic composition of a place makes up its national identity (Van Creveld, 1999). For instance, the United States utilizes a democratic system of government, while our national identity is one that is a cultural mélange of various heritages and backgrounds based on the influx of immigrants to this nation over time.

Given their sovereignty and territorial control, nation states have the capacity to exert influence over their citizens, as well as other nation states, in order to further their interests. As a result, some nation states may utilize their citizen populations to engage in illegal activities in order to either gain economic or political advantage over another nation. For instance, a nation state might encourage individual citizens to engage in the theft of trade secrets or intellectual property in order to gain economic advantage over another country they must compete with in the open market. The originating nation may provide indirect economic support to actors in order to facilitate their activities, but it does not provide any overt recognition or direct orders that can be traced back to the government. Thus the use of state-sponsored actors allows a government to perform illegal activities without directly engaging in the act.

The role of state sponsorship in cyber attacks that involve hacking and data theft has gained substantial attention since 1996. The evolution and history of nation states developing cyber network operation capabilities, often through state sponsorship, elucidates how these cyber attack capabilities have burgeoned over the years. With the maturity and increasing sophistication of these cyber programs, many nation states not only sponsor cyber attack capabilities, but have integrated these programs into their formal military and intelligence apparatuses. Traditional, linear methods of implementing *psychological operations*—or operations to affect perceptions, attitudes, emotions, opinions, or behavior of a targeted audience[2]—have notably been replaced with Internet-based tactics. Nation states have effectively adapted elements of traditional strategic denial and deception (D&D)[3] across the cyber sphere, manipulating environments, personas, and hiding behind virtual false flags[4] as an element of cyberwarfare.[5]

China: Enter the Digital Dragon

China was an earlier adopter of the World Wide Web (1994), and its users were excited and curious about pushing the boundaries of the technology (Reveron, 2012). By 1997, Chinese hacker sites had already sprouted up, with influential hacking groups, such as the Green Army and the Chinese Eagle Union, forming and growing (Henderson, 2007). The late 1990s were indeed formative, with a number of global hacking organizations that

[2] Joint Publication (JP) 3-53, Doctrine for Joint Psychological Operations, p. 17.

[3] *Denial and Deception*, or D&D, is a term used, particularly in military and intelligence operation contexts to describe information operation efforts by one party, typically a nation, to block information that could be used by an opponent to learn a truth, and to cause the adversary to believe something that is not true. Godson, R., & Wirtz, J. J. (2002). *Strategic denial and deception: The twenty-first century challenge*. New Brunswick, NJ: Transaction Publishers.

[4] *False flag operation*, or using artifices to disguise one's true country or group affiliation by deceptively claiming association or origin from another country or group. This technique has been used in numerous manners and means over history, whether by pirate ships seeking to gain access to unsuspecting victim vessels or in military strategies to overcome and surprise the adversary. Konstam, A. (2007). *Blackbeard: America's most notorious pirate*. John Wiley & Sons. *See also*, Ryan, D., & Ryan, J. (March 2012). Attribution: Accountability in cyber incidents. In V. Lysenko (Ed.), *Proceedings of the 7th International Conference on Information Warfare and Security*: University of Washington, Seattle, (referencing the Gleiwitz Incident of 1939, a false flag maneuver leading up to World War II wherein the German SS dressed as Polish rebels during the attack at the Gleiwitz radio compound and bodies of several murdered concentration camp inmates were dressed as Polish rebels where left at the Customs house; the attacks were falsely reported as Polish aggression).

[5] See: Bertram, S. K. (2016). *False flags in cyber intrusions – Why bother?* Retrieved from https://www. digitalshadows.com/blog-and-research/false-flags-in-cyber-intrusions-why-bother/.
Guerrero-Saade, J. A. & Bartholomew, B. (2016). *Wave your false flags! Deception tactics muddying attribution in targeted attacks*. Retrieved from www.virusbulletin.com/conference/vb2016/abstracts/wave-your-false-flags-deception-tactics-muddying-attribution-targeted-attacks/; https://threatpost.com/juan-andres-guerrero-saade-and-brian-bartholomew-on-apt-false-flags-and-attribution/121126/.
Hill, J. (2014). *Cyber-security expert warns of 'false flag' digital attacks*. Retrieved from http://www.forbes.com/sites/jasperhamill/2014/07/31/cyber-security-expert-warns-of-false-flag-digital-attacks/#20fe127e2bb0.
Hopping, C. (2016). *False flags making it harder to find root of cybercrime*. Retrieved from http://www.itpro.co.uk/security/27360/false-flags-making-it-harder-to-find-root-of-cybercrime.
Schindler, J.R. (2016). *False flags: The Kremlin's hidden cyber hand*. Retrieved from observer.com/2016/06/false-flags-the-kremlins-hidden-cyber-hand/.
Mitigating Risks arising from False-Flag and No-Flag Cyber Attacks. Retrieved from https://ccdcoe.org/.../mitigating-risks-arising-false-flag-and-no-flag-cyber-attacks.html.

had existed since the 1990s, such as the United States based Cult of the Dead Cow and the Germany-based Chaos Computer Club, gaining international attention for developing malicious code (such as the CDC's "Back Orifice" Trojan horse), conferences, and media attention. Like these groups, burgeoning Chinese hacker groups, such as the Green Army, were gaining traction and capabilities (Henderson, 2007).

Adverse actions and geopolitical atmospherics sparked and fanned the flames of China's cyber sovereignty. Through these international conflicts, nationalistic Chinese hacking groups, such as the Honker's Union of China and Javafile, were drawn to act to defend China's honor and demonstrably exert China's cyber network attack capability in the then-nascent cyberwarfare space. In 1999, NATO forces bombed Belgrade, Yugoslavia during military conflict in Kosovo, resulting in errant bombs striking the Chinese Embassy, killing three Chinese reporters (Henderson, 2007; Reveron, 2012). Chinese outrage resulted in a number of cyber attacks against US websites, including defacements declaring "Protest USA's Nazi Action! Protest NATO's brutal action!"[6] denial of service and malicious code attacks (Krekel, U.S.-China Economic and Security Review Commission, & Northrop Grumman Corporation, 2009; Ventre, 2009).

Later that same year the "Taiwan–China Hacker War" erupted after then Taiwanese President Lee Teng-hui gave a speech entailing his "two states theory," advocating for the bifurcation of Taiwan from China. This catalyst, and cascading Taiwanese independence issues, resulted in hackers from both countries engaging in cyber attacks intermittently over the course of approximately 4 years, causing reciprocal website defacements and denial of service attacks against numerous web servers (Fig. 8.1). Notably, in 1999 a far more understated and foreshadowing event occurred: the Chinese People's Liberation Army (PLA) colonels, Qiao Liang and Wang Xiangsui, published *Unrestricted Warfare* (ultimately translated into English[7]), a military strategy book describing the uses and benefits of asymmetric warfare to defeat adversary nation states, including cyberwarfare (Mazanec, 2015).

FIGURE 8.1 A website defaced by the Chinese hacking group Javaphile during the "Taiwan–China Hacker War."

[6] www.cnn.com/TECH/computing/9905/12cyberwar.idg/.
[7] https://www.amazon.com/Unrestricted-Warfare-Chinas-Destroy-America-ebook/dp/0971680728/ref=sr_1_1?s=books&ie=UTF8&qid=1476070989&sr=1-1&keywords=unrestricted+warfare.

Chinese tensions with the United States were reinvigorated in April 2001 when a United States Navy spy plane collided with a PLA Navy fighter jet near China's Hainan Island, killing the Chinese pilot[8] (Henderson, 2007; Krekel, Adams, Bakos, Northrop Grumman Corporation, & U.S.-China Economic and Security Review Commission, 2012; Krekel et al., 2009; Reveron, 2012). Hackers from both countries engaged in a vitriolic battle of denial-of-service, website defacements, and malicious code attacks, marking what is historically observed as the first "China–America Cyber War." From this engagement, burgeoning Chinese hacking groups such as the Honker Union of China and Red Crack demonstrated their tenacity and capabilities (Figs. 8.2 and 8.3); this importantly and tacitly translated as an extension of Chinese nationalism and a burgeoning asymmetric warfare platform.

FIGURE 8.2 A website defaced by the Honker Union of China during the "China–America Cyber War."

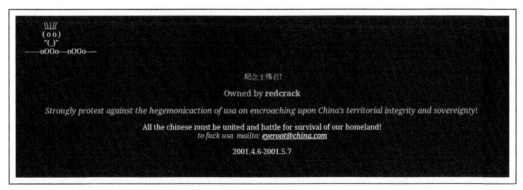

FIGURE 8.3 A website defaced by Red Crack during the 2001 "China–America Cyber War."

---

[8] http://www.nytimes.com/2001/04/02/world/us-plane-in-china-after-it-collides-with-chinese-jet.html; http://edition.cnn.com/2001/US/04/01/us.china.plane.06/.

China's successes in the cyber conflict realm were soon documented for online display on the New Hacker's Alliance website (Figs. 8.4 and 8.5). This virtual trophy room of website defacements further stoked the coals of ambition for Chinese cyber superiority.

FIGURE 8.4 The New Hacker *Alliance website banner.*

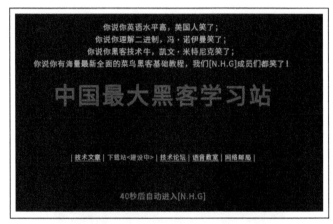

FIGURE 8.5 The New Hacker *Alliance* **website.**

From Cyber Nationalism to Cyber Espionage

These catalyzing events forever changed the landscape of China's cyber network operations posture and ideology. The years that followed revealed offensive weaponization of this powerful intelligence and information warfare tradecraft believed to be initiated through the Third Department of the PLA General Staff (3/PLA), China's signals intelligence agency, and the Fourth Department of the PLA General Staff (4/PLA), responsible for information and electronic warfare (Krekel et al., 2012; Lindsay, Cheung, & Reveron, 2015; Mattis, 2015; Reveron, 2012).

In 2004, it was publicly disclosed that China had engaged in computer network exploitation operations against (code named "Titan Rain") the Department of Defense and NASA systems; this was the first time that China had been publicly accused of cyber espionage (Stiennon, 2015).[9] Only a few years later, between 2006 and 2007, news reports globally

---

[9] See also, Titan Rain – how Chinese hackers targeted Whitehall
https://www.theguardian.com/technology/2007/sep/04/news.internet.

revealed that numerous Western government networks had been similarly breached, with China as the surmised culprit (Krekel et al., 2009; Reveron, 2012).

In 2009, a group of very sophisticated Chinese hackers compromised multiple high-level targets including Google, Adobe, Juniper Networks, Yahoo, Symantec, Northrop Grumman, and Dow Chemical (Schmugar, 2010; Zetter, 2010). In what was dubbed *Operation Aurora* by the security vendor McAfee, attackers were able to gain access to these institutions through the use of a website hosting malware, which would exploit a zero-day vulnerability in the Internet Explorer web browser. From there, the attackers appeared to use these infected systems as launch points to identify and compromise source code repositories within these companies (Markoff & Barboza, 2010; Zetter, 2010). While it is possible that these attacks were driven by individual hackers without state support, the complexity of the attacks and the sophistication of the actors would have required a high degree of cooperation in order to be successful. Additionally, the targets of the attacks appear to be more in line with the interests of a corporate entity or government in order to achieve a competitive advantage in the market, without the need for research and development. Finally, the source of these attacks appears to come from two Chinese universities with links to both the Chinese search engine company Baidu and the Chinese government (Markoff & Barboza, 2010; Schmugar, 2010). All of these points provided circumstantial evidence that the attacks were the result of state-sponsored actors working on behalf of the Chinese government (Fritz, 2008).

Later that year, researchers from the *Information Warfare Monitor* of the Citizen Lab at the University of Toronto's Monk School uncovered a massive cyber-spying operation, dubbed "GhostNet" (Lindsay et al., 2015).[10] The investigation revealed that thousands of computers, on networks related to ministries of foreign affairs, embassies, and systems associated with the Dali Lama, had been breached and implanted with malicious code with monitoring capabilities. Similarly, in 2011, information security researchers at McAfee published their findings of *Operation Shady Rat*: a massive, protracted, computer intrusion campaign against government agencies, private corporations, and international organizations (Krekel et al., 2012).[11]

Despite these revelations, China's typical response to the allegations was denial.[12] The lack of concrete evidence that the Chinese government conducted, ordered, or sanctioned these activities made it difficult to wield a "smoking gun"; it also made it challenging to identify a clear response to the intrusions.

In 2013, the information security firm Mandiant released the technical report, *APT1: Exposing One of China's Cyber Espionage Units,* a groundbreaking exposé into Chinese cyber network operations.[13] The report detailed the attacks conducted by members of 3/PLA, Second Bureau, Unit 61398, against 141 different victims across 20 different industries.

---

[10] See also, http://www.reuters.com/article/us-security-spying-computers-idUSTRE52R2HQ20090328; http://news.bbc.co.uk/2/hi/americas/7970471.stm.

[11] http://www.mcafee.com/us/resources/white-papers/wp-operation-shady-rat.pdf.

[12] http://news.bbc.co.uk/2/hi/americas/7972702.stm.

[13] https://www.fireeye.com/content/dam/fireeye-www/services/pdfs/mandiant-apt1-report.pdf.

A little over a year later, five members of Unit 61398 were federally indicted by the United States Department of Justice in the Western District of Pennsylvania for criminal activities relating to their computer intrusions, marking the first time that criminal charges had been brought against nation state actors for hacking.[14]

Virtual "No-Flag" Operations: Non-nation State Cover and Concealment

By contrast, individuals operating without state sponsorship, or *non-nation state sponsored*, tend to have fewer resources at their disposal and may differentially target resources in order to affect operational capabilities of a government or corporation, gain a direct profit from data theft, or cause fear among a population. Their attacks may not be as sophisticated as those used by nation states, but they can still prove effective, depending on the target of an attack. Additionally, actors without state sponsorship do not have to operate within specific military hierarchies of command and may organize in any way necessary in order to succeed. That does not mean there are not leaders within groups; they may be driven by a small core of actors who come together and rally others to their cause. Often, this may be done through the use of web forums, Internet Relay Chat (IRC), instant messaging groups, and social networking sites that enable the rapid formation of groups. Thus non-nation state-sponsored actors can more quickly come together to complete attacks with a wide network of participants who can just as rapidly disband upon completion of the act.

Over the years, through the use of deception narratives, nation states have intentionally contrived stratagems cloaking their nexus to attacks by appearing as non-nation state-sponsored organizations. These rogue-appearing groups or persons use passive misdirection techniques, such as self-presentation using exotic, mysterious names and graphics, to heighten curiosity and gain attention. Through this misdirection the true scope and purpose of the attacks is misjudged and often misattributed to non-nation state actors.

One excellent example of this was the series of distributed denial of service (DDoS) attacks against US financial institutions beginning in the fall of 2012 by the group *Cyber Fighters of Izz ad-Din al-Qassam* (Gonsalves, 2013). The attacks themselves were directed at US Bankcorp, JP Morgan Chase & Co., Bank of America, PNC Financial Services Group, SunTrust, and other institutions. The group utilized compromised web servers located in the United States as a launch point and caused some interruptions of service for the banks. It is not clear how successful the attacks were, though one estimate suggests at least seven banks were taken down for minutes to hours, depending on the institution (Gonsalves, 2013).

The group indicated in posts on the website Pastebin that they were engaging in the attacks because of the treatment of the Islamic faith by the West and the US government's refusal to remove clips of a movie that disparages the prophet Mohammed from YouTube (Figs. 8.6 and 8.7). They claimed that they would engage in attacks against banks

---

[14] https://www.justice.gov/opa/pr/us-charges-five-chinese-military-hackers-cyber-espionage-against-us-corporations-and-labor; https://www.justice.gov/iso/opa/resources/5122014519132358461949.pdf.

as retribution for these videos and base the duration of their attacks on the perceived damages that will result against these institutions relative to the number of times these videos have been viewed and the length of time they have been posted. While some of these institutions were able to use mitigation services to reduce the effectiveness of the DDoS attacks, the attacks were protracted and effective.

```
Dear Muslim youths, Muslims Nations and are noblemen
When Arab nations rose against their corrupt regimes (those who support Zionist regime) at the other hand when, Crucify infidels are
terrified and they are no more supporting human rights. United States of America with the help of Zionist Regime made a Sacrilegious
movie insulting all the religions not only Islam.
All the Muslims worldwide must unify and Stand against the action, Muslims must do whatever is necessary to stop spreading this
movie. We will attack them for this insult with all we have.
All the Muslim youths who are active in the Cyber world will attack to American and Zionist Web bases as much as needed such that
they say that they are sorry about that insult.
We, Cyber fighters of Izz ad-din Al qassam will attack the Bank of America and New York Stock Exchange for the first step. These
Targets are properties of American-Zionist Capitalists. This attack will be started today at 2 pm. GMT. This attack will continue
till the Erasing of that nasty movie. Beware this attack can vary in type.
Down with modern infidels.
```

FIGURE 8.6 Pastebin posting by the "Cyber Fighters of Izz ad-Din al-Qassam."

```
1.  "Operation Ababil" started over ███ :
2.
3.  http://pastebin.com/████████
4.  http://pastebin.com/████████
5.
6.  In the second step we attacked the largest bank of the united states, ███ ██████ bank. These series of attacks will continue untill
    the Erasing of that nasty movie from the Internet.
7.
8.  The site "www.████ com" is down and also Online banking at "████████ ██████ .com" is being decided to be Offline !
9.
10. Down with modern infidels.
11.
12. ### Cyber fighters of Izz ad-din Al qassam ###
```

FIGURE 8.7 Pastebin posting by the "Cyber Fighters of Izz ad-Din al-Qassam."

Since the individual hackers engaging in these attacks appeared to be motivated entirely based on their religious backgrounds to target and affect business endeavors, it appeared reasonable to surmise that the activity was merely criminal. Further, the religious component and the desire to change the attitudes and behaviors of the nation and the stance of those who posted the content may also lead some to call these attacks *hacktivism.* However, in March 2016, The United States Department of Justice indicted seven Iranian defendants for conducting these attacks on behalf of Iranian Islamic Revolutionary Guard Corps, revealing that the *Cyber Fighters of Izz ad-Din al-Qassam* narrative was purely to misdirect and deceive.[15]

[15] https://www.justice.gov/usao-sdny/pr/manhattan-us-attorney-announces-charges-against-seven-iranians-conducting-coordinated; https://www.justice.gov/usao-sdny/file/835061/download; http://www.forbes.com/sites/thomasbrewster/2016/03/24/iran-hackers-charged-bank-ddos-attacks-banks/#5e3816027f8d.

The indictments resoundingly revealed that Iran was gaining traction as an international cyber power. Researchers and information security experts prior to this public disclosure certainly perceived Iran's cyber network operation posture as a burgeoning threat,[16] but the revelation of Iran's nuanced and effective *no-flag* deception campaign caused many to revisit and reconsider attribution to prior attacks only years earlier. The 2012 destructive "Shamoon" malware attack that wiped over 30,000 Saudi Aramco systems, claimed by the hackivist group the "Cutting Sword of Justice" (Fig. 8.8), now seemed to come into clearer focus under information research lenses as Iranian originated (Geers, Kindlund, Moran, & Rachwald, 2014).[17] Similar clarity emerged in the destructive attacks against the Las Vegas Sands Corp.[18]

```
We, behalf of an anti-oppression hacker group that have been fed up of crimes and atrocities taking place in various countries
around the world, especially in the neighboring countries such as Syria, Bahrain, Yemen, Lebanon, Egypt and ..., and also of dual
approach of the world community to these nations, want to hit the main supporters of these disasters by this action.
One of the main supporters of this disasters is Al-Saud corrupt regime that sponsors such oppressive measures by using Muslims
oil resources. Al-Saud is a partner in committing these crimes. It's hands are infected with the blood of innocent children and
people.
In the first step, an action was performed against Aramco company, as the largest financial source for Al-Saud regime. In this
step, we penetrated a system of Aramco company by using the hacked systems in several countries and then sended a malicious virus
to destroy thirty thousand computers networked in this company. The destruction operations began on Wednesday, Aug 15, 2012 at
11:08 AM (Local time in Saudi Arabia) and will be completed within a few hours.
This is a warning to the tyrants of this country and other countries that support such criminal disasters with injustice and
oppression. We invite all anti-tyranny hacker groups all over the world to join this movement. We want them to support this
movement by designing and performing such operations, if they are against tyranny and oppression.

Cutting Sword of Justice
```

FIGURE 8.8 A message left on Pastebin by the "Cutting Sowrd of Justice" during the Saudi Aramco cyber attack.

Another serious deception and psyop event was the result of efforts of a pro-Assad Syrian group aptly named the Syrian Electronic Army. Founded sometime around May 2011, the Syrian Electronic Army had its roots in the Syrian Computer Society with direct connections to the ruling Assad family (Grohe, 2015). As Grohe (2015) points out, the Syrian Electronic Army encouraged the formation of a virtual hacking academy and early on focused particularly on website defacements and DDoS attacks on electronic versions of traditional media entities such as the Washington Post, the New York Times, CBS news, the BBC, and more. It was during the early parts of 2013 that the Syrian Electronic Army seemed to become more directly detached from the Syrian government, its leadership began changing, and new members emerged, demonstrating some independence from the official Syrian regime (Perloth, 2013).

---

[16] http://www.securityweek.com/irans-cyber-attack-capabilities-growing-quickly-experts.
[17] See, http://www.nytimes.com/2012/10/24/business/global/cyberattack-on-saudi-oil-firm-disquiets-us.html?pagewanted=all&_r=1.
[18] http://www.bloomberg.com/news/articles/2014-12-11/iranian-hackers-hit-sheldon-adelsons-sands-casino-in-las-vegas; http://money.cnn.com/2015/02/27/technology/security/iran-hack-casino/.

It was during this time of change that the Syrian Electronic Army launched a deception that rocked the US economic marketplaces. Having hacked the Twitter account of the Associated Press, on April 23, 2013, the Syrian Electronic Army put out this tweet.

The response from the US economic markets was immediate. During the 3 min that the tweet stood uncorrected, the New York Stock exchange lost 136 billion dollars in equity, thereby causing probably one of the largest examples of direct economic loss due to a single deceptive electronic communication by a non-nation state actor (Fisher, 2013). It is likely that we will see more of these types of deceptive attacks designed to negatively affect the economic stability of nation states. As Karppi and Crawford (2015, p. 73) point out, "Twitter and social media are becoming more powerful forces, not just because they connect people or generate new modes of participation, but because they are connecting human communicative spaces to automated computational spaces in ways that are affectively contagious and highly volatile."

Cyberwar and the Nation State

As cyberspace plays an increasingly critical role in managing the everyday aspects of communication and critical infrastructure, governments and military agencies are increasingly attempting to establish their role in cyberspace. Many industrialized nations recognize the threat that cyber attacks can pose to military and governmental infrastructure. Some consider cyberspace to be a new warfare domain just like land, sea, air, and space (Andress & Winterfeld, 2013). As a consequence, it is necessary to consider how fighting a war in this domain may operate and what constitutes an act of *cyberwar*.

There is no single agreed upon definition for warfare, even among the United Nations. The historical literature on war and warfare tactics, however, suggests that it can be viewed as an act of force or violence which compels the opponent to fulfill the will of the victor (Andress & Winterfeld, 2013; Brenner, 2009; Schwartau, 1996). When applied to cyberspace, the use of war tactics appears designed to control and affect the activities of an opposing force. Brenner (2009) defined cyberwarfare as nation states' "use of military operations by virtual means… to achieve essentially the same ends they pursue through the use of conventional military force" (p. 65). Thus the domain of conflict for cyberwar is different from traditional conflicts in that the operations take place in a virtual space (Rid, 2013). The weapons of cyberwar are also different from that of traditional combat, in that actors may utilize malware and hacking techniques in order to affect system functionality, access to information, or critical infrastructure (Rid, 2013). The outcomes and goals of cyberwar, however, are similar to physical war in that fighters may attempt either targeted tactical strikes against a specific target or try to cause as much damage as is possible to the operational capacity of a nation state.

Though there has been some debate about the actual threat of cyberwarfare and the utility of this term generally (see Andress & Winterfeld, 2013; Rid, 2013), we must recognize why it may be a fruitful environment for attack. Nearly all critical systems in modern industrialized nations depend on the Internet for commercial or logistic support. For example, water and sewage treatment plants and nuclear, hydroelectric, and other power grids are dependent on the Internet for command and control. Virtually all facets of banking, stock exchanges, and economic systems are run through the Internet. Even aspects of the military and related defense contractors of the world are run through civilian or commercial telephony. Any attack that could effectively disrupt the communications capacity of the Internet could effectively cripple our society, which would have ripple effects throughout the real world. At the same time, the sensitive data maintained by government or military agencies could be compromised and/or stolen in order to gain an economic or defensive advantage (see the Operation Aurora story covered earlier). Thus hacking sensitive systems would be an easy and immediate way to affect an enemy through cyberwarfare.

Over the last 10 years, there have been an increasing number of incidents that might practically be viewed as cyberwar. A key example is the conflict between Russia and Estonia in 2007. A conflict developed between Russian and Estonian factions in April 2007 when the Estonian government removed a Russian war monument from a memorial garden in a national cemetery (Brenner, 2009; Jaffe, 2006; Landler & Markoff, 2007). The statue, called The Bronze Soldier of Tallinn, was installed as a monument to the Russian involvement in World War II and was viewed as a relic from Estonia's time as part of the former Soviet Union. Now that Estonia was its own independent nation, the government felt it appropriate to have the statue removed (Guadagno, Cialdini, & Evron, 2010). Russian citizens living in Estonia and elsewhere were enraged by this action, leading to protests and violence in the streets of both countries. Over 1300 were arrested during protests in Estonia, many of whom were ethnic Russians living in the country.

The conflict quickly grew into online spaces, with hackers in both Estonia and Russia attempting to engage in different hacks and spam campaigns (Brenner, 2009; Jaffe, 2006). Russian hackers also leveraged online forums and hacker sites in order to rally attackers together to increase the volume of their attacks and used huge botnets of compromised computers for DDoS attacks (Clover, 2009; Davis, 2007). The attacks incorporated many individuals who were interested in attacking Estonia out of their love and respect for their homeland, many of whom had little knowledge of computer hacking. As a consequence, Russian attacks were able to shut down critical components of Estonia's financial and government networks, causing significant economic harm to citizens and industry alike (Brenner, 2009;

Landler & Markoff, 2007). The Estonian parliament and almost every governmental ministry website were affected. In addition, three of the six national news agencies and two of its largest banks also experienced problems (Clover, 2009). In fact, banks were knocked off-line for hours and lost millions of dollars due to DDoS attacks (Landler & Markoff, 2007).

In the wake of this onslaught, the Estonian government accused the Russian government of supporting and encouraging these attacks. To date, there has been no concrete evidence provided to support Russian state sponsorship (Denning, 2010). Many observers, however, have argued this incident is a clear demonstration of how nation states may engage in conflicts in the future. The actors involved may have been driven by their own sense of duty to their country or by actual military doctrine. Regardless, the severity of the attacks demonstrated the need to identify how cyber resources might be affected by conflicts in the real world.

The cyber attacks against Estonia provided a new visibility into Russia's cyber network operation capabilities. Soon after, the aperture was opened further. In 2008, while embroiled in conflict with Georgia surrounding cessation of South Ossetia, Russia augmented its conventional military operations with a disruptive cyber attacks against Georgian network infrastructure; denial of service attacks and website defacements (including those depicting then Georgia President Mikheil Saakashvili as Adolph Hitler, Fig. 8.9) disabled or degraded Georgian government servers (Segal, 2016). As with the Estonian conflict, Russia ultimately denied knowledge and involvement in the attacks; however, researchers have pointed to circumstantial evidence and Russia's psychological warfare and deception operations capabilities as an effective cloak of plausible deniability.[19]

Another significant example of nation state cyberwarfare is the appearance of a piece of malicious software called **Stuxnet**. This computer worm was used in attacks against the Natanz uranium enrichment facility in Iran (Clayton, 2010; Kerr, Rollins, & Theohary, 2010, pp. 1–9). As Heckman, Stech, Thomas, Schmoker, and Tsow (2015, p. 62) point out, Stuxnet specifically "built upon and exploited the Iranians' knowledge of earlier attempts to sabotage nuclear enrichment equipment, and the ability of the malware to hide itself from detection and defenses. This accentuated the deception effects of the malware attacks – making the centrifuges and their controllers seem responsible for the accidents".

Stuxnet was designed to specifically compromise and harm computer systems in order to gain access to the SCADA systems and related Programmable Logic Controllers (PLCs) inside of centrifuges in these plants (Clayton, 2010; Kerr et al., 2010, pp. 1–9). Specifically, the code would allow the PLC to be given commands remotely by the attacker, while shielding the actual behaviors of the centrifuges from the plant's SCADA control systems. As a result, attackers could surreptitiously disrupt the plant's ability to process uranium and cause confusion among operators and controllers. It is unknown how long the malware was able to operate inside of the facility, though estimates suggest it may have

---

[19] See, Weedon, J. (2015). Beyond 'Cyber War': Russia's use of strategic cyber espionage and information operations in Ukraine. In K. Geers (Ed.), *Cyber war in perspective: Russian aggression against Ukraine.* Tallinn: NATO CCD COE Publications (Chapter 8); Ottis, R. (30 June–1 July, 2008). Analysis of the 2007 cyber attacks against Estonia from the information warfare perspective. In D. Remenyi (Ed.), *Proceedings of the 7th European conference on information warfare and security.* University of Plymouth, UK.

impacted 1000 of the 5000 centrifuges in the plant and delayed the overall functionality of the nuclear plant by months or years (Kerr et al., 2010, pp. 1–9; Sanger, 2012).

Recent evidence suggests that Stuxnet was developed by the United States under the Bush administration as evidence grew regarding the Iranian nuclear program aspirations. The program, called **Operation Olympic Games**, was proactively implemented by an executive order of President Obama because it was thought that this sort of attack would be more targeted, difficult to detect, and produce fewer civilian casualties or collateral damage than a physical strike (Sanger, 2012). In addition, the use of this code was thought to have reduced the likelihood of a conventional military strike by Israel, which would have dangerous consequences for the region as a whole. The United States has not acknowledged any of the claims made related to Stuxnet, though its release in the wild has given computer security professionals and hackers access to this extremely sophisticated malware. The program may serve as a basis for the development of tools in order to exploit or attack critical infrastructure across the globe (Brodscky & Radvanovsky, 2010; Clayton, 2010). The US Department of Homeland Security expressed substantial concern over the use of Stuxnet-like code in attacks against US power installations (Zetter, 2011). Thus cyber attacks may be an increasingly common way for nation states to engage one another to cause harm.

FIGURE 8.9 Defacement image from a compromised Georgian website during the Russian–Georgian conflict.

In the last couple of years, Russia has engaged in what has been called "hybrid warfare". As Umland (2016) describes it, hybrid warfare constitutes the use of a number of tactics beyond conventional military forces to include economic and political pressure as well as deception and psychological manipulation through propaganda as well as cyber attacks.

One of the most recent examples of hybrid nation state cyber conflict involves the suspected involvement of Russia in influencing the 2016 national presidential election in the United States. The Director of National Intelligence for the United States has stated that they have been able to attribute efforts to influence the US presidential elections to "Russian directed efforts" (Office of the Director of National Intelligence, 2016). This attribution is made in regard to efforts by external parties to influence the election through the leaking of stolen email documents eventually released through third parties including the WikiLeaks organization as well as the hacker known as Guccifer 2.0. The statement by this office stops short of stating that they have evidence that the Russians are responsible for a number of attacks on US election-related electronic systems.

The likely overall objective of this campaign by the Russians is to keep a key partner in NATO (the United States) off balance and reduce its ability to make decisive responses to current and near-future Russian political and military moves against nation states along its borders. The current environment within the United States is particularly conducive to this type of conflict involving deception and manipulation. The American public has been split by a political divisiveness that has not been present in the United States for decades. One of the two major political parties in the United States is currently in crisis and there is significant political chaos within that party, adding to a fertile environment for further disruption by outside forces.

There are two pathways that appear to be active in this strategy to influence the US presidential elections. The first is to cast doubt on the integrity of the results of the presidential election held on November 8, 2016. It is important to note that there does not have to be any actual manipulation of the US presidential vote by a nation state or non-nation actors in order to have an effect. Indeed, just the knowledge that there are ongoing efforts in the form of cyber attacks on electronic systems involved in the US presidential election is enough to create significant suspicion and doubt about the true outcome of the election. This is likely to throw both the American people and the US government into considerable chaos and contribute substantially to the efforts to keep the United States off balance and less able to counter Russian political and military moves near the Russian borders.

The second effect that is particularly linked to the release of stolen emails from US political figures is the ability to produce movement in the political opinions of American voters. Russian President Vladimir Putin knows that he will face one of two individuals acting as the President of the United States as a result of the 2016 election. He will certainly have a preference for who that individual is and if there is a way to increase the probability that this preferred individual is elected, then it is likely that Putin will take steps to increase those odds. The selective release of these emails by third parties, and it is thought at the direction of the Russian government, is an effective way in which the Russian government may deceptively influence the US election. It is also a possibility and there is some evidence that in addition to assisting in the release of these documents, the Russian government has altered the content of them to damage one of the presidential candidate's position and promote the opponent, although this theory is not currently supported by the US intelligence community (Eichenwald, 2016).

Future of Nation State Cyber Conflict

As Martin Libicki (2012, p. 30) has pointed out, deception is the "sine qua non of cyberwar." He also notes that cyber attacks may have aftereffects that are just as damaging or even more damaging than the initial attack and points out as an example that after Stuxnet, the Iranians initiated an 18-month halt in the buildup of centrifuges because of the suspicion that there might be "further surprises" from Stuxnet or that further Stuxnet-like attacks might be on hand (Libicki, 2016). As Gartzke and Lindsay (2015) point out, digital technology is a critical component in what they have termed "the deception revolution."

The future of conflict, especially as it applies to cyber conflict, may belong in what Fitton (2016) calls the gray zone. According to Fitton (2016, pp. 111–112) the gray zone is "defined as the region between peace and war, which is not yet fully understood." He suggests that the gray zone is utilized by both nation states and non-nation state actors. He further argues that conflict in the gray zone camouflages who the real enemy is, as well as their intentions, and this ambiguity makes responding to attacks in the gray zone particularly difficult in terms of determining the legitimacy of responses, particularly for liberal democracies. This conclusion, Fitton suggests, reveals that offensive actions within the gray zone are especially attractive to more autocratic nation states as well non-nation state actors.

It also appears fairly likely that non-nation state actors will continue to expand their roles in conflict between nation states, particularly in the cyber domain. The advantages of deniability and nonattribution that non-nation state actors provide nation states makes relationships between these two types of entities attractive. During the past few years, we have seen a variety of relationships form between nation states and non-nation state actors that vary from very loose couplings to situations where there is virtually almost no separation between nation states and non-nation state actors. This continuum has been investigated by Healy (2012), who has created a 10-class taxonomy of relationships between nation states and non-nation state actors that varies across their level of positive relations with each other. One hand of Healy's scale are state-prohibited non-nation state actor groups whose existence is forbidden by the government but exists nonetheless, while the other end of Healy's scale contains a class of non-nation state actors that are essentially "state integrated."

Kilger (2017) suggests that there are four stages to the lifespan of relationships between nation states and non-nation state actors. In stage 1, nation states and non-nation state actors become salient to each other; that is, they become aware of each other, especially in the case of the nation state side of the equation. Nation states may become aware of non-nation state actors in the cyber domain through various means that include but are not limited to (1) attribution of recent attacks either on their organizations or that of others, (2) identification of non-nation state actors through ongoing investigations to cyber attacks, (3) informal contact between representatives of nation state governments and non-nation state actors through hacker conferences or meetings, and (4) capitalizing upon existing relationships between individuals already in the employ of a nation state's security services and hackers who reside outside those government entities.

The second stage involves the recruitment of these non-nation state actors by the nation state through various means. In some cases this may mean that representatives from a nation state's security services will draw upon the nationalistic or patriotic feelings that a non-nation state actor may have for their own homeland. In other cases recruitment may be facilitated by coercion in the form of negative consequences to the non-nation state actor in terms of their own or their families' well-being. One often publicized tactic is to offer a non-nation state actor who has been caught committing offenses the opportunity to delay or eliminate negative legal consequences for their actions. Another method that has been mentioned previously in this chapter is the use of false flag tactics that deceive the non-nation state actor into committing actions that they believe further the objectives of their homeland when in fact just the opposite is the case. Finally, one often overlooked motivation that is often played upon by nation states is the attraction of associating with a nation state's security services and the subsequent prestige legitimacy that entails that association.

The third stage is the maintenance stage of the relationship. In this stage, there are efforts particularly on the part of the nation state to maintain a constructive relationship between the nation state and non-nation state actors. The strategies by which this process takes place include continued immunity from prosecution for the non-nation state actors' illegal acts on behalf of the nation state and also a willingness to "look the other way" at some of the illegal outside activities that the non-nation state actors may be conducting. The nation state may also supply non-nation state actors with access to substantial resources such as computers, networking hardware, high-speed Internet access, and software, as well as occasional access to highly skilled technical experts within specific nation state entities. During this maintenance stage there is also likely to be continued "grooming" of the non-nation state actors in terms of positive feedback by nation state representatives (including things like medals) to keep them working at their most effective pace.

The fourth and final stage involves the dissolution of the relationship between the nation state and the non-nation state actor or actors. Relationships of this kind are often volatile in nature and their lifespan may be quite short. The initiation of the dissolution may reside either with the nation state or the non-nation state actors or both. In a number of cases the dissolution may be the result of the collapse of the covert nature of the relationship itself. Once a nation state–non-nation state relationship is uncovered, its covert nature is lost and therefore it is likely that the nation state will no longer have use for the services of the non-nation state actors and terminate the relationship. In other cases the often fragile nature of non-nation state actor groups may cause the group to break up of its own accord, so the group's relationship with the nation state fractures. In other cases the relationship dissolves because the nation state has found another more skilled set of non-nation state actors and no longer has a use for the relationship.

One final note about the dissolution stage of the relationship should be noted here. As Kilger (2017) points out, non-nation state groups of actors in the cyber domain have the opportunity during their existence to accumulate resources and subsequent power that may cause them in the end to break away and perhaps even challenge their former nation state "friends". That is, non-nation state actors are able to accumulate financial resources through the theft of financial assets in the form of stolen credit cards, bank accounts, ransomware payments, and other means. During their time spent in the relationship, they have been able and encouraged to develop more technical skills among the group's actors. Additionally, these non-nation state actors have accumulated some legitimacy through the association with a nation state's security services, even if the knowledge of the relationship is known only within the underground hacking community. Given these events, the power, prestige, and capabilities of the non-nation state actor or actors has grown to the point where they may be an actual threat to the nation state that formerly counted them as coopted. That is, they may become a technical, economic, and political force that may threaten the very nation state that formerly enlisted them. This is an outcome that is particularly interesting and may play an important role in the relationship of nation states and actors in the near to intermediate future.

Summary

In this chapter we have examined a number of important concept and ideas. The role of the cyber domain in terms of psychological operations is one that is going to continue to evolve in interesting and important ways in the future. A number of recent historical examples of nation state conflict in cyberspace has demonstrated the significant utility of warfare that may occur within the digital world and extend beyond that to the physical world. We have also explored both recent examples of digital deception in the form of false flag operations as well as the role of deception in cyber conflict and cyberwarfare. Finally, we have examined the potential for non-nation state actors to have a very significant effect on the nature of the conflict in the cyber domain and how relationships between these actors and nation states may develop and evolve. It is quite evident from the earlier discussions that deception in the cyber domain is going to continue to grow in importance to nation states, in particular as they migrate their political, ideological, economic, and military conflicts from the physical world to the virtual world. It is important that we gain a better, more comprehensive understanding of the nature of these conflicts and the role that deception plays in that realm.

References

Andress, J., & Winterfeld, S. (2013). *Cyber warfare: Techniques, tactics and tools for security practitioners.* Waltham, MA: Syngress.

Brenner, S. (2009). *Cyberthreats: The emerging fault lines of the nation state.* Oxford: Oxford University Press.

Brodscky, J., & Radvanovsky, R. (2010). Control systems security. In *Corporate hacking and technology-driven crime: Social dynamics and implications* (pp. 187–203). Hershey, PA: IGI-Global.

Clayton, M. (2010). *Stuxnet malware is 'weapon' out to destroy ... Iran's Bushehr nuclear plant?* Christian Science Monitor. Retrieved from http://www.distributedworkplace.com/DW/Government/Government%202010/Stuxnet%20malware%20is%20weapon%20out%20to%20destroy%20Iran%20Bushehr%20nuclear%20plant.doc.

Clover, C. (2009). *Kremlin-backed group behind Estonia cyber blitz.* Financial Times. Retrieved from http://www.ft.com/cms/s/0/57536d5a-0ddc-11de-8ea3-0000779fd2ac.html?ft_site=falcon&desktop=true#a xzz4bLRoZ1Ce.

Davis, J. (2007). Web War One: The botnet attack on Estonia last spring nearly shut down Europe's most wired country. Behind enemy lines with the foot soldiers of the digital age. *Wired, 15*(9), 162.

Denning, D. (2010). Cyber conflict as an emergent social phenomenon. In *Corporate hacking and technology-driven crime: Social dynamics and implications* (pp. 170–186). IGI Global.

Eichenwald, K. (2016). *Dear Donald Trump and Vladimir Putin, I am not Sidney Blumenthal.* Retrieved from http://www.newsweek.com/vladimir-putin-sidney-blumenthal-hillary-clinton-donald-trump-benghazi-sputnik-508635.

Fisher, M. (2013). *Syrian hackers claim AP hack that tipped stock market by $136 billion. Is it terrorism?.* Retrieved from https://www.washingtonpost.com/news/worldviews/wp/2013/04/23/syrian-hackers-claim-ap-hack-that-tipped-stock-market-by-136-billion-is-it-terrorism/.

Fitton, O. (2016). Cyber operations and grey zones: Challenges for NATO. *Connections: The Quarterly Journal, 15*(2), 109–119.

Fritz, J. (2008). How China will use cyber warfare to leapfrog in military competitiveness. *Culture Mandala: The Bulletin of the Centre for East-West Cultural and Economic Studies, 8*(1), 28–80. Retrieved from http://epublications.bond.edu.au/cm/vol8/iss1/2/.

Gartzke, E., & Lindsay, J. (2015). *Cross-domain deterrence: Strategy in an era of complexity.* Retrieved from https://quote.ucsd.edu/deterrence/files/2014/12/EGLindsay_CDDOverview_20140715.pdf.

Geers, K., Kindlund, D., Moran, N., & Rachwald, R. (2014). *World War C: Understanding nation-state motives behind today's advanced cyber attacks.* Technical report. FireEye.

Gonsalves, A. (2013). *Islamic group promises to resume U.S. bank cyberattacks.* Retrieved from http://www.csoonline.com/article/2133049/malware-cybercrime/islamic-group-promises-to-resume-u-s–bank-cyberattacks.html.

Grohe, E. (2015). *The cyber dimensions of the civil war: Implications for future conflict.* Laurel, MD.

Guadagno, R., Cialdini, R., & Evron, G. (2010). Storming the servers: A social psychological analysis of the First Internet War. *Cyberpsychology, Behavior and Social Networking, 13*(4), 447–453.

Healy, J. (2012). *Beyond attribution: Seeking national responsibility for cyber attacks.* Washington, DC: The Atlantic Council.

Heckman, K., Stech, F., Thomas, R., Schmoker, B., & Tsow, A. (2015). *Cyber denial, deception and counter deception: A framework for supporting active cyber defense.* New York: Springer.

Henderson, S. J. (2007). *The dark visitor: Inside the world of Chinese hackers.* Foreign Military Studies Office, United States Army.

Jaffe, G. (2006). *Gates urges NATO ministers to defend against cyber attacks.* Retrieved from https://www.wsj.com/articles/SB118190166163536578.

Karppi, T., & Crawford, K. (2015). Social media, financial algorithms and the hack crash. *Theory, Culture and Society, 33*(1), 73–92.

Kerr, P., Rollins, J., & Theohary, C. (2010). *The stuxnet computer worm: Harbinger of an emerging warfare capability* (pp. 1–9). Washington, DC: Congressional Research Service.

Kilger, M. (2017). The evolving nature of nation state – malicious online actor relationships. In T. Holt (Ed.), *Cybercrime through an interdisciplinary lens* (pp. 76–91). London: Routledge.

Krekel, B. A., Adams, P., Bakos, G., Northrop Grumman Corporation, & U.S.-China Economic and Security Review Commission (2012). *Occupying the information high ground: Chinese capabilities for computer network operations and cyber espionage.* McLean, VA: Northrop Grumman Corp.

Krekel, B. A., U.S.-China Economic and Security Review Commission, & Northrop Grumman Corporation (2009). *Capability of the People's Republic of China to conduct cyber warfare and computer network exploitation.* McLean, VA: Northrop Grumman Corp., Information Systems Sector.

Landler, M., & Markoff, J. (2007). *Digital fears emerge after data siege in Estonia.* New York Times. Retrieved from http://www.nytimes.com/2007/05/29/technology/29estonia.html.

Libicki, M. (2012). *Crisis and escalation in cyberspace.* Santa Monica, CA: RAND Corporation.

Libicki, M. (2016). Second acts in cyberspace. In *Paper presented at a workshop on the strategic use of offensive cyber weapons March, 2016, Stanford Cyber Policy Program.*

Lindsay, J. R., & Cheung, T. M. (2015). In D. S. Reveron (Ed.), *China and cybersecurity: Espionage, strategy, and politics in the digital domain.* New York: Oxford University Press.

Markoff, J., & Barboza, D. (2010). *2 Chinaschools said to be tied to online attacks.* Retrieved from http://www.nytimes.com/2010/02/19/technology/19china.html.

Mattis, P. (2015). *Analyzing the Chinese military: A review essay and resource guide on the People's Liberation Army.*

Mazanec, B. M. (2015). *The evolution of cyber war: International norms for emerging-technology weapons.* Lincoln: Potomac Books, an imprint of the University of Nebraska Press.

Office of the Director of National Intelligence. (2016). *Joint statement from the Department of homeland security and office of the director of national intelligence on election security* Issued October 7, 2016. Retrieved from https://www.dni.gov/index.php/newsroom/press-releases/215-press-releases-2016/1423-joint-dhs-odni-election-security-statement.

Perloth, N. (2013). *Hunting for Syrian hackers' chain of command.* Retrieved from http://www.nytimes.com/2013/05/18/technology/financial-times-site-is-hacked.html.

Reveron, D. S. (2012). *Cyberspace and national security: Threats, opportunities, and power in a virtual world.* Washington, DC: Georgetown University Press.

Rid, T. (2013). *Cyber war will not take place.* Cary, NC, USA: Oxford University Press.

Sanger, D. (2012). *Confront and conceal: Obama's secret wars and surprising use of American power.* New York: Crown.

Schmugar, C. (2010). *More details on Operation Aurora.* Retrieved from http://blogs.mcaffee.com/mcaffee-labs/more-details-on-operation-aurora.

Schwartau, W. (1996). *Information warfare: Chaos on the electronic superhighway* (2nd ed.). New York: Thunder's Mouth Press.

Segal, A. (2016). *The hacked world order: How nations fight, trade, maneuver, and manipulate in the digital age.* New York: PublicAffairs.

Stiennon, R. (2015). *There will Be cyberwar :b how the move to network-Centric Warfighting set the stage for cyberwar.*

Tzu, S., & Giles, L. (2009). *The art of war: The oldest military treatise in the world.* Auckland, NZ: Floating Press.

Umland, A. (2016). *Russia's Pernicious hybrid war against Ukraine.* Retrieved from http://www.atlanticcouncil.org/blogs/new-atlanticist/russia-s-pernicious-hybrid-war-against-ukraine.

Van Creveld, M. (1999). *The rise and decline of the state.* Cambridge: Cambridge UniversityPress.

Ventre, D. (2009). *Information warfare.* London: John Wiley & Sons.

Zetter, K. (2010). *"Google" hackers had ability to alter source code.* Retrieved from http://www.wired.com/threatlevel/2010/03/source-code-hacks/.

Zetter, K. (2011). *DHS fears a modified Stuxnet could attack US infrastructure.* WIRED. Retrieved from https://www.wired.com/2011/07/dhs-fears-stuxnet-attacks/.

9

Sweet Deception: Honeypots

ABSTRACT

This chapter provides the reader with a description of a set of technologies collectively known as "honey" technologies. The beginning discussion provides the reader with a brief history of early and often unintended honey technology experiences from the likes of Cliff Stoll, Bill Cheswick, and Fred Cohen. The next section focuses on the idea of honeypots and honeynets featuring the work of Lance Spitzner and the Honeynet Project and adds additional relevant theoretical concepts such game theory and practical commentary relevant to these particular forms of deception by information security professionals. The final section of the chapter is a discussion of honeytokens: informational objects of value that are used to entice malicious online actors to compromise digital devices that are either honeytokens in and of themselves or contain honeytokens that are susceptible to being stolen.

Keywords: *Deception toolkit; Decoy; Game theory; High interaction honeypot; Honeychannel; Honeynet; Honeynet Project; Honeypot; Honeytoken; Low interaction honeypot; Mimicking; Phoneytoken.*

CHAPTER OUTLINE

Introduction

This chapter explores the some of the theoretical aspects of the class of deception objects typically known as honeypots or honeynets. It should be noted that in reality this class includes a somewhat larger class of objects beyond traditional honeypots to include other elements such as honeytokens and honeycreds. Many of these types of deception entities, particularly honeypots and honeynets, are currently in large-scale deployment by commercial entities, security companies, government agencies, and military groups around the globe. They have been used not only in traditional information warehouse settings but have also been extensively utilized in other settings such as industrial control systems (Koltys & Gajewski, 2015), as well as in voice over IP phone systems (Aziz, Hoffstadt, Rathgeb, & Dreibholz, 2014). We will briefly examine the role of deception in two classes of honey objects: (1) honeypots and honeynets and (2) honeytokens.

A Bit of History

Likely the earliest examples of "honey technologies" are that of honeypots, and some of the early examples of honeypots can be traced at least back to the narratives of Cliff Stoll and the Cuckoos Egg. After noticing a 75 cent discrepancy in the computer billing records at Lawrence Livermore National Laboratories, Stoll discovered an intruder in one of the servers and proceeded to expend a significant amount of energy to uncover who this individual was and what he was interested in (Stoll, 1988). He set up a series of files on the compromised computer containing misinformation about the Strategic Defense Initiative in order to attract the attacker's interest. This computer became a primitive honeypot. Provos (2003) describes honeypots as useful in that they "distract adversaries from more valuable machines on a network, they can provide early warning about new attack and exploitation trends, and they allow in-depth examination of adversaries during and after exploitation of a honeypot." Eventually the attacker was identified as living in Germany and was later apprehended.

A similar effort occurred in January of 1991 when Bill Cheswick noticed an intruder on one of his machines, which happened to be named Berferd. During the next 5 months, Cheswick made various changes to the compromised computer in order to thwart and track the intruder, thus developing another variation of an early honeypot. What is perhaps just as interesting about Cheswick's account is that he describes his experiences in first person, and one can get the sense from his account that he is quite surprised that anyone would try to compromise another machine. It is a sense of curiosity that motivates him to expend efforts to learn more about the individual attempting to compromise his Berferd machine.

A more organized and later example of deceptive digital machines arose with the emergence of the Deception Toolkit by Fred Cohen (1998). Cohen's account in the journal *Computers and Security* is among the first to not only discuss technical details of using a decoy machine to learn more about the technical attacks in the wild, but importantly, his account describes at length some of the theoretical principles behind deception and applies them to the digital world. Cohen examines the roles of some of the basic principles of deception, including concealment, camouflage, false and implanted information, ruses, displays, demonstrations, lies, and the role of insight in the execution of deception. He is also one of the early pioneers in digital deception in terms of discussing how deception extracts an economic price from the attacker in terms of workload.

One of the outcomes of the deployment of the Deception Toolkit was the discovery that unlike earlier work (Howard, 1997) that suggested a rather low rate of online attacks, the use of the Deception Toolkit provided evidence that the actual rate of attacks in the wild was many times what was previously thought. Cohen also recognized that the techniques utilized in the Deception Toolkit were somewhat simplistic in nature and that a simple check of port 365 would indicate to an attacker that the machine being examined was being run as a deception host.

The next milestone in the use of digital deception is likely the formation of a new group that called themselves the Honeynet Project.[1] Founded by former Army tank officer Lance Spitzner, this small group of individuals on a discussion board eventually evolved into an organization that today lists 54 teams of information security experts in 44 countries. One of the main innovations to come out of the efforts in the early years of this organization was a set of tools that allowed individuals to set up honeypots: computers whose sole purpose was to capture and record the details of any attack against it. The honeypot also served to gather additional information about attackers through monitoring the content of chat services such as Internet Relay Chat that were set up on the honeypot by the attackers.

One of the early amusing stories from this era concerns the attack on a honeypot by an individual who then proceeded to set up a video chat channel on the server. The Honeynet Project members who set up the honeypot noticed the video chat traffic and tapped into it so they could actually see the attacker in the video in real time. Unfortunately, as word spread among the Project members about the video feed of the attacker, more and more Honeynet Project members jumped onto the compromised machine to watch the attacker go about his business and eventually the attacker noticed the significant additional load on the machine from all this attention; he realized that he had been discovered and he quickly left.

During the early years the Honeynet Project evangelized their knowledge and software tools for deception among a number government agencies, the military, and in the commercial sector as well. These efforts likely played a nontrivial part in popularizing the idea that deception played an important part in digital defense through the collection of intelligence on specific attack methods, the identities of attackers, and their motivations. In later years the Honeynet Project has development a significant body of work in terms of defensive information security software tools and is still active in the area. There will be additional discussion about honeypot and honeynet technologies in a later section in the chapter.

Today in the field of information security, deception has become one of the hot new topics. While the original work done in the area of honeypots often was open source in nature and freely distributed among information security researchers and professionals, their deployment often required significant technical expertise to deploy them effectively and to generate value from the data that they collected. In more recent years, there have been a number of commercial and noncommercial projects and products that make the deployment and analysis of the data collected significantly easier than in the past. Projects like Modern Honey Network, a free software tool created by Google-backed ThreatStream (Higgins, 2014), and products produced by commercial entities such as Cymmetria's Mazerunner (Cymmetria, 2016) are providing software deception tools that require less effort and technical expertise to properly deploy and utilize.

---

[1] Disclaimer: The primary author of this chapter is a founding member of the Honeynet Project and currently is a member of the board of directors of this organization.

The next section of this chapter will discuss some of the theory of deception that powers some of the software tools. These deception principles are deployed in some of these software tools and digital objects in this chapter, and so learning more about them will be useful to gain a more comprehensive understanding of how digital deception works.

Honeypots and Honeynets

Many researchers point to Spitzner's definition of a honeypot (Spitzner, 2002), where he states that "a honeypot is a security resource whose value lies in being probed, attacked or compromised." Spitzner goes on to elaborate on just what a security resource is "whatever we designate as a honeypot, our expectations and goals are to have the system probed, attacked, and potentially exploited. It does not matter what the resource is (a router, scripts running emulated services, a jail, an actual production system)." Provos (2004) provides a definition of honeypots that fits more with their objectives when he describes them as "closely monitored network decoys serving several purposes: they can distract adversaries from more valuable machines on a network, they can provide early warning about new attack and exploitation trends and they allow in-depth examination of adversaries during and after exploitation of a honeypot." During this same time period Pouget, Dacier, and Debar (2003) observed that there were also a number of other roughly similar definitions proposed by other researchers.

Similarly, Spitzner (2002) notes that honeynets "represent the extreme of research honeypots. They are high interaction honeypots, which allow learning a great deal; however they also have the highest level of risk. Their primary value lies in research, gaining information on threats that exist in the Internet community today. A Honeynet is a network of production systems." Spitzner suggests that within a honeynet, nothing is emulated on the machines within the honeynet, and all services are available for an attacker to take advantage of.

As more researchers began to experiment with and extended the open source core honeypot and honeynet tools being developed by the Honeynet Project, two different classes of honeypots tended to emerge. The first class was what was called a "low interaction" honeypot. A low interaction honeypot, according to Spitzner (2002), is one where only certain functions or services were running and available to be compromised by attackers. He explains that high interaction honeypots have all of the typical services and operating system processes of a normal production computer.

Provos (2004) also points out that honeypots may be either virtual or physical machines. Virtual machines have a significant advantage in terms of not requiring additional physical hardware for each additional honeypot that is put online. However, often this turns out to be a disadvantage to researchers in that attackers often get suspicious that a system they are attempting to compromise may be a honeypot if they detect that it is a virtual machine rather than a traditional computer with dedicated hardware.

The emergence of deception activities into a relatively new and rapidly evolving area such as digital technology suggests that it may be useful to apply some theoretical structure to this novel setting. This structure can provide some additional knowledge that may be applied to develop a foundational groundwork to build a better, more comprehensive understanding of how this phenomenon operates in the environment. One such example is that of Endicott-Popovsky et al. (2009), who apply Bell and Whaley's deception planning loop. Bell and Whaley (1991) divide deception into two broad categories: hiding the real and showing the false. Within each of these classes are specific activities that help accomplish these goals. On a fundamental level, hiding the real consists of masking, repackaging, and dazzling. Honeypots most certainly mask the data recording components present that collect data on the actions of the attacker, both during the initial attempts to compromise the honeypot as well as what the attacker does once the honeypot has been compromised. If the attackers realize that their actions are being recorded, they will quickly determine that the machine they have compromised is a honeypot that has no value and actually presents a serious risk to their activities and security.

Showing the false also has three different dimensions according to Bell and Whaley: mimicking, inventing, and decoying. Honeypots are designed to mimic real production machines, so the attacker believes that the target is real and there is information of value present on that particular target. The longer the honeypot can deceive the attacker into believing the honeypot is a real production machine, the more data the defender can collect for analysis. This suggests that high interaction honeypots are better at mimicry than low interaction honeypots because they contain many more of the markers that suggest that the machine is engaged in true production activities within the organization and not a honeypot. Similarly, honeynets that contain multiple high interaction honeypots in a typical networked setting provide additional mimicking value that provides additional false clues that the machines targeted in the network are true production machines that may contain information of value.

Decoying is also an important function of honeypots. In terms of economy of effort, efforts spent by an attacker on a honeypot are efforts that are not being expended on a target of value within the organization under attack. Economy of effort is an important factor in cyber defense. One of the objectives in the defense of a network is to force the attacker to expend as much effort as possible to compromise machines in the network. Similar to traditional property crime, attackers are driven toward return on investment, and if they perceive that there is not an attractive return on investment between the potential payoff of compromising a network and the efforts involved, they are likely to move on to a more vulnerable and potentially valuable target elsewhere.

Another positive aspect of deception through decoy is one discussed by Rowe, Custy, and Duong (2007). Their excellent paper points out that attackers have been shown to avoid honeypots for several reasons. The first reason is echoed in the previous discussion above: they are focused upon their investment in effort versus the potential payoff that resides in compromising a honeypot. Rowe et al. suggests that the second reason why attackers try to avoid honeypots is that they do not wish to expose their specific attack techniques and tools to a honeypot, where those strategies and tools will be noted and recorded and researchers will soon spread word of their details as well as possible defenses against that particular type of attack.

Rowe et al. cite other researchers who have noted that honeypots often are characterized by specific markers such as specific hardware parameters, specific "magic numbers," or traces of honeypot processes in memory that are clues that give the fact that the machine is a honeypot. These clues are often picked up by attackers who then move on to another machine, network, or target. They got the idea that if they could make a true production machine with valuable information on it appear to be a honeypot, attackers would avoid the machine and move on elsewhere. While quite a novel idea, one of the real challenges to this strategy is to make the evidence convincing enough that attackers will see only the first layer of deception—that this is a honeypot—and will not uncover the second layer of the deception—that this is a true production machine posing as a honeypot.

This challenge is more difficult than one might expect at first glance. For example, Rowe et al. discuss the concept of honeychannels and the challenges in managing the correct level of information (Rowe et al., 2007, p. 6):

> Maintaining similar information flow rate during deception has several implications for communications with honeypots, by what we can call "honeychannels." It is desirable that the information content of the honeychannel be similar to that of typical victim machines in the words and characters it transmits and their rate of transmission. This means it will be important to simulate the frequencies of words and data in the normal messages of a real computer system as much as we can during deception. But it also means that the semantics of information transmitted must preserve a similar information content. This means that fake information we present to a user must have roughly the same number and kinds of internal logical connections as real information flow.

Rowe et al. apply some game theoretic probabilities to the actions of the attackers and then design and execute an experiment to test their model as well as provide some foundational learning from empirical evidence about the concept of a fake honeypot. They exposed their honeypot to the Internet without a firewall and then varied the number of clues that it was a honeypot over time. As they suspected, the more clues present that suggested the machine was a honeypot, the fewer Snort alerts that they got as attackers shied away from the honeypot once they discovered its true nature. They also surmised that when they took the honeypot offline, the number of attacks decreased, and so they suggest that one possible defense for a production machine is to reuse an IP address that has already been investigated and discarded as worthwhile of attention.

The application of game theoretic theory to describe the behavior of attackers against a honeypot or honeynet is one that has gained popularity in recent years. The use of game theory in studying the economic behavior of attackers making attacks on honeypots and the decisions about deploying honeypots on the defender side of the equation seems like a reasonably natural fit. You have two players, an attacker and a defender, who are engaged in an actor-dependent activity or game in the form of the situation where defenders incur some cost to deploying a honeypot, while attackers incur some cost in discovering whether or not the machine they intend to compromise is a true production machine or a honeypot. Provided that there is some element of randomization in the process, it is possible to attempt to develop Nash equilibriums for each type of game where each player perfectly predicts the actions of the other player and so conducts an optimal or best outcome strategy.

Kiekintveld, Lisý, and Píbil (2015) discuss how game theory can apply to the behaviors found surrounding honeypots, and they develop a number of models to illustrate their usefulness in information security in general and in developing a better understanding of the dynamics of attacker-defender behaviors regarding honeypots more specifically. In demonstrating the usefulness and value of game theory in optimizing defensive measures, they observe (Kiekintveld et al., 2015, p. 6):

> *The key question in security games is to decide how the defender should allocate limited protective resources to maximize protection against an intelligent attacker who reacts to the security policy. The optimal deterministic strategy is simply to protect as many of the most valuable targets as possible. However, a randomized strategy can use deterrence to improve the overall level of protection by spreading the resources out over a larger set of targets. Since the attacker does not know exactly which targets will be protected (only the probabilities), the attacker has some risk of being unsuccessful when attacking a larger set of targets. Essentially, the defender is able to gain an advantage by concealing information about the defense strategy using randomization.*

In addition, Kiekinveld et al. point out that the value of each of the machines that the defense is protecting varies and that it is desirable for the defender to put more resources and effort toward defending more valuable machines and to put less toward machines with lessor value. They construct a set of game theoretic models where machines have different values, the defenders choose which machines they wish the honeypot to resemble, and both the attacker and defender know the number of honeypots in the network. They then plot the defenders expected against the number of honeypots in the network for three different scenarios: random attacker, maximum value attacker, and Nash equilibrium attacker. Additionally, they extend and complicate the scenarios by adding the ability for the attacker to probe the machines to better simulate conditions in the wild. Their conclusion is that game theory has the potential to add considerable value to the understanding of the dynamics that occur in network defense situations and that further research is likely to make inroads into better understanding the interactions involved in defender–attacker utility and actions in honeypot-laden computer networks.

There appears to be significant potential in applying game theory to understanding the utility and dynamics of attacker–defender actions in honeypot-infused networks.

Future work in this area may involve the application of a more complex extension of game theory models such as hypergame theory models to more realistically represent behaviors in honeypot or honeynet scenarios in the wild. In hypergame theory, an information asymmetry may occur, where actors may base their actions on either misperceptions about specific elements of the game, such as payoffs or costs that are internal in origin, or they may come from misperceptions about these elements due to deception on the part of other players in the game (Kovac, Gibson, & Lamont, 2015). The application of this extension to game theory should provide researchers with a richer universe of models from which to choose as well as enhance the ability to develop theoretical models that more realistically represent the dynamics of attacker–defender dynamics in the real world.

Honeytokens

The second class of related honey objects is labeled honeytokens. Although the term has been credited to Lance Spitzner, the actual origin of the term, according to Spitzner, was coined by Augusto Paes de Barros in 2003 on a Honeynet Project internal mail list (Spitzner, 2003). Spitzner (2003) described a honeytoken as "a digital or information system resource whose value lies in the unauthorized use of that resource." More specifically, unlike honeypots that are systems made up of computer hardware and software, honeytokens are objects that usually inhabit these digital systems. Examples of honeytokens might include credit card numbers, bank account numbers, authentication credentials, specific computer files, medical records, a specific image or set of pixels within an image, or other objects that can be uniquely identified. The idea behind a honeytoken is that it is something that some actor or a device possesses that they should not possess; that is, it is an object that has been acquired by malicious or illegal means.

A honeytoken in and of itself may or may not have intrinsic value. That is, it might be a credit card that is actually still valid and can be used by the individual who illicitly acquired it for goods or services. On the other hand, the credit card might have been specially created for use as a honeytoken and may have no or limited value to the person who possesses it. However, the real value of the honeytoken is accrued to the individual or group that has created the honeytoken for its own purposes.

Typically, honeytokens are created and then incorporated into an object that is subject to attack by malicious actors. For example, a credit card-based honeytoken might be set of related records within a database, where those records reflect the credit card number, its expiration date, the card verification value (CCV) security code, name of the cardholder, and their billing address, although often this information has been manufactured and does not represent the details of a real cardholder. The idea is that, similar to a honeypot where there should be no traffic and any traffic that is there is malicious, no one should legitimately possess the honeytoken. If they do, they obtained it by nefarious means.

Juels (2014) describes two important characteristics of honeytokens or equivalently honey objects. These characteristics are indistinguishability and secrecy (Juels, 2014, p. 1):

Indistinguishability: *To deceive and attacker, honey objects must be hard to distinguish from real objects. They should, in other words, be drawn from a probability distribution over possible objects similar to that from which a real object S* was selected.*

Secrecy: *In a system with honey objects, j is a secret. Honey objects can, of course, only deceive an attacker that doesn't know j, so j cannot reside alongside S. Kerckhoffs's principle therefore comes into play: the security of the system must reside in the secret, i.e., the distinction between honey objects and real ones, not in the mere fact of using honey objects. The secret j may reside with either or both of two types of entity: An actor (generally a user) that selects objects from S and a honeychecker, a system that signals an attack when an object other than s*=sj is selected and is distinct from the system that stores S.*

So we know that a honeytoken should resemble other objects that are in its class and that would have come from the same or similar sources as to allay the suspicions of the attacker that the object might not be genuine. In addition, even if the process by which a honeytoken is created is known by the attacker, without additional key information, the attacker will not be able to identify specific honeytokens within a system. This is important because while you do not want the attacker to be able to identify honeytokens, your production system must be able to distinguish honeytokens from real objects in the system in order not to contaminate production systems with honeytokens.

This bit of secrecy means that one must specifically exclude having the detection system that holds the process secret and can identify a honeytoken from being a part of the system holding the true and honeytokens; that is, they must be separate from the system that stores nonhoneytoken objects and honeytokens alike. Guarding this secret or process by which honeytokens can be detected must be done with care, and the author of a honeytoken system must take care not to count upon security by obscurity to keep that process secret from potential attackers (Almeshekah & Spafford, 2014).

Juels goes on to observe that honeytokens that come from systematic algorithms such as credit card numbers may be fairly easy to manufacture. Passwords might also not be too difficult to manufacture as honeytokens, given that they obey typical password standards for security features such as mandatory numeric and case differences within the password. On the other hand, he points out that other honeytokens such as email messages provide a more difficult task in systematically generating them by machine because these honeytokens must make grammatical sense as well as the content must not be nonsensical. Juels also points out that honeytokens might take on the form of something other than a digital object, for example, a set of permissions that are much more liberal than what a particular account owner needs. This would allow the account owner to wander into areas of file systems where there is no justification, and so logging such access may count as uncovering a honeytoken.

Over the past few years, honeytokens have taken on many forms. Gupta, Srinivasan, Balasubramaniyan, and Ahamad (2015) discuss the concept of an IP telephony-based honeypot system and the use of what they call "phoneytokens," phone numbers that area associated with a telephony-based honeypot. They discuss the difficulties in seeding these phoneytokens so that they are not viewed with suspicion by malicious actors. They suggest, for example, that one might seed these phoneytokens by creating a simple "do not call" list of telephone numbers and placing this file on a server that resides on a honeypot inside an organization's system. It should also be noted here that if a phone call is received by one of the phoneytoken phone numbers, this may signal that the honeypot upon which the phoneytokens has been stored has been compromised, although this is subject to false positives in the case of a misdialed or wrong number scenario.

Gupta et al. then discuss how calls to the phone numbers or phoneytokens are handled, remembering that in reality there should be no or almost no traffic to these phone numbers given that they are not associated with a real person or company. They suggest that calls to these numbers may be handled either as no, low, medium, or high interaction schemas. No interaction means that the telephony honeypot outcome will be either a busy signal or a decline response. A low interaction response might be a voicemail box where an announcement and message may be left. A medium response, Gupta et al. suggest, might be an interactive voice response system where certain canned responses from the phoneytoken number might be made. Finally, a high interaction response to a call to a phoneytoken phone number might be a voice recognition system deployed to interact with the malicious caller, providing them with a menu of options, recognizing their responses to those options, and guiding them through some sort of customer service menu that ends up eventually going to a message system or perhaps even a live person.

Another form of honeytokens is discussed by Virvilis, Vanautgaerden, and Serrano (2014), which utilizes honeytokens within network traffic. They suggest that one method for detecting intruders in a network is to post false Domain Name System (DNS) records on a DNS server on the network. No internal machines should be attempting to resolve these particular addresses, so when an attacker attempts to brute force replies from an internal DNS server, they will eventually trip across one of these honeytoken DNS records, and the DNS server can be programmed to notify administrators that someone has attempted to contact the nonexistent machine that is listed in the honeytoken DNS record.

Virvilis et al. also suggest other strategies such as hidden links in web pages (links that have text that is colored the same color as the webpage background so that they are invisible) that an attacker might pick up by looking at the source code for the page. They also suggest a similar approach could use comments hidden in HTML code of a webpage that refer to default admin accounts that are supposed to be inactivated. When these honeytokens hidden in the source code of the webpage are utilized by the attackers, the system can notify administrators that someone is prowling about.

Another interesting scheme is described by Tyagi, Wang, Wen, and Zuo (2015) and Juels and Ristenpart (2014). This is a mathematically complex way of encrypting content so that it protects against brute force attacks. The honeytoken-based deception component of this is that as an added extra "bonus," brute force attacks against password-protected content will eventually turn up a message that appears to the valid, decrypted message. While the methodology behind this technique is complex and requires some knowledge of the principles of cryptology, the fact that this technique exists is somewhat unique in terms of the application of honeytoken deception strategies.

Another sophisticated application of honeytokens involves the generation of decoys that reside in a cloud computing architecture. Kontaxis, Polychronakis, and Keromytis (2014) describe a method by which they generate computational decoys or computational honeytokens within a cloud structure. They point out that shared access to resources within the cloud, as well as the relatively new area of cloud security, means that their environment is fertile for malicious actors to infiltrate cloud structures and monitor cloud computational and communications processes with an eye to exfiltrating valuable data from the cloud. They suggest that honeytokens in the form of computational cloud decoys may fulfill two purposes: (1) they add ambiguity to the cloud environment in that the decoys make it more difficult to determine which cloud computational and communications processes are real and which ones are the result of decoys and (2) they provide defenders with the opportunity to seed decoy cloud computational processes with additional, different forms of honeytokens such as credit card information, special files, credentials to other systems, etc.

Kontaxis et al. (2014) assume that one or more instances, but not all the instances, within a cloud have been compromised. They also assume that the attackers are smart enough to compare and correlate captured data from among the compromised cloud instances so that they are able to detect potential honeytokens. This means that the computational cloud decoys that the defender generates must carry content that resembles content from other nondecoy instances. They also point out that instances within the cloud are oblivious to whether the computational process they are working on is a real user-initiated process or whether the process is a decoy. They call their computational decoy system DIGIT, and DIGIT is placed near the edge of the cloud so that it may pass through traffic from true computational instances back to their rightful owners, while the decoy traffic is diverted to a null channel and thus disposed of. They also point out, as previously suggested, that additional honeytokens in the form of credit information or other information can be injected into the decoy so that if the attacker compromises the computational decoy, they will exfiltrate honeytoken-laden data that will eventually set off an alarm when it is later used.

The final type of honeytoken to be discussed is a special one that is often described as some digital object with a "beacon" hidden within that object. Chakravarty, Portokalidis, Polychronakis, and Keromytis (2015) discuss how anonymous communications channels such as Tor encrypt traffic from end to end, but as this traffic reaches the end of the Tor node and makes its way on its final pathway, this traffic near the "end of the line" is susceptible to being intercepted, and confidential information traveling this pathway may be disclosed unless the original content is already encrypted.

Chakravarty et al. discuss how traffic in these environments may be seeded with honey-token objects such as services credentials or URLs that lead to sensitive-appearing documents that in turn are honeytokens. These honeytokens contain beacons in the form of scripts or macros that "phone home" when the document object is opened by the malicious actors after exfiltration, thus alerting the defenders to the fact that someone has intercepted the traffic after it has left the Tor endpoint. Over a period of 30 months, the researchers left this honeytoken system in place and recorded 16 traffic interception incidents in that time. They noted that the time span between the moment the traffic was intercepted and the time at which the decoy server was contacted ranged from 1 to 16 hours.

Summary

In this chapter, we have taken a brief look at how deception has been utilized in a special class of objects that we can label honey objects. Whether that object is a honeypot, a honeynet, or a honeytoken, this particular technology has provided defenders with a very large amount of information about the tools and techniques of malicious online actors. As the concept of honey objects has matured, researchers have brought a more theoretical focus to the technology, such as in the case of game theorists who have been working on producing game theoretic models of attacker–defender behaviors with an eye toward not only understanding these behaviors, but also working toward improving the strategies of defenders to more efficiently protect their assets. Finally, in the area of honeytokens, we have seen how researchers have branched out and developed new and sophisticated forms of honeytokens in an effort to better detect and protect their digital networks and devices against compromise.

References

Almeshekah, M., & Spafford, E. (2014). Planning and integrating deception into computer security defenses. In *Proceedings of the 2014 workshop on new security paradigms workshop* (pp. 127–138).

Aziz, A., Hoffstadt, D., Rathgeb, E., & Dreibholz, T. (2014). A distributed infrastructure to analyse SIP attacks in the internet. In *Networking conference, 2014 IFIP* (pp. 1–9).

Bell, J., & Whaley, B. (1991). *Cheating and deception.* Piscataway, New Jersey: Transaction Publishers.

Chakravarty, S., Portokalidis, G., Polychronakis, M., & Keromytis, A. (2015). Detection and analysis of eavesdropping in anonymous communication networks. *International Journal of Information Security*, *14*(3), 205–220.

Cheswick, B. (1991). *An evening with Berferd in which a cracker is lured, endured, and studied.* Retrieved from http://www.cheswick.com/ches/papers/berferd.pdf.

Cohen, F. (1998). The deception toolkit. *Risks Digest, 19.*

Cymmetria. (2016). *Cymmetria Mazerunner.* Retrieved rom http://l.cymmetria.com/mazerunner-product-whitepaper.

Endicott-Popovsky, B., Narvaez, J., Seifert, C., Frincke, D. A., O'Neil, L. R., & Aval, C. (2009). Use of deception to improve client honeypot detection of drive-by-download attacks. In *International conference on foundations of augmented cognition* (pp. 138–147). Heidelberg: Springer Berlin.

Gupta, P., Srinivasan, B., Balasubramaniyan, V., & Ahamad, M. (2015). Phoneypot: Data-driven understanding of telephony threats. In *Paper presented at the 2015 NDSS symposium*.

Higgins, K. (2014). *Open source tool aimed at propelling honeynets into the mainstream*. Retrieved from http://www.darkreading.com/analytics/threat-intelligence/open-source-tool-aimed-at-propelling-honeypots-into-the-mainstream/d/d-id/1278726.

Howard, J. (1997). *An analysis of security incidents on the Internet*. Dissertation. Carnegie Mellon University.

Juels, A. (June 2014). A bodyguard of lies: The use of honey objects in information security. In *Proceedings of the 19th ACM symposium on access control models and technologies* (pp. 1–4).

Juels, A., & Ristenpart, T. (2014). Honey encryption: Security beyond the brute-force bound. In *Annual international conference on the theory and applications of cryptographic techniques* (pp. 293–310). Heidelberg: Springer Berlin.

Kiekintveld, C., Lisý, V., & Píbil, R. (2015). Game-theoretic foundations for the strategic use of honeypots in network security. In S. Jajodia, P. Shakarian, V. S. Subrahmanian, V. Swarup, & C. Wang (Eds.), *Cyber warfare* (pp. 81–101). New York City: Springer International Publishing.

Koltys, K., & Gajewski, R. (2015). SHaPe: A honeypot for electric power substation. *Journal of Telecommunications and Information Technology*, 4, 37.

Kontaxis, G., Polychronakis, M., & Keromytis, A. (2014). Computational decoys for cloud security. In S. Jajodia, K. Kant, P. Samarati, A. Singhal, V. Swarup, & C. Wang (Eds.), *Secure cloud computing* (pp. 261–270). New York: Springer.

Kovac, N., Gibson, A., & Lamont, G. (2015). Hypergame theory: A model for conflict, misperception, and deception. *Game Theory*, 2015, 1–20.

Pouget, F., Dacier, M., & Debar, H. (2003). *Honeypot, honeynet, honeytoken: Terminological issues*. Rapport technique. EURECOM. 1275.

Provos, N. (2003). Honeyd-a virtual honeypot daemon. In *10th DFN-CERT workshop, Hamburg, Germany* (Vol. 2) (p. 4).

Provos, N. (2004). A virtual honeypot framework. In *USENIX security symposium* (Vol. 173) (pp. 1–14).

Rowe, N., Custy, E., & Duong, B. (2007). Defending cyberspace with fake honeypots. *Journal of Computers*, 2(2), 25–36.

Spitzner, L. (2002). *Honeypots: Tracking attackers*. Boston: Addison Wesley.

Spitzner, L. (2003). *Honeytokens: The other honeypot*. Retrieved from http://www.symantec.com/connect/articles/honeytokens-other-honeypot.

Stoll, C. (1988). How secure are computers in the USA? An analysis of a series of attacks on Milnet computers. *Computers & Security*, 7(6), 543–547.

Tyagi, N., Wang, J., Wen, K., & Zuo, D. (2015). *Honey encryption applications*. Retrieved from https://courses.csail.mit.edu/6.857/2016/files/tyagi-wang-wen-zuo.pdf.

Virvilis, N., Vanautgaerden, B., & Serrano, O. (2014). Changing the game: The art of deceiving sophisticated attackers. In *Cyber conflict (CyCon 2014), 2014 6th international conference on* (pp. 87–97).

10

Looking Forward: Deception in the Future

ABSTRACT

This chapter looks to the future to discuss how the advancements of technology and cyber communications will impact deceptive techniques. While the future will no doubt bring about new and creative methods of deception, there several interesting topics that are already in development including nanotechnology, quantum stealth, and advanced drones. The impact of these new technologies, as well as several others, will have a direct impact the field of psychology, as definitions of what is real and what are hallucinations may be challenged. This chapter concludes with the impact on society, indicating that technologists and scientists must ardently keep in mind the social scientific and human consequences of their newly created magic.

Keywords: *Disruptive technology; Drones; Holograms; Man in the middle; Nanotechnology; Neurohacking; Neuromarketing; Online communities; Quantum stealth.*

Looking to the future is always a dubious task. In some cases, predictions can be so fantastic that they never come to fruition, and in other cases the futuristic developments seem to happen overnight. The future of cyber deception seems to have a breadth and depth as deep as the imagination can go, given that current technology is changing so rapidly. The future can only offer more opportunities to confuse people's perceptions. In ancient times, as mentioned earlier in Chapter 1, The Psychology of Deception, conjurers and magicians in Egypt, India, China, Babylonia, and other countries performed for audiences, mystifying them with a wide variety of slight-of-hand tricks, illusions, and magic. The future's

Deception in the Digital Age. http://dx.doi.org/10.1016/B978-0-12-411630-6.00010-4

version of these bygone deceits will most definitely be derived from the advances in physics, computer science, engineering, and to some degree from "movie magic" (i.e., CGI, special effects). People interpret the world around them by a myriad of stimuli including visual, audio, and kinetic inputs. Psychologically, these inputs will continue to impact perceptions, misdirecting what is believed to be true.

While the future will no doubt bring about new and creative methods of deception, there are six interesting topics that are already in development. Those six subject areas include: (1) false online communities; (2) disruptive technology; (3) holograms; (4) nanotechnology and quantum stealth; (5) advanced drones; (6) neurohacking/neuromarketing; and (7) the man in the middle conundrum. The impact of these new technologies will also have a direct impact the field of psychology, as definitions of what is real and what are hallucinations may be challenged.

False Online Communities

According to Facebook's Second Quarter Results Report (June, 2016), there are over 1.71 billion monthly active Facebook users worldwide. Of those users, Facebook has reported that an estimated 8.7% are fake users. For the most part, those fake user accounts are created by individuals who for their own motives and purposes have created fictitious personas, including intelligence and military personnel creating accounts for false-flag operations. For instance, Dell SecureWorks identified at least 25 fake LinkedIn profiles that were being used to gather intelligence on defense industry companies and government contractors (SecureWorks, 2015). The accounts were tied to Iranian state-sponsored hackers and were thought to be a mechanism to surreptitiously gather information by subverting a trusted online community.

But what has not been reported openly in the press is the existence of entirely created online fraudulent communities. There are plenty of "hidden" communities or communities that want to remain anonymous; however, it is entirely possible to create hundreds or thousands of made-up people and communities on social media and online. These fabricated communities could be created by and managed by automated bots, linguistically driven neural networks, and artificial intelligence. The creation of entire communities may act as influencers for political, economic, financial, or philosophic purposes.

A microcosm of this phenomenon occurred when Ashley Madison created more than 70,000 female bots to send male users millions of fake messages (Impact Team, 2015). The fabrication of these fake people was to create the marketing illusion that there were thousands of available women participating in this "dating/cheaters" online service. However, in this scenario, the thousands of bots were only visible to a very specific target audience. The message bots were somewhat obvious and simpleminded as the proliferated messages were reported to be "lines" such as: "Hi, how are you today?," "Want someone to chat with?," and "What are you doing right now?" The psychology behind the communication was also simplistic as it was geared to appeal to those people (predominantly men) who were seeking extramarital affairs. The fact that these individuals were doing something illicit combined with the lure of a potentially significant positive personal reward in a digital environment that did not transmit visual or aural deception cues likely lowered their ability to detect these relatively simple deceptions.

But what if the intent was more sophisticated and propagated on a much larger scale? And the technology used to create realistic bots actually mimicked real language, actual dialogue, and real people? Could a thousand or a million-person fake community populate the online airwaves with rhetoric, philosophies, and fabricated actions, including threats? Would the inclusion of a few "seeded" real humans make it more difficult to detect a false community?

The idea of a large volume false community interacting as a consolidated voice may present challenges (i.e., reach of influence, detection as false, countermeasures) and could be extremely disruptive. The devices and platforms that are the foundations of the potentially misdirected communication and action (i.e., hardware, software) can also be influential and disruptive. This suggests that large-scale false communities could be used to influence public opinion, sway political elections, or support psychological warfare operations. Could false communities spark, support, and sustain social movements among real human populations?

Disruptive Technology

The growth of entirely fictitious online communities would likely cause a substantial shift in our views on what is real and how we validate information. In the technology sector, the notion of a product that creates a whole new category and completely subverts the existing market for a certain device is referred to as a disruptive technology (Bower, 2002; Zeleny, 2009). An excellent example of disruptive technology is the iPhone, as its extremely simple design, intuitive user interface, and software engagement via applications were unseen before its release in 2007.

There is no way to know what technologies will serve as a point of disruption or how they will be accepted by the general public. For instance, the Google Glass wearable technology was released in 2011 but did not stand out as a success with early adapters and the general public as a whole (Wohlsen, 2014). The thin glasses incorporate a wearable computer, which projects a heads-up display within the glass frame and is activated and controlled by voice command and user eye movement. Klein, Sabino de Freitas, Pedrone, and Elaluf-Calderwood (2015) take a comprehensive look at why Google Glass might have failed, and they utilize Actor Network Theory (Law, 1992) in part to investigate the different components of that failure. Law (1992, p. 379) suggests that Actor Network Theory (ACT) is "a body of theoretical and empirical writing which treats social relations, including power and organization, as network effects." That is, objects (including technology objects) must be treated as elements similar to humans, and objects in fact connect one human to another in a type of network.

If extending Klein et al.'s argument, we can apply ACT to the Google Glass failure to see the failure of Google Glass to produce a symmetrical bidirectional connection between two individuals. The Glass wearer (sometimes derisively called a "Glasshole") was connected to the object (Google Glass), but that connection was asymmetrical in that information pushed to the wearer was not directly sharable or observable by another person engaged in social interaction with the wearer. This effectively "broke" the actor–object network. Breaking this network may have generated suspicions on the part of the nonwearer that the Google Glass owner was receiving information that they were not sharing and using that information for deceptive purposes in the interaction. Thus one consequence of this disruptive technology was at least the perception of deception on the part of the Glass wearer, and in fact it is possible that Google Glass might actually be able to facilitate deception.

A number of wearable Internet-enabled devices have become popular in the wake of Google Glass, gaining substantive market share. Devices like the Fitbit, iWatch, Pebble, and various Samsung Galaxy products can be connected to mobile phones via Bluetooth and give users the ability to track daily habits, exercise, heart rate, sleep cycles, and other personal data via applications. In turn, users can understand their health and calorie intake and find ways to engage in proactive behavior management to lose weight or feel better. The devices may not constitute a form of disruptive technology because they must work with other technology such as laptops or cell phones in order to capture and transform data points into useable information. Thus they are peripheral devices that do not replace any existing product category.

Instead, the information collected these wearable devices may serve a disruptive technology for data collection and information aggregation. For instance, the Fitbit and other health-tracking wearable technologies have been integrated into corporate health and wellness plans and tied to company health insurance plans (Olson, 2014). Generating first-hand data on the health practices of employees provides companies with ways to incentivize health care plan costs based on the lifestyles of the employee (Olson, 2014).

The use of wearable device data collection methods, coupled with massive data storage needs, creates massive opportunities for data breaches targeting health-based application services (Collins, Sainato, & Khey, 2011). There have been a number of attacks against the health care industry over the last few years. In fact, 18 health care providers lost sensitive data in 2014 due to hacking and external compromises (Ponemon Institute, 2015). One of the largest breaches targeted Anthem Health Care, leading to the loss of personal information from 80 million Americans, including full names, dates of birth, social security numbers, addresses, employer information, and income (Abelson & Creswell, 2015). Since hackers recognize the value of health care data, coupled with increasing connections between wearable devices and health care provider data sources, this may become a prominent target for compromise. One estimate puts the value of stolen health care data as worth as much as 10 times the value of stolen credit card information (Humer & Finkle, 2014). In fact, a Price Waterhouse Cooper study on wearable technology found that 86% of a sample of 1000 industry experts worried that wearable technology would increase their risk of data breaches (Price Waterhouse Cooper, 2014).

In much the same way, thermostats and home security systems that are connected to and managed via the Internet have become exceedingly popular in the last few years (see Curtis, 2013). These Wi-Fi-enabled devices allow consumers to manage their energy consumption and view goings on in their home with great ease through mobile and web-based interfaces. These devices, along with the wearable technologies mentioned above, create an Internet of Things (IoT), referring to all the noncomputing devices that are connected via the Internet (Curtis, 2013).

The security implications of a network of enabled devices may create a massive disruption point for both criminals and nation state actors. Almost everyone has some type of heating, ventilation, and air conditioning (HVAC) system running in their homes or offices. For example, having HVAC and security applications run through a smartphone or tablet turns that device into a set of house keys or a remote control that is dependent on the security protocols of the user and the vendor alike (Curtis, 2013). If a user's phone or tablet is not password protected, anyone would be able to gain control of their home systems if they were able to acquire the device. The same is true for the passwords used to secure and manage the systems in their home. The use of simple or default passwords would enable anyone to compromise the device. A study by HP (2014) found that 10 common smart devices sold to the general public, including smart thermostats, had common vulnerabilities that could be easily exploited to gain access to and control of the equipment (HP, 2014). The sensitive information captured by these devices could also be subjected to a data breach if compromised, which could lead to the loss of personally identifiable information.

Given that many in the general public do not recognize or understand the need to apply basic security protocols to their devices, there are now tremendous opportunities for offenders to compromise these devices. In fact, one of the possible scenarios for the IoT is for an individual to be "surrounded by hostile devices" in their own home (Macaulay, 2015). The potential to be situated in an environment that traditionally has been a bastion of security and safety (e.g., home) now holds the potential for devices in that environment to deceive the occupants and create a milieu of insecurity instead.

While it may seem that these vulnerabilities can be resolved through improvements in security protocols and security tools, the use of deception in order to compromise these devices cannot be understated. For instance, hackers could target HVAC devices during heat waves or extreme cold snaps and remotely shut off access to their management interface applications. The email address associated with that device could then be sent a message spoofing the manufacture's information and indicate that the recipient pay a fee in order to regain access to their devices. Such scams are regularly used in malware and phishing schemes and could be successful in targeting IoT devices with minor adjustments.

Extremist groups or nation state hackers could target IoT infrastructure in order to directly affect the population of an enemy nation to cause fear or disrupt services. During critical moments in time, such as in the recent coup attempt in Turkey, one simple Facetime video call to an ordinary iPhone at a television station by President Erdogan may have made all the difference in terms of the outcome of the coup. Imagine if nation state or coup-backed hacking groups were able to push malware to all of the smart televisions within a foreign country and then effectively cause them to fail during a coup attempt or even to forcibly redirect the programming to a deceptive misinformation campaign: the results could be very serious indeed.

Holograms

One rather simple app that hit the market in the summer of 2016 was Pokémon GO: an augmented reality smartphone game using Global Positioning System (GPS) data and mapping software where users collect Pokémon creatures in the real world. GPS is a United States owned utility that provides users with positioning, navigation, and time information services. As players view their current surroundings, Pokémons are digitally placed in the environment. While these Pokémon creatures are two-dimensional and displayed on the user's screen, it is plausible that the future will offer three-dimensional holographic images placed in the actual environment. For example, Microsoft already launched its gaming lenses called Hololens. Other companies have also started to develop and release holographic products, including Ostendo Technologies, who has spent about 10 years working on miniature projectors designed to present 3-D images for smartphones and giant screens without having to wear 3-D glasses (Rusli, 2014). Apple, HP, Samsung, Altice, and Leia are all currently working on their own 3-D imaging interface for smartphones. And a Chinese phone manufacturer, Estar Takee, has already launched a smartphone that renders a 3-D display by reading the eye movements of the user (Boxall, 2014).

Holograms present another dimension (literally and figuratively) to cyber deception and psychological manipulation. However, when it comes to using holograms for misdirection, researchers will have to consider the visual and perceptual capabilities of humans (Barabas & Bove, 2013). The technology itself will have to advance to a point where the projected image is difficult or near impossible to decipher from reality, if it is ever to be used as a mechanism to present false objects into an environment. In the meantime, the use of holographic images as deceptive presentations can certainly create diversions and interruptions.

For example, if anyone has ever flown in a small aircraft, the action of flying through a cloud for the first time can play visual and psychological tricks on the mind. Everyone knows that clouds are, for practical purposes, a gas–water vapor, and not a solid. However, on approach to that white fluffy thing, the brain says "it looks like cotton, it looks like a solid, oh, no, we are going to crash into a big snow drift." It is only the illusion that it is solid, but it does play on human instinct and emotion, if only for a few seconds or a minute. A similar type of human instinct and intuition may play a role in the application of holograms and the use of deceptive holographic images. According to Barabas, Smithwick, and Bove (2010), despite active research on perception relating to visual displays in general, very little work has been done to explore the viewing of holographic images. Thus the impact on humans and whether they can be deceived by holograms is yet to be seen.

Nanotechnology and Quantum Stealth

The implementation of holograms presents additional stimuli for the human brain to process, but advance stealth takes that stimuli away. The history of magic, deception, and illusion has always been filled with disappearing acts. An experiment allegedly carried out by the United States Navy during World War II made a warship disappear. The Philadelphia Experiment, as it is known, supposedly demonstrated the technology to render a destroyer, the USS Eldridge, invisible (Naval Historical Center of the United States Navy, 1998). The US Navy released a full report indicating that the experiment was never done and that making a destroyer vanish into thin air "does not conform to known physical laws." The purported cloak of invisibility may not have existed in 1943, but the science of nanotechnology or quantum stealth may be developing something that the Philadelphia Experiment received credit for decades ago. For the purposes of building invisibility cloaks, there are two applied theories that scientists have taken to tackle the challenge. One approach is to use technologies or methods that bend light around objects. A second approach is to incorporate materials into the objects (or around the objects) to create the illusion of disappearing.

Nanotechnology-based invisibility cloaks are already being tested in the field, and the use of light-bending nanotechnology for military camouflage is already in use (Walia, 2014). A Canadian-based company, Hyperstealth Biotechnology, has developed a technique called "Quantum Stealth," which is also a type of light-bending technology that surrounds the wearer of an object or piece of clothing to create the illusion of invisibility. Scientists in China have proven that they can make a cat "disappear" using similar methodologies, which hide objects using continuous streams of light with gaps and bend light around objects (Chen et al., 2013).

Another technique, using camouflaged fabrics, is proving successful by making an object, or a soldier, disappear. A material known as "squid skin" was developed by scientists at the University of California, Irvine. According to Gray (2013), these scientists "have created a new stealth coating that can change the way it reflects infrared light on command. The films, which are around 100,000 times thinner than a human hair, can be switched on and off using a chemical signal." The goal is to make soldiers invisible at night and to block their detection from night vision. According to the lead scientist at UC-Irvine, the squid skin stickers actually mimic the real camouflage used by squids as they alter their color to disappear into their underwater environment (Gorodestsky, 2015). Dr. Gorodestsky stated, "our long-term goal is to create fabrics that can dynamically alter their texture and color to adapt to their environments…basically, we're seeking to make shape-shifting clothing – the stuff of science fiction – a reality" (Gray, 2013).

While all of these developments in invisibility cloaking are relatively new, at some point they will be deployed in the field by the military, intelligence community, law enforcement, and perhaps by private industry to hide their assets. But, ultimately, almost everything that is used privately or professionally becomes available to the home user, or at least to those who are willing to pay for the innovative technologies. Thus to some degree, the ability to hide things may become part of our apps, our devices, and our clothing. It would be hard for people to psychologically resist the ability to vanish or to make things vanish. Invisibility has been a human pipedream as far back as 1897, when H.G. Wells published *The Invisible Man*. The ability to "disappear" in the hands of the masses would certainly create a new paradigm of reality detection and invisibility countermeasures.

Advanced Drones

The numbers of commercial drones, military drones, and now home-use drones have proliferated over the last few years. According to the Federal Aviation Administration (FAA), there are currently 2.5 million drones in 2016, and the number is supposed to increase to over 7 million by 2020 (Shen, 2016). While there is nothing new about drones or their current use, the future may bring some interesting twists to the use of these unmanned aerial vehicles (UAV). Similar to other new devices or technologies, drones can be turned into vehicles of theft, scams, or hacking. As a demonstration during a security conference, a security professional showed how a very expensive ($35K) law enforcement drone can be hacked from over a mile away (Greenberg, 2016). For several years, hackers have been offering code (e.g., SkyJack) to turn drones into command and control servers, which can take over other drones within the radius of a Wi-Fi connection (Fincher, 2013).

In order to account for all of these drones and to monitor the skies for disruptive or criminal behavior, the FAA has required drone owners/operators to register their UAVs.

However, drones outfitted with Wi-Fi scanning devices with the intent to conduct wireless network reconnaissance of government activities, neighborhoods, and office complexes will most likely continue undetected. The "bad guys" will find ways around the registration process using fake names and false credentials, or at some point may make themselves invisible or completely vanish. As discussed earlier, there are scientists and researchers working on ways to achieve invisibility. Specifically, The Defense Advanced Research Projects Agency (DARPA) put out a Request for Proposal (RFP) to create "vampire drones," which vanish when exposed to sunlight (Derla, 2015). According to the RFP posted by DARPA the requirements for the vampire drone include:

- size and flight specifications (i.e., 10 feet across, fly at least 90 miles in a straight line);
- design in which the drone must "vanish" within 4 h of its mission;
- design in which the drone must disappear within 30 min of sunset;
- include electronic materials that are capable of disappearing when triggered remotely; and
- include a self-destruct mechanism, as no evidence of the drone must be left behind postmission (DARPA RFP, 2015).

DARPA's self-destruct or vanishing mechanism is not isolated to their wish list, as other programs at the Pentagon have been focusing on self-destructive data and chips or a "disappearing electronics platform" (Lemos, 2015). Disintegration Upon Stress-Release Trigger (DUST) is a technology being developed by a Xerox Company (PARC), which enables microchips in devices to disintegrate on command, leaving behind only tiny glass-like shreds that are not visible to the human eye (Lemos, 2015). The ability to execute this "new magic" of making objects disappear or vanish entirely will no doubt impact human thought and human psychology. In addition to the need for parallel research to focus on technical countermeasures, social scientific research is necessary to understand the impact of these advancements.

Neurohacking/Neuromarketing and Texting by Thinking

So far, the future-leaning technologies have centered on devices or materials that are used, worn, seen, or directed by a human being. However, what if the future allows for the manipulation of thoughts? Neurobiologists and researchers are discovering ways to read and interpret brain waves (i.e., people's thoughts) in order to devise better treatments for Alzheimer's, Parkinson's, and dementia. But could the future's technology and advancements serve up misinformation and deception through accessing our neurotransmitters? Current research is certainly pointing in that direction. For example, researchers at University of California, Berkeley have created a "semantic atlas" by decoding brain waves (Huth, de Heer, Griffiths, Theunissen, & Gallant, 2016) that could potentially and eventually reveal a person's private thoughts. Canton (2012) takes the idea of this brain mapping one more step, predicting that once brain waves are deciphered in the future, neurohacking and neuromarketing will be potential issues.

Neuromarketing is the targeting of people's brains with the intent to manipulate what they want with carefully crafted advertising or the planting of desires. The ethics of neuromarketing are being challenged today and that is without the ability to actually read or transmit thoughts (Flores, Baruca, & Saldivar, 2014). If an actual form of neuromarketing (which may or may not include neurologically hacking one's brain) is possible in the future, how far can deception and misdirection be taken? At that point, the need for realistic holograms, fancy invisible drones, and disappearing chips is almost a moot point…just manipulate thoughts, beliefs, and perceptions.

Future Timeline (2012) predicts that by 2020, people will be "texting by thinking." This may not be entirely far-fetched, as technologists at Twitter back in 2009 were able to use, in essence, an EEG to send a Tweet (Keim, 2009).

The Man in the Middle Conundrum

The Man in the Middle (MitM) attack has been a classic and commonplace attack on digital networks for decades. In a MitM attack, a piece of hardware and/or a software package is inserted in the communications path of two or more digital devices. The MitM components typically work to deceive the two end points of the communication into thinking that they are communicating with each other without any interference or surveillance. Usually in a MitM attack the communication is intercepted from one end point of the communications path, and the content of that communication is monitored and altered in some way by the MitM code, either by changing some of the communication content or adding or deleting specific elements within that content. Once the alteration of the communications is achieved, the content is sent onward to the intended communications end point.

As individuals begin to place more and more digital devices between themselves (e.g., one end point) and the other intended end point, this opens up a number of opportunities to inject a MitM attack into that communications path with the intention of deceiving the human end point of that path. Assessing the temperature of a room is a simple example. A human may use their natural senses to perceive that the room they occupy seems hot to them. Because people cannot often produce a precise measure of the temperature of a room, they look to an IoT device—a Nest thermostat in this case—to see what their temperature is registering. Between the communications path of the temperature sensor in the Nest and the digital readout of that temperature, a MitM attack might consist of inserting code into the Nest thermostat such that it displays the incorrect temperature. Which piece of information is the human supposed to accept as accurate: their body's sense of the room temperature or the reading on the Nest thermostat?

As we inject more and more digital devices into the middle of the communications path and we begin to leave the traditional, simple path of phenomenon to human sensory organs behind and replace it with things like augmented or virtual reality, we increase the opportunities to have hardware or software or both interjected into the communications path with the objective deceiving either the human end point or perhaps even the digital one on the other end of the human–digital device chain. This also suggests that what humans have traditionally labeled "reality" that they directly sense with their bodies may become more and more altered by digital devices that stand between the person and the stimulus. It remains to be seen, as discussed in the next section, just how humans will adapt to this digitally facilitated sensory communications path.

The Impact on Humans and Psychology

Predicting future technologies that could provide platforms for misinformation and misdirection is a difficult task. What is more certain is that whatever technologies emerge, there will likely be opportunities to alter information or perceptions along the way. This suggests that it would be a good idea to initiate research that can provide us with some ideas and theoretical knowledge about the effects of such deceptions, along with developing methods to detect possible deception as well as providing some careful thought into the possibility of deception countermeasures. Most of the detection techniques and counter-deception methods will no doubt be technical: combatting engineering with engineering, science with science, and physics with physics. However, one of the areas that has not been considered is the impact that these new technologies will have on humans or the science of psychology.

Hypothetically, if holograms, invisibility cloaking, vanishing objects, and neurohacking/neuromarketing were to come to fruition, the social construction of how humans formulate their realities would likely be dramatically altered. Psychologists would likewise have to adjust how they evaluate "normalcy" or how they may diagnose psychological disorders. Today's Diagnostic and Statistical Manual of Mental Disorders, Fifth Edition presents common criteria for the classification of mental disorders. But what would or could be the consequences of technologies that distort the realities of what stable, sane, everyday people might experience? Will there be a diagnosis of "Virtual Reality Systems Disorder," which outlines the symptoms of people who cannot distinguish the differences between holographic images and real objects? Will the definitions of delusions, hallucinations, and "hearing of voices" have to be changed because it may be perfectly sane for someone to see things and then have them vanish? Would the inability to accept digitally constructed realities become a mental disorder in and of itself? How will practicing psychologists and psychiatrists differentiate between people who are hearing and seeing virtual or actual objects that "vanish into thin air" versus those people who are hallucinating in the classical sense?

On the flip side, will the field of psychology be able to take advantage of these new technologies to neurotransmit cures for obsessive-compulsive disorders and other ailments? If that is the case, what safeguards will be developed to prevent deceptive information from being transmitted in these cases? Whatever the future holds regarding the creation of new technologies, particularly those that will be applied to deceptive practices, technologists and scientists must ardently keep in mind the social scientific and human consequences of their newly created magic.

References

Abelson, R., & Creswell, J. (February 6, 2015). *Data breach at Anthem may forecast a trend.* The New York Times. Online source http://www.nytimes.com/2015/02/07/business/data-breach-at-anthem-may-lead-to-others.html.

Barabas, J., & Bove, M. V., Jr. (2013). Visual perception and holographic displays. *Journal of Physics: Conference Series, 415* 012056.

Barabas, J., Smithwick, Q. Y. J., & Bove, V. M., Jr. (2010). P-3: Evaluation of rendering algorithms for presenting layered information on holographic displays. *SID Symposium Digest of Technical Papers, 41*(1), 1233–1236.

Bower, J. L. (2002). Disruptive change. *Harvard Business Review, 80,* 95–101.

Boxall, A. (July 17, 2014). *Is this 'holographic' smartphone revolutionary, or just a fire phone clone?.* Online source http://www.digitaltrends.com/mobile/holographic-smartphones-thanks-takee/.

Canton, J. (2012). *Global futures forecast 2012 – Top trends that will shape the coming year.* Institute for Global Futures. Online source www.globalfuturist.com/images/docs/GFF2012.pdf.

Chen, H., Zheng, B., Shen, L., Wang, H., Zhang, X., Zheludev, N., et al. (June 7, 2013). *Natural light cloaking for aquatic and terrestrial creatures.* SAO/NASA Astrophysics Data System. Online source http://arxiv.org/abs/1306.1780.

Collins, J. D., Sainato, V. A., & Khey, D. N. (2011). Organizational data breaches 2005–2010: Applying SCP to the Healthcare and Education Sectors. *International Journal of Cyber Criminology, 5,* 794–810.

Curtis, S. (August 2, 2013). *Home invasion 2.0: How criminals could hack your house.* Telegraph. Online source http://www.telegraph.co.uk/technology/internet-security/10218824/Home-invasion-2.0-how-criminals-could-hack-your-house.html.

DARPA Broad Area Announcement and Request for Proposal. (October 9, 2015). *Inbound, controlled, air-releasable, unrecoverable systems (ICARUS)*. Solicitation Number: DARPA-BAA-16–03. Online source https://www.fbo.gov/index?s=opportunity&mode=form&id=6bf17b2b80ff386403bfc90b151a5dec&tab=core&_cview=0.

Derla, K. (December 17, 2015). *Forward to the future: DARPA predicts what the world will be like in 2045*. Tech Times. Online source http://www.techtimes.com/articles/116880/20151217/forward-to-the-future-darpa-predicts-what-the-world-will-be-like-in-2045.htm.

Facebook. (June 30, 2016). *Facebook second quarter 2016 results*. Online source http://www.prnewswire.com/news-releases/facebook-reports-second-quarter-2016-results-300305084.html.

Fincher, J. (December 8, 2013). *SkyJack: The drone that hijacks other drones in mid-air*. New Atlas. Online source http://newatlas.com/skyjack-hijacks-other-drones/30055/.

Flores, J., Baruca, A., & Saldivar, R. (2014). Is neuromarketing ethical? Consumers say yes, consumers say no. *Journal of Legal, Ethical and Regulatory Issues, 17*(2), 77–91.

Future Timeline. (2012). *Predictions for 2020 and beyond*. Online source http://www.futuretimeline.net/21stcentury/2020.htm#.V6Pme5Whepo.

Gorodestsky, A. (April 20, 2015). *Thermocomfort cloth inspired by squid skin*. University of California. Irvine ARPA–presentation. Online source www.arpa-e.energy.gov/sites/default/files/09_UCI_DELTA_Kickoff.pdf.

Gray, R. (September 10, 2013). *Stealth coating based on squid skin could make soldiers invisible to night vision*. The Telegraph. Online source http://www.telegraph.co.uk/news/science/science-news/10298803/Stealth-coating-based-on-squid-skin-could-make-soldiers-invisible-to-night-vision.html.

Greenberg, A. (March 3, 2016). *Hacker says he can hijack a $35K police drone from a mile away*. Wired. Online source https://www.wired.com/2016/03/hacker-says-can-hijack-35k-police-drone-mile-away/.

HP. (2014). *Internet of things research study, 2014 report*. Online source http://www8.hp.com/h20195/V2/GetPDF.aspx/4AA5-4759ENW.pdf.

Humer, C., & Finkle, J. (September 24, 2014). *Your medical record is worth more to hackers than your credit card*. Technology News. Online source http://www.reuters.com/article/us-cybersecurity-hospitals-idUSKCN0HJ21I20140924.

Huth, A. G., de Heer, W. A., Griffiths, T. L., Theunissen, F. E., & Gallant, J. L. (April 28, 2016). Natural speech reveals the semantic maps that tile human cerebral cortex. *Nature, 532*, 453–458.

Impact Team. (August 16, 2015). *We are the impact team. We are releasing the Ashley Madison data*. Online source https://www.reddit.com/r/AnythingGoesNews/comments/3h71ar/we_are_the_impact_team_we_are_releasing_the/.

Keim, B. (April 20, 2009). *Twitter telepathy: Researchers turn thoughts into tweets*. Wired. Online source http://www.wired.com/2009/04/braintweet/.

Klein, A., Sabino de Freitas, A., Pedrone, C., & Elaluf-Calderwood, S. (August 7–11, 2015). Who is afraid of Google Glass? Mapping the controversy about wearable and ubiquitous computing. In *Academy of management meeting, Vancouver, Canada*.

Law, J. (1992). Notes on the theory of the actor-network: Ordering, strategy and heterogeneity. *Systems Practice, 5*(4), 379–393.

Lemos, R. (October 15, 2015). *Turning computer chips to DUST*. TechBeacon. Online source http://techbeacon.com/3-cutting-edge-data-security-technologies-will-help-secure-future.

Macaulay, T. (February 27, 2015). *Social engineering attacks in the IoT: The shape of things to come*. Online source https://www.linkedin.com/pulse/social-engineering-attacks-iot-shape-things-come-tyson-macaulay?forceNoSplash=true.

Naval Historical Center of the United States Navy. (December 11, 1998). *Information sheet: Philadelphia experiment*. Online source https://ia802709.us.archive.org/28/items/PhiladelphiaExperiment/Philadelphia%20Experiment_text.pdf.

Olson, P. (June 19, 2014). *Wearable Tech is plugging into health insurance.* Forbes. Online source http://www.forbes.com/sites/parmyolson/2014/06/19/wearable-tech-health-insurance/.

Ponemon Institute. (2015). *2014 cost of cyber crime study.* Traverse City, MI: Ponemon Institute.

Price Waterhouse Cooper. (2014). *The wearable future. Consumer intelligence series.* Online source http://www.pwc.com/us/en/industry/entertainment-media/publications/consumer-intelligence-series/.

Rusli, E. M. (June 2, 2014). New chip to bring holograms to smartphones. *Wall Street Journal.* Online source http://www.wsj.com/articles/new-chip-to-bring-holograms-to-smartphones-1401752938.

SecureWorks. (October 7, 2015). *Hacker group creates network of fake LinkedIn profiles.* Online source https://www.secureworks.com/research/suspected-iran-based-hacker-group-creates-network-of-fake-linkedin-profiles.

Shen, L. (May 25, 2016). *Drone sales have tripled in the last year.* Fortune. Online source http://fortune.com/2016/05/25/drones-ndp-revenue/.

Walia, A. (March 3, 2014). *Quantum stealth – Scientists unveil invisible cloak technology.* Online source http://www.collective-evolution.com/2014/03/03/quantum-stealth-scientists-unveil-invisible-cloak-technology/.

Wohlsen, M. (April 15, 2014). *Failure is the best thing that could happen to Google Glass.* Wired. Online source http://www.wired.com/2014/04/failure-is-the-best-thing-that-could-happen-to-google-glass/.

Zeleny, M. (January 2009). Technology and high technology: Support net and barriers to innovation. *Advanced Management Systems, 1,* 8–21.

Index

Note: Page numbers followed by "f" indicate figures and "t" indicate tables.'

Printed and bound by CPI Group (UK) Ltd, Croydon, CR0 4YY

03/10/2024

01040327-0012